A GUIDE TO
PREHISTORIC ENGLAND

For Susan, Harriet, Amelia and Daniel

A GUIDE TO
PREHISTORIC
ENGLAND

NICHOLAS THOMAS

B.T. BATSFORD LTD
London

First published 1960
Second edition 1976
ISBN 0 7134 3267 5 (Cased)
ISBN 0 7134 3268 3 (Limp)

Filmset by Servis Filmsetting Ltd, Manchester
Printed and bound in Great Britain by
Butler & Tanner Ltd, Frome
for the Publishers
B.T. BATSFORD LTD
4 Fitzhardinge Street, London W1H 0AH

CONTENTS

PREFACE

Our countryside is littered with the visible remains of communities who lived here for nearly 3,000 years before the Romans conquered England. Having lectured on the archaeology of these islands to many groups of adults and children, and taken them into the fields to see such remains, I have noticed that most people are quite unaware of the existence of these signs of prehistoric habitation. Given even a brief explanation, however, the simplest earthwork takes on a new significance and provides an altogether broader setting for the objects in museums which their builders made and used. I have compiled this gazetteer for people who love the countryside, who are interested in the past and may wish to plan their excursions around visits to pre-historic sites of various types. I have, I must confess, listed only those sites which I think people *should* see and have had to leave out many places which may draw enquiries from those coming upon them for the first time. I think nevertheless that most of the major pre-Roman earthworks of England have been included.

In a compilation of this sort, accuracy of detail and selection of the right sites depends to a great extent upon the assistance of archaeologists with detailed knowledge of particular areas. My own shortcomings have to some extent been lessened by the generous help of many friends and colleagues and my gratitude to them is heartfelt. They are: A.M. ApSimon (Somerset), B. Blake (Cumberland), J.W. Brailsford (Dorset), Miss L. Chitty (Salop), R.R. Clarke (Norfolk), Mrs E.M. Clifford (Glos.), J.F. Dyer (Beds., Bucks. and Herts.), Miss C.I. Fell (Cumberland), Lady Fox (Devon), J.F. Head (Bucks.), J.P. Heathcote (Derbys.), Miss K.S. Hodgson (Cumberland), J.D. Jones (I.O.W.), A. Oswald (Notts.), Dr A. Ozanne (Cambs.), H. Ramm (Yorks.), G. de G. Sieveking (Cumberland), Dr J.E. Spence (Cumberland), C. Thomas (Cornwall), F.H. Thompson (Cheshire), J. Wacher (Leics.). H.C. Bowen has examined my lists for most of Wessex and has helped me with innumerable points of detail; Mrs M.A. Cotton has read and augmented almost all my material concerning Iron Age hill-forts. C.W. Phillips and the staff of the Ordnance Survey at Chessington placed their maps and card indices at my disposal (together with many cups of tea) during lengthy visits to their premises. Prof R.J.C. Atkinson read the Introduction and several of the county lists, and offered much valuable criticism L. V. Grinsell answered enquiries on many sites. The selection of sites for each county was based upon the gazetteer listed by Jacquetta Hawkes in *A Guide to the Prehistoric and Roman Monuments in England and Wales*, 1954.

While seeking out the museum whereabouts of antiquities found or excavated on sites listed in the gazetteer, I received help from the following colleagues: H.J. Case, Miss E. Dance, F. Jenkins, Miss E. Pirie. For help with proof correction and checking of typescript with drafts, I am greatly indebted to my mother and to Miss C. Johnson. To Miss Ivy Scott-Rogers especially, and to Mrs K. Dunham, I am grateful for typing. I would also like to express my thanks to the scores of people who allowed me to examine sites on their property. I wish here to emphasise, as I have done at the beginning of my gazetteer, that visitors should always seek permission from the land-owner before leaving a right-of-way to look at an earthwork.

Preface to the Second Edition

An enormous volume of archaeological field research has taken place since this guide was first published. Many of the sites described in it have been examined extensively by excavation and I have tried to include as much as possible of the results of this activity in the second edition. As with the first, I am greatly indebted to friends and colleagues who have supplied information and helped in other ways, especially Alan Aberg, David Addison, David Ball, Collin Bowen, Alan Burchard, Caroline Dudley, James Dyer, Peter Fowler, Leslie Grinsell, Roy Hughes, David Kelly, Harry Lane, Fiona Marsden, Susan Pearce, Joan Taylor and Geoffrey Wainwright. Professor Leslie Alcock has kindly allowed reproduction of fig. 44. I am also extremely grateful to Madeleine Canney, Janine Ringwood and, especially, Valerie Macfarlane, who undertood the retyping. My wife has been a great support and I am very grateful for the way she has enabled me to devote the necessary time to prepare the second edition.

LIST OF
ILLUSTRATIONS

ACKNOWLEDGMENTS

The publishers acknowledge their obligation to the following organisations and photographers for illustrations which appear in these pages:

Aerofilms Ltd. for fig. 59; Ashmolean Museum, for figs. 43 and 62, from photographs by the late G.W.G. Allen; W.A. Baker, for fig. 35; City Museum and Art Gallery, Birmingham, for figs. 1, 4, 5 and 36; The City Museum, Bristol for figs. 12 and 13; The Trustees of the British Museum, for figs. 2, 7, 9, 52, 60, 64, 65 and 69; G.P. Bustow, F.S.A. and G.A. Holleyman, F.S.A., for figs. 45 and 46 (from *Proceedings of the Prehistoric Society*, 1957); J.O. Carter, for fig. 6; the late Brian C. Clayton, for figs. 15, 18, 20, 30 and 63; the late Mrs. E.M. Clifford, O.B.E., F.S.A., for figs. 31 (from *Proceedings of the Prehistoric Society*, 1940), 32 (from *Proceedings of the Prehistoric Society*, 1938) and 33 (Bristol and Gloucestershire Archaeological Society); the late M.B. Cookson, for figs. 54, 55 and 58; Dorset Natural History and Archaeological Society, for fig. 23; Dept of PreSistoric Archaeology, University of Edinburgh, for fig. 49; Lady Fox, F.S.A., for fig. 19 (from *Transactions of the Devon Association*, 1954); the late H. St George Gray, O.B.E., F.S.A., and the Society of Antiquaries, for fig. 48; J.P. Heathcote, M.A., F.S.A., for fig. 17; the Institute of Archaeology, for figs. 25–8 and 37; Methuen and Co. Ltd, for fig. 11 (from *The Ancient Burial-Mounds of England* by L.V. Grinsell, O.B.E., F.S.A.); the Ministry of Works (Crown Copyright), for figs. 40 and 54–8; City of Norwich Museums, and Hallam Ashley, for fig. 41; the late G.H.L.F. Pitt-Rivers, for fig. 22 (from *Excavations in Cranborne Chase, Vol. IV*); Miss K.M. Richardson, F.S.A. and the Society of Antiquaries, for fig. 29; the Royal Commission on Historical Monuments, for fig. 24 (reproduced by permission of the Controller of Her Majesty's Stationery Office, Crown Copyright); Prof J.K. St Joseph, O.B.E., F.S.A., for figs. 16, 21, 34, 39, 42, 47, 51 and 61; Prof. J.K. St Joseph and the Cambridge University Collection, for fig. 67 (Crown Copyright); Salisbury, South Wilts and Blackmore Museum and Fowler Smith for fig. 3; the Society of Antiquaries, for figs. 25–8, 38, 68 and 70; Nicholas Thomas, F.S.A., for figs. 10, 14, 56 and 57; Wiltshire Archaeological and Natural History Society and Peter Francis, for figs. 8 and 50; Reece Winstone, A.R.P.S., for fig. 53; the Yorkshire Archaeological Society, for fig. 66.

INTRODUCTION

*'Antiquities are history defaced, or some remnants of history,
which have casually escaped the shipwreck of time.'*

FRANCIS BACON

The earliest inhabitants of England lived as hunters, fishermen and
food-gatherers. Not yet tilling the soil, they fed upon what nature had
to offer. Since this way of life involved almost no control or exploita-
tion of their environment, their personality left little mark upon the
land in which they struggled to survive.

Here and there we catch a glimpse of these Palaeolithic and Mesolithic hunters at work, a hearth or a scatter of flint implements in a
cave, a hollow in the ground where a small family had sought a night's
shelter. The inhabited caves on Mendip or in the Peak, the pit-shelter
at Abinger (Surrey), such and a few more are the visible structural
remains of this period. They were the prelude to the earthworks of a
more developed prehistoric England, just as the all-but perfection of
stone and bone tool production by these hunters, together with their
successful efforts to tame or even domesticate dogs and control
gregarious wild herds such as cattle and pigs were essential stages in
the emergence of a settled farming society in the Neolithic period
which followed.

Before 3,500 BC (see p. 36), groups of farmers began crossing the
Channel to Britain, probably in wooden-framed skin boats, bringing
with them seed grain of wheat, barley and oats, their domesticated
livestock – cattle, sheep and goats – and pet dogs. They appear to have
settled first in the south west but traces of the bearers of this so-called
Windmill Hill culture have been found widespread in the British Isles,
with evidence to suggest that their expansion was rapid.

The introduction of farming to our islands early in the 4th millenium,
with its necessarily more sedentary way of life, marked the completion
of a process in which the knowledge of cultivation and domestication
had been carried from the Near East over a period of about 4,500
years. This spread of peoples and of knowledge seems to have been
carried along two main routes, the Danube and the north Mediterranean coasts and it reached the Rhineland and SE France by c. 5,000
BC. Neolithic culture in NW Europe shows, from the first, a mixture of
Mediterranean and European characteristics in seemingly endless

variation and nowhere is this more evident than in the remains of the
Neolithic and succeeding communities who peopled our islands.

The impact of the first farming communities upon our landscape
must have been gradual. Although evidence for sudden change in
natural vegetation caused by cultivation and by clearance for settlement can be seen in pollen analyses from archaeological excavations,
it may have been generations, even centuries, before the settlers were
sufficiently established to begin building the sort of structures which
can still be visited and by which their material culture is recognised in
Britain. The causewayed camp on Windmill Hill (Wilts.) and the
mound of a long barrow nearby have yielded evidence that both these
early sites overlay ground which had already been cultivated.

The earliest Neolithic sites in Britain would, then, have been settlements, open or fortified according to local conditions (including the
reactions of indigenous Mesolithic hunters surviving in the areas of
settlement). Carn Brea (Cornwall) is currently the earliest known
fortified settlement in Britain, its rampart sheltering unsophisticated
timber-framed buildings and its inhabitants tilling small plots
immediately outside as well as keeping flocks and herds.

Hembury (Devon) is perhaps the earliest of a class of domestic site
which began to be built in southern Britain from about 3,000 BC – the
causewayed camp; continued absence of convincing prototypes in NW
Europe implies that such camps were a product of insular Neolithic
culture and as such they probably post-date considerably the initial
settlements. Fifteen such camps have been recorded, of which the
majority can still be seen. They are enclosures formed by one or more
earthworks whose ditches – and sometimes the banks – are interrupted,
a construction technique suggesting gang-work. Sometimes the camps
are located in situations as if for defence, on hill-tops or at the ends of
spurs. They also occur on level ground or beside rivers. Except for the
remains of dense, permanent occupation at Hembury (Devon), the
causewayed camps appear to have been used only seasonally; and
from the domestic refuse, including human bones, found deposited
and carefully covered over in the ditches of some, it appears that ritual
practice may have been one of their functions. Pottery and other
artifacts brought from a distance are also a feature and it seems likely
that most causewayed camps served as fairs, or rallying points, where
Neolithic farmers foregathered at certain times of the year for social
contact, for barter, for exchange of ideas and perhaps for worship.
Whatever the purpose served by these camps, it became deeply
engrained: most were in use for nearly a millenium and provided
regional foci recognised in some places until the coming of the
Romans.

1 *West Kennet chambered long barrow, Wiltshire: early Neolithic bowl, c. 3,000 BC. Diam. 6½ ins.*

2 *Norton Bavant, Wiltshire: early Neolithic bowl, c. 3,500 BC. Diam. 5 ins.*

Domestic rubbish from the camps includes fragments of the earliest pottery to be found in Britain (one of the innovations of Neolithic culture in Europe), round-based, leathery-looking vessels (figs. 1, 2) belonging to a west European tradition. The earliest evidence for the grinding of stone (hitherto shaped only by flaking) also occurs in the Neolithic, on axe-heads made of flint and stone. Crop-raising is attested by flint blades for sickles as well as by elongated querns for grinding, while hunters used the bow and arrows tipped with leaf-shaped flint heads.

These farmers learned to extract good flint by mining in early Neolithic times and they were also able to recognise and exploit our islands' considerable wealth of hard, workable volcanic rocks which were ideal for axe-heads and hoe-blades.

The second class of field monument by which the so-called Windmill Hill culture of these farmers is recognised is the long barrow. This is a specialised form of tomb which provided, with local variations, a formal structural setting for communal burial, whose essential elements occurred in many parts of western and central Europe.

The earliest long barrows are those whose mounds are composed of earth and subsoil and whose burials, concentrated at the easterly end of usually wedge-shaped mounds, were occasionally housed in wooden chambers or other structures, or else laid in disorder on a prepared platform of some kind. Almost always, the skeletal remains suggest that the long barrow represented the final resting-place for corpses whose flesh and sinews had rotted while the bodies lay elsewhere – sometimes in a wooden or earthen enclosure on the same site, or close by, as at Wor Barrow (Dorset, fig. 22) or Skendleby (Lincs.), or the ditched enclosure beside the long barrow on Normanton Down (Wilts.). Burials varied in number from one or two to more than 50;

some long barrows appear to have been cenotaphs. Earthen long barrows in Britain incorporate a variety of structural features which can be matched from Scandinavia to south Poland: as houses of the dead, it is possible that their overall shape originated in the domestic houses of Danubian farmers who had reached Denmark by 4,000 BC. In our islands, such burial mounds were built during more than 1,000 years, from beginnings in the 4th millenium BC.

A second long barrow tradition, which may have originated in Brittany at least as early, saw the construction of stone burial chambers at the easterly end of wedge-shaped, or sometimes circular mounds built usually of stone. Called respectively gallery and passage graves, the burial area in the former combined a parallel-sided passage usually with side chambers, while the passage led to one main chamber in the latter. At Wayland's Smithy (Oxon.) a gallery grave was found to overlie a much smaller earthen long barrow, suggesting that the stone-built chambered tombs were introduced to Britain after the appearance of earthen long barrows; both styles, however, continued alongside each other until the end of the Neolithic. Essentially, each represents different ways of communal disposal of the dead. The entrance to a chambered tomb could be unblocked whenever a corpse was to be added, rendering unnecessary the kind of separate storage areas associated with earthen long barrows.

The Cotswolds and North Wiltshire contain many chambered tombs of gallery type, passage graves being very rare in England. In the Penwith area of Cornwall, however, stone chambers beneath small, circular mounds belong to the passage-grave tradition and are probably as early. In Kent there is a small series of burial chambers set at the end of mounds which are (or were) strikingly rectangular and narrow. The origins of these may be found in Scandinavia, north Germany and Holland but they appear to be as early as the gallery graves elsewhere in Britain. Standing before the huge stones of the facade to West Kennet (Wilts.), then moving into the tomb itself, it is not difficult to imagine the elaborate ritual – feasting, dancing and chanting – not to speak of the sense of awe, with which each burial would have been accompanied: we must marvel, also, at the ideals which compelled the construction of such massive monuments, some of them destined to house so few dead people.

The essentially continental culture of our first Neolithic population gradually became transformed into something insular. In the south this is seen in the excessive lengthening of earthen long-barrow mounds, producing the bank barrows of Dorset. The religious symbolism seen here may also have inspired a type of apparently ritual earthwork, the cursus, which evidently originated in England. These avenues defined by two parallel banks and ditches about 100 yds. apart, with enclosed ends, can be of immense length and several of them have been laid out to incorporate or be in association with long barrows. Their wide distribution in Britain shows how relatively uniform was the spread of religious practice in these islands. The ideas which compelled the erection of stone avenues and alignments in the later Neolithic and Bronze Age must have originated here, in the long barrows and cursuses of our Neolithic farmers.

In the north of England, the fairly rapid achievement of insular characteristics in the long barrows of the early Neolithic farmers is seen in the practice of burning the timber structure containing the disarticulated human bones before construction of the mound, its collapse usually resulting in partial burning of the bones beneath.

It also appears here and across into Scotland, in the construction of trapezoidal mounds of stones incorporating small, isolated burial chambers or cists, which constitute another form of long barrow, the long cairns. In the north, moreover, inhumations and multiple burials after cremation were occasionally covered by round barrows in this period.

During the third millenium BC, Neolithic culture in Britain gradually evolved, inspiration coming in part from within itself, with its varied European inheritance, in part from continued fertilisation across the Channel through trade and settlement. Of the many ways in which the material equipment of our Neolithic peoples evolved during the thousand and more years which followed the initial colonisation of these islands, pottery shows the most obvious developments. From the original, generally undecorated, round-based bowls

3   *Amesbury, Wiltshire: grooved ware, c. 1,700 BC. Diam. 6 ins.*

4   *West Kennet chambered long barrow, Wiltshire: Peterborough ware, c. 1,700 BC. Diam. 6 ins.*

of west European tradition which were brought to Britain, we can trace the evolution of a series of highly decorated wares (figs. 3, 4). In due course the rounded base gave way to a flat base (fig. 4) and the rim was emphasised and deepened until, in the Early Bronze Age of the 2nd millenium BC, a collar evolved (fig. 6).

Of various known classes of structure which appear in Britain during the 3rd millenium BC, the type of sacred site called a henge monument appears to have originated here, for convincing European prototypes have not yet been demonstrated.

These sites are roughly circular areas of ground up to 1,500 ft. in diameter, defined by a ditch with a bank outside it. One or two entrance gaps break the earthworks (Avebury has four). Henges are usually set on low ground, often near water. Rivers and the material prosperity which in part depended upon them, fertility of wives and of crops and livestock, such no doubt were the elements sought after and worshipped by the builders of these places.

Insular Neolithic burial practices which emerged during the 3rd millenium BC were varied. The habit of depositing cremated bones in a circular earthwork enclosure owed much to the construction of henge monuments for worship. The digging of pits during burial ceremonies, presumably to receive libations offered to some sort of earth goddess, again was a practice found in the henges. In phase 1 at Stonehenge there is a combination of sacred site and cremation cemetery which shows how deeply religion now embraced the desires of the living and the needs of the dead in an after-life.

The increasing need to clear the ground and till it, using flint and stone axes and hoe-blades, led to the development of a sophisticated industry, incorporating the mining and quarrying of the raw materials and their trade all over the British Isles. The organisation which this implies – quarrying, making and selling, feeding the working communities – reached its climax in the supply of more than 80 pillars of Pembrokeshire bluestone for Stonehenge II and is the most astonishing aspect of life at this time.

Fresh impetus to the late Neolithic way of life in all its aspects was given by the arrival of well-armed and equipped settlers from homelands in the Low Countries and the mouth of the Rhine a little before 2,000 BC. The newcomers are distinguished by their sophisticated pottery – beakers (fig. 5) – and by possession of trinkets of gold and knives and awls of copper. Their chiefs wielded stone battle-axes with a shaft-hole for attachment to the handle. More important than these material innovations, which included stone wrist-guards as part of their impressive archery equipment, was their distinctive burial practice. In place of communal, they introduced individual interment.

5 *West Kennet chambered long barrow,
Wiltshire: bell-beaker, c. 1,800 BC. Max.
diam. 8 ins.*

6 *Snail Down Bronze Age bell-barrow,
Wiltshire: collared urn, c. 1,500 BC. Diam.
of rim, 13 ins.*

The round barrows of the Beaker Folk, each covering one main grave, were the link between multiple cremation and communal burial of Neolithic traditions and the elaborate, formalised, round-barrow architecture of the Bronze Age which followed.

Though the culture of the Beaker Folk remained essentially stone-using, they appear to have had an ability to organise and the power to dominate the Neolithic communities with whom they came into contact, which made a considerable impression upon the face of the country. It can be seen in farming, for example, in the preference for barley at the expense of wheat; but it appears even more forcibly in the quantities of Beaker pottery and other artifacts found in the debris associated with virtually all the great structures (for whatever purpose) erected at the end of the 3rd millenium BC.

Few purely Beaker earthworks have been identified in England. Everywhere, the picture which emerges is of Beaker and local Neo-lithic peoples working together – or with the former as the dominating partner – whether in construction of great henge monuments like Durrington Walls with its huge timber buildings; or timber and stone structures like the Avebury/Overton Hill (Wilts.) complex; or in more flimsy settlements whose heavily eroded traces occasionally reward the patient excavator. The long barrows continued to be honoured, flint mines and quarries maintained production under the new stimulus: indeed, the Bluestone phase at Stonehenge has been attributed to the Beaker Folk.

These new settlers must have re-established close contact between Britain and northern Europe and their discovery of the rich metallic ores of south-east Ireland, the west of England and the west Midlands enabled a copper- and bronze-using culture to emerge. The earth-works of Bronze Age England must be seen against this background of insular tradition and European innovation.

A sophisticated bronze technology had been developed in Britain by c. 1,700 BC, which ushered in our Early Bronze Age. The working of sheet gold and an incredible facility for fashioning ornaments and other articles out of jet, shale, amber and bone, as well as weapons and heavy tools in copper and bronze, mark this as an era of brilliant and versatile craftsmen. No doubt their skills in wood, leather and textiles were equally great, as witness the traces of leather-lined wooden sheaths on their bronze dagger blades, while the enlarged range of often highly decorated pottery (figs. 6–9) shows that the

7   *Aldbourne, Wiltshire: Aldbourne cup and cover, c. 1,600 BC. Rim diam. 4 ins.*

traditional crafts were being maintained. As befits a well-established, probably prosperous society, fresh contacts were made with NW Europe, principally through trade, although it also seems possible that there was movement of peoples between Brittany and Wessex. Cylindrical segmented beads made of faience – a blue glaze applied to a prefired glassy core – found in barrows in southern England, are exact copies, if not actual imports from the Near East and there is other evidence to show that at this time Britain, like western Europe, was in contact by trade, at least, with countries bordering the east Mediterranean.

8   *Badbury Barrow, Dorset: food vessels, c. 1,600 BC. Diam of rim (left), 4¾ ins.*

9   *Wiltshire: Typical Early Bronze Age incense cups. Top row (L. to R.) Snail Down, Normanton, Lake. Bottom row (L. to R.) Winterbourne Stoke, Manton (2, the first a grape cup). Diam. of smallest, 1½ ins.*

With little evidence to support it, any assessment of the character of society which developed during the Neolithic and Early Bronze periods must remain largely guess-work. The transition from communal – often family – burial during the Neolithic to individual burial and an increasing use of cremation could, however, suggest profound changes in social structure. While there is little surviving evidence for chieftainship and priesthood before c. 2,500 BC, thereafter we find an increasing quantity of equipment which suggests the possibility of both: and in the so-called Wessex Culture of the Early Bronze Age there is a series of graves whose furnishings – daggers, axes, gold-work and other ornaments – suggest exceptional wealth among certain men and women.

During the last ten years the research of Professor Thom has also established the distinct possibility that from c. 2,500 BC there was increasing knowledge of astronomy and of the mathematical precision

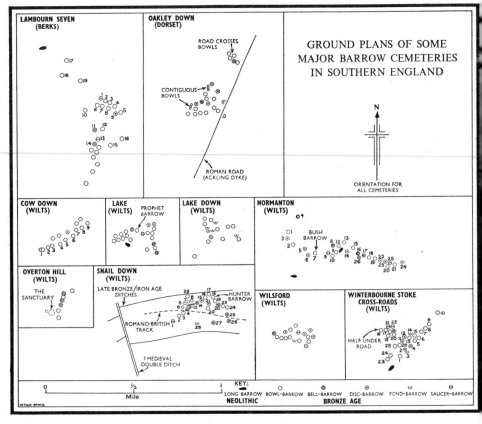

10   *Barrow cemeteries*

required to measure the passing of years and of periods within the year by constructing permanent structures for calculation.

However sophisticated the social stratification may have been, however wealthy the patrons of craftsmen and of priests and seers, the way of life for most Bronze Age people, in a warm, dry climate probably altered little during the earlier 2nd millenium BC. The food supply was sustained by a mixture of arable farming and stock-raising, augmented by hunting, fishing, fowling and the gathering of what nature had to offer. Erosion of the surface of most of the areas of early settlement in Britain, together with silting of valleys, has removed or hidden virtually all trace of their dwellings but here and there remains of fields have been found, sufficient to show (with other evidence) that Early Bronze Age farmers and pastoralists were making a not inconsiderable impact upon the landscape.

Today, however, the chief witnesses to the engineering and organising abilities of the Late Neolithic and Bronze Age communities in Britain are to be found in the round barrows, the henge monuments and the stone circles and alignments which belong to this period. When a death occurred in the family of a chief or master craftsman (assuming that only the select few were granted barrow-burial), or when their leader himself died, the whole social group involved would gather at the traditional burial ground and sometimes spend weeks in elaborate burial ceremonies, which occasionally included the storage of the corpse (as in the Neolithic) until the time for construction of the barrow was propitious: the preferred time seems to have been in late summer, when the harvest was gathered and the springtime additions to flocks and herds were safely established.

Nearly two centuries of barrow-digging has shown that in detail no Bronze Age burials are quite alike. More broadly, however, inhumation was gradually replaced by cremation, the later Neolithic preferred rite re-establishing itself. Each barrow was erected principally for one person, male or female, adult, juvenile or infant. Other corpses sometimes accompanied the primary interment, suggesting that human sacrifice may have been a common practice. In addition, secondary burials – perhaps of lesser members of the same family or group – were frequently placed in the sides of a barrow at a later date.

Ceremonies during burial were often involved and prolonged. When cremation was the rite, the funeral pyre was sometimes built near the centre of the area later to be covered by the mound. More often the burning took place elsewhere, the bones of the deceased – usually washed clean of ashes – being brought to the site of the burial in a special container. Before cremation or inhumation, the corpse was sometimes laid out for a period of days or weeks for the flesh to decay and wooden platforms were occasionally built for this purpose. Some pond-barrows (fig. 57) were also used as enclosures for the dead before final burial.

Inhumed corpses were generally buried fully clothed. The more durable parts of their dress – shale or bone buttons, bone and bronze pins – provide all too inadequate hints at the fashions of the time. Grave goods were appropriate to the sex of the deceased. With men, hunting-knives, arrowheads and battle-axes were frequently deposited; offerings of beads, awls and small knives were placed with women.

In Wessex the sex of a corpse seems sometimes to have been commemorated in the type of barrow raised over it. Bell-barrows, large mounds separated by a berm or space from their surrounding ditch (fig. 11), usually covered male interments. Females were placed beneath disc-barrows – small mounds at the centre of a large circular space defined by a ditch and outer bank. Saucer-barrows were built more often over females than males. Bowl-barrows, the least sophisticated of barrow forms, covered burials of either sex.

In chalk country, the ditch around a barrow provided white chalk as a final covering for the mound (fig. 54). In Bronze Age times the great barrow cemeteries of Wessex, the Chilterns, East Anglia and the Yorkshire Wolds would have appeared as blazing circles of white in a landscape of greens and browns.

In stone country, barrows were less frequently surrounded by a ditch. Retaining walls or kerbs of well-laid stone, and complicated internal structures replaced the ditch as a focus of attention. Burial rituals were in other respects as elaborate and individual. Nowhere outside Wessex, however, were the accompanying grave goods so rich. A few henge monuments were built in the Bronze Age. The Thornborough Circles (fig. 67) and those about Ripon (north Yorks.) can be attributed to the Stonehenge period by the concentration of round barrows among them and by the presence of a filled-up and forgotten Neolithic cursus which underlies the central Thornborough Circle. Here, in low-lying, river-gravel country, crystals of gypsum had been deposited on the bank in an attempt to whiten it – clearly the designer's response to what he or his patron had seen in the nearby Wolds, or perhaps in Wessex itself. The Neolithic henge monument was replaced generally, however, by the simple stone circle, particularly in areas where stone for uprights was available. In Cornwall and Devon, parts of Dorset, the Peak and in the north, circles of greatly varying diameter and height were raised in large numbers. Single uprights can often be found at their centres or just outside. It used to be thought that the exact shape of stone circles was immaterial, as

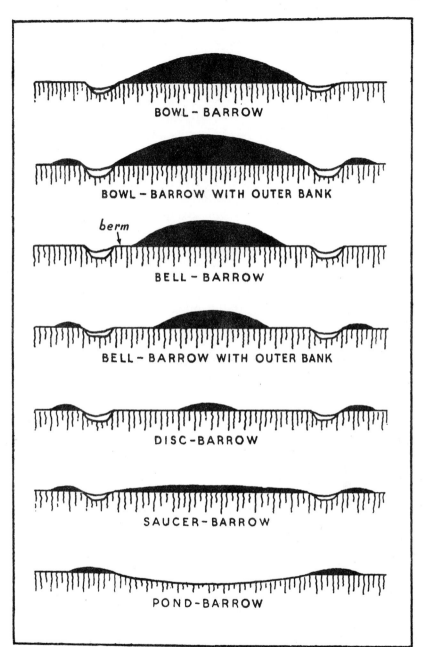

11   *Ideal cross sections to show barrow types*

long as the layout approximated to the circular. Today, thanks to the work of Professor Thom, to which attention has already been drawn, we have come to appreciate that the apparent irregularities in the ground plans of many stone circles are possibly deliberate, the product of relatively advanced field geometry and that the purpose of such structures may be more sophisticated and practical than merely an architectural setting for religious practices focused upon the worship of some earth goddess. In late Neolithic henges like Avebury (Wilts.) and Arbor Low (Derbyshire), the bank and inner-ditch arrangement included a circle of stones in the area thus defined.

Stonehenge remains the greatest tribute to the organising ability and the wealth necessary to command massive human and natural resources that was wielded by one group in the Early Bronze Age anywhere in Europe. The uncertainties now attached to the interpretation, in calendar years, of radio-carbon determinations (p. 36) have suggested that the Mycenaean background to Stonehenge in its third phase, hitherto assumed, has now to be reconsidered – that Stonehenge III may have been conceived before the rise of that great prehistoric Greek civilisation. At the present time this problem must remain unresolved until more is known of the variations in the rate at which Carbon-14 is absorbed by living organisms but it emphasises the flimsiness of assumptions which are not based upon irrefutable evidence.

The engraving of ritual symbols upon stone monuments and on the surfaces of natural rocks was a widespread practice in Bronze Age England. In the south, the signs are often easily understood, axe-heads (of bronze) being most commonly depicted. In Yorkshire and further north, the commonest symbols are small circular depressions, often surrounded by rings and with an occasional channel leading away from the central 'cup mark'. All these signs must have been derived from the more monumental engravings of the Atlantic seaboard of Europe. They were brought by the builders of passage-graves, who introduced those great communal burial mounds to Ireland, North Wales and to Cornwall in the 4th or 3rd millenium BC.

Current belief suggests that the barrow-building phase in Britain ended about 1,300 BC; perhaps by c. 1,400 BC, however, the material products of the Early Bronze Age were changing sufficiently to enable us to distinguish a Middle Bronze Age period, marked by considerable diversification of bronze tools, weapons and ornaments, by new burial practice and above all by the development of a new life-style which made a real impact upon the countryside. Life in Britain henceforth appears to have changed but little between the emergence of the Middle Bronze Age and the first appearance of iron technology about the 7th century BC and with it the beginning of our Iron Age. The so-called Late Bronze Age, beginning c. 10th century BC, saw considerable development in bronze casting techniques, coupled with mass production of a great variety of metalwork – rapiers and slashing swords with shields for defence, spears and knives for hunting; axes, chisels, hammers and saws for the carpenter. Although a massive increase in weapon production and the appearance of slashing swords and horse-gear suggest the rise of a new style of warrior prince, the remains to be seen on the ground – the chief interest of this guide – are indistinguishable from those of the Middle Bronze Age.

Styles in Middle–Late Bronze Age pottery betray an unmistakable Neolithic ancestry. The barrel- and bucket-shaped pots (fig. 13) with their finger-tip decorated bands applied so as to resemble rope-work carriers for these usually large containers, recall grooved ware of c. 1700 BC. The Early Bronze Age collared urns (fig. 6) continued, simplified, with finger-tipped bands added. Only the food vessels and the incense cups (figs. 7–9) disappeared, with the round-barrow burials for which they were made.

The bronzes characteristic of the Middle phase were rapiers, socketed spears and palstaves – evolved from the flat and flanged axes of the Early Bronze Age, no doubt through European stimulus. Bronze ornaments, mainly bracelets and neck-rings, became common

12 *Deverel Barrow, Dorset: Middle Bronze Age globular urn, c. 1,200 BC. Height 9 ins., rim diam. 7 ins.*

13 *Deverel Barrow, Dorset: Middle Bronze Age bucket urn, c. 1,200 BC. Height 13½ ins., rim diam. 10½ ins.*

for the first time, while goldsmiths left sheet gold in preference for bar gold; in due course the use of solder became widespread. Middle Bronze Age hoards of metalwork are known, but they became common – and really large – only in the Late Bronze Age, suggesting that the tinker of the 2nd millennium could hardly have been commercially conscious.

The effect made upon the landscape by the farmers of the later 2nd millennium was the most striking aspect of this period. As we have indicated, Early Bronze settlements are unknown, the mellow climate perhaps making substantial buildings unnecessary. From Middle Bronze Age times, in a gradually deteriorating climate, we find well-preserved remains of settlements. These comprised small groups of circular houses, usually enclosed within fenced or stone-walled paddocks and linked by trackways to fields and watering places. Evidently the social units involved were small and land hunger had not yet arisen. Hence personal weapons do not stand out in the archaeological record and fortified settlements are almost unknown. These farmers seem to have lived in peace, continuing to plough and to raise stock as their ancestors had done for more than 2,000 years.

The settlements were set among fields, square or oblong in shape, seldom exceeding $\frac{1}{2}$ an acre in area and known as 'Celtic' fields. Rare instances of round barrows overlying 'Celtic' fields show that their development dates from the Early Bronze Age or before: they flourished from the Middle Bronze until the end of Roman times and have left an unmistakable pattern upon the English landscape – a unique heritage – which is only now – alas – being erased by the deep ploughing and bulldozing techniques of modern farming.

Middle Bronze farmers worked blocks of 'Celtic' fields whose boundaries, often edged by trackways, are still visible in many parts of England. Sometimes the fields are aligned on an axis whose orientation is followed across many square miles of countryside, as if master-minded by a few exceptionally influencial communities or individuals. Here and there occur blocks of fields differently aligned, as if rival farming interests were being asserted. Invariably, however, those who tilled the 'Celtic' fields respected the earlier round barrows, using them on occasion as markers for the laying out of the fields and trackways but never ploughing over them.

The settlements and fields of our Middle and Late Bronze Age vary little in general layout whether in Wessex or on Dartmoor or in the north of England and they suggest a uniformity of arable and pasture farming, augmented no doubt by hunting, which is echoed in material equipment.

In Wessex, at least, a notable change occurred, probably during the latter part of this period, when much of the land appears to have been reorganised and divided up by massive, v-shaped boundary ditches into larger, generally rectangular areas which, as on Snail Down (Wilts.) have sometimes cut across earlier 'Celtic' fields. This rationalising of the landscape, in which the v-shaped ditch systems have been shown (at Snail Down and elsewhere) to supersede earlier, usually flat-floored boundary ditches, may reflect a growing shortage of arable land as population increased and more powerful communities began to take in the land of weaker neighbours.

It is almost impossible to reconstruct the religious beliefs of these Middle and Late Bronze Age farmers. Barrow-building in the south of England had ceased probably before 1,200 BC. In Yorkshire and other northern centres of population, remains of the dead, inhumed or cremated, were covered by small stone heaps (cairns), concentrated in their hundreds close to the settlements. In Wessex, the link with the barrow-builders was maintained by burying the cremated dead, often in a characteristic urn, in a hole in the sides of an earlier mound, with large numbers of additional burials extending away from the barrow in a flat cemetery, or so-called urnfield. No stone or earthwork structures have survived which can be interpreted as ritualistic in purpose, although the remains of timber dwellings suggest that structures for religion could have been built of wood, in the tradition of Woodhenge.

Although a climatic deterioration early in the 1st millennium BC must have necessitated improved buildings and permanent settlements, sites datable to this period are rare. From the 8th and 7th centuries BC, however, we find an increasing number of well-preserved settlements, whose owners were using new styles of pottery and tools or weapons occasionally made of iron, which serve to usher in our final period in prehistory, the Iron Age.

In Iron Age Britain, there was a dual character in the population. The foundations of society were the small, mixed-farming communities of the Bronze Age, living mostly in enclosed settlements of round houses among 'Celtic' fields. Mingling with them were Celts, coming from France and the Low Countries as migrants or in small groups as princely adventurers and through trade and other social contact.

The continuity of the Bronze Age is seen in the tradition of circular houses, which were built throughout the Iron Age. The architectural contributions of the Iron Age period are found in elaboration of the round-house style, particularly its increase in size to the proportions hitherto recorded only at Woodhenge and similar religious structures of the Neolithic. Where no stone was available, these houses were entirely timber-framed: their roofs were probably thatched or skin-covered, with walls infilled with wattle-and-daub. In stony country, footings were often of stone, supporting a timber superstructure (figs. 25, 36). A porch sometimes, channels to take off rain water, a hearth, such were the normal built-in amenities of an Iron Age dwelling. The innovation of the period is the appearance at Crickley Hill (Glos.) and at a few other places of large rectangular buildings. These represent the continental tradition and were brought to Britain by settlers or by other direct contacts with western Europe.

Farming practice, the basic Iron Age occupation, shows the same trends: while 'Celtic' fields continued, large-scale storage of grain in underground pits was new. The simple Bronze Age scratch-plough, probably drawn by a pair of oxen, continued in use although a heavier, more useful variety may have been introduced just before the Roman conquest. But the efficiency in crop-raising was increased by a greater awareness of the importance of manure (explaining the potsherds found in the soil of 'Celtic' fields, presumably incorporated in the refuse brought from the settlement for spreading on the fields). It is possible that some form of crop rotation may also have been practised. To the basic crops of barley and wheat a number of other cereals were introduced which, coupled with meat and fruit, fish and game gave Iron Age society an ample and varied diet: it helps to account for the considerable increase in population during the last centuries before the Roman conquest.

Domestic economy in the Iron Age revolved around the successful storage of seed and the preservation of artificially dried grain for food. Cereals harvested for flour were dried in the sun on wooden racks, threshed and then preserved in square granaries or shelters erected on 4–6 posts, or else, along with seed grain, stored in deep pits, lined with basketry or clay and covered with lids. These protected the harvest from wild animals, vermin and fire. Their life would have been short: when contaminated with mildew, they were converted into rubbish pits and replaced by freshly dug silos for the next yield from the fields (fig. 26). At Little Woodbury (Wilts.) the stockade around a farmstead which was inhabited for several generations contained about 360 such storage pits. North of a rough line joining the Severn Estuary to the mouth of the Humber, storage pits are less commonly found, although recent aerial photography is beginning to reveal their existence in Yorkshire and elsewhere. Nevertheless, it seems clear that northern Iron Age peoples developed a different economy, concentrating on cattle-breeding, some sheep-farming, keeping pigs and perhaps rearing ponies.

Hunting was pursued on horseback and on foot, with dogs playing an important part in the chase. The principal long-range weapon was the sling. For the kill there were iron-headed spears, with swords and a variety of dirks and knives. The range of iron tools and weapons was almost limitless. Huntsman, butcher, blacksmith, carpenter, farmer, each had his own specialist kit which would still look practical to a modern craftsman.

Sheep provided wool for clothing which was woven on a vertical loom, a piece of apparatus which would have been found in almost every house at this time. Only the stone or clay weights which kept the vertical threads taut survive – with holes in the ground marking where the loom posts stood. An array of bone weaving combs, needles and other things hint at the doubtless prettily decorated cloth which was made in each home. Indeed mirrors, toilet articles, pins, beads, all suggest that as the time of the Roman Conquest approached, the people of Britain were well clothed and conscious of personal style.

Beauty and design were now a part of craftsmanship. In the home, cooking pots no longer appeared at table, a range of finer wares being used for eating. In woodwork (which has been so well preserved in the Somerset lakeside villages) and above all in bronze and precious metals, the artistic sense which western Europeans had gained from contact with the Greek world reached a height not matched before nor since excelled. British 'Celtic Art', its greatest pieces located in most of our national museums, its lesser achievements best represented at Glastonbury and Taunton, was a noble contribution to the artistic heritage of western Europe.

The general absence of change between the way of life of the Bronze Age farmer and his Iron Age successor, with 'Celtic' fields being tilled and small farmsteads continuing into the Roman period, must be set against the appearance of hill-forts which, from the 7th century BC, were built in great numbers in most parts of England.

Many – perhaps most – hill-forts were built on ground which had been a focus of occupation, sometimes including ritual, since Neolithic times. Maiden Castle (Dorset), where the causewayed camp was overlaid by a bank barrow, followed in turn by (ill-defined) Bronze Age occupation and then by hill-forts of two periods, enclosing an Iron Age ritual building and then a Romano-Celtic temple both located suggestively close to the east end of the Neolithic bank barrow, is one among many to feature such continuity. Generally, our earliest hill-forts enclose less than ten acres, with a tendency to increase in size as the period progressed, often reflecting the growth in Celtic population which we have already noted.

As with size, so in development of defences. Most early hill-forts comprise one bank and ditch, additional earthworks following in time to form the multivallate enclosure. In most of the latter, the banks and ditches are juxtaposed. Occasionally, especially in the south west – e.g. Milber Down (Devon), Buzbury (Dorset) or Bredon Hill (Hereford and Worcester) – wide spaces were left between the ramparts, possibly to provide areas for herding stock or, as at Bredon, to double the size of fortified ground in response to local needs.

Most hill-forts were built on high, dominating ground and it is often possible to see a pattern in which naturally defined areas of several square miles usually contain at least one major hill-fort. Hill-slope forts are sites where the earthworks were deliberately sited below the highest ground: many such enclosures also have widespread defences. Forts are not infrequently located on low ground, although here a command of country may nevertheless occur through its flatness, while proximity to rivers may provide natural protection. Spurs and promontories were used frequently, the hill-fort being located so that maximum advantage could be taken of natural slopes to keep earthwork-building to the minimum.

Cliff castles, single or multivallate in defences and a peculiarity of the south west, are a version of the inland promontory forts but their resemblance to the cliff castles of Brittany may also suggest close cultural contact between the two regions. Hill-forts, the most spectacular of English prehistoric earthworks, are monuments to military engineering and tribal organisation. Ladle Hill (Hants.) and Bindon (Dorset) are half-finished examples which show how the work was done. First came the marking out trenches of the planners, then the deepening and widening of ditches, the heightening of banks behind by gangs of labourers carrying out the design. Carpenters or stone-masons provided the vertical rampart facings behind wide, deep, v-shaped ditches which confronted an enemy (figs. 24, 29). The greatest ingenuity and building skill was necessary at the entrances. These were the weak points in a hill-fort. They had to be kept to a minimum and were frequently defended by elaborate outworks. In many forts, however, entrances were simple breaks in the earthworks, especially among the earliest single-rampart forts. Frequently, the rampart ends were built to curve inwards, defining a funnel-shaped passage. Wooden gates, sometimes with a footbridge for sentries over the top, were hung near the inner end of the funnel. Guard houses of stone or timber have been found beside many gates. Within, the area immediately behind the ramparts was the favourite site for huts but, as with the attendant storage pits, granaries and paddocks, they could also occur in the central area more generally.

The main concentration of hill-forts in England, particularly those with multiple ramparts, lies to the south of Yorkshire and Lancashire.

Genuine hill-forts, it is true, occur in the north, for example the Stanwick (North Yorks.) earthworks and Yeavering Bell (Northumberland). The general pattern of settlement in these northern areas, however, seems to indicate a large population (particularly in Northumberland and Cumbria) divided into small units. Even where sites described in the gazetteer as 'hill-fort' occur, they tend to be well under 5 acres in area.

In the decades following c. 120 BC, south-eastern England witnessed large-scale settlement of peoples from the area of modern Belgium, the so-called Belgae. From initial landings at the mouth of the Thames and in Kent, these newcomers spread rapidly north of the Thames into Hertfordshire. Later, c. 60–50 BC, a second wave of Belgae settled in Sussex, Berkshire, the Thames valley and parts of Hampshire (map of late Iron Age tribes, fig. 14). The history of the last pre-Roman

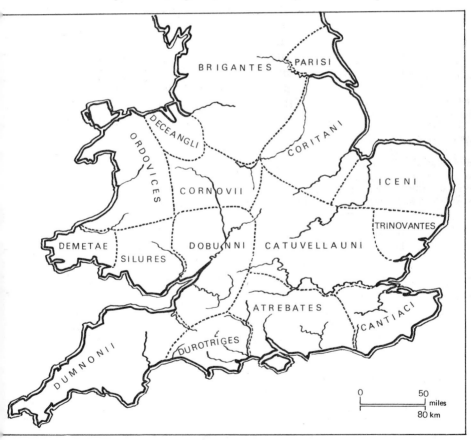

14 *Late Iron Age tribes in southern Britain*

years in England concerns the rivalry of these two Belgic tribes in the south east – the Catuvellauni and Trinovantes of Herts. – Essex, and the Atrebates and Regni of Berkshire, Hampshire and Sussex, and the attempts by the non-Belgic tribes north and west to contain them.

The Belgic settlements introduced a number of important inventions to Britain. The principle of the wheel had perhaps the most far-reaching effect. Wheeled vehicles came into general use throughout southern England. A plough drawn by a large team of oxen and sometimes mounted on wheels broadened the scope of the farmer, enabling him to move down on to the heavier soils of the valleys. For the potter, the introduction of a kick-wheel allowed an almost limitless repertoire of shapes for cooking pots, dishes, flagons and drinking cups. The housewife, moreover, now received a new type of handmill – the rotary quern – for grinding her corn. Instead of rubbing the grain between a circular upper stone and an elongated lower grindstone, she could do this daily chore more efficiently and quickly by rotating two circular stones, one pivoting upon the other and turned with a handle. The flour was finer and less was wasted. Finally, the Belgae introduced a coinage of gold, silver and bronze. Coins began to circulate in small numbers in the south of England before 120 BC (the arrival of the first Belgic people). It seems, however, that after the Belgic settlements these became a regular part of life in southern England. Through contact with Roman Gaul, the Belgic chiefs in particular began to inscribe their names, in Roman characters, upon their coins. For the first time, some, at least, of the inhabitants of England cease to be anonymous. They take on a new individuality. In the commentaries of Caesar we have the first eye-witness account of those who had built and inhabited our hill-forts, tilled our 'Celtic' fields, made the pottery, the tools, coins and other things which now fill our museums.

Some new and distinctive earthworks were introduced to England by the Belgic invaders. They did not normally build or inhabit hill-forts. Instead they fortified their capitals and defined their often hard-won lands by large enclosures and elaborate systems of dykes. The earthworks north of Verulamium (St Albans) and at Wheathampstead (Herts.), those west of Camulodunum (Colchester), at Bagendon (Glos.) and at Chichester (Sussex) are examples of tribal defences in the new style.

Burials and evidence for ritual throughout the Iron Age are scanty. Before the Belgic invasions, a small series of inhumation burials widely distributed in England suggests that this was the normal rite. Some cemeteries, such as those at Harlyn (Cornwall) and the Humberside Danes Graves, together with war cemeteries such as that outside Maiden Castle (fig. 28), imply that most communities buried their dead in single graves (sometimes beneath small mounds), concentrated near the settlements. So far very few cemeteries have been discovered. The Belgae cremated their dead, the ashes being contained in urns of pottery or sometimes in bronze buckets and deposited in pits. These were usually concentrated into cemeteries. Grave goods deposited with these people ranged from a few pots to elaborate furnishings of bronze and iron, with glass, ornaments and personal equipment. It is possible on these grounds to distinguish between the graves of chiefs, noblemen and ordinary folk. Dedication burials during the erection of hill-forts and dwellings (for example at Maiden Castle, Dorset, fig. 27) may have involved human sacrifice and show the continuation of a religious belief which may first have appeared in England in Neolithic times. Structures built specifically for worship are extremely rare. The religion of henge monument, stone circle and stone upright had either died out in the Iron Age or else was practised in places less artificially defined. While, as we have already noted, the location of hill-forts and their internal arrangements reflect a continuity with earlier ritualistic and domestic sites, just as Stonehenge still attracted attention in the Iron Age, it is probable that during the last centuries before the Christian era religious ceremonies were usually performed in the open or in forest clearings. Here and there, however, excavation has revealed circular structures along with crude versions of the square Romano-Celtic temples which remind us of the varied setting in which the Druids and other Iron Age priests and seers performed their rituals.

During his campaign in Gaul, Julius Caesar tested the strength of our south-eastern Belgae by landing in Kent in 55 and 54 BC. He conquered the area as far north as Hertfordshire and brought the Catuvellauni to terms. These Britains at least were to send annual tribute money to Rome. The arrangement appears to have lapsed on his death, and during the years preceding the final conquest of AD 43 the Romans maintained an uneasy peace with the Britons more by diplomacy than by military discipline. The pre-Roman coins provide ample evidence for the dynastic struggles which raged within England and for the support which the rival houses sought, at intervals, from Rome. The Belgae of Berkshire–Hampshire–Sussex, the Atrebates and Regni, came down heavily on the side of Rome; the Catuvellauni remained nationalist to the last, the ear of barley on their coins being struck in defiant opposition to the Roman vine leaf which the supplicants to Caesar had placed upon theirs. Cunobelin (Cymbeline), the greatest chief of the Catuvellauni, never challenged Rome by a direct assault upon his Belgic rivals to the south west, but attempted to expand into their territories by his own forms of diplomacy. On his death (c. AD 40) his less prudent heirs precipitated the Roman conquest of AD 43 by direct acts of aggression against those who had allowed themselves to become dependent upon Rome.

A Note on Dating

An attempt has been made to suggest dates in years for many of the sites in this guide. Sometimes, for lack of precise information obtained by excavation or other means, the brackets within which the construction and primary use of the site are likely to fall can span up to a millenium. Other sites can be dated relatively closely, either because of characteristic finds made there or else because radiocarbon, or Carbon-14 dates have been obtained (for up-to-date explanations of the method, including corrections now apparently necessary in the light of recent research using the long-lived bristlecone pine, see the sections in M. Magnusson, *Introducing Archaeology*, Bodley Head, 1972, and C. Renfrew, *Before Civilization*, Jonathan Cape, 1974). For Iron Age hill-forts, experience gained by scientific excavation during the last 20 years shows that it is pointless to hazard precise dating within the Iron Age period (c. 650 BC–AD 43) unless extensive excavation has been carried out. Here, the comment 'not dated' indicates this lack of precise information.

The dates quoted in this guide are based on C14 determinations which have not been corrected to allow for the variations which bristlecone-pine research, mentioned above, now suggests is necessary if a date in calendar years, not C14 years is required. It is gradually emerging that C14 years become increasingly younger than the true, calendar years (obtained by correction) for any sample, in proportion to its date before the start of the Christian era; by the 4th millenium BC, the true date of a sample can be more than 700 years older than its C14 date. Thus the calendar date for the beginning of Stonehenge, phase III, now appears to fall some centuries before the *floruit* of Mycenaean civilisation (its own date immovably fixed by cross reference to Egyptian dating), upon whose architectural experience its builders had been thought hitherto to have drawn. Because of these uncertainties in the carbon-dating technique, the author has thought it best to quote C14 years, leaving it to his readers to apply the corrections when they judge that research upon the subject makes the necessary correction charts sufficiently reliable. For the same reason, he has decided to use capital letters for BC, as of old, instead of following the modern practice of employing lower case letters – bc – for uncorrected C14 dates.

GLOSSARY OF ARCHAEOLOGICAL TERMS

Abingdon ware An early decorated style within the Neolithic pottery family in southern England, characterised by pounded shell grit, strap handles, heavy rims, pricked and incised decoration. Named after causewayed camp at Abingdon (Oxon.).

adze Carpenter's and farmer's tool, the head shaped like an axe but hafted with cutting edge at right angles to line of handle.

agger Made-up foundation of Roman road; also hill-fort and other ramparts, a term now rarely used.

Aldbourne cup Miniature ritual cup of Early Bronze Age (c. 1,700–1,400 BC) characterised by incised and dot-filled decoration (fig. 7). Perhaps French origin; Wessex distribution.

awl Copper or bronze boring tool, one end fitted into handle. Usually found with females in graves (2,100–1,300 BC).

bank barrow p. 16.

barrow Circular or elongated mound raised over burials. Mound derived from surrounding quarry-ditch or by scraping in vicinity. Neolithic–Iron Age.

battle-axe Stone weapon or ceremonial axe-head, attached to handle by shaft-hole. Usually one cutting edge, with flattened butt. Late Neolithic–Early Bronze Age.

beaker Drinking vessel with S-shaped profile, flat base, decorated by impressed cord or notched tool (fig. 5). European origin still uncertain; British vessels derived from Rhineland, c. 2,200 BC.

Beaker Folk p. 18 ff.

Belgae p. 33 ff.

Belgic Pertaining to Belgae.

bell-barrow Large Early Bronze Age (c. 1,700–1,400 BC) burial mound separated from surrounding ditch by flat space (berm). Concentrated in S. England chalk country. Usually covers male burial. Fig. 11, p. 25. Two or three mounds can be surrounded by one ditch (double or triple bell).

bell-beaker See beaker.

belt-hook Part of large hook-and-eye belt fastening common in Early Bronze Age (c. 1,700–1,400 BC). Usually of bone.

berm Flat space separating bank from quarry-ditch. Characterises bell-barrow (fig. 11). Also found at some long barrows.

blind entrance Dummy entrance at broadened end of chambered long barrow, with burial chambers located elsewhere in mound. Belas Knap (Glos.) the classic example (fig. 30).

bowl-barrow Circular barrow mound, surrounded by a ditch (fig. 11). Commonest type of barrow, especially Neolithic–Early Bronze Age, but wide range in time and distribution.

Brigantes Non-Belgic Late Iron Age tribe in N. of England (fig. 14). Final centre at Stanwick (N. Yorks.); p. 251.

Bronze Age p. 20 ff.

cairn Heap of stones covering burial. Wide range in size, date and distribution.

capstone Roofing stone to burial chamber or cist.

Catuvellauni Chief Belgic tribe of SE England in late Iron Age (fig. 14); p. 33.

causewayed camp p. 14.

cella Here, main room of Romano-Celtic temple.

'Celtic' field p. 28.

Chysauster-type house Iron Age stone dwelling with series of rooms leading off roughly circular courtyard. Local origin in Britain.

cist Burial pit dug into subsoil; sometimes lined with stones and roofed with capstone; usually covered by barrow. Also stone burial container built on land surface beneath barrow, too small to be classed as a 'chamber'.

collared urn (fig. 6) Chief storage jar of Early Bronze Age, c. 1,700–1,300 BC, derivative forms extending to Iron Age. Majority have been found associated with cremated burials and there used as containers for human ashes.

corbelling Method of roofing stone chambers whereby upper layers of wall stones overhang increasingly until they meet to form roof, or else leave space small enough for a single capstone.

cordoned urn Regional version of collared urn where lower edge of collar is replaced by strip (cordon) of clay and profile has become slack. North English style, c. 1,700–1,300 BC.

counterscarp bank Small bank on outer (downhill) edge of hill-fort ditch.

cove U-shaped setting of stone uprights associated with stone circles and other ritual sites of Neolithic and Bronze Age.

cup-and-ring marks Rock carvings comprising circular depressions with one or more surrounding rings (also hollowed), brought to Britain in later Neolithic period and concentrated in N of England. Use extended into Bronze Age.

cupmark See above.

currency bar Flat bar of iron, edges at one end squeezed up. Made in various lengths up to 3 ft.; supposed to be currency in Iron Age, c. 100 BC. Concentration in south-central Midlands.

cursus p. 16.

Deverel-Rimbury culture Middle Bronze Age culture in s and central England from c. 1,300 BC. Stockaded settlements; new pottery styles and metalwork (figs. 12, 13).

disc-barrow (fig. 11) Small mound on wide circular plateau defined by ditch and outer bank. Chalk-country type, usually covering female cremated interment; c. 1,700–1,400 BC. Two or three mounds can be located on the plateau.

Dobunni Non-Belgic Late Iron Age tribe, settled in Cotswolds with capital latterly at Bagendon (Glos.), fig. 14. Perhaps conquered by Catuvellauni c. AD 15.

Durotriges Non-Belgic Late Iron Age tribe of Dorset/Somerset; fig. 14.

entrance-grave See gallery-grave, passage-grave.

faience Form of glass having quartz core fused, by heat, with lime or alkali, and covering glaze of soda–lime–quartz; often coloured blue with copper salts. Origin perhaps Near East. Used as close dating evidence for Early Bronze Age, but believed by some to be of local origin and so less useful.

flange Term used particularly to describe ridges along top and bottom edges of early bronze axe-heads, hammered or cast, to keep head rigid in handle.

fogou Passage cut into subsoil, roofed and concealed, associated with Iron Age settlements in Cornwall. Often has one or more branches and side chambers. Considered to be escape route or hideout, also perhaps for storage.

food vessel (figs. 8, 65) Early Bronze Age (c. 1,700–1,400 BC) flowerpot-shaped vessel with ridged or hollowed upper part and thick bevelled rim. Decorated more profusely in north than in south where it can be plain. Later Neolithic origins.

forecourt Semicircular end (usually at E) of chambered long barrow, with entrance to burial chambers at centre. Focus of burial rituals.

gallery-grave Neolithic chambered tomb where rectangular burial chamber is not clearly differentiated from approach passage. Covered by long or round mound (Scillonian entrance graves). 'Transepted' gallery-graves have series of side chambers leading off parallel-sided gallery which was also used for burials (Cotswold tombs classic examples). Simple gallery-graves are concentrated in England, in the Peak District.

grape cup (fig. 50) Miniature ritual vessel found in graves of Wessex Early Bronze Age (c. 1,700–1,400 BC). Sides covered with decorative knobs. French origin probable.

grooved ware (fig. 3) Late Neolithic style, characterised by flat base, profuse decoration including grooves, dots, fingertip and applied bands.

halberd, halberd pendant Early Bronze Age weapon (c. 1,700–1,400 BC), heavy dagger-like blade fixed by rivets at right angles to shaft. Models (pendants) in gold and amber strung on necklaces by women in Wessex.

Hallstatt First (c. 8th century BC) iron-using culture in central and w Europe, named after type-site in Austrian Alps. Introduced iron to Britain.

henge monument p. 18.

hill-fort p. 31 ff.

hill-slope fort p. 32.

Iceni Non-Belgic late Iron Age tribe of East Anglia (fig. 14). Revolted against Roman authority AD 51, under their queen Boudicca.

incense cup (figs. 7, 9) Miniature ritual vessel of Early Bronze Age (c. 1,700–1,400 BC), usually highly decorated. See grape cup, Aldbourne Cup.

Iron Age p. 29ff.

La Tène Second (5th century BC–1st century AD) Iron Age culture of central and w Europe, named after type-site in Switzerland.

long barrow p. 15ff.

long cairn p. 17ff.

lynchet Bank of soil accumulated at downhill side of 'Celtic' (and medieval) fields caused by ploughing on sloping ground.

megalithic Made of large stones; term usually applied to burial chambers.

Mesolithic Middle Stone Age, c. 8,000–4,000 BC. Characterised by composite hunting weapons, barbed or pointed with flint blades less than 1 in. long (microliths).

microlith See Mesolithic.

monolith Large stone, associated with structure or else erected alone for ritual purposes.

mortuary enclosure Earthwork or timber structure built for storage of corpses prior to erection of barrow; usually Neolithic, p. 18.

Mousterian A Palaeolithic culture of the last glacial period of the Ice Age, defined by distinctive stone tool-making techniques and tool types, e.g. heart-shaped hand-axes, side-scrapers and choppers: associated on some sites with Neanderthal man.

Neolithic p. 13 ff.

Palaeolithic Old Stone Age, period prior to c. 8,000 BC. Upper Palaeolithic includes last major cold phase of Ice Age, inhabited caves, paintings, etc.

passage-grave Chambered tomb covered by round mound; burial chamber clearly differentiated from approach passage. Scillonian entrance-graves combine elements of passage- and gallery-graves. Extending through Neolithic in Britain.

Penwith chamber tomb See portal dolmen.

platform-barrow Form of Bronze Age bowl-barrow with flat-topped mound.

pond-barrow (figs. 11, 57). Used for burial, ritual and as mortuary enclosure; Early Bronze Age.

portal dolmen probably early form of Neolithic communal burial chamber, usually covered by long mound. Side-wall stones project at one end to form portal entrance, with slab between; roofed by one slab, usually tilted. Exceptionally massive stones used throughout.

port-hole entrance Perforated slabs forming entrance to some Neolithic chambered long barrows, particularly in Cotswolds.

promontory fort p. 32.

revetment A facing designed to prevent slip or collapse of rampart or barrow sides; usually of timber, stone or turf.

ritual pit Hole dug presumably to receive libations and other offerings: feature of pre-barrow rituals in Neolithic, Bronze Age.

round barrow Circular burial mound. See barrow and p. 23ff.

saucer-barrow (fig. 11) Early Bronze Age, chalk downs type. c. 1,700–1,400 BC. Usually covers female cremation.

scarped Part of hillside artificially steepened to strengthen Iron Age hill-fort defences.

Scillonian entrance-grave See gallery-grave, passage-grave.

shaft-grave Vertical shaft for burials, here referring to those royal graves of s Greece (16th–15th centuries BC), containing material possibly showing two-way contact with Wessex during Stonehenge period. But see 'A Note on Dating', p. 36, for problems raised by recalibration of Carbon-14 dates.

tesserae Small cubes of brick, stone or glass set in cement to form pavement. Introduced to Britain by Romans.

Trinovantes Belgic Late Iron Age tribe in Essex. Constant feud with Catuvellauni one cause of Roman invasion, AD 43 (fig. 14).

timber-lacing Technique of Iron Age hill-fort rampart construction, where horizontal timbers are laid across rampart and sometimes attached to vertical timbers at front and back. Often associated with stone revetting of rampart.

timber-revetting Facing of hill-fort rampart with horizontal timbers attached to wide-spaced vertical wooden posts.

transepted gallery-grave See gallery-grave.

Upper Palaeolithic See Palaeolithic.

Windmill Hill culture Term for the best-documented, but not the earliest, group of Neolithic people in s England, named after causewayed camp near Avebury (Wilts.). Way of life probably represents that of most early Neolithic groups in Britain.

Windmill Hill ware One of the earliest pottery styles (figs. 1, 2) in England, belonging to Windmill Hill culture.

wrist-guard Rectangular plate usually of slate, perforated at corners for attachment to wrist. Afforded protection against recoil of archer's bow-string. Part of equipment of Beaker Folk.

THE GAZETTEER

It must be remembered that inclusion of a site in this gazetteer does not imply that the public has access to it. Visitors should always obtain the landowner's permission before inspecting an earthwork which is on private land, however close to a right-of-way.

Directions for reaching a site include the names of nearby large towns (with the main A. or B. roads on which these stand), followed by those of the nearest town or village to the site, with road numbers. Many sites can be found with this information used in conjunction with the normal AA or RAC handbook road maps. It is assumed, however, that the appropriate 1 in. (or 1:50,000) O.S. maps will be used.

Where the present location of finds from a site is known, it is recorded after the directions for finding the site.

This gazetteer is not an exhaustive list of the pre-Roman earthworks of England. It is a selection, and should form the basis for expeditions into the countryside in search of earthworks of specific type. Nevertheless, the majority of major earthworks in England has been included. For counties abounding in prehistoric sites of all types, those which are particularly well preserved have been emphasised at the expense of others. For Wiltshire, barrows have been given more space than hill-forts; for Dorset the emphasis has been reversed. Hill-forts and Neolithic long barrows in the Cotswolds have been listed more exhaustively than round barrows, despite the large number of the latter. In the Midlands, where sites of all types are rare, an attempt has been made to include every pre-Roman earthwork which is still well preserved. It has been impossible to do more than hint at the number and variety of late prehistoric settlements and other sites in Northumberland, Cumbria and the Yorkshire counties. In any case, many of these northern sites may have been built in Roman or immediately post-Roman times: their dating is notoriously difficult.

Some prehistoric sites are closely associated with Roman structures. Where this happens, a description of the Roman remains is included.

An asterisk placed before the name of a site indicates that there is a reference to it in the bibliography (pp. 258–264).

Avon

PALAEOLITHIC

Aveline's Hole (ST/477587), $\frac{1}{2}$ mile N of A368/B3134 junction, on E side of B3134. Finds in the museum of the University of Bristol Spelaeological Society.

This cave is in 2 parts, an inner chamber approached through an outer one. Finds from the cave include not only a wide range of Upper Palaeolithic flint tools and weapons but also a series of apparently contemporary skeletons, some perhaps buried intentionally. Among the objects recovered were 60 sea-shells perforated for threading into a necklace. A link with the contemporary continental culture represented in the painted caves of the Dordogne, France, was provided by an antler harpoon head with two rows of barbs.

This cave, which has been cleared down to bedrock by a series of excavators, would have provided a snug shelter for hunters c. 12,000 BC.

NEOLITHIC

Felton Hill, chambered long barrow (ST/516648) 1$\frac{1}{2}$ miles W of Winford (B3130), $\frac{1}{2}$ mile SW of Felton.

A roughly oval long barrow, c. 75 × 45 ft. and 4 ft. in height, this small example of a probably chambered tomb is orientated NNE/SSW. Its mound is made up of earth and stones and now damaged. At the NNE there are several large stones, 2 still in position, which suggest the remains of a chamber; indeed there are enough to provide for a transepted chamber. Date c. 3,500–2,500 BC.

Hautville's Quoit, standing stone. See **Stanton Drew.**

*Stanton Drew, circles, avenues, cove and standing stones (ST/603630) 6 miles S of Bristol, E of village of Stanton Drew (off B3130).

This group of monuments, which must belong to the period 2,200–1,400 BC, represents a centre of worship comparable to those at Avebury (Wilts., below), Knowlton (Dorset, below) or Thornborough (N Yorks., below). In the use of stone throughout, the Stanton Drew complex belongs essentially to the West.

The largest circle, Great Circle, is the central one of 3 orientated NE/SW. It has a diam. of about 360 ft. and would originally have contained at least 30 stones. Twenty-seven are still visible. On the E side, an avenue, of which 8 stones survive, leads towards the river Chew; it is joined by an avenue from the N circle. The latter is the smallest circle, having a diam. of about 100 ft. It contains its original complement of 8 stones. Like the Great Circle, it has an avenue, 7 stones of which can still be seen. These lead towards the river Chew, joining up with the other avenue. Neither is visible beyond this junction.

The third circle stands 700 ft. to the SW in an orchard. It still has 12 stones and would have had a diam. of 140 ft.

The cove, a U-shaped setting of 2 large uprights with a fallen stone between them, lies behind the Druids Arms Inn. It should be considered an integral part of the complex. Though its purpose is not known it seems likely that it continues the tradition of the concave forecourt of the long barrows which, in earlier Neolithic times, must have been the focus of religious activity – at least during burials. With the development of circles and avenues (and in Britain henge monuments and cursuses) something of the continental long barrow tradition was retained.

A line drawn from the SW circle through Great Circle will strike an isolated stone, Hautville's Quoit, which lies on the N side of the river Chew, 500 yds. to the NE (E of Hautville Farm, S of road to Pensford). It appears that in the 18th century a second stone was near it and both were standing. The survivor today, much damaged, is 7 ft. long and fallen.

The stones used in this complex are mostly the local conglomerate; some are of oolite and Hautville Quoit may be sarsen.

Stoney Littleton, chambered long barrow (ST/735572) 3 miles NE of Radstock (A362, A367) ¾ mile SW of Wellow. Reached via Stoney Littleton Farm. Finds in Bristol City Museum.

An elaborate and well-restored example of the Cotswold series, Stoney Littleton is 107 ft. long and 54 ft. wide. It is wedge-shaped, and orientated SE/NW; it has a max. ht. of 10 ft. A deep funnel-shaped forecourt leads to the tomb entrance; within, an ante-chamber gives access to a walled passage just over 40 ft. long, from which 3 pairs of side chambers lead off. There is also an end chamber. In plan all these are carefully squared up. The roof of chambers and passage is carried out in corbelled vaulting. One of the uprights defining the outer entrance to the tomb seems to have been selected because it bears the well-defined cast of an ammonite.

Restored in 1858, it was first opened in 1816 and many human bones were found in 4 of the side-chambers. It is a fine example of a Cotswold–Severn transepted gallery tomb. Date, c. 3,500–2,500 BC.

Waterstone, burial chamber (ST/501644) on Cornerpool Farm, 1 mile N of Redhill (A38).

Behind the farm a group of stones can be seen which may represent the collapsed burial chamber of a long barrow now destroyed. There are 3 recumbent stones 3–8 ft. long, made of the local lias; a fourth stone, lying across them, measures 10 × 9 ft. and must weigh 6–7 tons. It might have been used as a roofing stone. These stones may be the remains of a portal dolmen. Date, c. 3,500–2,500 BC.

BRONZE AGE

*Lansdown, round barrows (ST/712689) 3½ miles NW of Bath, just E of Little Down Iron Age hill-fort, ½ mile E of North Stoke. Finds in British Museum.

There must have been a number of round barrows on Lansdown in Bronze Age times. Today 2 are clearly visible within the ramparts of Little Down Camp

and 2 more lie just to the E. Both of the latter are small. They were examined about 1905 and found to have been already opened. Each had contained a cremation placed in a cist covered with a stone. One of the cists had escaped careful attention: in it, together with burnt bones and the remains of urns, was found a gold-covered copper disc, 6¾ ins. in diam. and usually called a 'sun-disc'. It has not been satisfactorily identified and is impossible to date. One theory is that it is part of a bowl of the Danish Middle Bronze Age, c. 13th century BC: it could also be post-Roman.

IRON AGE

Bathampton Down, enclosure and 'Celtic' fields (ST/774650) 1¾ miles E of Bath, E of Sham Castle, on golf course.

This enclosure occupies 78¼ acres. It is defended by a single bank and ditch. A modern wall stands on the rampart along the W side. Original entrances cannot now be identified.

The earthwork overlies part of a field system which must therefore be earlier. The roughly square and rectangular fields extend N and S of the enclosure. Their boundary banks are packed with stones, suggesting that originally they were dry-stone walls. A sunken track connected with the fields cuts across the hill-fort nearly 600 yds. E of its W side.

Not dated. Fields possibly in use again after abandonment of the hill-fort.

Blaise Castle, hill-fort (ST/558784) 1 mile NW of Westbury-on-Trym (Bristol), ½ mile SW of Henbury (B4055, B4057); 500 yds. SW of Folk Museum. Finds in Bristol City Museum.

This hill-fort is oval in plan and encloses about 7 acres. The defences are slight along the S and SE where steep hillsides make elaborate earthworks unnecessary. Along the N and W there are 2 banks and ditches, now obscured by trees. Original entrances cannot be identified without excavation. Extended occupation here started c. early 2nd century BC.

Bristol, hill-forts. See **Blaise Castle, Clifton** and **Kings Weston.**

*Bury Hill, hill-fort (ST/652791) 5½ miles NE of Bristol, ½ mile S of Winterbourne Down (between A432 and B4058).

This camp is roughly pear-shaped, its defences enclosing about 5½ acres. On the w side quarrying has obscured the earthworks. Here the ground slopes steepest but is not sufficiently precipitous to warrant absence of fortifications. On the other 3 sides there are 2 banks and ditches with possible entrance gaps facing NE, NW and SE. In view of the Roman occupation of this site it is not clear which of the entrances are of the Iron Age.

Excavation has revealed that the banks are composed of stone rubble dug from the ditches and faced on the outer sides by well-built stone retaining walls. In places the inner rampart still has a height of 9 ft. The ditch was U-shaped, in places 20 ft. wide and 5 ft. deep.

Most of the features within the earthworks of the camp are Romano-British, the long mound near the centre, on the w side, being an early Roman dwelling house. A well was found just s of the NW entrance of the camp.

The camp has not been dated by excavation. Occupation followed all through the Roman period.

Cadbury Camp, hill-fort (ST/454725) 3¼ miles E of Clevedon (B3124, B3130, B3133), ¾ mile N of Tickenham (B3130). Finds in Taunton Museum.

This fort is roughly oval in plan and its defences enclose about 6 acres. Almost everywhere there are 2 banks with corresponding ditches outside them. There is an outwork 150 yds. to the w which was perhaps designed to cover the easy approach from this direction. There is an original entrance at the N. Here the innermost bank is in-curved and the outer banks on the E side (there is a third bank and ditch here) turn outwards, providing a well-covered approach. All these ramparts are probably revetted with drystone walling provided by material from the rock-cut ditches. Not dated.

Clifton Camp, Borough Walls and ***Stokeleigh,** promontory forts (ST/566733, Clifton; ST/559733, Stokeleigh), respectively NE, SW and NW of Clifton suspension bridge, Bristol.

Overlooking the Avon Gorge, close to Clifton suspension bridge, 3 promontories have been fortified by earthworks. Though separated by the Gorge, each camp is within 800 yds. of the other. All are more or less identical in design and size and they are likely to be contemporary.

The camp on Clifton Down is the most accessible. It has 3 banks with ditches between them, well-preserved on the N side. These enclose about 4 acres. The main entrance was probably through the gap in the E side; a second entrance may have exited close to the cliff-edge at the NW. There are some slight earthworks, including a rectangular enclosure, within the camp on the SW side. These have not been explained by excavation and may not even be contemporary.

The promontory fort of Borough Walls is on the s side of the Gorge, facing Clifton Camp and cut across by the road from the Suspension Bridge. It had 3 banks with 2 ditches, enclosing an area of about 7 acres. The inner or middle rampart had internal tie-beams which had been set alight, altering the entire nature of the rubble forming this bank. Its entrances have never been found and it is now almost destroyed by quarrying.

Stokeleigh Camp, also on this side of the Gorge, faces Borough Walls across a short valley. Its main defence consists of 2 banks and ditches: additional banks were built on the NW and also at the SE, overlooking Nightingale Valley. There is an entrance close to the SW corner and the area thus enclosed is about 6½ acres. Undated.

Dolebury, hill-fort (ST/450589) 1 mile SE of Churchill (A38, A368), ¼ mile E of A38.

This impressive fortress is roughly rectangular in plan, defended by a bank, ditch and counterscarp bank which enclose about 20 acres. There are slight additional outworks cutting off this hill 100 yds. further E. An original entrance occurs at the w end, possessing outworks which make use of 2 small spurs projecting w.

The ramparts were built of stone and the inner one still stands 18–20 ft. high in places.

The area thus enclosed has been badly cut up by lead mines, but there is a series of small isolated earthworks, running across the axis of the camp, which needs to be explained by excavation. There is another small earthwork which cuts off the sw corner of the main fort. Not yet dated.

*King's Weston, promontory fort (ST/ 556781) 2½ miles E of Avonmouth (A4, B4054), NE end of King's Weston Hill, ¼ mile sw of Blaise Castle (above). Finds in Bristol City Museum.

The NE end of this long narrow hill is cut off by a bank and ditch which fortify 1 acre. Steep hillsides on the N and E make this earthwork an adequate protection. There is another, slighter bank and ditch across the hill 850 ft. to the w. There are some gaps in these defences but none has yet been established by excavation as an entrance. The ditch of the E rampart has been shown to be cut into the rock, 6 ft. deep and over 15 ft. wide, with a flat floor and vertical walls.

There is a circular enclosure midway between the main fort and its w earthwork. It consists of a slight bank about 60 yds. in diam., with a shallow ditch outside it. It may have contained a dwelling. Excavation has shown that it is contemporary with the fort and that both were built c. 250 BC.

*Maes Knoll Camp, hill-fort (ST/600660) 4½ miles s of Bristol, 1¼ miles sw of Whitchurch (A37).

This triangular hill-fort of c. 30 acres occupies the E end of Dundry Hill. Much reduced by the plough, it is of exceptional interest because its concave N side, NE and NW corners are overlain by the bank and ditch of West Wansdyke, a boundary earthwork of c. 7th century AD. The NW corner of the hill-fort is covered by a massive section of Wansdyke called Maes Knoll Tump, its bank rising 21 ft. above level ground, its ditch c. 100 ft. wide and 17 ft. deep. The NE corner of the hill-fort extends 200 ft. beyond the NE corner of Wansdyke, showing as a bank, ditch and counterscarp, before turning s and now destroyed by the plough. Here Wansdyke runs due s, within the hill-fort, before crossing its E side and continuing SE down the hill. The E and W sides of the hill-fort show only as slight scarps, but at the s corner the bank becomes distinct, forming an in-turned entrance. Not dated.

West Wansdyke, extending from Maes Knoll to Horscombe, 2 miles s of Bath, was probably built by the West Saxon,

King Cynegils, to define his frontier with Mercia following defeat at the hands of Penda and a treaty signed in 628. It was intended to control movement westward from the Cotswolds and lower Avon. This earthwork is weaker than the Wiltshire Wansdyke and may be about 40 years later.

*Sodbury Camp, hill-fort (ST/761826) 2 miles E of Chipping Sodbury (A432, B4060), ¼ mile w of A46.

This rectangular camp encloses c. 11 acres. It has an inner bank with a ditch immediately outside, 30 ft. wide and 7 ft. deep. Along the w, steep hillsides make extra defence unnecessary, nevertheless the inner rampart continues along part of the crest, with a ditch and counterscarp on the hillside below.

The outer rampart is set 50 ft. beyond the inner ditch, its irregular outline suggesting it is unfinished. In places it is 11 ft. high. It is separated by a 12 ft. berm from its outer ditch, 45 ft. wide.

The main entrance is in the centre of the E side, the inner rampart-ends staggered and showing traces of fire-reddened stonework. There is a second out-turned entrance through the outer rampart towards the NE corner. Not dated.

Stokeleigh, see **Clifton Camp** p. 46.

*Worlebury, hill-fort (ST/314625) immediately NW of Weston-super-Mare. Finds in Weston-super-Mare and Taunton Museums.

This site overlooks the mouth of the Severn. It lies E/W, its N side being defended by the natural fall of the land into Sand Bay. The defence on its s side consists of a single massive rampart and ditch: these are multiplied at the E end where the ground becomes level. Here there are the remains of 2 banks separated by a great ditch, and 4 smaller ditches beyond these. The area so enclosed is over 10 acres. Further still to the E there are 2 banks of slighter proportions but presumably all part of the defensive system. There is an in-turned entrance, 13 ft. wide, at the SE, at the junction of the single and multiple defences; there is another opposite it, at the NE, and a third at the w end.

The ramparts were shown by excavation in the mid 19th century to have been built with cores of unlaid stone, faced on either side with well-laid masonry and containing as many as 3 internal (i.e. hidden) walls to ensure stability. Today this work is everywhere obscured by collapsed masonry.

Many storage pits were found, and can still be seen, at the E end of the fort, dug 5–6 ft. into the solid rock. They suggest that it was permanently occupied. The finds from them (such storage pits becoming rubbish pits when fouled by their original contents) suggest that their builders were of the same culture as those who erected villages in the marshes at Glastonbury and Meare. The discovery of about 18 skeletons, many showing evidence of violent death, suggests that this camp was conquered either by the Romans or perhaps by a rival tribe in the Iron Age.

Bedfordshire

NEOLITHIC

Five Knolls, round barrow; see Bronze Age. Northernmost bowl-barrow is Neolithic.

*Maiden Bower, causewayed camp and Iron Age hill-fort (SP/997225), 1¼ miles NW of Dunstable (A5, A505, B489), approached through Sewell, off A5. Finds in Luton Museum.

Part of the Iron Age rampart (below) has been dug away by the chalk quarry to reveal a flat-bottomed ditch underlying the later bank. Early Neolithic pottery found in this proves that here lies the most N example of the causewayed enclosures built by the first farmers and herdsmen to reach Britain, c. 3,500 BC. Neolithic ditch sections can still be seen exposed in the SE face of the quarry.

The Iron Age fort consists of a single bank about 8 ft. in height, quarried from a ditch originally 10 ft. deep, V-shaped and 25 ft. wide at chalk surface. Sections of bank and ditch can be seen in the quarry on the NW side of the site. This roughly circular earthwork encloses about 11 acres. There is an original entrance on the SE, the gap on the N not yet having been proved to be original. Two lines of post-holes found by excavation at the SE gap represent a typical entrance closed by a gate perhaps with sentry walk above it. Numerous 'Celtic' fields around the camp can be seen from the air, with numbers of storage pits and hut circles within it. Occupation probably began in the 5th–4th centuries BC and lasted until the arrival of the Romans.

*Waulud's Bank, domestic site (TL/062246), ¼ mile N of Leagrave railway station (B579), 2¾ miles NW of Luton town centre. Finds in Luton Museum.

This is the only defensive late Neolithic earthwork identified in England. It consists of a massive chalk bank heaped up inside a ditch originally 30 ft. wide and 8 ft. deep, enclosing a semicircular area of some 18 acres. The W side is formed by the river Lea which rises within the earthwork. Late Neolithic grooved ware of c. 2,200–1,700 BC has been found on the ditch-floor during excavation, together with the post-holes of a hut on the outer edge of the ditch in Sundon Road Recreation Ground. One must suppose that people lived here with their flocks and herds, conveniently close to water, at the end of the Stone Age.

BRONZE AGE

*Five Knolls, barrow cemetery (TL/006211), on Dunstable Down, ¼ mile S of junction of B489 (Icknield Way) and B4541. Grave goods in Luton Museum.

This cemetery consists of a triple bell-barrow, 2 bowls and 2 possible pond-barrows. The N barrow, a bowl, contained a crouched inhumation accompanied by a long flint blade-flake with one edge ground smooth. This object places the barrow in the late Neolithic period, though we find it here in a cemetery typical of the Bronze Age. Fragments of early Neolithic (Abingdon ware) and beaker pottery have been found in the S mound of the triple bell-barrow. The whole group must have accumulated early in the Bronze Age, c. 1,700 BC, when Neolithic elements were still strong.

A fine secondary collared urn containing a cremation, found in the N bowl-barrow, must belong to the developed Bronze Age, c. 1,350 BC. The pond-barrows have never been excavated.

Galley Hill, barrow cemetery (TL/092270), 1¾ miles SE of Streatley (A6), approached by lane off A6, 3 miles N of Luton railway station. Finds in Luton Museum.

One of the 2 genuine barrows here is kidney-shaped. A pit was found beneath each lobe, one containing the skeleton of a young man associated with Windmill Hill pottery, the other more than 20 ox-jaw bones. There was also a central grave but it has been robbed without record.

In the 4th century AD a large number of corpses, the result perhaps of a mass execution, were added to this barrow whose initial date must be c. 3,000–2,500 BC. The second barrow here may be Iron Age: it has been robbed.

IRON AGE

Caesar's Camp, hill-fort (TL/179489), ¼ mile NE of Sandy railway station (A1, A603). Finds in Museum of Archaeology and Ethnology, Cambridge.

This is a much damaged hill-fort strategically placed on a steep-sided spur overlooking the river Ivel to the SW. Surviving parts of the single bank and ditch follow the contours and enclose 7 acres. Undated.

Maiden Bower, hill-fort. See Neolithic.

Berkshire

*NEOLITHIC

Combe Gibbet, long barrow (SU/365623) on Inkpen Beacon, 1¼ miles SE of Inkpen, 1 mile NW of Combe.

This long barrow is about 150 ft. in length, 50 ft. wide at its E and broader end, and here 6½ ft. high. There are side-ditches which are still 3 ft. deep. It is orientated E/W. Records of burials or excavation do not survive. Date, c. 3,500–2,500 BC.

Inkpen Beacon, long barrow. See **Combe Gibbet.**

*Lambourn, chambered long barrow (SU/323834), 2¾ miles N of Lambourn (B4000, B4001) 1 mile W of B4001. At S end of Westcot Wood (wrongly placed on 1 in. O.S.).

Discovered about 1850, the NE end of the site is in the wood and crossed by the cart track. It is c. 220 ft. long, 70 ft. wide at its E end and here 4½ ft. high. Parallel side-ditches originally 7 ft deep, flank the mound, whose ends are open. Excavation has shown that their contents provided a turf cover with chalk crust to a core of sarsens which constitute the mound. Near the E end a contracted female burial has been found, associated with extra human bones and a necklace or bracelet of polished common dog whelk. Date (C14) c. 3,400 BC.

The Lambourn Seven Barrows Bronze Age cemetery (pp. 50–51) lies about ¼ mile to the E; the proximity of round barrows to an earlier long barrow is a not infrequent occurrence.

BRONZE AGE

Holden's Firs, barrow cemetery. See **Mortimer Common.**

Idstone Down, barrow cemetery. See **Three Barrows.**

*****Lambourn Seven Barrows,** cemetery (SU/ 328828) 2½ miles N of Lambourn (B4000, B4001), W of B4001. Finds in British Museum, Ashmolean Museum, Oxford (dog's skeleton).

This is one of the finest barrow cemeteries in England (fig. 10). Its 26 mounds can be divided into 2 groups, those immediately N of the minor road from Lambourn to Kingston Lisle, and those W and E of this. The N group has accumulated in 2 rows aligned E/W, with 7 outlying barrows W towards the Neolithic long barrow (p. 49).

Taking the N row of the main group first, there is (from N to S):

(1) A disc-barrow about 120 ft. in diam., its central mound now spread all over the area within the ditch. The ditch has a bank outside it. No burials recorded.

(2) A bowl-barrow 70 ft. across and 6–7 ft. high, with surrounding ditch. No burial records.

(3) Another ditch-surrounded bowl-barrow, similar size. No burial records.

(4) Two bowl-barrows, their mounds run together and their ditches hour-glass shaped in plan. One may perhaps be earlier than the other. Their mounds are now about 100 ft. long and are 6–7 ft. high. No burial records.

(5) A bowl-barrow about 60 ft. in diam. and 6 ft. high, with a surrounding ditch. The burnt bones of a woman were found in a sarsen cist with capstone, enclosed in a collared urn. Sarsens and flints covered this cist.

The S row of barrows, parallel to that above, has the following types, starting at the N end:

(6) A barrow with 2 mounds, one 4 ft. high, the other 6 ft. high: their total length is over 100 ft. They are enclosed by an oval ditch separated from their edges by a slight berm. The bones of an ox and a dog were found in the N mound.

(7) A bowl-barrow with ditch, 10 ft. high and about 100 ft. in diam. No burial records.

(8) A barrow, either a bell or a bowl, with the remains of a tree-ring around it. Its diam. is about 70 ft., its ht. 7–8 ft. No burial records.

(9) A disc-barrow with a total diam. of over 100 ft., its central mound 1 ft. high and some 60 ft. across. No burial records. South of the Lambourn/Kingston Lisle road, and W of the trees along it, the barrows are scattered irregularly. From N to S there are:

(10) A bowl-barrow with ditch, 70 ft. in diam. and 4 ft. high. There are no records of burial.

(11) A prominent barrow, perhaps a bell, confused by a tree-ring. The mound is 70 ft. across and 9 ft. high. There are no burial records.

(12) Due E of (11) a small bowl-barrow 3 ft. high and over 70 ft. in diam. It has no visible ditch and shows a robber pit at its centre.

(13) A saucer-barrow, its diam. about 40 ft. It has a slight mound and traces of an outer bank. It covered 2 graves. In one were the crouched bones of a boy, provided with a beaker and flint tools. In the same grave, overlying the boy, there were the bones of a man who had with him a fine flint dagger of Beaker type. In a grave to the S, but in the same barrow, were the bones of a child with the remains of a beaker.

(14) The only bell-barrow in the cemetery. It is partly covered by a plantation. The mound is 6 ft. high and about 60 ft. in diam. The surrounding ditch is separated from it by a berm 12 ft. broad. The only recorded burial was a cremated one, added after the barrow had been built and enclosed in a sarsen cist with capstone. With it there was a bronze awl and a jet pendant.

(15) A bowl-barrow, 140 yds. E of (14). It is only 1 ft. high and has a diam. of about 60 ft. No burial records.

(16) About 100 yds. NE of the last, a bowl-barrow, 4 ft. high and some 70 ft across. No burial records.

For the rest of the cemetery, there are 3 visible barrows (with 2 others almost disappeared) between the long barrow and all the round barrows so far described:

(17) The N is a bowl-barrow 9 ft. high, over 70 ft. across and with a surrounding ditch.

Its mound has a core of turf and soil, then a casing of chalk, with an uppermost covering of soil. At the centre, there were the remains of a funeral pyre and a human cremation. With the bones had been deposited a bronze awl, riveted dagger wrapped in cloth and an incense cup. Also in the barrow, all later than its construction, were an inhumation, a cremation in a collared urn furnished with a bronze riveted knife, 2 small heaps of cremated bone sealed beneath the chalk casing, and 112 cremations above the chalk casing, all of the Middle Bronze Age, c. 1,250–1,000 BC. Of these, 58 were in urns and all were surrounded by sarsen stones. There was an inhumation of a child, perhaps Roman, in the topsoil. Probably the barrow was originally a bell, enlarged in the Middle Bronze Age to receive the 112 cremations. (18) 140 yds. to the sw there is another bowl-barrow with ditch, confused by a tree-ring. It is 6 ft. high and about 75 ft. in diam. There are no records of burial.

(19) To the SE there is a bowl-barrow with about the same diam. but 7–8 ft. high. It has no recorded burials.

Finally, to the s of all these sites, but still part of the same cemetery, there appear to be at least 7 more barrows. They are small or else not yet proved by excavation, and need not be described.

This is a typical cemetery of the Wessex Bronze Age. It must be contemporary with Stonehenge in all its phases, spanning the period c. 2,200–1,400 BC. Its later burials belong to the period 1,250–1,000 BC.

The contrast in its layout between the 2 neat rows and the scatter of other mounds among them should be noted.

Mortimer Common, barrow cemetery (SU/ 643651) 3¼ miles E of Aldermaston (A340), ¾ mile SW of Three Firs public house: at Holden's Firs.

There are at least 5 barrows in this cemetery, now in a plantation with the SE mounds partly overlaid by the road from Stratfield Mortimer. The mounds are in a line, almost touching, NW/SE. At the NW end there is a disc-barrow over-lapped by a small bell-barrow. The disc is easily overlooked. It is 178 ft. across with a central mound 42 ft. in diam. and 1 ft. high. Ditch and outer bank are intact. The

bell is 4½ ft. high and 84 ft. in diam. Its berm is 9 ft. wide. Very few disc-barrows in England were impinged upon by barrows of different type. To the sw there is a second bell, 133 ft. in diam., its mound 6 ft. high and berm 26 ft. wide. On the sw side there are 2 bowl-barrows, 40–50 ft. in diam. and 1–2 ft. high. Nothing is known of the contents of these mounds. Date, c. 1,700–1,400 BC.

Three Barrows, cemetery (SU/276811) 3½ miles NE of Aldbourne (A419), ¾ mile NE of Russley Park, on Idstone Down s of Old Ditch.

These 3 bowl-barrows are in a line and almost touch each other. They are all about 50 ft. in diam. and 4–5 ft. high. There are no records of excavation but 2 have central hollows suggesting prior opening. Date, c. 1,700–1,400 BC.

IRON AGE

*Grimsbury Castle, hill-fort (SU/512723), 4½ miles NE of Newbury (A4, A34, A339), ½ mile s of Hermitage (B4009); s of road to Bucklebury.

This camp is roughly triangular in plan, the area enclosed being about 8 acres. Its irregular outline may be explained by the care with which its builders followed the contours of the hill on which it is situated. It has a bank and ditch with a counterscarp bank. There is an original entrance, slightly in-turned, through the w side. There is a second entrance, perhaps original, facing N and a third at the SE. There are 2 additional earthworks which may belong to some phase in the history of this camp: one runs N from the N entrance for about 400 ft.; the other lies beyond the camp to the w and describes a wide arc following the line of its w side.

Not yet dated by excavation.

*Membury, hill-fort (SU/302753) 2¾ miles sw of Lambourn (B4000, B4001), 2¼ miles SE of Baydon, w of B4001.

This camp, on level ground, is cut by the Wiltshire/Berkshire county boundary. Its defences comprise a bank and ditch with a counterscarp bank; the original entrance is at the NE. An area of 34 acres is thus enclosed. The site, which has been damaged by cultivation and is much overgrown, is undated.

*Walbury, hill-fort (SU/374617) 3¼ miles sw of Kintbury, 1¾ miles SE of Inkpen.

This enormous enclosure has an area of 82 acres. It is trapezoid in plan. Its defences consist of a slight bank and ditch with entrances on the SE and NW sides. The latter appears to be slightly in-turned. Undated.

Buckinghamshire

NEOLITHIC

*Whiteleaf, short long barrow and supposed Bronze Age pond-barrow (SP/821040) 1 mile NE of Princes Risborough (A4010, A4129), above Whiteleaf Cross. Finds in University of London Institute of Archaeology.

This damaged burial mound appears kidney-shaped, perhaps caused by subsidence, 70 × 50 ft. and with a surrounding quarry-ditch originally perhaps with a U-plan. The mound lies SE/NW, 7 ft. high at the s. Traces of a wooden burial chamber were found at the centre of the mound, measuring 8 × 5½ ft. A pit surrounded by stakes had been dug N of the chamber before the barrow was built. The remains of a middle-aged, arthritic male were scattered on the original land surface, left foot and 1 tooth in the chamber, the rest outside to the E: the body must have been brought to its final resting place here as a collection of bones. Fragments of about 60 Neolithic pots and many flints lay throughout the mound, perhaps products of a funeral feast. Date c. 2,500 BC.

A pond-barrow lies to the NE (SP/822041). Its 'pond' is 36 ft. across and 3 ft. deep. There is a surrounding bank 2½ ft. high and 6 ft. wide. There is also an outer ditch giving this site a total diam. of 60 ft. The cross-shaped depression at the centre may have been the base of a windmill. Date, c. 1,700–1,400 BC but possibly modern.

BRONZE AGE

*The Cop, round barrow (SP/773011) 2½ miles sw of Princes Risborough (A4010, A4129), 1 mile E of Chinnor church (B4009), 350 yds. NE of Bledlow Cross: lane sw from Bledlow Church, then track through wood. Finds in Aylesbury Museum.

This bowl-barrow is about 60 ft. in diam. and 7 ft. high. Recent excavations revealed that the main burial had been robbed in antiquity; it was probably an inhumation. Several burials had been added afterwards: one cremation was doubtless of the Bronze Age, while other cremations and inhumations were Anglo-Saxon. The barrow was found to have no surrounding ditch. Date of construction 1,700–1,400 BC.

Whiteleaf, pond-barrow. See Neolithic.

IRON AGE

*Beacon Hill, hill-fort (SP/960169) 5 miles sw of Dunstable (A5, A505), s of Ivinghoe Aston and B489. Finds in the County Museum, Aylesbury.

Along the N and E sides of this triangular hill-fort there was a bank and ditch of which only the latter survives, as a level platform. The w side has traces of a second platform and possibly the hill-fort was abandoned before the second bank and ditch were extended round the site. The entrance was in the E corner and nearly 5½ acres are enclosed.

Excavation revealed that the inner rampart had been faced back and front (c. 6–7 ft. apart) by timbers, horizontals retained by spaced uprights. The ditch was about 8 ft. wide and 8½ ft. deep. The entrance was in-turned, a series of timber uprights supporting a single gate. A circular and a semicircular hut (diams. 27½ ft.) lay 150 ft. w, with 2 granaries c. 12 ft. sq. and other structures. More signs of habitation occurred towards the highest point; storage pits were absent. Date, early 6th century BC, occupation short-lived.

Boddington Camp, hill-fort (SP/883080) 1 mile E of Wendover (A413, A4011).

This site occupies the end of a high ridge and can almost be classified as a promontory fort. Its defences, which consist of a bank and ditch, enclose 17 acres. On the E side the bank is still 13 ft. high in places. The entrance was probably at the NW and has now been destroyed by the farm. Undated.

Bulpit Wood, hill-fort (SP/832050) 1¾ miles NE of Princes Risborough (A4010, A4129), ¾ mile SE of Great Kimble (A4010).

Steep hillsides protect the NW and SW sides of this camp. On these sides a single bank and ditch were considered adequate. Facing the flatter ground to the E, the curved third side of the camp consists of 2 banks and ditches with a wide entrance through the middle. About 4 acres are thus protected. Undated.

Bulstrode Park Camp, hill-fort. See **Gerrards Cross.**

*Cholesbury, hill-fort (SP/930073) 2¾ miles S of Tring (A41), on N side of village. Finds in Aylesbury Museum.

About 11 acres are enclosed by this oval hill-fort. The defences comprise 2 banks and ditches on the N side and 3 around the S half of the site. These have been damaged where they come nearest to the village street. At the NW, where the banks swing round to the NE, the outer ditch continues straight for a short distance before stopping; a smaller bank and ditch link its end to the main rampart, defining a triangular area between the 2.

Excavation has shown that the hill-fort is of the 2nd–1st century BC.

Church Hill, hill-fort. See **West Wycombe.**

Danesborough Camp, hill-fort (SP/921348) 2¾ miles E of Bletchley (A5, B488, B4034)

between Woburn Sands (A50, B557) and Bow Brickhill (B557); in Wavendon Wood.

Almost a promontory fort, this site is protected by steep hill slopes on all except the SW side. It is roughly rectangular and encloses about 8½ acres. A deep, wide ditch surrounds the site except at the NE where it has disappeared. Traces of a slight bank can be seen along the S and SW; at the latter there is also a counterscarp bank.

The only likely entrance is in the SW side, which is approached by a hollow way. A similar track approaches the NE corner of the fort where also there may have been an entrance.

The relationship between this site and the undated earthwork to the W has not yet been established. Undated.

Gerrards Cross, hill-fort (SU/995880), in W angle of Gerrards Cross (A40/A332).

The largest site in the county, this fort encloses 22 acres. It is significantly close to the Misbourne R. In plan it is oval, the defences comprising a bank, ditch and counterscarp bank. The former is 12 ft. high in places. There are 3 entrance gaps but excavation has not yet established which is ancient. Occupation here does not appear to have been permanent. Undated.

Ivinghoe Beacon, hill-fort. See **Beacon Hill.**

Medmenham, hill-fort (SU/807847) 2¾ miles SW of Marlow (A409, A4155) NE of church and A4155.

This fort overlooks the Thames. It encloses 17 acres. The defences now consist of a bank and ditch but on the W side there are traces of a second bank. Here the main bank is over 15 ft. high in places. The NW entrance may be original. Undated.

Pulpit Hill, hill-fort. See **Bulpit Wood.**

West Wycombe, hill-fort (SU/828950) ½ mile NW of A40/A4010 junction. Surrounds church.

This fort is small, enclosing 3 acres. It has a bank, ditch and counterscarp bank, the former still 11 ft. high. The entrance may have been where the NW gate of the churchyard now is. Undated.

Cambridgeshire

IRON AGE

*Wandlebury, hill-fort (TL/494534), 4¾ miles SE of Cambridge, on N side of A604, 2¾ miles NW of A11/A604 crossroads. Finds in Museum of Archaeology and Ethnology, Cambridge.

In plan this hill-fort is circular, the area enclosed being 15 acres. It is defended by 2 banks and ditches and a counterscarp bank. Of the series of gaps in the earthworks, that in the SE, which carries a road to the stables, is an original entrance.

The area within the outer ditch has been levelled so that only this feature and the counterscarp bank can now be seen clearly: but a slight rise and a hollow indicate the existence of the outer bank and inner ditch.

Excavation has revealed that the outer bank and ditch were dug in the 3rd century BC and were the only defences of the earliest fort here. This bank was faced on both sides with timbers and was 14 ft. wide; the ditch outside it was steep-sided

and flat-floored, 14 ft. deep and 18 ft. wide at ground level. This defence, like so many of this period, was allowed to fall into decay.

Perhaps in the 1st century BC or early years AD the site was re-fortified on a more ambitious scale. An inner bank and ditch were built, the latter V-shaped, 18 ft. deep and 40 ft. wide. The rampart behind it was faced on the outside with timbers. The first bank and ditch, now collapsed, were refurbished, the ditch being re-dug to twice its width, the material going outside to form the counterscarp bank.

This rebuilding may represent a reaction by the Norfolk Iceni to the expanding Belgae from Essex.

There was always permanent occupation within the camp. Excavation has revealed a great concentration of storage and rubbish pits, post-holes and other traces of domestic and agricultural activities. The 3 periods of fortification indicated above were carried out by people of the same culture.

Cheshire

BRONZE AGE

*Sponds Hill, round barrow (SJ/970803) 3¾ miles SW of New Mills (A6015, B6101), 1¼ miles WNW of Kettleshulme (B5089). Trig. station on barrow top.

This mound has a diam. of 45–50 ft. and a ht. of about 5 ft. There are traces of a ditch surrounding it. A human cremation without grave goods was found at its centre. Date, c. 1,700–1,400 BC.

IRON AGE

*Castle Ditch, hill-fort (SJ/553695) 9½ miles ENE of Chester, 2 miles NE of Kelsall (A54). On Eddisbury Hill.

The defences of this camp enclose the flat top of a hill and follow its contours. The area thus protected is 7 acres. There are 2 banks and 2 ditches. Excavation has shown that the site has a complex history of development. First, the hill was occupied by an Iron Age community who defended themselves with a simple palisade. The first fort which replaced the palisade had a single bank, ditch and counterscarp bank and enclosed the E half of the hill. There was an entrance in the E side, approached by a hollow way; it had a wooden guardhouse on either side, inside the main bank. Later, the defences were extended NW to take in the top of the hill. A second entrance was added, at the centre of the NW end. The rampart was of earth and stone, with a V-shaped ditch outside it and was 'timber-laced' at the entrance.

Finally, the whole circuit of the camp received a second (outer) bank and ditch; the entrances were in-turned more deeply and were faced with drystone walling.

Date of earliest hill-fort, c. 2nd century BC: reconstructed early 1st century AD. The hill-fort was dismantled by the Romans and refortified c. 10th century AD.

*Kelsborrow Castle, promontory fort (SJ/ 532675) 2¾ miles E of Tarvin (A51, A54), ½ mile SE of Kelsall (A54).

An oval area of about 7 acres is cut off from the N by a bank and ditch. Steep hillsides protect the SE and W sides. In places the ditch is 25 ft. wide and the bank 40 ft. thick. Entry was probably obtained around the E end. Not dated.

*Maiden Castle, promontory fort (SJ/ 497529) 5½ miles E of Fardon (A534, B5102, B5130), 1½ miles SE of A534/A41 crossing. On NW side of Bickerton Hill.

This promontory fort is protected around its NW side by steep hillsides. On the SE there are 2 banks with a ditch between, enclosing 1½ acres. There is an entrance through the ramparts 40 yds. from their N end; here the inner bank is in-turned. Excavation has revealed that the main rampart has an inner core of layers of timbers laid criss-cross (timber lacing) and sand, with a covering and facing of boulders. It was 17 ft. wide and would have been about 12 ft. high. The outer bank consists of a heap of sand against a stone revetting wall. There was evidence that this bank had been rebuilt at least once, a vertical timber revetment being replaced by the stone wall. The ditch was originally about 24 ft. wide and only 2 ft. deep, with a flat floor.

The inner in-turned entrance provided a passageway 50 ft. long; at the outer end it is 16 ft. wide and it narrows to 8 ft. It was cobbled, the surface showing wheel-ruts. A wooden gate was hung across the inner end of this passage. There was a hut for sentries in a hollow in the angle of the S in-turn. Date c. 2nd century BC.

Cleveland

IRON AGE

*Eston Nab, promontory fort (NZ/568184) 3 miles NW of Guisborough (A171, A173), 1 mile S of Lazenby (A174).

The NW side of this promontory fort is protected by a steep hillside and cliff. The earthworks around the SE side consist of a bank, ditch and counterscarp bank; an area of nearly 2½ acres is thus enclosed. The rampart is 9–14 ft. high. Excavation has shown that it comprises a clay bank 16 ft. wide, backed by a 14 ft. thick stone wall. On the hill-top, occupation has been found associated with a palisade enclosure 200 ft. across, parallel to the rampart; this is not visible on the surface. Not yet dated.

Cornwall

NEOLITHIC

There are two types of chambered tomb in Cornwall – Scillonian entrance graves and Penwith chamber tombs. The former, concentrated in the Scillies, spread into w Cornwall. They are probably a form of passage grave (p. 16) where chamber and passage are not distinguished; certainly their use continued into the Middle Bronze Age. Penwith tombs are versions of the portal dolmen (p. 40), a type of burial chamber found on both sides of the Irish Sea and thought to be possibly the earliest form of communal tomb in the British Isles. No early Neolithic finds have yet been made in a Penwith tomb; in origin probably early, they had a long life.

Ballowal, chambered tomb. See **Carn Gluze.**

Brane, chambered tomb (SW/401282) 2¾ miles SE of St Just (A3071, B3306), between Brane and Tredinney.

This Scillonian entrance grave is covered by a round barrow about 20 ft. in diam. and 6½ ft. high. The chamber, 7½ × 4 ft., is orientated SE/NW. It has a roof of 2 capstones and may originally have had a third. The mound is edged with stone uprights. Date, c. 2,500 BC.

Carn Brea, walled settlement. See under Iron Age.

*Carn Gluze, composite burial mound (SW/355313) 1 mile w of St Just (A3071, B3306), on Cape Cornwall. Finds in Truro Museum, British Museum.

This unusual composite barrow, max. diam. c. 75 ft., ht. c. 12 ft., excavated in 1874, has the following sequence. First a deep, rock-cut pit reached by rough steps was dug, with 4 cists built nearby containing Middle Bronze Age pots. Next, an oval double-walled cairn, 30 × 37 ft., its walls 5 ft. apart, was heaped over these, another cist containing an offering of lamb being added near its top. It would originally have been a dome c. 15 ft. high. Two more empty cists were built outside this cairn, at its base. The whole was then enlarged

to its present size, with an outer surrounding wall, after which an entrance grave was inserted at the SW. Its paved floor was found to cover burnt human bones and potsherds. All the finds from this site belong to the Middle Bronze Age, c. 1,250–1,000 BC.

Carwynnen Quoit, burial chamber. See **Giant's Quoit.**

*Castilly, sacred site and Bronze Age barrows (SX/031627) 3¾ miles SW of Bodmin (A30, A38, B3269), ¼ mile s of A30, beside road joining A30 and A391.

This is characteristically situated close to water. It is an oval earthwork comprising a bank and ditch, the latter on the inside. There is a single entrance facing NW and a modern gap facing SW. Its max. diam. is 217 ft. Today the ditch is still 7 ft. deep and 18 ft. wide, while the bank outside it is 6 ft. high. The site has been built from the local weathered slate and perhaps remodelled in medieval times.

This site stands close to a series of important prehistoric trackways: like **Castlewitch** (below), Castilly may have been connected with trade, its builders anxious to further their prosperity by worship. Date, c. 2,500–1,900 BC.

At least 5 round barrows can be found close to Castilly. Three are opposite, on the w side of the road to the farm. Another is 300 yds. w and a fifth is on the N side of the A30. Air photographs show several more hereabouts. Date, c. 1,700–1,400 BC.

*Castlewitch, sacred site and stone-axe quarry (SX/371685) 1 mile SE of Callington (A388, A390), s of A388.

This is probably a Neolithic sacred site. It is nearly circular, with an original diam. of about 300 ft. Its ditch is inside its bank and a single entrance faces S. There is no evidence that a circle of stones had ever stood within the ditch.

On Balstone Down, ¼ mile to the N (by Bench Mark 628), there occurs an outcrop of igneous rock – a greenstone – extensively quarried in Neolithic and early Bronze Age times for the manufacture of axe-heads, which were traded to Wiltshire, Dorset, Devon and Somerset. The henge monument may have been built by the group of people engaged in this trade. Date of Castlewitch, c. 2,500–1,700 BC.

*Chapel Carn Brea, chambered tomb (SW/386281) 2¼ miles SE of St Just (A3071, B3306); between A30 and B3306. Marked as 'tumulus' on map.

This cairn, which once had a medieval chapel built on top of it, is 62 ft. in diam. and was originally at least 15 ft. high. It had a drystone surrounding wall and 3 more incorporated in the mound. At the centre was a stone-built tomb, 9 × 4 ft., orientated NW/SE, the NW end being brought to a point. Cremation burials may have been associated with this tomb. The mound was badly damaged, 1939–45. Only a small secondary burial cist in the side can now be seen. Date, c. 3,200–2,500 BC.

Chapel Euny. See **Brane.**

Chun Quoit, portal dolmen (SW/402340) 2½ miles NE of St Just (A3071, B3306), between B3318 and B3306; 100 yds. w of Chun Castle (p. 63).

At the centre of a round barrow 35 ft. in diam. stands a large burial chamber. This is nearly 6 ft. square and its capstone is about 12 ft. square. Stones on its s side may indicate the remains of a short passage. The base of the mound is still visible. This Penwith chamber tomb is dated c. 3,200–2,500 BC.

Devil's Frying Pan, burial chamber. See **Giant's Quoit.**

Giant's Quoit, portal dolmen (SW/650372) 1¾ miles s of Camborne (A30, B3303), N of Carwynnen.

This burial chamber must originally have been covered by a barrow mound, traces of which suggest that it was long. Its capstone, set on 3 uprights, fell in the 19th century and has been replaced. Date, c. 3,200–2,500 BC.

Lanyon Quoit, chambered long barrow (SW/430337) 2 miles SE of Morvah (B3306), on N side of road to Madron and Penzance.

This group of stones, re-erected in 1824, stands at the N end of a long barrow. The mound, of which scant traces remain, lies N/S. It measures 90 × 40 ft. This Penwith chamber tomb must originally have been larger than it is today. At the opposite end

of the barrow other stones may indicate additional burial cists. Date, c. 3,200–2,500 BC.

Mulfra Quoit, portal dolmen (SW/452354) 2 miles s of Zennor (B3306), s of road from Porthmeor (B3306) to Penzance.

This chamber is now ruined, its capstone resting partly on the ground and only N, s and E walls surviving. There are traces of a barrow 40 ft. in diam. which must have covered this Penwith chamber tomb. Date, c. 3,200–2,500 BC.

Pawton, portal dolmen (SW/968683) 3 miles sw of Wadebridge (A39, A389), 2½ miles NW of Withiel: on St Breock Downs.

A burial chamber stands at the s end of a mound which measures 70 × 50 ft., orientated S/N. The chamber has 9 uprights, defining a rectangular area and supporting 1 large capstone. This Penwith chamber tomb may be dated c. 3,200–2,500 BC.

Pennance, The Giant's House, chambered tomb (SW/448376), ¾ mile sw of Zennor, s of B3306. Marked as 'tumulus' on 1-in. O.S.

This is a fine Scillonian entrance grave. The barrow is about 25 ft. in diam. and 6 ft. high; it has a well-built kerb around it. A parallel-sided burial chamber leads in from the SE. It is 13 ft. long and there are 5 capstones in position. Date, c. 2,500 BC.

*Stripple Stones, sacred site (SX/144752) 6¾ miles NE of Bodmin (A30, A388, B3269), 1 mile N of A30; on Hawkstor Downs.

This sacred site consists of a roughly circular bank and ditch, with a diam. of 225 ft. enclosing a flat area which contains an irregular ring of 15 stones, with another at the centre. The ditch is inside the bank. There is an original entrance through the bank and ditch facing sw. Three stones lie outside the circumference of the circle within the earthwork; it is probable that these are not now in their original position. Excavation has revealed that the ditch has an original width of 9 ft. and a depth of about 3 ft. It had been cut irregularly. In sites like this we see combined the simple stone circle, which is found wherever building stone was available, and the earthen circle with inner ditch and entrances, the British contribution to the design of sacred sites. Proable date, c. 2,200–1,400 BC.

Treen, chambered tombs (SW/438371) ½ mile E of Porthmeor (B3306): W of track from Gurnard's Head Hotel to Bosporthennis.

There are 4 Scillonian entrance graves close together in a line N/S, and apt to be overgrown. The most N is about 25 ft. in diam. and 5 ft. high. There are traces of a chamber in the S part of the mound. The third from the N, about the same size, has a well-built rectangular chamber 12½ ft. long and 4 ft. wide. It is likely that the other mounds in this group cover chambers of this type. Date, c. 2,200–1,400 BC.

Trethevey Stone, portal dolmen (SX/259688) 2¾ miles NE of Liskeard (A38, A390, B3254), ¾ mile NE of St Clear.

This Penwith chamber tomb consists of 8 stones, 1 of them a huge capstone, the others forming the sides of the chamber. One of these is fallen. The chamber is divided in 2 by 1 of the stones: a corner of this has been broken away so that access to the chamber is made possible. The sides of the structure project beyond the cross-stone, forming a sort of ante-chamber. The capstone covers all the uprights. This tomb was originally enclosed by an oval mound measuring 130 × 60 ft. in the last century but now almost disappeared. Date, c. 3,200–2,500 BC.

Wooley, long barrow (SS/263166) 3¼ miles N of Kilkhampton (A39, B3254), ½ mile E of Woolley, on S side of A39.

This long barrow is orientated E/W. It is about 225 ft. long and 130 ft. in breadth. There may originally have been a chamber at the E end but nothing now shows. Date, c. 3,200–2,500 BC.

Zennor Quoit, portal dolmen (SW/469380) 1 mile SE of Zennor (B3306). Finds in Truro Museum.

This fine Penwith chamber tomb is divided by a cross-stone into a burial chamber and ante-chamber. Communication between these compartments is impossible. Furthermore, here the ante-chamber is reached through a gap between 2 large stones which form a facade like those found in front of most chambered long barrows in the Cotswolds and elsewhere. The capstone is probably not in its original position. It is thought that the structure was covered by a round mound of stones now totally robbed.

Finds from the chamber and ante-chamber suggest that this tomb was built c. 3,200–2,500 BC, but remained in use into the Early Bronze Age.

BRONZE AGE

The traditions and religious practices of the Neolithic communities in Cornwall lingered on into the Bronze Age. Many stone circles and chambered tombs were still in use at a time when, in Wessex, altogether new burial architecture had been evolved and Stonehenge was nearing completion. Some of the small hut circles and associated fields may belong to the Bronze Age. So few have been dated by excavation, however, that only those on Rough Tor and Trewey Down have been included in this section.

Bodrifty, Bronze Age village. See Iron Age.

Boleigh Circle, see **Merry Maidens.**

Boscawen-Un, stone circle (SW/413274) 1 mile N of St Buryan (B3283), ¼ mile S of A30.

This circle, having a diam. of about 75 ft., comprises 19 uprights with a space for a 20th stone. There are 4 more, placed close together on the circumference at the NE and another stone, the largest, near the centre. Date, c. 2,200–1,400 BC.

Boskednan, circle. See **Nine Maidens.**

Braddock, barrow cemetery (SX/142634) 3¼ miles NE of Lostwithiel (A390, B3268), ¾ mile W of West Taphouse; N of A390.

This is a barrow cemetery in the Wessex manner. Unlike the Pelynt cemetery to the SE (p. 60) it extends in a straight line E/W. There are 8 bowl-barrows in the group, none of which has been excavated with known result. Date, c. 1,700–1,400 BC.

Camelford, triple bowl-barrow (SX/136834) 2 miles E of Camelford (A39, B3283), W of Crowdy Marsh.

This site consists of 3 mounds set within an oval ditch with a bank on the outside, c. 200 ft. long. This layout must have been derived from Wessex where the multiplication of mounds within one ditch is not unusual. Nothing is known of burials here. Date, c. 1,700–1,400 BC.

*Carn Creis, barrow (SW/356305) 1 mile sw of St Just (A3071, B3306): on cliffs s of Carn Laskys. Grave goods in British Museum.

The grave goods found with a burial in this barrow are important. The mound was only 18 ft. in diam. It had a surrounding kerb and incorporated a large natural granite block 4 ft. high. The barrow had been disturbed but among the cremation burials found there 1 was associated with an urn of Cornish Bronze Age type and some segmented faience beads. Whether imports from the E Mediterranean or of British manufacture, these beads which are common in Wessex suggest an Early Bronze Age date, c. 1,700–1,400 BC.

Castilly, barrows. See Neolithic.

Crousa Common, round barrow (SW/774196) 1½ miles sw of St Keverne (B3293), s of Beacon and B3293, close to track of Coverack.

This is a good example of the type of large barrow often built of stones hereabouts, and on the Goonhilly Downs to the w. This example is about 40 ft. in diam. and 4 ft. high. Its mound is retained by a kerb and at the centre there are traces of a burial chamber. Date, c. 1,700–1,400 BC.

Dawns Men, circle. See **Merry Maidens.**

Duloe, stone circle (SX/235583), at s end of Duloe (B3254), by turning E off B3254.

This circle is remarkable because its diam. is small (37 ft.) and the size of its 8 stones unusually large. One is about 9 ft. tall. Moreover, while all the other Cornish circles, together with the chambered tombs, are of granite, Duloe circle is of quartz. Date, c. 2,200–1,400 BC.

*Fernacre, stone circle (SX/144800), on Roughtor Moors, Bodmin, 3¼ miles SE of Camelford (A39, B3266), 1¼ miles SE of Stannon China Clay Works.

This flattened circle, max. diam. c. 150 ft., has about 52 small granite stones, 39 still standing. Prof. Thom has recently demonstrated the complicated geometry of its layout. Earliest likely date c. 2,200 BC.

*The Hurlers, stone circles (SX/258714) 4¼ miles NE of Liskeard (A38, A390, B3254), 1½ miles w of Upton Cross (B3254).

The Hurlers are 3 stone circles set out in a line orientated NE/SW. From N to s their diams. and number of stones are: (1) 110 ft., 13; (2) 135 ft., 17; (3) 105 ft., 9. Originally each circle would have had 25–35 stones.

Excavation has shown that the stones of these circles were dressed to shape and that care was taken to see that the tops of the uprights were at roughly the same level above ground. They stand in pits, their bases packed around with granite blocks. A fallen stone has been found at the centre of the central circle. The area within the N circle seems originally to have been paved with granite slabs. Date, c. 2,200–1,400 BC.

*Leaze Circle, stone circle (SX/137773) 2½ miles E of St Breward (E of B3266), ¼ mile NE of Leaze Farm (ruined).

This is a small circle, with a diam. of 81 ft. It has 16 stones, 10 of them still standing. A modern bank crosses the site, accounting perhaps for its mutilation. The average ht. of the stones above ground is 3½ ft. Probable date, c. 2,200–1,400 BC.

Men-an-tol, holed stone (SW/427349) 1½ miles E of Morvah (B3306), ½ mile N of Lanyon Farm.

A block with a hole in it is set between, and in a line with 2 upright stones. These are not now in their original positions. While they are likely to be prehistoric, it should not be assumed that they formed part of a burial chamber. Likely date, c. 2,200–1,400 BC.

Merry Maidens, stone circle and standing stones (**The Pipers** and **Fiddler**) (SW/432245) 1½ miles SE of St Buryan (B3283), on s side of B3315 to Boleigh. Beaker from area in St Buryan Church.

This fine circle has 19 evenly spaced stones and a diam. of about 80 ft. It is complete except for a gap facing NE, which may constitute an entrance. The granite blocks are naturally shaped and about 4 ft. high. They have been carefully selected, each having a roughly rectangular section.

Nearly ¼ mile NE there are 2 large standing stones (The Pipers), one 15 ft. high, the other 13½ ft. They lie on a line drawn from the centre of the Merry Maidens and must be considered as part of it. Several burials have been recorded from this area, including one deposited with a beaker now in St Buryan Church. The Fiddler is an upright to the w. Date of sites, c. 2,200–1,400 BC.

Nine Maidens, stone circle (SW/434353) 1

mile s of Porthmeor; reached by lanes NW of Newmill (Gurnard's Head/Penzance Road).

There were originally about 20 stones in this circle. Of these, 5 have fallen and 6 still stand. All are about 2½ ft. high. It has a diam. of some 25 ft. There is a stone at the centre. Date, c. 2,200–1,400 BC.

Nine Maidens, stone row (SW/937676) 3 miles NE of St Columb Major, E of A39.

This is the only alignment of stones in Cornwall. It is orientated NE/SW and has a length of 350 ft. There are 9 stones in it, irregularly set out. They have a ht. of 5–6 ft.

These single rows of uprights must be ritual sites, like the stone avenues and the earthen cursuses of Britain and Western Europe. This one may have been set up c. 2,200–1,400 BC.

*Pelynt, barrow cemetery (SX/200545) 2¼ miles N of Polperro (A387), ½ mile sw of Pelynt (B3359). Grave goods in Truro Museum.

This must be considered the most important barrow cemetery in Cornwall. There are at least 10 bowl-barrows concentrated here, their hts. ranging from 1 ft. to 5 ft.; the largest of them has a diam. of about 80 ft. Since the area has long been under the plough, some smaller mounds may have been destroyed. Burials by cremation were found in all the barrows excavated in the last century. In several instances the bones had been placed in, or were accompanied by urns of Cornish type. Several barrows were found to cover areas of charcoal suggesting cremation on the spot. One of the burials had been placed in a pit lined and covered with stone slabs. More than one grave had been covered by a heap of stones beneath the barrow-mound.

One interesting object found in these barrows is a battle-axe made from local greenstone. Even more important is the fragment of a bronze sword said to have come from the same cemetery, because it is undoubtedly Mycenaean Greek in type, datable to the period 1,450–1,300 BC. Thus, the axe suggests local trade while the sword fragment, if a genuine find, shows contacts extending to the Mediterranean late in the Early Bronze Age.

*Rillaton, round barrow (SX/260719) 3 miles ssw of North Hill (off B3254), on E edge of Craddock Moor. Grave goods in British Museum.

This barrow is significantly close to The Hurlers stone circles (p. 59). It is circular, about 120 ft. in diam. and 8 ft. high. It has been mutilated at the centre and W; E of the centre a stone burial-cist survives. This was opened in 1818 and found to contain an inhumation accompanied by a Wessex-type bronze dagger, beads which probably included segmented faience (?) from Egypt, an urn and in it a superb copy in sheet gold of a bell-beaker fitted with a flat handle. The sides of this vessel are corrugated. The technique employed recalls the gold cups from a shaft-grave at Mycenae and specimens found recently in Germany and Switzerland. The cist containing these fine things was rebuilt c. 1890 and may originally have been located at the centre; date, c. 1,700–1,400 BC.

Rosemodress Circle, see Merry Maidens.

Roughtor, settlements, fields and defended site (SX/144803), 3¼ miles SE of Camelford (A39), on Bodmin Moor.

A fine group of huts and fields is to be found below the sw end of Roughtor. They are bounded on the E by a track. On the higher end of Roughtor, now obscured by fallen boulders, the remains of a stone fort can be made out which may be contemporary with this settlement. The stone circles of **Fernacre** and **Stannon** (pp. 59, 60) may also be part of the complex, though none of the sites has been dated by excavation.

The Roughtor settlement consists of a series of irregular enclosures, some with lynchets and circular huts, extending s for about ½ mile. They represent fields and paddocks, with the dwellings of their owners scattered among them. Date, most likely period c. 1,200–800 BC.

*Stannon, stone circle (SX/125799) 2½ miles NE of St Breward, 2½ miles SE of Camelford (A39). Close to Stannon Farm.

This flattened circle resembles Fernacre. It has a max. diam. of c. 130 ft. About 59 stones can be seen of which 41 still stand. The highest of these is 3¾ ft. above ground. A fallen stone is near the centre of the circle and may originally have stood there. Probable date, c. 2,200–1,400 BC.

Tregaseal, stone circles (SW/387324) 1¼

miles NE of St Just (A3071, B3306), ¼ mile N of Bostraze.

There are 2 circles E and W., separated by a hedge. The E circle has 16 stones standing; it has a diam. of 69 ft. and originally 20 stones. Only 2 stones of the W circle survive. Date, 2,200–1,400 BC.

*Tresvennack, standing stone (SW/442279) ¾ mile SSE of Lower Drift (A30), via Tresvennack Farm. Finds in Penlee Museum, Penzance.

This stone is 11½ ft. high and may be partly worked. A burial pit and large urn were found near its base, with a smaller pot nearby. Date, c. 1,200 BC.

Trevelgue Downs, round barrows (SW/834637) 1¾ miles NE of Newquay (A392, A3075), ¼ mile NW of Trevelgue, between road and sea. Grave goods in Truro Museum.

The 2 massive barrows here were opened in 1872. The E was found to cover a stone cist containing the crouched skeleton of an adult with a stone battle-axe. The cist in the other mound also contained unburnt human bones. It appeared that a huge fire had been kept alight upon this cist for several days before the barrow was heaped over it. Date, c. 1,700–1,400 BC.

*Trewey-Foage, settlement with fields and round barrow (SW/465373) 1¼ miles SE of Zennor (B3306); approached by track from Zennor via Foage Farm.

Though not easily found in the coarse downland grass, this settlement, which has an area of about 6 acres spreading W from the 'old St Ives Road', is important because it represents one of the few groups of 'Celtic' fields in Cornwall, and because it has been scientifically excavated.

The site comprises a series of nearly rectangular fields, each of about ½ acre, with huts scattered among them and contemporary tracks linking huts and fields. A barrow, 3 ft. high and 20 ft. in diam., stands on the edge of the settlement. It might be contemporary.

The fields are marked by overgrown banks of stones about 2 ft. high. They run parallel to the contours of the gently sloping down.

The huts are circular, with an internal diam. of about 16 ft. The walls have stone facings with earth and rubble cores, and with an entrance gap. There were hearths

near the centres of each. Trewey-Foage must have been in use c. 1,400–1,200 BC.

*Trippet Stones, stone circle (SX/128750) 6 miles NE of Bodmin (A30, A38), on Manor Common, 1 mile N of A30. Close to track to Bradford.

The Trippet Stones circle is W of and close to the Stripple Stones (above, p. 57). There are 12 stones in this circle, 8 standing. Originally there would have been about 26. The diam. is 108 ft. These stones are above the average ht. found in Cornish circles; all stand 4–5 ft. above ground. Date, c. 2,200–1,400 BC.

Veryan, round barrow (SW/913387) 3¾ miles S of Tregoney (A3078, B3287), ½ mile SSW of Veryan. At trig. point 342.

Nothing is known of the burial beneath this mound but it should be noted because it is one of the largest round barrows in England, being over 15 ft. high. It shows how large some of the numerous round barrows in this part of Cornwall were; they recall the great chalk barrows of Wessex and confirm the direct contact between the areas, attested also by grave goods from other Cornish barrows. Date, c. 1,700–1,400 BC.

IRON AGE

*Bodrifty, village (SW/445354) 3 miles N of Penzance, 1½ miles SE of Porthmeor (B3306), 700 yds. W of Mulfra Hill, 300 yds. NW of Bodrifty Farm. Finds in Truro Museum.

This village was occupied mainly in the Iron Age, but at least 1 of its huts appears to have been built in the Late Bronze Age and reused later. In its present form, the village consists of about 8 circular huts surrounded by a boundary wall with an entrance in the SW corner, enclosing 3–4 acres of land. There are also field lynchets and other enclosures, particularly to the NE. Most of the huts are about 20 ft. in diam. Their walls have well-laid inner and outer facings and rubble cores. Most have a central hearth (the village has been scientifically excavated recently). Drains have been found in at least 1 hut. The largest hut, on the E side of the village, appears to have been rebuilt in the Iron Age, on Bronze Age foundations. Within its circular wall of 2 periods, a ring of post-holes has been found, suggesting supports for a roof. The hut walls have each been set on a level platform cut back into the hill. The finds suggest a level of poverty, with cereals being grown, and leather and textiles for clothing. The village appears to have received no stimuli from trade.

The first settlement here, from c. 7th century BC was not set within an enclosure but was scattered among its fields. The evolving of a more regular village within an enclosure wall extended from c. 2nd century BC to the mid-Roman period.

Caer Brane, hill-fort (SW/408291) 2¾ miles SE of St Just (A3071, B3306), ½ mile NE of Brane.

This fort is almost circular, with a total diam. of 430 ft. Its defences comprise an inner rampart of drystone and an outer bank made of earth derived from an external ditch. The drystone wall has been destroyed and an original entrance cannot now be identified.

Though presumably of the Iron Age, this fort may stand on the site of a Neolithic camp.

*Carn Brea, hill-fort and Neolithic settlement (SW/686407), between Camborne (A30, B3303) and Redruth (A30, A393), s of A30, ¼ mile s of Carnbrea village. Reached by track from Carnkie. Finds in Truro Museum and Ashmolean Museum, Oxford.

A single rampart around the N side of this hill, doubled (wide-spaced) around the s side, are Iron Age, not yet dated more closely. About 36 acres are enclosed. An entrance through the inner rampart close to the monument at the w end of the hill is lined with upright slabs with a rock-cut step at the inner end. Excavation (continuing) has shown that these ramparts are drystone-faced, with rock-cut ditches outside: at least 15 large circular huts have been identified.

There are traces of a tumbled wall, linking up with natural rock outcrops around the summit of the E end of the hill which have been shown to be Neolithic, associated with a settlement within (irregular huts and at least one lean-to attached to this wall) and possible cultivation plots outside. These have a date-range (C14) c. 3,109–2,687 BC, forming the earliest village in Britain.

*Carn Euny, village and fogou (SW/402289) N of A30, midway between Land's End and Penzance, ½ mile NNW of Brane. Finds in Penzance and Truro Museums.

Carn Euny Iron Age village – first occupied before 400 BC – continued in use until the end of the Roman period. The landscape was more wooded than today and early huts were timber-built. The superb stone fogou may belong to the early period. Stone huts now visible belonged to later occupants, especially those of the 1st century BC. The intervening centuries saw the blocking of the fogou and much demolition and rebuilding of Iron Age houses, but 3 main complexes emerge on the NE, E and s, with another possible one by the ruined cottage. These form a series of interlocking circles around the fogou, sharing party walls and having impressive paved entrances. A smaller hut is situated in the SE and remains of comparable huts are visible on the sw of the site.

The fogou with its unique round chamber was built in several stages: the round chamber with entrance passage may date back to the Bronze Age and have been roofed with timber around a central post. Then the long passage was built – probably closed at both ends originally. Later, the E end was opened up with an entrance flanked by two uprights.

Castle-an-Dinas, hill-fort (SW/485350) ½ mile NW of Castle Gate (B3311).

This hill-fort is ¾ mile E of **Chyauster** village (p. 63) and may have had some connection with it. The fort is circular, having a max. diam. of about 750 ft. It has 3 ramparts of stone with ditches outside each, and the remains of a fourth bank and ditch beyond. The middle stone wall is 13 ft. thick. There is a well near the centre of the fort and huts have also been traced. A modern tower now obscures these. Undated.

*Castle-an-Dinas, hill-fort (SW/945624) 2¼ miles ESE of St Columb Major (A39, A3059), 1 mile N of A30.

Like so many of the circular hill-forts in Cornwall, this site appears to have been connected with the late Iron Age tin trade; rich tin deposits exist close to it.

Its defences, which cover an area of 6

acres, comprise 3 massive ramparts which would originally have had ditches outside them. The remains of a fourth earthwork can be traced outside the others. The total diam. is about 850 ft. An entrance faces SW. Recent exploration has shown that the 2 outer ramparts were built late in the life of this 2-period site.

As at **Chun** (below) huts would have been built around the inside of the innermost rampart and there was also a well. Date, c. 2nd–1st century BC.

*Castle Dore, hill-fort (SX/103548) 2¼ miles NW of Fowey (A3082), on E side of B3269. Finds in Truro Museum.

Though small, this earthwork is of importance; it is well preserved and was excavated in 1936 and 1937. The defences of the site are roughly circular, the inner bank and ditch having a diam. of 320 ft., the outer defences being about 420 ft. across. There is an entrance gap through both rings at the E; here the outer bank and ditch are thrown outwards nearly 100 ft., making their overall plan egg-shaped. The inner bank still rises 7 ft. above the interior; its ditch is 22 ft. wide and is now 4 ft. deep. The outer bank is 6 ft. high in places and its ditch is the same size as the other. Both entrances were about 25 ft. wide.

Excavation revealed that at first the banks had been made by heaping up a stone and earth core between turf retaining walls, and then covering everything with turf and soil. Subsequently the inner bank was given revetments of stone, the outer face presenting a vertical wall to the enemy. During this work it was heightened by material dug out of the inner ditch. The outer bank was not reformed in this way. Both ditches had been cut in bedrock, the inner one to a depth of 8 ft., the outer one 12 ft. They were V-shaped. A series of post-holes representing an elaborate inturned timber gateway was found at the inner entrance. It included a narrow entrance passage 30 ft. long, lined with timbers, and a bridge over the gates. This entrance belonged to a second phase in the history of the site – perhaps that in which the inner rampart was faced with drystone walling. When first built, the entrance was no more than a gap in the bank and ditch, filled with brushwood at night to keep out intruders and wild animals.

The area between the earthworks on the E side seems to have been used as a paddock for animals. Post-holes for hurdling and the foundations of huts were found here. The passage between the entrances through the earthworks was found to have been flanked by banks and ditches, with a gap in each; these effectively cut off the paddock areas from those going through to the centre of the site. There were also huts in the central area.

Castle Dore was built c. 200 BC and altered c. 50 BC. After the Roman period it was re-occupied c. 6th century AD.

*Chun Castle, hill-fort (SW/405339) 2½ miles NE of St Just (A3071, B3306) 1 mile S of Morvah (B3306). Finds in Museums at Truro and Penzance.

Chun Castle is cleverly sited and must have been almost impregnable. It is nearly circular in plan, with defences consisting of 2 ramparts faced with granite blocks, and with a rock-cut ditch outside each bank. The outer bank has a diam. of about 280 ft. In places the inner rampart is nearly 10 ft. high; it is recorded that it stood more than 12 ft. in the last century.

The original entrance faces SW. The gaps through the banks are staggered so that those coming in could be covered by fire from all sides. A series of stone-built rectangular and (earlier) circular huts existed around the walls inside. Some of these have been excavated: one had a paved floor and yielded evidence of tin and iron smelting in the 5th–6th century AD. A well has been found on the N side of the interior. Pottery and other finds suggest that Chun was built in the 3rd–2nd century BC, probably in connection with tin trading from this area, down the W coasts of France and Spain to the Mediterranean. See also **Chun Quoit**, p. 57.

*Chysauster, Iron Age and Roman village (SW/473350) 2 miles N of Trevarrack (B3311), approached by road from Badger's Cross, off B3311. Finds in British Museum and museums at Penzance and Truro.

This is perhaps the most rewarding of the village sites of Cornwall and Devon because most of it has been excavated and is now maintained by the Department of the Environment. The site consists of 4 pairs of circular houses set on opposite sides of a street which connects them. Five of the houses have been cleared completely: the other 3 can be traced on the ground without difficulty.

Each house consists of a courtyard, surrounded by a circular or oval wall, in the thickness of which there is a series of rooms opening on to the courtyard. When excavated, hearths were found in many of the rooms, together with hand mills for grinding corn, pottery and other domestic rubbish. It is not known how all the houses were roofed: some of the rooms had traces of stone corbelling, others would probably have been thatched. The courtyards at the centre were open to the sky. Floors were paved and under at least 1 of the houses there was a well-built drain. Behind the houses there were garden plots, terraced and marked off with stone walls. That behind House 3 is particularly clear. House 3 appears to be double; being the largest in the village, it may have belonged to the chief. It is the only house which has yielded Iron Age remains alone. Date, c. 2nd century BC–3rd century AD. A ruined fogou and other buildings lie SE.

Courtyard houses of this type are found also in Wales and further N. Their origins have not yet been worked out but in Cornwall they may be a translation into stone of the wooden houses found in Iron Age Wessex and elsewhere in lowland Britain.

*Gurnards Head, promontory fort (SW/433385) 5½ miles W of St Ives (A3074, B3306), 1 mile N of Porthmeor (B3306). Finds in Penlee House Museum, Penzance.

Tin and copper occur hereabouts and the fort on Gurnards Head, like so many similar sites in Cornwall, probably owes its origin to the extensive trade in these ores during the Iron Age. The defences of this period – 2 banks and 3 ditches – run across the narrowest part of this promontory, effectively cutting off an area 380 yds. long. Here there is a series of hut-circles where the people thus protected lived.

The earthworks cutting off the Head consist of an inner, main bank, originally a formidable wall of stones 17 ft. wide at its base and still 6 ft. high. The inner face was found to be stepped. Both faces are carefully built, with a rubble core between them. Outside this, the innermost ditch,

now hardly visible was 15 ft. wide and 3 ft. deep, rock-cut. A recent field wall to the s of this is built on the second bank: this is now only 2½ ft. high. It has no stone construction, being of small rubble and earth. The middle ditch is about 14 ft. wide and also some 3 ft. deep. It runs from cliff-edge to cliff-edge. The outermost ditch is 30 ft. to the s. It had steep sides and a V-shaped profile, 9 ft. wide and 4 ft. deep. The entrance, which runs through the middle of the earthworks, was made by building the banks and ditches out of alignment, so that the breaks in each are staggered. This defence in depth implies use of the sling as the chief weapon.

The huts within are in 2 groups, 170 ft. and 550 ft. N of the inner rampart, on the E side of the head. Some have been shown by excavation to be circular and 20–30 ft. across. They had central hearths, well-marked entrances and walls with rubble cores and stone facings.

Occupation (and the fort-building) dates from the mid 2nd century BC. It probably continued into Roman times.

Halligye, fogou and destroyed fortified homestead (SW/712238) 4 miles SE of Helston (A394, A3083), ½ mile N of B3293 and Garras. Visitors will need a torch.

At one time there was a homestead here, defended by 2 ramparts and a ditch. The fogou connected with it alone survives. This was built so that much of it lay beneath the inner rampart of the fort and it provided a form of entry to the interior from 1 of its passages which opened on to the fort ditch.

The fogou is considered the finest in the county. Though irregular in outline, it is T-shaped, with a slight foot to the T. The cross of the T is formed by a long passage running N/S: the N end of this, now blocked, used to open on to the ditch. This part comprises a long, wide gallery with a narrower and lower chamber at the N end, with a lintel (and originally a door) separating them. The upright of the T is curved and lies E/W. It is 54 ft. long. The modern entrance comes into it. Its W end has a small side chamber or passage running S; close to this there is a ridge or stumbling trap across the main passage. This would have warned those hiding here that someone unfamiliar with the retreat had entered it.

This fogou has heavy lintels and supports for the small doorways, and smaller masonry for the walls and roof and the relatively roomy passages. Date, 1st century BC–3rd century AD.

Harlyn Bay, cemetery (SW/877754) 2½ miles W of Padstow (A389, B3276), on coast road 1 mile NW of St Merryn (B3276). Museum on site.

No satisfactory account has ever been written of the uncovering of these burial cists, nor is it possible to date them closely. Over 100 cists have been found. They are made of the local slate and comprise walls and covering slabs. It has been claimed that all the graves were orientated to the N, but contemporary plans and accounts do not confirm this. Each grave contained a skeleton buried in a crouched position. Some of these had been accompanied by bronze rings, pins and safety-pins belonging to a period of transition from the Late Bronze to the Iron Age. Five of the graves are now preserved under glass in ground adjoining the museum. The cemetery may be dated c. 400–300 BC. It must have served a settlement situated nearby and may have been in use down to the 1st century BC.

Kelsey Head, promontory fort (SW/765608) 3¼ miles W of Newquay (A392, A3075), ¾ mile W of West Pentire.

A roughly rectangular headland, protected on the N and W by cliffs, is defended on the S by a V-shaped bank and ditch. An area of 2½ acres is thus enclosed. There is an original entrance 10 ft. wide through the centre of the earthwork, where it changes direction; there is a scatter of loose masonry around the E side of this gap. The ditch is about 15 ft. wide and still 2 ft. deep. The bank rises at least 5 ft. behind it. Undated.

***Maen Castle,** promontory fort (SW/348258) ¾ mile N of Land's End, W of path to Sennen.

A very small area is protected on the W by steep cliffs and on the E by 2 ramparts with a medial ditch, extending 190 ft. from cliff-edge (N) to escarpment (S). The inner bank is separated from the ditch by a berm, which is broadened towards the S end to provide a wide space at the entrance to the fort. N of the entrance, the inner bank

bulges out sharply and nowhere conforms closely to the line of the ditch. The outer bank follows the edge of the ditch exactly.

Excavation has shown that the ditch was originally about 9 ft. deep, broad and U-shaped. The inner edge has been pounded until it is too slippery to climb (at least where exposed by the spade). The outer bank is mainly of soil, revetted on the W with a stone wall. The main rampart is faced with large stones, set vertically in holes in the subsoil to contain a rubble bank 5–11 ft. thick. Some of these facing stones are 4 ft. high. At the entrance, there are traces of curtain walls forming a passageway in from the ditch causeway. The entrance through the inner bank was originally 11 ft. long but has been lengthened at the inner end as a recent shelter for shepherds. The Iron Age portal was defined by 2 uprights 5 ft. high (1 now on its side). At the inner end, 2 post-holes were found which would have supported a door or timber hurdle. No evidence of permanent occupation has been found inside the fort, except for a concentration of potsherds and charcoal within the bulging inner rampart N of the entrance. There are ample traces of field plots on the hillside E of the fort. Date, c. 4th–3rd century BC.

Pendeen Vau, fogou (SW/384355) 1¼ miles WNW of Morvah (B3306), behind Pendeen House (private property).

This is a well-preserved example of a fogou. In plan it is Y-shaped, entry being down the stone-built branches of the Y. Only 1 of the branches is now used as an entrance. It extends above ground level and may have been connected with a dwelling on the surface. The stem of the Y is 24 ft. long and, with the SW branch, is lined and roofed with stones. The SE branch, however, is cut into solid clay with D-shaped cross section: access is via a carefully built entrance leading from the stone-lined passage. Undated.

Treen Dinas, promontory fort (SW/398220) 4 miles SE of Land's End, ½ mile S of Treen (B3315).

This headland is cut off by a series of earthworks probably built at different periods. The most N is a bank and ditch of immense proportions. Some distance behind this there is a series of 3 much slighter banks and ditches. Of these, the outer one is very low. Behind it is the largest of the 3, with 1 of intermediate proportions to the s. The middle earthwork not only spans the headland but also appears to curve s at each end, following the sides of the headland.

The extreme tip of the headland carries the most interesting fortification, which is also probably the latest of the series. A bank faced with heavy masonry and with a central entrance spans the narrowest part; a ditch with a central causeway has been dug immediately outside it. This earthwork lies a few yds. N of the loggan stone. There is the outline of a circular hut immediately behind this rampart at its E end. This cliff castle is undated but its most N defence is probably the latest since it renders the other earthworks unnecessary.

*Tregeare Rounds, hill-slope fort (SX/ 034800) between Port Isaac (B3267) and St Teath (B3267), on s side of B3314. Finds in Truro Museum.

This is an example of the type of earthwork deliberately sited off the crest of a hill, in contrast to normal hill-fort practice; it is overlooked by higher ground to the NW. Tregeare is roughly circular, the diam. of its innermost earthwork being about 500 ft. It has 2 main banks and ditches, the entrances through both facing SE and downhill. A sunken track leads from the entrance to a stream. There is a third and slighter earthwork covering this trackway, on the SE side of the fort. As elsewhere, the ends of the bank at the innermost entrance are raised up, presumably providing vantage points for those overseeing the herding of cattle into the centre of the fort. This seems to have been the purpose for which these hill-slope forts were designed. Traces of occupation have been found between the 2 main ramparts, but not in the central area – another indication that cattle were kept in the middle. Probable date, 2nd–1st century BC.

Trencrom, hill-fort (SW/518362) 2¾ miles w of Hale (A30, B3302), N of road from Start (A30, A3074) to Cripple's Ease (B3311).

This superbly situated fort is protected by a single wall which follows the contours of the hilltop; it takes advantage of outcrops of boulders and other natural features which lie in its path. It is roughly rectangular in plan, enclosing about 1 acre. There are original entrances on the E and w. The wall comprises 2 rows of large upright stones with small rubble filling the space between them. Within the defences, the flat ground contains traces of more than 17 circular huts. This site has not been excavated, but finds of surface pottery suggest a date c. 2nd century BC.

*Trevelgue Head, promontory fort and Bronze Age barrows (SW/825630) 1 mile NE of Newquay (A392, A3075), ¼ mile NW of St Colomb Porth. Finds in Truro Museum.

This site must have been of special importance in prehistoric times because it protected a harbour probably used by those trading the local tin. Indeed evidence has been found for bronze-smelting during the Bronze Age. The earthworks that are visible, however, belong to the Iron Age, with habitation lasting through the Roman period.

This site is divided today by a narrow cleft through which runs the sea. On the landward side 3 pairs of banks and ditches guard the approach, a fourth earthwork lying further to the E and cutting off nearly 200 yds. of the Head. A second group of 3 banks and ditches (the cleft forming the island constituting the third ditch) defends the E end of this island. These rock-cut ditches and banks are all massive, the outermost being 12 ft. deep and its bank 6–8 ft. high. They enclose an area of nearly 6 acres.

Within, a series of huts has been excavated. They belong to the Iron Age, Roman and Dark Age periods. The foundations of some have been cut back into the natural rock and walls were of good quality drystone. Finds included Iron Age bronze horse harness and a small bronze foundry on the s side of the castle. Date of early occupation, c. 3rd century BC. Habitation continued beyond Roman period.

There are 2 round barrows close to the outermost rampart (about SW/825630). One has a diam. of 70 ft. and a ht. of 12 ft.; the other is nearly 50 ft. across and 10 ft. high. Nothing is known of their contents. Date, c. 1,700–1,400 BC.

Cumbria

It is difficult to assign all the sites of this county to periods as they have been for counties further s. They have therefore been separated into 2 groups. Period 1, approximately 2,200–1,200 BC and Period 2, 1,200 BC to 1st century AD. A more precise date is given only where the results of excavation warrant it.

PERIOD 1

Aaron's Apron, enclosure and cairns. See **Sampson's Bratfull.**

Addingham, barrow. See **Long Meg.**

Barnscar, cairns and Period 2 settlement (SD/135958) 4¼ miles SE of Holmrook (A595, B5344), 1½ miles NE of Bridge End.

The character of this group of huts and cairns (at least 368 in number) has not yet been established. Some of the cairns, which follow the ridge for 800 yds., have been dug into in the last century and burials, including 'urns' are reported. They have diams. of 5–25 ft. and all are very low. On the w side of these stone heaps there is a group of at least 6 huts which are likely to be prehistoric. They cover nearly ¾ acre and are now in ruins.

It has been plausibly suggested that the greater part of these cairns may really be stone heaps resulting from field clearance in early medieval times. Twelve cairns were tested in an excavation conducted by Dr Donald Walker in 1957 and no funerary deposits came to light. However, both the palaeobotanical evidence and the evidence of a complex structure of individual cairns make this hypothesis less likely. Also in 1957 the small group of huts was planned by the Ordnance Survey, and 1 large circular hut was cleared revealing a central hearth. A single sling-stone was found during the excavation.

Barron's Pike, cairn ditch (NY/595752) 7¼ miles NW of Greenhead (A69, B6318), 2 miles E of Bewcastle Roman fort.

The mound which lay within this ditch is now almost removed. The ditch is about 60 ft. in diam. and 7 ft. wide, with an entrance gap facing sw. There are no burial records.

*Birkrigg Common, circle, barrows, enclosures, 2¼ miles s of Ulverston (A590, A5087, B5281), between Great Urswick and Bardsea. Finds in Barrow-in-Furness Museum.

Circle, SD/292739. This is a double stone circle with paved floor, the inner ring having 10 stones and a diam. of 30 ft., the outer having 15 stones and an approx. diam. of 85 ft. Unlike the first, it is irregular and very incomplete. The hts. of all surviving stones are 1–2 ft. above ground. Within the smaller circle, 5 human cremations have been found, 1 covered by an inverted collared urn.

Barrow, SD/282740. The mound of this barrow is about 50 ft. in diam. It belongs to the type called a 'platform barrow', the mound being flat on top; the edge of the mound, its highest part, is about 1 ft. high. There are no traces of a surrounding ditch. The edge of the barrow is of larger limestone blocks than those found at the centre. Burnt bones of at least 10 humans have been found in the mound.

Barrow group, SD/286742. There is a group of 4 barrows here, their diams. 12–21 ft. and all about 1 ft. high. Only one shows any trace of a surrounding ditch; all are of earth and stones. These barrows have been excavated but no burials have yet been found.

Barrow, SD/284743. This turf-covered mound of earth and stones is nearly 2 ft. high and 25 ft. across. It has no surrounding ditch. There is a disturbance at the centre, but no records of burials have survived.

Barrow ('tumulus' on 1-in. O.S.), SD/285744. This mound is about 40 ft. across and nearly 3 ft. high. There are no signs of a surrounding ditch. A large tilted stone at the centre may have covered a burial cist, but no records survive.

Barrow, SD/289743. This barrow is about 40 ft. in diam. and nearly 2 ft. high.

Remains of 3 inhumations have been found in it, together with a bronze awl. Near the E edge of the mound a series of deposits of black earth were found, each covered by stone slabs and the whole area surrounded by a circle of large boulders all covered by the barrow. This feature cannot now be interpreted.

This circle, originally perhaps surrounding a cairn or barrow, is about 30 ft. in diam. It has 12 stones, 2–2½ ft. high.

*The Carles, Castlerigg, circle (NY/292236) 1½ miles E of Keswick (A591, A594, B5289), ¾ mile NE of Castlerigg.

This site is a circle, flattened around the NE. It has about 38 stones and a max. diam.

15   *The Carles (Keswick): stone circle*

All these sites, c. 1,700–1,400 BC.

Barrow (between enclosures) SD/288746. The mound is roughly rectangular, 27 × 30 ft. and nearly 2 ft. high. There is no evidence of a surrounding ditch. It is made of earth and stones. Excavation revealed a concentration of 7 cremations in the NE quarter of the barrow. Three of these were in Bronze Age cordoned urns. Date, c. 1,400–1,200 BC.

Enclosures. These lie NE and SW of the barrow described above, almost touching each other. That to the NE is roughly oval, its longer axis measuring nearly 300 ft. It has an in-turned entrance in the E side and 3 depressions representing huts, within. The bank is 10–15 ft. wide and nearly 2 ft. high.

The larger enclosure to the SW is a more regular oval in plan and is 6 times as large as the first. There is an original entrance at the NW. Its bank is everywhere now very slight. These 2 enclosures were probably a fortified homestead and cattle pound for a group of families living in the period 500 BC–1st century AD.

Blakeley Raise, circle (NY/068132) 4 miles NE of Egremont (A595, A5086), 2 miles S of Ennerdale Bridge.

of 107 ft. There is a rectangular setting of 10 stones within the circle, touching it at the E and an outlying stone about 300 ft. SW (fig. 15).

Cardonneth Pike, cairn (NY/559520) 6 miles SSW of Brampton (A69, A6071, B6292), 1 mile NE of Cumrew (E of B6413).

This cairn has been erected on a skyline. It measures 74 × 72 ft. and is about 8 ft. high. In its NW sector there is a recess which is probably the site of a cist; the lowest stones here may be in their original positions. At least 40 'urns', now lost, have been found in the cairn.

Castlerigg, circle. See **The Carles.**

Casterton, circle (SD/640799) 2 miles NE of Kirkby Lonsdale (A65, B6254) 1 mile E of Casterton (A683).

This circle has a diam. of 59 ft. It consists of 20 stones, though there may originally have been more. These have hts. up to 2 ft. The stones are set on a low, flat-topped platform, itself built on a slight spur.

The Cockpit, stone circle or enclosure (NY/483222) 1½ miles SE of Pooley Bridge (A592, B5320), on S side of Roman road called High Street.

Two concentric rings of small stones,

inner diam. 84–86 ft., probably represent the inner and outer facings of a stone wall forming a roughly circular enclosure. On the wall at the SE, there are traces of a small cairn or dwelling, its relationship to the wall not clear. There are 2 less clearly defined groups of stones on the W arc of the wall.

Cold Fell, cairn (NY/606556) 6 miles SE of Brampton (A69, A6071, B6292), 3 miles SE of Hallbankgate (B6292). Trig. station on mound.

This cairn is about 50 ft. in diam. and over 4 ft. high. The stone heap appears to be surrounded by a ditch. There are no burial records.

Cop Stone, standing stones, cairns (NY/496216), c. 1,500 yds. SE of **The Cockpit,** 1 mile SW of Helton. Finds in British Museum.

Cop Stone is a megalithic upright, $4\frac{3}{4}$ ft. high. It appears to be enclosed by a slight bank, much of which has disappeared since recorded by early observers. A small standing stone can be found c. 400 yds. NW and several cairns occur in the vicinity. Of these, a cairn c. 420 yds. NW of Cop Stone is now c. 38 ft. in diam. and includes a setting of 10 stones projecting above the mound's surface. This setting, diam. c. 18 ft., may have acted as a surround to the cairn before it became spread. A food vessel and adult cremation have been found here.

Crosby Ravensworth, barrow circles, $3\frac{1}{2}$–$4\frac{1}{4}$ miles NW of Orton (B6260, B6261):
(1) **Oddendale** (NY/593129) comprises a low mound edged with stones and surrounded by an outer stone circle 90 ft. in diam. Remains of a cremated burial were found under the mound.
(2) At NY/597148 there are 2 mounds 60 yds. apart. That to the N is 45 ft. across and 3 ft. in ht. The other is 30 ft. in diam. and 1 ft. high. Both mounds have kerbs of stones. An inhumation has been found in one of these.

The Currick, long cairn (NY/537827) $4\frac{1}{2}$ miles SE of Newcastleton (B6357), in Kershope Forest $2\frac{1}{4}$ miles ESE of Kershope Bridge.

Though now much damaged, this retains the 'flat-iron' outline characteristic of Neolithic cairns in this area (chiefly across the Border). It is about 145 ft. long and is

orientated SE/NW. Its SE end is squared off with well-laid stones; here it is about 60 ft. wide. The indentation in each side may be the site of a burial chamber which, tradition suggests, was dug out some time ago. There are no records of burials. Date, c. 2,500 BC.

Elva Plain, circle (NY/177317) $3\frac{1}{2}$ miles ENE of Cockermouth (A594, A595, A5086, B5292), $\frac{3}{4}$ mile NNE of Embleton.

There are still 15 stones in this circle, which give it a diam. of 100 ft. There is an outlying stone 182 ft. to the SW. The circle is incomplete and the tallest stone is $3\frac{1}{2}$ ft. above ground.

*Eskdale Moor, circles and cairns (NY/173025) 2 miles SE of Wast Water, 1 mile NNW of Boot.

There are 5 stone circles enclosing cairns on Burnmoor, all about 1 mile NW of Gillbank. Of these, the Eskdale Circle, its N side flattened, max. diam. 105 ft., has 39 stones mostly fallen. There is an outlying stone to the NW. There are the remains of 5 small cairns within the circle; all have a retaining circle of stones about 25 ft. in diam. Opened in 1866, each was found to cover a cist containing a human cremation. Two stone circles, both containing a cairn, lie 100 yds. to the W. They have diams. of about 50 ft.

On Low Longrigg, $\frac{1}{4}$ mile further W, there are 2 more circles, one 50 ft. across with 9 stones, the other 65–75 ft. in diam. The first circle contains a cairn; the other encloses 2 cairns.

Gamelands, circle (NY/640082) $1\frac{1}{4}$ miles E of Orton (B6260, B6261), N of road to Raisbeck.

This circle has a diam. of 138 ft. Most of the granite stones are fallen and none now stands more than $2\frac{1}{2}$ ft. above ground.

Giant's Grave, standing stones. See **Lacra.**

Glassonby, barrow circle. See **Long Meg.**

Goggleby, avenue. See **Shap.**

*Grey Croft, circle (NY/034024) $2\frac{1}{4}$ miles WSW of Gosforth (A595), $\frac{3}{4}$ mile N of Seascale (B5344). Finds in Tullie House Museum, Carlisle.

This circle has been dug out and restored recently. It is approx. circular, with a diam. of about 80 ft. There are 10 stones, their ht. above ground being 4–7 ft. and their wts. 1–4 tons. Originally there may have been 12 stones in the circle. They are volcanic lava agglomerates brought by glacial action from the dome of the Lake District. During restoration of the circle, an oval heap of small stones measuring 22 ft. by 15 ft. was found at the centre. Originally this heap would have risen to a ht. of about 3 ft. Evidence of burning, including the cremation of a human, was found among these stones. Part of a jet ring placed with the bones suggests that circle and burial may be dated c. 2,200–1,400 BC.

Keswick, stone circle. See **The Carles, Castlerigg.**

*King Arthur's Round Table and **Mayburgh,** sacred sites (NY/523284) 1¼ miles SE of Penrith (A6, A66, A594), s side of Eamont Bridge (A6, A592).

The Round Table is in the sw angle of A6/A592. It is nearly circular, with a diam. of about 300 ft. Originally there were 2 entrances, of which the SE survives. There is a surrounding ditch with a bank outside, about 5 ft. high. The berm which separates ditch and bank is not original, for the site was considerably disturbed in the 19th century. The low mound on the central plateau is also recent.

A 17th-century plan shows 2 standing stones outside the N entrance. Excavation in 1937 and 1939 revealed that the ditch was cut with a flat floor, to a width of 30 ft. and depth of 4–5 ft. Near the centre of the plateau defined by ditch and bank there was a trench 8 ft. long, 3 ft. wide and 10 ins. deep, which had been used to cremate the corpse or bones of a human: hazel had been used for fuel. This was covered by a stone structure which was too damaged for interpretation, but the feature is presumed to be contemporary with the henge monument.

Mayburgh lies ¼ mile to the w. It is also circular (diam. 360 ft. crest to crest of bank), with 1 original entrance facing E. The area enclosed is about 1½ acres. Its rampart is 8–15 ft. high. This has been formed by collecting surface stones instead of the more normal method (as at the Round Table) of digging a ditch inside. There is a stone near the centre, 9 ft. high: it is known that this is the survivor of a central rectangular setting of 4 stones, with 4 more flanking the entrance.

Both are close to a river, a characteristic situation for these late Neolithic sacred sites. Date, c. 2,500–1,700 BC.

Kirkby Moor, earth circle with stone avenue, cairn; 1½ miles SE of Grizebeck (A595, A5092), 1 mile NE of Beck Side.

'The Kirk' (SD/251827). This circle has a diam. of 75 ft. Its bank is of earth and stones 6–10 ft. wide and nearly 2 ft. high. Around the inner edge of the bank on the E side there are the remains of a retaining circle of large stones. No entrance or surrounding ditch can be seen. About 100 ft. to the NE, the first of 3 pairs of stones forming, perhaps, an avenue with a sinuous course, can be seen. They stand 1–2 ft. above ground.

One thousand ft. NNE there is a cairn (at SD/251830). It is about 80 ft. in diam. and 3–4 ft. high, and is made up of rough stones. There is no trace of a surrounding ditch. In the ssw side a stone-lined cist has been found and can still be seen. A cremation has been recorded from it. Date of both sites, c. 1,700–1,400 BC.

*Lacra, burial circles, standing stones (Giant's Grave) and avenues (SD/150814) 1½ miles NW of Millom (A5093), ½ mile NE of Kirksanton. Finds in Barrow-in-Furness Museum.

Remains of 5 circles and 2 possible avenues can be seen s and SE of Lacra. Circle A (map ref. above) is 330 ft. E of the house. It is nearly 50 ft. in diam. and has 6 surviving stones, 2 placed close together facing E. Circle B lies 400 yds. due S. It has 6 stones and a diam. of 48 ft. Originally it would have had 11 equally spaced uprights. Excavation has revealed a low central mound 32 ft. across. Near its centre there was an inner ring of stones 14 ft. in diam. placed on top of the mound with their long axis pointing towards the centre. The mound itself, of earth with rubble above, covered traces of a cremation burial. There are the remains of a third circle (C) 350 ft. ESE of Circle B. The longest of its 4 stones measures 5 ft. The original diam. would have been about 70 ft. Circle D and 2 possible avenues are 500 ft. ESE. They are irregular and confused by an outcrop of natural stones hereabouts. Circle D has a diam. of 50–60 ft., and there is a double (but ragged) line of stones extending 152 ft. ENE. A large flat stone lies near the centre of the circle. Parts of a collared urn (originally perhaps with a burial) have been found at the base of the N stone of Circle D. There are traces of a small circle of 6 surviving stones 25 ft. NW of D, 16 ft. across and with a stone at its centre. About 160 ft. SW there are remains of a second possible avenue, 50 ft. wide and extending WSW for 230 ft. Most of the N side of this avenue is missing. Giant's Grave is on the S side of Kirksanton (A5093). It comprises 2 upright stones, one 10 ft. high, the other 8 ft. There is a cup-mark on the larger stone, 3 ins. across and 1½ ins. deep.

Langdale, axe factory. See **Pike of Stickle.**

Leacet Plantation, barrow-circle (NY/ 563263) 4 miles SE of Penrith (A6, A66, A594), ¾ mile NE of Melkinthorpe, on S side of Leacet Plantation.

Seven stones forming a circle 37 ft. across are the retaining circle of a round barrow. When excavated in the 19th century, a cremation was found at the centre. A series of urns, a food vessel and an incense cup had been placed at the base of some stones of the retaining ring.

Long Meg and her Daughters, Little Meg, circles and barrow (NY/571373) 2¼ miles N of Langwathby (A686, B6412), ¾ mile NE of Little Salkeld. Carved stone in Penrith Museum.

This circle has a flattened N side, max. diam. 360 ft. There are 65 stones (the Daughters), of which 27 still stand. There were originally about 70 stones, all nearly 10 ft. high. Long Meg is an outlying stone, about 60 ft. to the SW. It is 12 ft. high. There are 2 other outlying stones, 28 ft. apart, between this one and the main circle. There are traces, particularly on the W side, of a surrounding bank. A series of cup-and-ring marks has been discovered on the NE face of Long Meg.

Little Meg (or **Maughanby Circle**), 700 yds. NE, is a circle of 11 stones which originally surrounded a barrow. This mound covered a burial cist containing an urn filled with burnt human bones. Two of the stones (one still in position) have been decorated by hollows and spiral engravings.

At NY/573394, ¼ mile NW of Glassonby, there is a ring of 31 stones with a diam. of 45 ft. This was the retaining circle for a mound which was found to cover a cist in its SE quarter. The contents of this is not known but outside the stone circle a collared urn was found inverted over a cremation (of a male). Date, c. 2,200–1,400 BC.

Maughanby Circle. See **Long Meg.**

Mayburgh, sacred site. See p. 70.

*Mecklin Park, round barrow (NY/ 126019) 3¼ miles NE of Holmrook (A595, B5344), 1 mile ENE of Santon Bridge. Finds in Tullie House Museum, Carlisle.

The mound is 30–32 ft. in diam. and about 3 ft. high. A stone kerb of granite boulders was revealed by excavation. A scatter of charcoal was found at the centre of the mound but no burial. A sherd of Beaker pottery suggests that this barrow was built c. 2,000–1,700 BC. Other cairns in this area have yielded food vessels and jet beads.

*Mount Hulie, hut circle (NY/578747) 9 miles NE of Brampton (A69, A6071, B6292, B6413) ¾ mile E of Bewcastle; 860 yds. N, 83 yds. E of Woodhead Farm. Finds in Tullie House Museum, Carlisle.

The diam. of this hut is 26 ft. It has been cut back into the hillside and has a wall 2½ ft. thick, on a 3–4 ft. footing. The entrance faces S. It is wider on the outside and is clearly splayed. Excavation revealed 2 holes in the floor of the interior which may have held wooden supports for a timber-framed roof. A hearth stone was found inside and E of the doorway. A jet conical button and a ring pendant found on the floor suggest a date c. 1,700–1,400 BC for the hut.

Oddendale, barrow. See **Crosby Ravensworth.**

Orton, barrow. See Period 2, **Castle Folds.**

Pike of Stickle, axe factory (NY/272072) on N side of Gt. Langdale, 7½ miles NW of Ambleside (A591, A593), 3¼ miles WNW of Chapel Stile (B5343). Finds in Tullie House Museum, Carlisle, British Museum, Cambridge Museum of Archaeology and Ethnology, etc.

On the steep hillside leading up to Pike of Stickle from the 500 ft. contour, the 'workshops' of one of the highest-output Neolithic axe factories in Britain are located (map ref. is to centre of area). Flakes, roughed-out axe-heads and debris can still be found lying on the surface of the screes. The rock which outcrops naturally here is a tuff of the Borrowdale Volcanic Series and is an ideal raw material for axes and other heavy tools. It is easy to flake, can be ground down to a sharp edge and is very hard. It was eagerly sought after throughout the later Neolithic and the factory may have remained in production down to c. 1,400 BC. So far, only axe- and adze-heads have been found made of this rock. They were traded to all parts of England, Wales and Scotland, with a concentration in Wessex.

Sampson's Bratfull, long cairn, cairns and enclosure (NY/098080) 3¾ miles NE of Calder Bridge (A595), on Stockdale Moor, ¾ mile ENE of Scalderskew.

This mound lies E/W. It is 90 ft. long and 45 ft. max. width. Its greatest ht. is 6 ft. No record of burials or internal structures survives: without excavation nothing can be said of the depressions and traces of walling visible in the mound of this stone-built long cairn. Date, c. 2,500 BC.

Immediately to the N (Stockdale Moor), S and W of the long cairn, some scores of small stone heaps can be identified. These have not been excavated but, like all small cairns of this class in the N of England, are likely to have covered burials, since dissolved by the acid soil.

Another concentration of cairns can be found on Nether Wasdale Common, about 1 mile ESE (at NY/115077). There are about 8, mostly some 9 ft. in diam. and 1 ft. high. They seem originally to have been surrounded by a stone enclosure which may have been contemporary. Remains of this can be seen to the E of the cairns.

Seascale, stone circle. See **Grey Croft.**

Shap, circles and avenue (NY/567133) 1¼ miles S of Shap (A6), on E side of A6, 600 yds. N of junction with B6261.

Shap circle (map ref.) is now damaged by the railway line. Originally it had a diam. of 80 ft. Six large granite stones, now all fallen, can be seen. All are 8–9 ft. long. From this circle, the remains of an avenue can be traced up to Thunder Stone (NY/552157), ¾ mile NW of Shap. Other stones of this avenue (described in the 18th century) can be found at the following distances SE of Thunder Stone: 660 yds., 980 yds., 1,035 yds. (Goggleby Stone), 1,665 yds. (and 110 yds. W of King's Arms

Inn); 4 more stones, probably belonging to the avenue, can be found E and W of the main road between the last and the circle. All these stones are 6–8 ft. long. There are 2 cup-and-ring marks on the stone at 980 yds.

A second circle lies 1½ miles NNE of Shap Church (NY/568178), 250 yds. SW of Gunnerwell. It includes the remains of a mound in which there is a circle of stones 52 ft. in diam.: 1 of these still stands. The mound has an outer circle of stones 105 ft. across. Three of these stand. A burial cist was found at the centre of the mound.

There is a third circle at NY/553189, diam. c. 24 yds. It has a cairn at its centre with its own retaining wall and traces of another to the W.

Stockdale Moor, cairns and enclosures. See **Sampson's Bratfull.**

Studfold, circle (NY/040224) 2 miles ESE of Distington (A595, B5296), 400 yds. N of Greyhound Inn.

This incomplete circle is cut across by a modern wall which incorporates 1 stone. At least 11 other stones can be found, though some are only a few inches above turf-level. The diam. cannot now be estimated.

Sunbrick, round barrow. See **Birkrigg Common.**

Sunken Kirk, circle. See **Swinside.**

*Swinside, circle (SD/172883) 2½ miles ENE of Broughton (A593, A595), NW of Broadgate and Crag Hall (off A595).

There are 55 stones giving this circle a diam. of 90 ft. Two outliers 9 ft. apart at the SE, where there is a gap in the circle, suggest an entrance. When complete, the stones must have been almost contiguous. Excavation has shown that the stones are bedded on a layer of small rammed pebbles.

Thunder Stone, avenue. See **Shap.**

White Borran, cairns (SD/266891) 3 miles NE of Grizebeck (A595, A5092), 1½ miles W of Blawith (A5084).

The first cairn consists of a pile of large rubble, 40 ft. in diam. and over 3 ft. high. There is no trace of a surrounding ditch. The centre has been dug out but without recorded results. Date, c. 1,700–1,400 BC.

There is another cairn of the same period at SD/267890, 280 ft. ESE of the last. It is 20 ft. across and 1 ft. high. Several boulders form a retaining wall around the N side, but cannot be seen elsewhere. The centre has been dug out, likewise without result.

PERIOD 2

(c. 1,200 BC – Roman Conquest)
Barnscar, settlement. See Period 1.
Birkrigg Common, enclosure. See Period 1.
Burwens, village. See **Crosby Ravensworth.**
*Carrock Fell, hill-fort and Period 1 cairns (NY/343337) 5 miles NW of Trout-beck (A594, A5091), 1¼ miles NW of Mosedale.

This fort is oval in plan, protected on all sides by steep hill-slopes which are precipitous at the W end. About 5 acres are enclosed. The defences consist of a single rampart of stones. In places well-built stone facings can be seen. Of several gaps of different widths, that at the W end and another W of the cottage at the SE corner are original entrances.

The cairn is at the E end of the ridge within the fort. It is 40–50 ft. in diam. A cist can be seen at its centre, placed NE/SW. Nothing is known of its contents.

Some hundreds of cairns can be found in the area N of Carrock Fell, especially centred on NY/342347, NY/347353 and at NY/351349. Many are small cairns which have not yet yielded evidence of burial. At the last of these map refs., however, there is an oval barrow, 36 × 25 ft., 3 ft. high. A thick jacket of soil and rubble was found to cover a bottom layer of gravel. At the base of this there was a small pit containing a cremation and a piece of bronze.
Castle Crag, hill-fort (NY/469128) 6 miles WSW of Shap (A6), on W side of Hawes-water Reservoir.

Natural slopes protect the N and NE sides of this oval fortification, though excavation has revealed traces of a parapet here. The main defence is a stone rampart along the S side with 2 ditches outside it. There is a possible entrance at the W, approached by a pathway. Traces of hut floors and hearths have been found within the fort, on an an area of about 1/10th acre.
Castle Crag, hill-fort. See **Shoulthwaite.**
Castle Folds, hill-fort and Bronze Age barrow (NY/650094) 1¾ miles NE of Orton

(B6260, B6261), ¾ mile NW of Sunbiggin.

This fortified settlement of 1¼ acres occupies the top of a flat knoll. It is irregular in plan, with 4 sides. There is an entrance in the surrounding stone wall in the S side, approached by a pathway through the broken rock outside the fort. The wall of the fort must originally have been about 8 ft. thick. The outlines of circular and oval huts can be seen built against the inside of this wall.

There is a barrow 500 yds. SSE. It has a diam. of 49 ft. and is 4 ft. high. A pit at the centre, cut 2 ft. into the rock, contained an adult inhumation with an implement of chert. Three other adults had been buried in the mound. Date, c. 1,700–1,400 BC.
*Castlehead, promontory fort (SD/421797), ½ mile SE of Lindale (A590, A5074), 1¾ miles NE of Grange-over-Sands (B5277).

An area of c. 1⅓ acres is defended by steep slopes on all except the N side and only here have defences been built. These consist of an inner rampart running across the spur from E to W, curving S slightly at the latter and stopping short of the plateau edge to provide an entrance 10 ft. wide (used by the footpath), perhaps original. The rampart has no ditch; its outer face was revetted by vertical dry-stone walling which is still c. 4 ft. high in places. In front of the W half of this defence there is a scarp defining a triangular area, which may represent an outwork here protecting the entrance. Not dated.
Castle Hill, settlement (NY/702230) 2 miles NE of Appleby (A66, B6260), 1½ miles SE of Dufton.

This settlement commands Burthwaite Beck. It consists of 7 circular huts and a rectangular enclosure surrounded by a roughly oval earthwork. The area protected by this slight defence is 1 acre. There is an entrance gap at the NW. The earthwork has a ditch with a bank outside it.
*Castle How, hill-fort (NY/202308) 5 miles E of Cockermouth (A594, A595, A5086), SE of Bassenthwaite Lake Station; N of A594.

This small but heavily defended fort is protected on the N and S by steep hillsides. On the W there are 4 ditches and counter-scarp banks, the second from the top being the largest. Beyond the outermost ditch the natural slope has been artificially scarped to form an extra defence. At the E end there are 2 banks, ditches and counter-scarp banks. The innermost ditch has vertical sides, flat floor and is at least 6 ft. deep s of the original entrance here. The area enclosed is about 1½ acres. Some tooled stones found incorporated in the ramparts suggest that this fort was used, if not built, in the Roman period – but by natives, in a pre-Roman tradition.

Castlesteads, fortified settlement (NY/ 518252) 2¼ miles ssw of Eamont Bridge (A6, A592), 1 mile NE of Askham.

An area of ¼ acre is enclosed by 3 concentric banks with 2 ditches between them (all virtually destroyed on the E side). The interior is divided into a series of small enclosures. Original entrances cannot now be made out. Though without close parallel, this site is akin to the Iron Age hill-forts. To some extent it also resembles the site ½ mile to the N (called **Yanwath Wood**).

Crosby Garrett, settlements (NY/719064) 9 miles SSE of Appleby (A66, B6260) 1¼ miles NE of Newbiggin-on-Lune; E and s sides of Begin Hill.

There are 3 villages, set among contemporary square fields and bounded by limestone scarps. The settlement has an area of 160 acres. The main village, and perhaps the earliest, is on the SE slope of Begin Hill (map ref. above). It comprises a series of sub-rectangular hut enclosures with, on the w and s, a series of paddocks. There is a rectangular building with stone door-posts on the s side of the village. A trackway runs NW and there is another leading sw. The second village lies 700 yds. to the NE. It has the same collection of huts and paddocks but covering only half the area of the first village. There is a possible entrance on the N side. The third village is 300 yds. NE of the second and is about the same size. It is more regular in plan than the others, being almost rectangular: it also has paddocks and hut-sites. All 3 villages are integrated with the surrounding system of fields, boundary banks and trackways. Without excavation, nothing is known of the type of hut or the size of the groups living here.

Crosby Ravensworth, village sites. Area 3

miles N of Orton (B6260, B6261), 1½ miles s of Crosby Ravensworth. Finds in Tullie House Museum, Carlisle.

There is an important series of settlements in this area, most of which are likely to be pre-Roman in origin, though Ewe Close was certainly in use after the Conquest.

Ewe Close (NY/609135). An extensive village covering 1¼ acres.

The main part consists of 2 groups of circular huts and paddocks, each roughly rectangular and surrounded by a wall. The w group has a very large round hut at its centre and a main entrance facing s. South of these groups there is a third rectangular embanked enclosure, with huts and paddocks in and N of it. The huts have heavy stone-built walls usually 6 ft. thick. The floor of the largest hut (centre, w group) was paved. Objects excavated here were mainly Roman, but may represent the final phase of a prehistoric village.

Ewe Locks (NY/612128), 700 yds. s of above. Here there are 2 groups of round huts and paddocks 60 yds. apart. The NE and larger group is set within an oval and a square enclosure, covering 1 acre. The sw group includes 1 hut and some paddocks. The foundations of 2 rectangular buildings, probably post-Roman, can be seen among the huts in the NE group.

Cow Green (NY/617121), 1,000 yds. SE of last. Two groups of sub-rectangular huts and paddocks are almost joined. A more recent house lies just s of these groups. The huts in the E group are more rectangular than those to the w. Both groups have entrances facing ssw. Hut walls are 5–6 ft. thick.

Burwens (NY/622123), 200 yds. NE of Crosby Lodge. A rectangular wall encloses nearly 1 acre and contains a series of circular and less regular huts. There is an entrance to the village in the w side and a 'street' runs SE from it, through the village. Several of the huts have courtyards; some are built against the main enclosure wall, others stand detached. Fields N and E of this village cover 3–4 acres. **Howarcles** (NY/627132), 1,200 yds. NE of last, covers 1½ acres. A series of oval and sub-rectangular huts and paddocks lies either side of a roadway running N/s. The group is dominated by 1 very large oval hut at the NE.

At NY/633124, 1,000 yds SE of the last, there is another settlement, covering 2 acres. A modern wall overlies the main village enclosure along the NE. There are about 20 circular or oval huts set among irregular paddocks. A main entrance may be at the SW.

Dunmallet, hill-fort (NY/468246) 4½ miles SW of Penrith (A6, A66, A592, A594), on W side of Pooley Bridge (A592, B5320), N end of Ullswater.

The fort is at the top of a cone-shaped hill whose sides are unusually steep. An oval area of about 1 acre is protected by a bank and ditch with traces of a counterscarp bank. There is a probable entrance at the SW, where the hillside affords the easiest approach.

Ewe Close, village. See **Crosby Ravensworth.**

Ewe Locks, village. See **Crosby Ravensworth.**

Holme Bank, enclosure (SD/276734) 3 miles ESE of Dalton-in-Furness (A590, A595), 1 mile NW of Baycliff (A5087).

Though not yet dated by excavation, this is likely to have been a fortified farmstead inhabited by Britons 1st century AD. It has a 5-sided bank of earth and stone, faced originally with large slabs set up on edge, 10–14 ft. wide and 2–3 ft. high, with an entrance facing E. It measures 60 × 160 ft. There is a slight ditch round the E and SE sides. Inside, there are traces of 2 huts, 15–25 ft. in diam., and 1 cross bank on the N, probably to contain livestock. Outside the enclosure, 80 ft. to the NW, there is a third hut with a bank and ditch around its N side.

Howarcles, village. See **Crosby Ravensworth.**

Hugill, settlement (NY/437009) 2¼ miles NE of Windermere (A591, A592), ¼ mile E of High Borrans.

The modern wall around this settlement is built upon the original enclosing bank. There were entrances in the middle of the W side, at the W end of the S side and towards the N end of the E side (where the original bank curves in behind the modern wall). Within, there is a series of terraces and paddocks in the E half, with a preponderance of hut-like enclosures in the W half. The huts are generally circular.

About 2 acres are enclosed.

*Lanthwaite Green, settlement (NY/161209) 2¾ miles NW of Buttermere (B5289); 500 ft. SE of Lanthwaite Gate. Finds in Keswick Museum.

The site appears as a hollow 200 ft. across. A rampart once surrounded the settlement, with an entrance facing W. There is a series of internal divisions, particularly around the SE half of the main enclosure, which may be either hut sites or paddocks for stock.

Peel Wyke, hill-fort. See **Castle How.**

Shoulthwaite, hill-fort (NY/300188) 3¾ miles SE of Keswick (A591, A594, B5289), 1 mile W of A591/B5322 junction.

This fort commands the Gill. It is protected by precipitous slopes on the W and N. Roughly oval in plan, it is defended on the E and S by a rampart constructed of earth and stone, over 6 ft. high; there is an additional rampart between 2 ditches at the SE. A simple entrance interrupts the defence at the E. About ½ acre is enclosed. Not dated.

Smardale Demesne, settlements (NY/730072) 3 miles SW of Kirkby Stephen (A685, B6259), SE of SE corner of Crag Wood.

These are 2 settlements lying close together astride a ridge. The larger, of 1¼ acres, comprises 2 groups of rectangular paddocks and enclosures with traces of at least 1 large circular hut in each. The other site is 500 yds. NE of the first (NY/735075). It is a roughly oval enclosure, subdivided by an internal crossbank at the N and with a circular hut near the middle. The entrance may have been at the NE.

*Threlkeld Knott, settlement and Period 1 cairns (NY/329241) 4 miles E of Keswick (A591, A594), ¾ mile SE of Birkett Mire (B5322).

The settlement covers an area over 400 × 300 ft. Its long axis E/W, it comprises a series of at least 5 rectangular enclosures or paddocks, with 4–5 hut circles among them. An original entrance to the site faces NW. The largest hut is near the centre. Excavation showed that it has an internal diam. of 20 ft., with walls 5–6 ft. thick. Its entrance faces SE. The other huts are slightly smaller in diam.

To the N and E are remains of a field system with lynchets and heaps of stones gathered by surface clearance. These are probably contemporary with the settlement.

Towtop Kirk, enclosure (NY/494179) $4\frac{1}{2}$ miles NW of Shap (A6), $1\frac{3}{4}$ miles W of Bampton.

A roughly oval enclosure wall, 55×42 yds., contains at its centre the U-shaped outline of a hut, with a second enclosure and other features to the E. There are traces of a second hut, now obscured by a much later structure, to the NW. The entrance to the enclosure is at the NW.

Urswick Stone Walls, enclosures (SD/260741) $1\frac{3}{4}$ miles E of Dalton-in-Furness (A590, A595), $\frac{1}{4}$ mile NW of Little Urswick. Finds in Barrow-in-Furness Museum.

There are 2 enclosures here, that to the W being roughly oval, the other rectangular. The oval enclosure has an area of $1\frac{1}{2}$ acres. It has a stone surrounding wall 10–12 ft. wide and now about 1 ft. high. Originally this wall would have been considerably higher. An original entrance is at the SE (with modern field wall through it). Within, there is a series of roughly rectangular cattle pounds or paddocks, with walls 4–5 ft. thick and made of large stones set upright or laid horizontally, with rubble between them. Traces of 5 hut circles, 20–30 ft. in diam., can be seen near the centre of the enclosure: all their entrances face E. Finds from the huts suggest a 1st century BC–1st century AD

date. The rectangular enclosure to the SE has a rampart (or wall foundation) 15–20 ft. wide and 1–2 ft. high. There is an original entrance at the SE corner. Both enclosures must have protected a group of families with their livestock. NW and NE of these sites there is a cultivation terrace 500 ft. long.

Waitby, settlements (NY/755074) $1\frac{1}{2}$ miles SW of Kirkby Stephen (A685, B6258), on N side of railway embankment 1,100 yds. NW of Kirkby Stephen West Station.

Two settlement sites 60 yds. apart are just overlapped by the railway embankment. The NW site is very rectangular in plan, with a series of sub-rectangular divisions inside and an in-turned entrance in the W side. The SE site is more irregular in outline, with several internal divisions and traces of at least 3 circular huts. The entrance may have been in the E side. Each site has an area of about 1 acre.

Yanwath Wood, fortified settlement (NY/519260) $\frac{1}{2}$ mile N of Castlesteads (p. 74).

This is a roughly D-shaped enclosure associated with a bank and ditch forming the straight side of the D and running N/S for about 250 yds. The enclosure is protected by 2 banks (? the remains of walls) with a ditch between them: it has an area of 1 acre. There is an entrance at the NW. The gap at the SE may also be original. There are several small enclosures within.

Derbyshire

NEOLITHIC

*****Arbor Low,** sacred sites and Bronze Age round barrows (SK/160636) 5 miles SW of Bakewell (A6, A619), $\frac{3}{4}$ mile E of Parsley Hay Station (A515). Finds in Sheffield Museum, British Museum, Buxton Museum.

This site has a circular bank with a diam., crest to crest, of 250 ft. and an average ht. of 7 ft. Within it there is a ditch nearly 30 ft. wide, from which the limestone for the bank has been quarried. Both are broken by entrances facing N and S. On the ground so defined, there are nearly 50 stones and fragments belonging to a circle which had a diam. of about 150 ft., and a central U-shaped setting – a cove. Today all these stones are fallen. It is likely, however, that they would originally have been upright. They are all of the local limestone (fig. 16).

Excavation in 1901–2 revealed that the ditch was irregular in shape and size. It has an average depth of 6 ft. At the entrance-gaps its ends are slightly squared-off. No holes have yet been found in which the stones of the circle and cove could have stood. They may have been wedged upright in natural hollows in the limestone; this might account for their collapsed state today. A skeleton was found just to the E of the cove but its relationship could not be ascertained. Arbor Low must belong to the phase 2,500–1,700 BC.

A slight bank and ditch approach Arbor Low from the s reaching it just w of the s entrance. This bank is about 1½ ft. high. Digging showed that its ditch was irregular in shape, 4 ft. deep and 8 ft. wide, and that this inexplicable little earthwork was contemporary with, or later (and likely to be much later) than the henge monument.

A round barrow (c. 1,700–1,400 BC) impinges upon the bank of Arbor Low E of its s entrance. This is 7 ft. high and about 70 ft. in diam. A gap in the bank of the henge monument where the barrow stands suggests that the latter had in part been made from the sacred site. The barrow may have been augmented by material from its surrounding ditch, but the existence of this has not yet been proved by excavation. A cremation has been found in the barrow, associated with a bone pin, flint strike-a-light and 2 food vessels. These had been placed in a carefully made stone cist, paved and roofed with stone.

*Gib Hill, 350 yds. sw of Arbor Low, is 15 ft. high and oval in plan, c. 120 × 70 ft., with traces of a surrounding ditch. It appears that an earlier oval barrow has had a circular mound added to it, like the barrow overlying the bank of Arbor Low. The limestone burial cist found here in 1848, containing a cremation and food vessel, would belong to the added mound, c. 1,700–1,400 BC. The oval mound could be c. 2,500 BC. Immediately NW can be traced a circular ditched enclosure with slight outer bank, diam. c. 180 ft., which may be a henge monument. Excavation has shown its ditch to be 20 ft. wide and 3½ ft. deep.

*Bull Ring, sacred site and Bronze Age

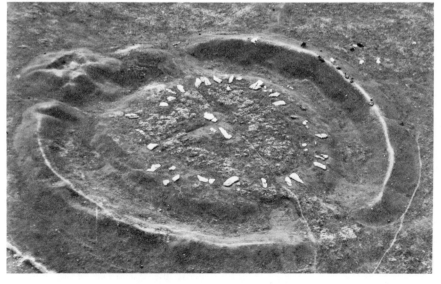

16   *Arbor Low henge monument: barrow impinging on bank at top left*

round barrow (SK/078783) E of school in Dove Holes (A624), 3 miles NE of Buxton. Finds in Buxton Museum.

This sacred site comprises a nearly circular bank about 250 ft. in diam., with a ditch within it, 30–40 ft. wide. Both are broken by original entrances at the N and s. Today the bank is 3–4 ft. high. The site was excavated in 1949. The bank had been made by heaping up limestone rubble from the ditch within; the latter was irregular in shape, with a depth of 4–7 ft. Its wall tended to slope down more steeply on the inside than on the outside.

An 18th century report shows that a ring of stones had stood on the plateau defined by bank and ditch : these have now disappeared. Such a stone circle would make the Bull Ring resemble **Arbor Low** (above) : both belong to the period 2,500– 1,700 BC.

A large round barrow can be found sw of the Bull Ring, occupying a position analogous to Gib Hill, beside Arbor Low. This mound is still 8 ft. high. No records of its contents survive. It is likely to belong to the period 1,700–1,400 BC.

*****Five Wells,** chambered tomb (SK/124711) 1 mile w of Taddington (off A6), N of footpath to Chelmorton. Finds in Sheffield Museum.

An oval barrow, 70 × 65 ft., covers 2 separate burial chambers set back-to-back, each approached by a passage, one from the E, the other from the w. Like all the burial chambers in the Peak these are wedge-shaped, with 2 pillar-like stones defining the break between chamber and passage. Originally both structures would have had roof slabs and the whole covered with a mound. The passage-entrances are simply sharp breaks in the line of the well-built drystone wall which revetted the mound.

At least 12 burials have been found in the chambers, together with a fragment of doubtful early Neolithic and some Peterborough pottery and flint tools. This type of circular mound with chambers approached by passages represents mixed architectural and cultural elements: their derivation is western, perhaps partly Irish. They must belong to the period 2,500– 2,000 BC.

*****Green Low,** chambered tomb (SK/

233580), 1 mile NW of Grangemill (A524, A5012), ¼ mile s of A5012. 1½ miles E of **Minninglow** (below) and E of Bronze Age round barrow.

Excavation has shown that this roughly circular cairn, c. 57 ft. in diam. and 2 ft. max. ht., covered a burial chamber of 2 compartments, lying nearly N/S. A straight facade recessed into the s side of the cairn, 33 ft. long, had a near-central entrance giving access to the chamber : a large stone of the facade on the w and a stone slab set at right angles to the facade on the E form door-jambs. The chamber is 15 × 15 ft. internally; there were traces of a paved floor. Disturbed in Roman times and dug by Bateman in 1843, we cannot estimate the number of inhumations originally buried here. The forecourt was blocked at the end of the tomb's use; Beaker pottery in the cairn suggests a building date c. 2,000 BC.

*****Minninglow,** chambered tomb (SK/ 209573) 2¼ miles w of Grangemill (A524, A5012), ¼ mile E of mineral line.

The largest Peak chambered tomb, this much robbed mound measures 141 × 121 ft. and is 8 ft. high. There is a central wedge-shaped chamber with capstone resting on portal pillars and the rear upright, its unexcavated passage running E. A second chamber, its passage running s, lies 17 ft. to the s. Remains of a third chamber lie to the w, with another near the edge of the mound at the sw. Other stones hereabouts suggest that the site includes more burial features. The tomb was robbed in Roman times and there are no records of burials. Date, c. 2,500– 2,000 BC.

*****Ringham Low,** chambered tomb (SK/ 169664) 650 yds. E of Ricklow Dale, 450 yds. N of Lathkill Dale, 2½ miles E of A515/B5055 junction; partly covered by plantation. Bronze Age round barrow to s. Finds in Sheffield Museum.

Crossed by a field wall and its s half in a plantation, this site is the only Peak tomb to have a truly elongated mound. It is about 150 ft. s–N and c. 110 ft. wide at the s, where its concave plan suggests the presence of some kind of forecourt. Traces of 4 chambers have been found across the central part of the mound, all lying E–W and wedge-shaped. The most E is a double chamber, whose E half yielded 4 skeletons and a bone pin and whose W half, its floor paved, held 2 skeletons with 2 leaf arrowheads. The big paved chamber further W contained remains of 12 skeletons and more bones occurred in that to the SW. Date, c. 2,500–2,000 BC.

BRONZE AGE

Arbor Low, round barrow on sacred site. See Neolithic.

***Beeley Moor,** cairns (SK/281668), 7 miles sw of Chesterfield (A61, A619, A632), 1¾ miles SE of Beeley (A623). Finds in Sheffield Museum.

This is a group of 3 contiguous cairns, aligned E–W, restored after recent excavation. All comprise piles of locally collected stones with surrounding kerbs, the stones of the central cairn alone being carefully laid slabs: they have diams. of 25–27 ft. and hts. of 2–3 ft. They had been built on a layer of white sand for some reason of ritual. The E cairn may be the earliest. Its centre had been robbed but a secondary cremation was found off-centre. Outside the kerb on the E, a natural rock had been joined to the kerb by slabs to form a cist. The central cairn incorporated an inner kerb. Its centre was also robbed but retained traces of a cremation. The W cairn yielded a rough central cist with cremation and late collared urn. There were 2 secondary cremations, one with a collared urn. At its N junction with the central cairn there was an external slab cist holding a cremation and food vessel while nearby a slab laid close to the outside of the kerb held another cremation.

Twelve yds. W of the tripple cairn is a rectangular cairn, c. 9 × 6 ft. and 1 ft. high. The carefully made mound within a kerb covered a shallow central depression containing traces of a cremation, with a Near Eastern segmented faience bead. Date of all cairns, c. 1,700–1,400 BC.

Bull Ring, round burrow. See Neolithic.
Doll Tor, circle and burials. See **Stanton Moor.**
***End Low,** round barrow (SK/156606) 9 miles N of Ashbourne (A52, A515, A517), ¾ mile NW of A515/A5012 junction. Grave

goods in Sheffield Museum.

This mound is about 70 ft. in diam. and 7 ft. high. It has a crater at the centre and disturbance on the W side. There is no evidence for a surrounding ditch. The mound appears to be made of heavy rubble. Excavation in the last century uncovered a secondary inhumation of a juvenile 6 ft. from the S edge, with a cremation near it. The main burial, that of a middle-aged male, lay in a central grave-pit sunk 6 ft. below the Bronze Age land surface. A large flat bronze dagger with 3 rivets for attachment to a wooden handle, and a flint blade-flake were with the corpse. Date, c. 1,700–1,400 BC.

Eyam Moor, circle (SK/225790) 1½ miles ssw of Hathersage (A622, A625), ½ mile N of minor road from Nether Padley (A622) to Gt Hucklow.

This circle has a diam. of about 100 ft. It has 16 small stones set within a circular bank of earth. Date, c. 2,200–1,400 BC. Nearby cairns are probably contemporary.

Froggatt Edge, circle (SK/249768) ¼ mile NE of Froggatt (B6054); 3¼ miles SE of Hathersage (A622, A625).

This circle has a diam. of 36 ft. It consists of 2 concentric rings of stone uprights set on the inner and outer edges of a bank. Of these stones there are 6 on the inside (one 4 ft. tall) and 5 on the outside. There are entrances N and S, a tall inner upright acting as a portal stone. Date, c. 2,200–1,400 BC.

Gib Hill, round barrow. See Neolithic, **Arbor Low.**

***Harthill Moor, Nine Stones,** circle (SK/225625) 2 miles S of A6/A524 junction; ¼ mile W of A524.

Today this circle consists of 4 stones, all upright. If 9 in number originally, they would fit into a circle about 45 ft. in diam. The stone in the gateway to the S probably belongs to the circle. The uprights are the largest in Derbyshire: the most S stone was found by excavation to be 11½ ft. long, 4½ ft. being buried below ground. Date, c. 2,200–1,400 BC.

***Hob Hurst's House,** round barrow (SK/287692) 3 miles SE of Baslow (A619, A623), S of track from Chatsworth, past Bunkers Hill Wood to Upper Loads.

Today this site appears more square than circular. Its mound has a diam. of about 33 ft. and is 4 ft. high. It has a ditch around it and a bank around that. Unpublished reports suggest that stone uprights may have been set in this bank in the customary Derbyshire manner (e.g. on **Stanton Moor**). A stone cist with no capstone was found at the centre of the mound. It measured 10 × 9 ft. A body may have been cremated in this pit, after which the burnt bones were carefully placed in one corner of it. Date, c. 1,700–1,400 BC. **King's Stone,** standing stone. See **Stanton Moor.**

*****Lean Low,** round barrow (SK/149623) 1 mile NNW of End Low (above). Grave goods in Sheffield Museum.

The mound of this barrow is about 50 ft. in diam. and 5 ft. high. It has a central crater and disturbance at the E edge. Its composition is heavy rubble, with no sign of a surrounding ditch. Excavation in the last century uncovered a secondary inhumation just S of the centre, its head protected by large stones. N of the centre a secondary cremation with a food vessel and a flint knife was found in a stone cist. The primary burial was a contracted inhumation of a youth about 16. It had no grave goods but was surrounded by rats' bones. Date, c. 2,000–1,400 BC.

Mam Tor, round barrows. See Iron Age.

*****Stanton Moor,** barrow cemetery and circles (around SK/247634) 1½ miles SE of A524/B5056 junction; ¾ mile NE of Birchover. Cars may be left in the quarry by the site of Cairn (1) (see plan, fig. 17). Grave goods in Heathcote (private) Museum, Birchover and Sheffield Museum (Doll Tor Circle).

At least 70 stone cairns, a number of circles and a standing stone can be found on top of Stanton Moor, an area of about 150 acres, bounded by the roads from Birchover to Stanton-in-Peak and Stanton Lees.

The area must have been used as a burial ground and considered as a place for worship by a Bronze Age tribe or group of tribes living in the area within the period 2,200–1,400 BC. The burial architecture is relatively simple and the cairns are not impressive in size: indeed, some are most difficult to find. The Moor is remarkable, however, because it gives the visitor an opportunity to see a large group

of burial places, with circles and standing stones set among them and all of 1 period and culture. Furthermore, since 1926, a large number of these sites has been excavated and restored by the Heathcotes, a family of archaeologists living in Birchover. Here in their private museum are to be found the urns, bronzes, flints and other objects recovered from the cairns on the Moor. Nowhere else in Britain can such a complete picture of burial customs, barrow architecture and grave goods be obtained in one day. Details of cairns and circles *excavated* are given below, numbered according to the plan (fig. 17).

(2) This cairn has a diam. of 54 ft. and a max. ht. of 5 ft. The mound was of stones and sand. A ring of large horizontal stones, one a natural one in its geological position, stood just within the edge of the mound. There was a smaller concentric ring of stones set about 3 ft. within larger. Twelve separate deposits of cremated human bones were found in the mound, some accompanied by collared urns, a food vessel, an incense cup and flint tools. At the centre there was a stone burial chamber measuring 4½ × 2½ ft. With the cremation in it there were pieces of an urn and fragments of bronze. Cairn partly restored.

(3) This cairn is oval, measuring 28 × 20 ft. and having a ht. of 2 ft. The mound of stones and sand with a curb of larger stones, covered 4 burials by cremation, 1 at the centre, the others W of it. The central burial, a female, was in a collared urn which also contained a smaller collared urn and a bronze knife. These stood in a hole dug down to bedrock and not protected by a stone cist. Two of the other burials were accompanied by urns and there were also pieces of bronze, perhaps a pin, with one.

(4) This cairn has a diam. of 14 ft. and a ht. of 1 ft. The mound of stones and soil had been retained by a ring of larger stones. At the centre a pit cut down to bedrock was found to contain a cremation, charcoal, flint tools and a piece of bronze. There were no other burials.

(5) This site is 12 ft. in diam. and 9 ins. high. One burial was found in a pit at the centre covered by a stone. There were no grave goods.

(6) The cairn here, disturbed in antiquity, is 14 ft. in diam. There had been a burial at the centre and another was found in 1930 on the E edge, beside a ring of stones which edged the cairn. The site had been enlarged slightly at the sw and a collared urn containing a cremation had been buried there.

(7) A cairn of sandy soil and stones 14 ft. across and 2 ft. high: it was ringed with larger stones. There were 3 cremation burials, 1 at the centre. One of the others was contained in a collared urn.

(8) This cairn is 15 ft. in diam. and very low. It has an outer circle of larger stones. A stone-covered pit at the centre contained a cremation furnished with an incense cup and the remains of bronze tools or pins. A burial at the N edge consisted of 2 cremated adults also accompanied by burnt pieces of bronze.

(9) This mound, 18 ft. in diam., was found to cover no burials at all.

(10) A mound 10 ft. in diam. covering a small amount of burnt human bone.

(11) This was found to be a natural rise in the ground.

(12) A tiny mound 7 ft. across. Traces of a cremation were found on the E side, under a stone in its retaining circle.

(13) A rectangular cairn, 40 × 22 ft. and 3½ ft. high, orientated nearly N/S. There were 13 burials by cremation here. Males and females were represented. The grave goods included collared urns, flint tools and a bone bead divided into segments and perforated in 2 directions. One urn contained an incense cup besides bones. Another had in it a clay stud.

(15) A small mound with some large stones around its circumference. It contained 3 groups of burnt bone, 1 in a rough cist at the centre.

(16) This appears as a depression surrounded by stones set in 2 concentric rings touching each other. A burial in a collared urn was found at the centre, 1½ ft. below the surface. A ring of jet was found here during the dig. In a circular extension of stones on the N side 2 other cremations were found, 1 in a collared urn. The pond-like shape of the main barrow may link it with the specialised pond-barrows of Wessex (p. 40).

(17) This is an oval cairn, 16 × 8 ft. It has a surround of large stones. It appeared never to have had a mound. There was a burial N of the centre, in a collared urn and furnished with flint tools and a bone pin, another at the E edge and central, and a third at the NW; the latter was in a collared urn and with it there was a flint arrowhead.

(18–19) Two cairns almost touching, on a line NW/SE. The N cairn, about 9 ft. across and stone-ringed, covered a single cremation, an adult female, at its centre. At the centre of the other, a slightly larger circle with an extension S, there was a cremation with a collared urn under a stone. There were 2 other cremations, one in the extension. Cairns restored.

(20) This cairn is about 16 ft. in diam. and 2 ft. high. It has an extension on the N side covering a cremation, while 5 other cremations lay in the material of the main mound. Two collared urns were found with the burials.

(21) This consists of a cairn with 2 extensions, measuring 22 × 16 ft. It had almost no mound. Near the centre there was a large rough cist containing the burnt bones of a young female adult and pieces of a collared urn. Cremations occurred in both extensions, 1 furnished with a collared urn, incense cup and flint tools.

(22) This cairn has a diam. of 17 ft. and a ht. of 2½ ft. It has a stone ring around it. There were 2 burials here, neither central. One was deposited in a collared urn.

(23) Only 8 ft. in diam. and added late to the group of cairns around it. There was a pile of burnt bones under a stone at the centre.

(24) An oval cairn, 16 × 9 ft., built beside a stone 5½ ft. long. No burials were found here.

(36) A barrow with a diam. of 30 ft. and a ht. of 2½ ft. The mound had no well-built stone kerb and the only burial found in it was well S of the centre. This was a heap of cremated human bones placed in a pit but not otherwise protected. At the bottom of this pit was a stone battle-axe perforated for a haft. It is of dolerite, probably quarried from one of several outcrops of this rock in Derbyshire. Although the burnt bones appear to be female, battle-axes were usually buried with men.

(43, 56, 61) These 3 sites are similar in design but differ slightly in size. They

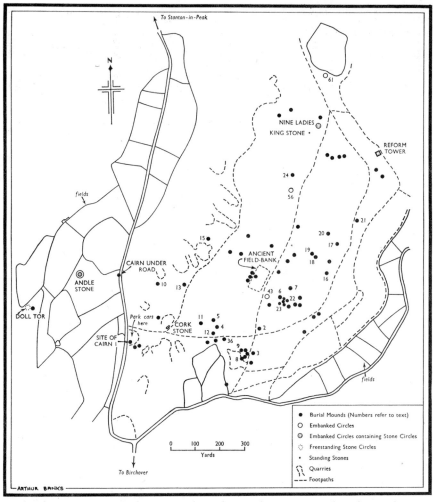

17   *Stanton Moor: barrows and ritual sites of a Bronze Age burial ground,*
                        c. 2,200–1,400 BC

comprise circular banks of rubble (diams. about 60 ft., 80 ft., 40 ft. respectively), broken by entrances facing N and S. Some large recumbent stones on the inner edge of their banks may originally have stood upright. Such circles must have been for rituals connected with the burials and cairn-building of the Bronze Age tribe using Stanton Moor. They were also for burial, since cremations were associated with some of the 7 collared urns, incense cups and awl recovered from (61) and also with the faience bead from (56). **Doll Tor.**

This site was built as a free-standing stone circle. It must have been associated with the cairns and other sites on Stanton Moor. Its map ref. is SK/238628; close to the N edge of a plantation.

This circle had 6 upright stones, 2 of them now fallen and all joined by a ring of smaller horizontal stones. It has a cairn-like extension on the E side containing the remains of 3–4 collared urns and as many incense cups at the centre of the circle. Five more burials were found in 1931–3, 3 of them close to the stones of the main circle; there were collared urns with some of these.

In the mound of the extension there were 4 cremations around the E edge, 3 with collared urns and 1 with a star-shaped bead of blue faience. At the centre, in a hollow beneath a large stone acting as a cist, the cremated remains of a female adult were found: a segmented faience bead probably from the Near East had been put with her ashes: both may have been made c. 1,400 BC and argue that the site belongs to this period or a little later. **Nine Ladies.** This circle, with its outlying upright stone to the sw (both surrounded by modern stone walls) must be considered an integral part of the Stanton Moor complex. Its stones (ht. 2–3 ft.) give it a diam. of about 33 ft. It has a slight surrounding bank of earth and a small mound at the centre. It should be contemporary with the barrows round about. The single upright stone outside it, the King Stone, is a feature found commonly all over Britain.

*Swarkeston Lowes, barrow-cemetery (SK/365295) 4 miles s of Derby, ½ mile N of A514/B5009 junction. Finds in Derby Museum.

There are 4 round barrows in this cemetery, all but the most w disappearing under the plough. They have diams. of 120–200 ft. but they have been spread by ploughing.

The second mound from the w was excavated in 1955. Its single ditch, only roughly circular in plan, was about 105 ft. in diam.; its mound today is 4½ ft. high. The ditch was very irregularly dug but tended to have a U-shaped profile; it was about 2 ft. deep and 6–7 ft. broad. Originally this had been a bell-barrow, the mound itself being 55 ft. in diam. and having a space or berm 13–25 ft. broad between its edge and the surrounding ditch. The mound consisted of a core of turves stacked neatly in layers and covered by soil from the ditch. A pile of cremated bones had been placed at the centre, on the old land surface but in no receptacle; nor were there any grave goods with it. Pagan Saxon burials had been added to the top of the mound.

The next barrow to the E is of 2 periods. Its first mound, with a diam. of c. 60 ft.,

lacked a ditch. It covered remains of a wooden coffin (the unburnt burial had disappeared) which contained a flint knife. Later the mound had been increased by adding a surrounding ditch, with a berm, to form a bell-barrow. The associated burial was a cremation with collared urn, dug into the top of the original mound; it has a C14 date of 1395 ± 160 BC. The mound of this barrow covered well-preserved traces of a Beaker period habitation site. It comprises a mass of small post-holes, some forming a double row at least 40 ft. long. Date of cemetery, c. 1,700–1,400 BC.

IRON AGE

*Ball Cross, hill-fort (SK/228691) ¾ mile NE of Bakewell (A6, A619), overlooking golf course to s. Finds in Sheffield Museum.

This site, which has an internal area of 1¾ acres, is set on a spur, 2 of its sides being protected by precipitous slopes to the valley. Its N and E sides are protected by a stone wall, rock-cut ditch and counterscarp bank. The ditch has a roughly V-shaped profile and a depth of 6–8 ft. The wall would have been more than 5 ft. thick at its base, carefully faced with drystone inside and out and with a rubble core. It must have been built to a ht. of about 8 ft. The original entrance is likely to have been near the NW corner.

The site has been deliberately levelled, probably by the Romans in their advance N after the landings in AD 43. Earlier, the camp had been permanently occupied. Date, perhaps 1st century BC.

*Castle Naze, promontory fort (SK/055784) 1½ miles sw of Chapel-en-le-Frith (A624, A625), on spur of Combs Moss overlooking Combs.

This fort occupies a triangular area of c. 2¼ acres. The N and s sides are protected by natural slopes. The E side is protected by 2 banks with a ditch beyond the outer. Excavation has shown that the inner bank is the earlier and is of dump construction. Traces of a drystone facing to the outer bank were found: this is the larger earthwork, dominating the inner. The entrance through the middle is probably not original. Access seems to have been gained through the gap between the N ends of the earthworks and the cliff-edge, approached today by a prominent hollow way up the hillside. Not dated but probably late Iron Age.

*Castle Ring, hill-fort (SK/221628) 3½ miles s of Bakewell (A6, A619), w of road from Alport (B5056) to Elton: on NW side of Moor Farm.

A small fort enclosing less than 1 acre, the defences of Castle Ring consist of a main bank, a ditch outside and a counterscarp bank. Only on the SE side are these earthworks interrupted – probably because of the nearby farm. In the 18th century an entrance was recorded on this side. Perhaps built in the 1st century BC.

*Fin Cop, hill-fort (SK/174710) 3 miles NW of Bakewell (A6, A619), ½ mile N of A6, overlooking Monsal Dale.

This site is built on the w end of a limestone hill whose steep N and W sides would have afforded sufficient protection without artificial additions. Two banks and ditches form the E side of the fort: only the N end of the line is now preserved. The earthworks were probably never continuous. A simple entrance is through the E side, 370 ft. from the N end. Date, perhaps 1st century BC.

*Mam Tor, hill-fort and Bronze Age round barrows (SK/128837) 1½ miles w of Castleton (A625), 1¼ miles s of Edale. Finds in Manchester University Museum.

This is the largest hill-fort in Derbyshire. Its proportions link it with forts in s Britain. The site occupies the sw and higher end of a long ridge. An area of 16 acres lies within the earthworks. A bank, ditch and counterscarp bank have been built with a triangular plan, the apex at the N where the ridge is crossed. The average ht. of the inner one above the present surface of its silted-up ditch is 25 ft.

Excavation has shown that the main bank is about 18 ft. wide and 10 ft. high.

Originally its front and rear had stone revetments. The ditch is 8 ft. wide and c. 8 ft. deep. The area thus protected contains abundant traces of occupation including hut-platforms cut into the hillsides. One of these, when excavated, revealed a semicircular gulley or foundation trench following the edge of the platform and enclosing a series of post-holes. Elsewhere post-holes, gulleys and traces of hearths have been found. Not yet closely datable, this site has a longer history than the other Derbyshire hill-forts, its beginnings possibly going as far back as the Late Bronze Age.

There are 2 Bronze Age round barrows within the ramparts at the sw edge of the ridge, both almost levelled by the plough. An urn and a bronze axe may have been found in one. Date, c. 1,700–1,400 BC.

*Markland Grips, promontory fort (SK/510751) 5½ miles sw of Worksop (A57, A60, A6009), 1¼ miles E of Clowne (A616, A618), s of A616. Finds in Sheffield City Polytechnic and City Museum.

Here a triangular promontory with steep N and S sides has been defended by triple banks and ditches, of which clear remains of the innermost only survive. The present central entrance through this earthwork may be original. Air photographs and excavations have shown that, N of the entrance, the 2 outer banks and ditches, now almost disappeared, had a U-shaped layout, joined to define the entrance passage and open at the N end, by the cliff (where the end of the middle bank survives). s of the entrance, the 2 inner banks had a U-plan, joined at their N end to define the entrance and all 3 open, but converging, at the s end. The innermost bank, in places 45 ft. wide and 9 ft. high, is a dump of clay and gravel with limestone slabs lodged horizontally into its face. The innermost ditch was 8–9 ft. deep. Date, probably late Iron Age.

Devon

PALAEOLITHIC

*Kent's Cavern, inhabited caves (SX/ 934641) 1 mile E of Torquay Harbour. Finds in Torquay Museum, British Museum and Natural History Museum, South Kensington.

Hunters of the Old Stone Age made use of Kent's Cavern at various times between 100,000 and 8,000 BC. Wild animals, including hyaenas, also competed for the shelter it provided.

The cavern consists of 2 parallel main chambers and a series of galleries and chambers leading off them. Evidence of human occupation has been found of all periods, getting dense at the end of the Ice Age; all that can now be seen of it is a series of flint implements with a wide range in time, and a few bone tools of greater significance. Three bone harpoons, a bone sewing needle and a rod of ivory which must have been ceremonial, have been found here. The latter must belong to the last cold phase in Britain, beginning c. 50,000 BC.

NEOLITHIC

Corringdon Ball, chambered long barrow (SX/670614), Dartmoor, 2 miles NW of South Brent (off A38), by track across Ugborough Moor from Aish.

This is the only true long barrow on Dartmoor. It is 140 ft. long, 60 ft. wide and 6½ ft. high. It is orientated SE/NW. At the SE end there is a collapsed burial chamber, made of massive stones. Nothing is known of the burials in this chamber. Date, c. 3,500–2,500 BC.

Hembury, causewayed camp. See Iron Age.

Spinster's Rock, chambered tomb (SX/ 700908), Dartmoor, 4¼ miles NW of Moretonhampstead (A382, B3212), ¼ mile E of A382, W of Shilstone.

Nothing now remains of the barrow which must once have covered this chamber. The 3 uprights and capstone now visible are not in their original position, the structure having been rebuilt after its collapse in 1862. Date, c. 2,500 BC.

BRONZE AGE

*Broad Down, barrow cemetery (SY/ 163970–SY/172933), N end of group 2¼ miles S of Honiton (A30, A373), on W side of minor road via golf course to Farway Hill and B3174. Main concentration at Roncombe Gate (B3174). Grave goods in Exeter Museum.

There are more than 57 barrows in the 3 mile stretch between Gittisham Hill and Broad Down. Those on Farway Hill (s side) and Broad Down (N side) are sufficiently concentrated to be considered as a cemetery in the Wessex manner. All the mounds are of bowl-type and some appear to have no surrounding ditches. Their diams. vary from 25–140 ft. and their hts. from a few inches to 12 ft. The larger mounds tend to have a ditch. Among those with diams. of 45–50 ft. there is a specialised type with a flat top and steep sides.

Many of these mounds have now been excavated or robbed. The records of this work show that all the Bronze Age burials were by cremation. Within many of the mounds a central heap of stones was found to cover the grave. The latter was sometimes a stone cist, at other times it was not clearly defined. One barrow had a ring of stones set around the outer edge of its ditch. One cremation had been placed in a food vessel.

The grave offerings are rich and indicate close connections with Wessex. There are 2 cups with handles carved from blocks of shale quarried from Kimmeridge in s Dorset or from the Bovey Beds in s Devon and probably worked up on a pole-lathe, the earliest recorded examples of the technique in Britain. There was a lone bead carved into segments to resemble the blue faience beads possibly imported from the Near East at this time; and a bronze dagger was associated with one of the shale cups. From one barrow an incense cup was found to have been used to hold the cremated ashes of an infant. The date of this complex is c. 1,700–1,400 BC.

*Chapman Barrows, cemetery (SS/695435), Exmoor, 2 miles SE of Parracombe (off A39).

This fine cemetery, strung out in a line along a ridge, contains about 11 mounds. Details of the burials beneath them are lacking but one has yielded a cremation. Date c. 1,700–1,400 BC.

The **Long Stone,** ½ mile to the s (p. 93) may belong to this complex.

DARTMOOR

For convenience, the selection of pre-historic sites (except the long barrows and hill-forts) on Dartmoor is described in one group alphabetically and is not divided chronologically. So few sites have yielded adequate dating evidence that the periods during which these religious and domestic structures were in use cannot be calculated. The majority belong to the Bronze Age. Many huts are of the Iron Age and a few sites of all types may be Neolithic. Only where the evidence permits it, has a date been suggested in this section.

Those who wish to examine the area in detail should obtain *Dartmoor* by R. Hansford Worth, published by his Executors, 1953, *Dartmoor*, National Park Guides, Number One, HMSO 1957, *Antiquity*, Dec. 1938, p. 444ff., *Proceedings of the Prehistoric Society*, XVIII, 1952, p. 55ff, and ibid., XX, 1954, p. 100ff. (list of settlements). Reasonably complete lists of sites are to be found in these indispensable works.

Most of the finds unearthed during excavations on the moor are to be found in the museums at Plymouth, Torquay and Exeter.

Dartmoor, a granite mass of 250 square miles, had much to offer to prehistoric settlers. Though more wooded than it is now, plenty of pasture would have been available for grazing; water was abundant and the ground was easily cleared for cultivation. Wood and stone made building easy and a variety of minerals, especially tin, provided valuable material for trade. River, sea and land routes connected Dartmoor (and the sw generally) with areas of wealthy settlers further E. Yet local conditions have combined to produce a succession of prehistoric inhabitants here whose way of life and religious beliefs, as seen in their material remains, are peculiar to this region.

*Archerton Newtake, cairn and cist (SX/636795) 1 mile WNW of Postbridge (B3212); 350 yds. NW of Archerton.

At the centre of a ruined cairn, 18 ft. in diam., there is a cist with 2 pairs of side-stones and 2 endstones, the cover missing. It measures about 4 × 1½ ft. and is nearly 2 ft. deep. It contained charcoal and an archer's wrist-guard of slate. The skeleton had decayed. The cairn may have had a kerb of uprights. Date, c. 2,000–1,700 BC.

Beardown Man, standing stone (SX/596797) 3 miles NNW of Two Bridges (A384, B3212), across moor via Beardown Hill; military danger zone.

This stone is wide and thin. It has a ht. of nearly 11½ ft., and does not taper much towards the top.

Broadun Ring, settlement (SX/637802) 3¾ miles NE of Two Bridges (A384, B3212), 1½ miles NW of Postbridge (B3212), w side of the Dart.

This group of 9 huts is set inside an unusually stoutly built enclosure. It commands a wide sweep of country. The East Dart provides a water supply, 200 yds. below. The pound wall would originally have been at least 5 ft. high. It is 6 ft. thick. The huts have diams. of 9–22 ft. One, 6 ft. in diam., may have been a store hut. Several had hearths and cooking holes.

Bush Down, settlement (SX/685826) 4¾ miles WSW of Moretonhampstead (A382, B3212), N side of B3212.

Here can be found 3 groups of huts, 9 in all, each over 20 ft. in diam. associated with fields further up the hillside to the s.

Butterdon Hill, cairn cemetery, stone row and standing stone (SX/655587), 1¾ miles NE of Ivybridge (A38, B3211), 1¼ miles SE of Harford.

There is a group of at least 6 cairns near the top of the hill, sufficiently concentrated to be considered a cemetery in the

Wessex manner. The largest of the cairns has a height of about 12 ft. and a diam. of 100 ft. From one, a single stone row leads N, a distance of 6,280 ft., ending in a large upright.

Challacombe, standing stone and stone rows (SX/690809), 5 miles SW of Moreton-hampstead (A382 and B3212), 1 mile E of Warren House Inn (B3212) and E of old tin mines.

A good example of a triple row, this alignment lies nearly N/S, the N end now destroyed, the other end being blocked by a large stone set across it. The rows narrow towards this point. During restorations, one large stone in the central row, towards the N end, was turned until it lay across the axis of the rows. To the W of this point several stones lie scattered, which might suggest the remains of a circle. These, however, are not now in their original positions. Today these rows are 528 ft. long.

Corringdon Ball, South Brent, long barrow. See Neolithic.

Cosdon Beacon, cairn, cists and rows (SX/643916) 1½ miles S of Sticklepath (A30), 1½ miles WNW of Throwleigh, on footpath S from Ramsley (A30).

There is a cairn here with a circle of stones around it: within are the remains of 2 cists with capstones. Leading SE for about 225 ft. there is a triple stone row: this changes direction slightly and becomes a double row for 120 ft.

Down Tor, cairn, row and standing stone (SX/589694) 4½ miles ENE of Yelverton (A386), 2 miles E of Burrator Reservoir.

This single row lies NE/SW and is 1,145 ft. long. At the W end there is a cairn with a free-standing circle around it. The stones of the row near it increase in size noticeably. There is a cairn on the line of the row 620 ft. from the E end: at this end there is a standing stone 7½ ft. high.

Drizzlecombe, cairns, circles, cists, rows and standing stones (SX/592670) 4½ miles E of Yelverton (A386, B3212), reached by track from Sheepstor to Ditsworthy Warren House and then up Plym valley.

At the centre of this group of structures there are 3 stone rows, aligned NE/SW. Two are almost parallel, the third lying to the S and being double, but depleted. Each has a cairn at its E end and a large standing

stone at its other end. The N rows are 500 and 300 ft. long, their standing stones respectively 7¾ and 14 ft. high. The third row is 488 ft. long and its standing stone 10½ ft. high.

A very large barrow lies close to the centre of these rows: there is a third cairn N of the E ends of the 2 single rows, and another 600 ft. further E. North of and between the latter there is the retaining circle of a cairn with its cist still visible: there is another cist 250 ft. to the W. A third cist can be found S of the S stone row.

Foales Arishes, settlement (SX/737758) 1½ miles ESE of Widecombe, ¼ mile SW of Hemsworthy Gate. Finds in City Museum, Plymouth.

This is an important site, obscured by fairly recent remodelling of the SE part of its fields. There are 8 huts to be found, having diams. of 18–30 ft. Their walls have a core of small rubble set between facings of larger stones. Some huts contained cooking holes and hearths.

The fields were originally small and rectangular, differing from each other in size. Their N and S banks can be seen underlying long rectangular medieval strips which extend from the crest between Top Tor and Pil Tor SE for 500–600 yds. Some of these ancient field banks run up to the huts and are clearly associated with them. Originally the prehistoric fields would have covered more than 25 acres. This settlement can be dated by pottery to the late Bronze and Iron Ages, c. 1,000–600 BC.

Green Hill, cairn and row. See **Stall Moor.**

Grey Wethers, circles (SX/638832) 2½ miles N of Postbridge (B3212), over moor via Hartland Tor.

There are 2 circles close together here, one N of the other. Both have been restored. The N one has a diam. of 103½ ft., the other 116½ ft. Before restoration there were 9 standing and 6 fallen stones in the N circle, with 7 standing and 20 fallen in the other. The highest stone in the former is about 4½ ft., that in the latter is nearly 4 ft.

Grimspound, settlement (SX/701809) 4¾ miles SW of Moretonhampstead (A382), by footpath E from road joining Wide-combe and Shapley Common (B3212).

This is a walled area of 4 acres, in which

24 huts can be seen. The main wall is of granite, with large facing stones and a rubble core. It is about 9 ft. thick and would originally have been at least 6 ft. high. The entrance is through the s, higher, side. It is about 7 ft. wide: the approach is paved. Within the enclosure, at the lower end, there is a stream – doubtless the main reason for the existence and situation of this village (fig. 18).

Most of the huts have a diam. of about 15 ft. The entrances to some of the huts were protected from rough weather by an extension or porch. Inside, apart from the usual fittings (hearths and cooking holes, for example) several of the huts contained a raised platform or bench occupying a segment of the circular area. These would have acted as resting-places and beds. The hut-walls were the footings for roofs made of timber, thatch and turf. A stone on the floor at the centre of the hut supported the main vertical roof-timber.

This village was occupied by a pastoral community, cultivating the land and quartering their flocks and herds within their enclosure at night – safe from marauding animals and with an assured and abundant water supply.

Heatree. Grave goods destroyed, 1939–45.

The 'Two Barrows', close together, are important because one (the N) produced a bronze dagger of Wessex form. The amber pommel of its handle was decorated with an inlay of tiny gold pins like those from **Winterbourne Stoke** cross-roads and **Bush Barrow** (Wilts., below) and also found in Brittany. These had been buried with cremated bones away from the centre of the barrow. This mound is about 4 ft. high and 40 ft. in diam. The s mound is a little smaller and its contents are not recorded. Date, c. 1,700–1,400 BC.

Harter Tor, cairns, stone rows (about SX/574717) 1½ miles sw of Princetown (B3212, B3357), ¼ mile E of B3212.

There are 2 rows close together here, the N one double and 450 ft. long, the s one is single and is 165 ft. in length. Both alignments are orientated NE/SW. There is a cairn with a retaining circle around it at the E end of the N row; a cairn without such a circle lies at the E end of the other row.

Hayne Down, settlement (SX/742798) 3¾ miles ssw of Moretonhampstead (A382, B3212), 1 mile sw of Manaton (B3344); ¼ mile E of track from Hedge Barton to

18   *Grimspound, Dartmoor: Bronze Age settlement*

*Hameldown, cairns (SX/706792) 1¾ miles NNW of Widecombe, 1 mile w of road from latter to Manaton (B3344) via

Manaton via Bowermans Nose.

There are 3 single-walled huts here, set among fields. The w hut is set into the

hillside, with its door facing SW. One orthostat still stands. The hut has a diam. of 26 ft. The central hut is 24 ft. across with large walling stones. Its door probably faced S. These 2 huts have banks around the outside. The stones of the third hut are large. Its entrance faced SE.

N of this small settlement there is a group of field banks and lynchets. It is possible that they and the huts are contemporary, perhaps in the Iron Age period.

built footings and an entrance facing S. Excavations revealed the remains of a ring of posts within, supporting a thatched or turfed roof, and a drain. There were the remains of a hearth, and an iron-smelting furnace and a forging pit. The irregularity of the roof posts suggests that part of the hut may have been open to the sky.

Other huts scattered about among the fields of Kestor, for instance one 300 ft. NE, (fig. 19) had conical roofs supported on a central post and additional struts, the

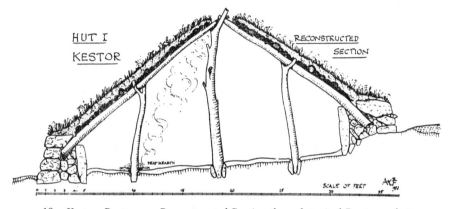

19   *Kestor, Dartmoor: Reconstructed Section through typical Dartmoor hut*

*Kestor, settlement (SX/665867) 5½ miles W of Moretonhampstead (A382, B3212), 2¼ miles SW of Chagford; cut on N side by road from Teigncombe to Batworthy. Finds in Exeter Museum.

A recently excavated site, this extensive settlement dates from c. 700–600 BC. A large group of rectangular fields spreads up the hill from the Teigncombe–Batworthy road. These follow the NE/SW axis of the ridge here. A drove-way follows the top of the ridge, associated with the fields: another can be found 200 ft. NW of the road referred to, and parallel to it. This one would have taken the cattle to water and grazing. Not all the fields were in use at one time, the smaller ones tending to be the earlier.

The main feature of the settlement is Round Pound, a large oval enclosure with an original entrance to the NW and containing a circular hut at the centre. This has a diam. of 37 ft. It has typical stone-

lower ends of the roof timbers everywhere being embedded in the circular stone wall-footings. There are 25 huts in the settlement, their diams. ranging from 12–37 ft.

Lakehead, cairn, cist, row (SX/645776) 2¾ miles NE of Two Bridges (A384, B3212), N of track to Bellever.

Here is a fine stone cist with its capstone, recently restored. Around it are 6 stones of a circle of diam. about 25 ft. Starting within the circle and leading E for 44 ft. is a single stone row.

Legis Tor, settlement (SX/573654) 3¾ miles SE of Yelverton (A386, B3212) on N bank of the Plym; reached by road and path from Meavy and Brisworthy. Finds in City Museum, Plymouth.

This is a large site which has clearly developed in stages. It comprises 4 enclosures or pounds (where sheep and cattle could be protected from wild beasts) and a series of huts. The first enclosure, the second smallest, is in the middle of the S edge of the settlement, overlooking the river. One hut is incorporated in its wall on the N side. From this pound there later was built a large pound on the W with a hut just outside it at the sw, an altogether larger one NE of these and, finally, a small enclosure in the SE corner of the largest pound. Huts are scattered within the whole area – 4¼ acres.

Originally the walls of these pounds may have been 7–8 ft. high, having turf or earth cores and stone facings. The hut walls would have been about 4 ft. high, their upper walls and roofs of timber and thatch. Some had paved floors, cooking holes and hearths.

Pottery found in the huts suggests that this settlement is Bronze Age, c. 1,250–1,000 BC.

for about 140 ft. There is a stone circle 350 ft. s of this row: immediately to the s there is a cairn and 2 standing stones (fig. 20).

Raddick Hill, settlement (SX/576714) 3 miles sw of Two Bridges (A384, B3212), between Princetown and Dousland (B3212), E of the Meavy, on s side of small tributary. Finds in City Museum, Plymouth.

This enclosure contains 10 small huts, their diams. ranging from 10–19 ft., and one large hut with a diam. of about 25 ft. Pottery from the smaller huts, some of it found in cooking holes, suggests that they are earlier in date than the large hut. It seems likely, in fact, that this oval enclosure with its 10 huts and with its entrance attached to one of these by a

20   *Merrivale, Dartmoor: double stone row, Bronze Age*

Merrivale, cairns, circle, cist, standing stones (SX/555744) 4½ miles E of Tavistock (A384, A386, A390), on s side of A384, ½ mile SE of Merrivale (A384).

This group consists of 2 double rows, parallel, running E/W, the N one 596 ft. long and blocked by a stone at the E end, the s one being 865 ft. long and likewise blocked. Near its centre there is a small cairn with a stone circle around it. There is a large stone cist 160 ft. to the SE of this circle; 150 ft. wsw there is a cairn which is at the N end of a single stone row extending sw

cross wall, was built before c. 1,400 BC. Later, c. 800–400 BC, it was reused, one large dwelling being built on the E side, with a new entrance through the pound wall close to it. It would thus appear that these isolated Late Bronze Age huts were built to house a shepherd or cowherd when he brought his herd to new pastures for the summer. At this site the old enclosure wall would have been used as a paddock for the herd at night.

Riders Rings, settlement (SX/680645) 3¾ miles wsw of Buckfastleigh (A38, A384), across moor from Shipley Bridge and South Brent (off A38).

There are 2 pounds or enclosures here, the s and earlier enclosing just over 3 acres, the N pound enclosing 7 acres. There are at least 17 huts in each pound. Most huts are concentrated close to the pound walls, mainly the NW wall. The entrance to the s pound is at the s corner: that to the N pound is in the SE side. The pound wall has a core of small rubble, faced with larger stones. Its original ht. would have been about 7 ft.

The circular huts within the pounds would have housed the villagers. The small enclosures against the pound wall must have been where sheep and cattle were stalled.

Hearths have been found in some huts, together with domestic rubbish.

Rippon Tor, settlement (SX/753759) 3¾ miles N of Ashburton (A38, A384), 2 miles W of Ilsington, s of road from Widecombe to Haytor Vale.

Rippon Tor is a small farmstead which probably provided for 1 family. It has 1 circular hut, 26 ft. in diam. with a door facing E. It is placed on the N side of a rectangular farmyard with stalls in the SE and SW corners. There are 3 rectangular fields on the s, E and W sides of this yard, with further traces of cultivation N and W. Just over 1 acre was thus cultivated. NE of the hut there is a spring, the source of the Sig.

Roundy Park, cairn and cist (SX/639797) 1 mile WNW of Postbridge (B3212). W of the Dart.

The cairn in Roundy Park has one of the largest cists on Dartmoor, though it may have been inaccurately restored. It measures 6½ × 3½ ft., and is nearly 3 ft. deep. There are 2 coverstones. The barrow originally covering it was about 16 ft. in diam. It has been robbed.

Scorhill, circle (SX/655874) 6¼ miles W of Moretonhampstead (A382, B3212), footpath from Berrydown, via Chagford and Gidleigh.

Many stones have been looted from this circle but it is still one of the finest on Dartmoor. Its diam. is about 90 ft. There are 23 stones standing and 7 more fallen. Originally there would have been 60–70 stones in the circle. The tallest stone stands

over 8 ft. above ground level.

Shapley Common, settlement (SX/695824) 4¼ miles SW of Moretonhampstead (A382, B3212), ½ mile s of B3212, on W road to Widecombe. Either side of road.

There are 2 groups of huts here, 3 in one, 10 in the other. The huts in the smaller (N) group are roughly twice as big as those in the s group. Hearths and charcoal, together with domestic rubbish, were found in several huts. Some have raised platforms occupying segments of the circle, indicating beds and resting places. Several huts yielded evidence of a central wooden post supporting a conical thatched roof. Fields are associated with this settlement.

Shovel Down, circles, rows, cairns, standing stones (about SX/660860) 2¾ miles SW of Chagford (B3344), footpath from Batworthy via Thorn.

Here there is a complex of monuments spread N/S. At the N end, ¼ mile s of Batworthy, there are the remains of 2 stone rows, each double, running N/S. There is a possible circle W of the N ends of these. The E avenue leads s to a circle of 4 concentric rings of uprights: these originally were part of a cairn. A third, almost complete, double stone row begins near the cairn circles and runs for 386 ft. SE to another cairn. Just to the s a single row begins, then a double row runs beside it towards a standing stone, the Longstone. This is 10 ft. 5 ins. high. To the s there are traces of a double row leading, after 550 ft., to another standing stone, the survivor of three known as the Three Boys. This one is 4½ ft. high. Three hundred ft. SE there is a stone burial cist.

Smallacombe Rocks, settlement (SX/756782) 2½ miles NE of Widecombe, 2 miles s of Manaton (B3344); on W edge of Haytor Down, E of Grea Tor. Finds in Torquay Museum.

There are the remains of 4 huts with diams. of 22–30 ft. here, together with fields, some remade at a later time. Traces of hearths were found in some huts, and pottery which suggested that they had been built c. 1,250–1,000 BC. The hut walls were of the type with core of rubble, faced on both sides with larger stones.

Soussons Common, cairn and cist (SX/676788) 1½ miles ESE of Postbridge (B3212), N of road to Widecombe.

This circle of about 22 upright stones is the retaining wall of a cairn now almost removed. At the centre can be seen 2 sides of a rectangular cist which would have been covered by the cairn.

Spinster's Rock, Drewsteignton. Long barrow, see Neolithic.

Staldon, cairn and stone row (SX/633621, s end) 1½ miles s of **Stall Moor/Green Hill** row (below).

This is a single row of large uprights on a hill-crest, curved slightly, 1,643 ft. long and lying N/S. Near its N end it touches the retaining circle of a cairn. A little to the N, there is a cairn to the E and W of the row. Staldon row has no feature at either end.

Stall Moor/Green Hill, cairn and stone row (SX/635644, s end) 6¾ miles W of Buckfastleigh (A38), 3½ miles NE of Cornwood.

This should be considered as 2 single rows which join, one descending from a cairn on Green Hill (at the N), the other beginning with the free-standing circle around a cairn on Stall Moor, to the s. The row is over 2 miles long, the longest on Dartmoor. It makes several changes of direction as it was laid out across country which rises and falls considerably.

Standon Down, settlement (SX/554824) 3½ miles NE of Mary Tavy (E of A386, N of Tavistock), via Wapsworthy and Bagga Tor. Military danger zone.

This is an open village, more than 60 huts being recognisable, many of them linked to each other by walls. Some of the walls form cattle and sheep pens, others fields. Most of the huts are small, few exceeding 20 ft. in internal diam. There is a spring near the s side of the settlement. Occupation here was probably of the Middle Bronze Age, c. 1,250–1,000 BC.

Trowlesworthy Warren, settlements (SX/575645) 4 miles SE of Yelverton (A386, B3212), s of the Plym over Cadover Bridge, and E across moor.

In this area there are 6 small enclosures, each with an area of about ½ acre and containing 5–10 circular huts. These have diams. of 15–33 ft. In places the massive enclosure walls are 9 ft. thick.

Two Barrows, cairns. See **Hameldown.**

Watern Down, cairn and stone row (SX/674825) 5¼ miles SW of Moretonhampstead (A382, B3212), 1 mile N of Warren

House Inn (B3212).

One of the best double rows on Dartmoor and quite complete, this site is 473 ft. long and orientated N/S. Its N end has a blocking stone across it: at the other end there is a cairn. The double row widens as it approaches this cairn.

Watern Oke, settlement (between SX/562837 and SX/569834) 3½ miles ESE of Lydford (off A386, between Tavistock and Okehampton) on N side of the Tavy, E of its junction with the Rattlebrook. Finds in City Museum, Plymouth.

This is an example of a large village, more than 90 small huts being recorded. Many of the huts are joined by walls which often form enclosures. Few huts exceed 19 ft. in diam. The entrances of some have external sheltering walls. Several of those excavated contained hearths. All are rather roughly made and would appear to belong to a poor farming community.

White Ridge, settlement (SX/643818, SX/646816) 1¾ miles NNW of Postbridge (B3212) on W side of White Ridge. Finds in City Museum, Plymouth.

There are 2 settlements consisting of huts associated with enclosures on the s and w slopes of White Ridge, at about 1,500 ft. O.D. That on the w slope has 6 huts; the s site has 4. Both groups of huts are associated with small irregular enclosures and fields, some being paddocks for flocks and herds, others fields. The huts are small, few exceeding 20 ft. in diam. Those in the s site have external walls protecting their entrances from draught. Some have yielded pottery which suggests that both settlements were in use in the Bronze Age before 1,000 BC.

Yellowmead, cairn and rows (SX/574676) 2½ miles ESE of Dousland (B3212), N of footpath E from Sheepstor.

Of this cairn its 4 retaining circles remain, recently restored: the outermost circle has a diam. of 65 ft., the innermost 20 ft. There are traces of at least 1 double row of stones leading W from this quadruple circle.

Yes Tor Bottom, settlement (SX/567729) 1½ miles SW of Princetown (B3212, B3357), s of railway to King Tor Halt. Finds in City Museum, Plymouth.

This site represents the enclosed farmstead of a small community. There are 2 pounds, the older and smaller at the NW. The area finally enclosed was about 2½ acres. Nine huts are associated with the enclosure walls. Most of these had a diam. of about 20 ft., but the hut furthest NW was over 26 ft. in diam. Pottery from some of these huts shows that this farm is of the Middle Bronze Age, c. 1,250–1,000 BC.

The sites which follow are outside Dartmoor.

Farway, round barrows. See **Broad Down.**

Five Barrows, barrow cemetery (SS/733368), Exmoor, 3 miles SW of Simonsbath (B3223, B3358), ½ mile N of road to Yardwells Cross.

This cemetery, concentrated on top of a round hill, contains at least 9 barrows. One of these is a bell-barrow. The W, 97 ft. in diam. and 9¾ ft. high, has 2 standing stones close to it on the SW. Each is about 2 ft. in ht.

Nothing is known of the contents of this cemetery. Date, c. 1,700–1,400 BC.

Hembury Castle, barrow. See Iron Age.

Long Stone, standing stone (SS/705431), Exmoor, ½ mile SE of **Chapman Barrows** (p. 86).

This upright stone lies between the **Chapman Barrows** cemetery (above) and **Longstone Barrow** (below). It is about 9 ft. high and unusually thin in proportion. It should be regarded as a part of the barrow concentration hereabouts, perhaps a fertility symbol in an area where Bronze Age structures were especially concerned with death and the after-life.

Longstone Barrow, round barrow (SS/707427) ¼ mile S of **Long Stone** (above).

This is a fine bowl-barrow, its surrounding ditch still clear. The mound is about 70 ft. in diam. and 8 ft. in ht. It appears to have been robbed but nothing is known of its contents. Date, c. 1,700–1,400 BC.

*North Molton, round barrow (SS/729317) 1¼ miles NNW of North Molton, on Bampfylde Hill, SW of minor road to Yard Gate. N of the wood. Grave goods in Exeter Museum.

Though not a conspicuous barrow, a necklace of unusual interest was found here in 1889. The barrow is 48 ft. in diam. and about 3 ft. high. No details are known about the burial by cremation beneath this mound, but a series of beads which

belonged to it has survived. These consist of 5 segmented and 3 biconical beads of faience from the Near East, 9 beads of lignite and 1 of amber. The lignite was probably obtained from Bovey Tracey in Devon; the amber is likely to have been carried across England from the E coast. This necklace, a product of widespread trade, was probably deposited in the barrow c. 1,700–1,400 BC.

Setta Barrow, round barrows (SS/725381), Exmoor, 2¾ miles SE of Challacombe (B3358), on county boundary 1¼ miles N of Simonsbath/Yardwells Cross road.

The mound of Setta Barrow is about 100 ft. in diam. and over 7 ft. high. It is retained by a well-preserved ring of stones. Remains of a similar peristalith are visible around the edge of the barrow immediately to the N. Likewise, the tops of stones are visible around the SW side of the barrow to the S of Setta Barrow. These are set 9 ft. within the edge of the mound. The latter is about 80 ft. in diam. and 8 ft. high. The remains of a double stone row approaches the site from the SW: 3 stones are in place and 1 is fallen. Nothing is known of the contents of these burial mounds but they can be dated c. 1,700–1,400 BC.

IRON AGE

*Blackbury Castle, hill-fort (SY/187924) 3 miles NW of Seaton (B3172, B3174), ¾ mile N of junction of A35 and B3174: on S side of minor road off B3174. Finds in Exeter Museum.

This fort is oval and has an internal area of about 4 acres. It is defended by a single bank and ditch. The entrance faces S. It is fortified by an unusually large triangular barbican, defining an approach passage 180 ft. long and enclosing 2 acres.

Excavation has shown that the earthworks have not altered significantly since they were built c. 200 BC. The bank, which stands 10 ft. high in places, is a dump of clay and flints without any structural features: it lies within a V-shaped ditch originally 8 ft. deep and 31 ft. wide. The entrance through the main bank was furnished with wooden gates and perhaps a bridge over the top. It was 8½ ft. wide. The end of the E rampart here, which is knobbed up and slightly out-turned, had been faced with wattle and daub. The barbican was found to be an unfinished addition, fitted with a pair of gates at its s end 15 ft. apart. The passage between the 2 pairs of gates was metalled with gravel. One hut has been found inside the fort, with a clay oven, cooking pit and hoard of slingstones, but occupation was not extensive.

Burley Wood, hill-fort (SX/495876) 7¼ miles sw of Okehampton (A30, A386), 1¾ miles sw of Bridestowe (A30). Reached from SE, via Watergate.

This fort comprises a main enclosure, roughly oval and enclosing about 2 acres, with a series of outworks across the higher ground to the s. The primary enclosure is defined by a bank and ditch, with traces of a counterscarp bank. It has an in-turned entrance at its s corner. This gives access to an annexe of half the size, protected by a bank and ditch. It has its own enclosure or pen in the NE corner. This annexe has an entrance at the w end, the N rampart here being in-turned. About 100 ft. s of the annexe there is the first of 3 cross banks running in straight lines E/W. The southernmost of these is much the largest and may be later than the other 2. There is a simple entrance through the central cross bank and 2 entrances through the most s cross bank. A medieval motte and bailey can be seen NE of the main enclosure. Undated.

Castle Dyke, hill-fort (SX/875787) 4¾ miles N of Newton Abbot, ¾ mile SE of Chudleigh (A38), in Ugbrooke Park.

This camp has a single bank and ditch enclosing about 6 acres. In plan it is oval, with original entrances on opposite sides, facing NE and sw. At both, the rampart is broadened, providing well-defended passageways. About 250 yds. to the s there is an outer line of defences comprising a bank and ditch; this lies across open ground protected further E and w by steep hillsides. There is a simple entrance through it at the centre. Undated.

*Clovelly Dykes, hill-fort (SS/311235) within angle of A39 and B3237 to Clovelly.

This site has not yet been excavated but it clearly belongs to the group of camps placed on hillsides, with wide-spaced defences forming concentric enclosures for herding places and cattle pens rather than as fortified settlements.

The site, which encloses 23 acres, may have been built in 2 stages, its 2 innermost earthworks first, followed by the 3 additional banks and ditches on the w and the semicircular earthwork around the s and E sides (which becomes double on the NE).

Of the first stage, the outer earthwork is 26 ft. wide, the inner one 16 ft. across. The entrance is through the E side.

Of the second stage, the outermost enclosure is also stronger than the earthworks inside it. The E entrance of Stage 1 continued in use, while 3 more entrances may be found along the NE side. The w one of these has an additional outwork: the central one is in-turned and the end of the bank knobbed up. All these entrances face towards springs at the heads of valleys running down to the coast. The whole site lies astride 3 ridgeways, running E/W and s. Clovelly Dykes is thus ideally situated for a community primarily concerned with stock-rearing activities such as milking and autumn slaughter. Undated.

*Cranbrook Castle, hill-fort (SX/739890) 2 miles NW of Moretonhampstead (A382, B3212), N of road joining Uppacott and Cranbrook.

This well-placed hill-fort is roughly square in plan, enclosing 8 acres. On the N side a steep hill-slope makes fortification almost unnecessary. But a small marking-out bank here suggests that a rampart had been intended but not completed. On the other sides the inner rampart, still 9 ft. high, has an outer facing of stone. It is separated from its ditch by a berm or flat space. The inner ditch is 11 ft. deep today, but it contains at least 3 ft. of silt. On the s side there is a smaller but distinct outer bank and ditch. On the E and w sides the second earthwork appears only as a slight bank whose outer edge falls slightly where the ditch should be. There are 2 entrances, one through the E side and the other (perhaps unfinished) at the sw. The former is slightly inturned. Undated.

Dumpdon Camp, hill-fort (ST/176040) 2½ miles NE of Honiton (A30, A373), 1 mile NW of Monkton (A30).

This camp crowns a spur overlooking the River Otter. It is triangular in plan, defended on all sides by 2 banks and ditches with traces of an outermost counterscarp bank. Steep hillsides are an added protection on the E and W. The earthworks are most massive where they cross the spur and face N. Three acres are thus enclosed. There is an elaborate entrance with outworks near the NE corner. Here the main ramparts are inturned, providing a funnel-shaped approach about 100 ft. long. Outside, there are additional earthworks which prevent a direct approach to the entrance. Undated.

*East Hill, promontory fort (SX/604941) 1¼ miles SE of Okehampton (A30, A385, B3217).

This fort cuts off the end of a spur overlooking the River East Okement to the E and S. It defends an area of 2 acres. There is a single bank and ditch, the former in places 8 ft. high. On the S and E sides the fall of the land is a sufficient protection, though there seems to be a slight bank along the E edge as an additional protection.

Excavation has revealed that the bank is made of earth and rubble, originally probably faced with drystone walling. The ditch had a flat floor and nearly vertical sides: it was originally about 20 ft. wide and 8–10 ft. deep. There is a simple entrance through this earthwork near its centre. Here excavation exposed a very well-laid facing wall, together with foundation trenches for a timber gate. Not dated.

Hawkesdown Castle, hill-fort (SY/263914) ¼ mile NE of Axmouth (B3172 off A35).

This camp is on high ground overlooking the River Axe to the W. It is roughly rectangular in plan, enclosing 2½ acres. Its W and N sides are protected by the steep hill falling to the river, though a bank follows each edge. On the E side, there is a massive bank and ditch, the former 10 ft. high. About 250 ft. further E there is a second and slighter rampart. Along the S side there is a fine bank, ditch and counterscarp bank, adding to an already steep hill-slope. The original entrance is at the SE corner. Here the earthworks have been arranged so as to flank the entrance passage. Undated.

Hembury Castle, hill-fort and Bronze Age barrow (SX/726684) 1¾ miles NNW of Buckfastleigh (A38, A384), 1 mile SE of Stoodley.

This camp is kidney-shaped, with an internal area of c. 7 acres. It is protected by a stout bank, ditch and counterscarp bank. There is a simple entrance facing SE. Not dated.

On the W side there is a mound within the rampart which is probably a bell-barrow of the Bronze Age. It is about 25 ft. high and nearly 50 ft. in diam., with a surrounding ditch. A depression at its centre shows that it has been opened – but without recorded result.

*Hembury, hill-fort and Neolithic causewayed camp (ST/113030) 3½ miles NW of Honiton (A30, A373), on N side of A373. Finds in Exeter Museum.

This must be considered the most important site in Devon. An imposing Iron Age hill-fort has been built upon the remains of a Neolithic causewayed camp; it has been scientifically excavated.

The Iron Age site is roughly triangular, its apex pointing S. It encloses about 8 acres. The defences consist of 3 banks and ditches on the W and N and 2 on the E. There are 2 original entrances, the main one in the middle of the W side, the other at the NE corner. Contemporary hollow ways approach both, one following the NW entrance, the other coming from Hembury Fort Cottage on the E side.

Excavation has revealed that the inner ditch is irregular in shape but at least 10 ft. deep. The banks were originally faced with timbers. Both entrances are of inturned type, the ends of the innermost rampart on the E side, and of the middle rampart on the W curving inwards to provide funnel-like passages to the interior. Massive gate-posts were found, with evidence for timber bridges over both gates. They had cobbled roadways. At each place, the entrance-passage runs obliquely through the banks and ditches. The first Iron Age fortification, of unknown date, was a palisade around the hill-top with a second palisade further down the hillsides. About 2,000 trees would have been needed. The main ramparts followed later, a rebuilding of c. 2nd century BC.

Later, in late BC or in the early years AD, 2 banks and ditches were erected across the fort, almost dividing it in half. They run due E from the W entrance and would have blocked it. Each has a V-shaped ditch 4 ft. deep, and the banks were timber-faced. There is a staggered entrance gap through the s bank and ditch near its centre, but not through the inner one.

The s half of the fort was found to over-lie a Neolithic camp with characteristic interrupted ditches. Nothing of this is now visible and the complete plan of the camp has not yet been uncovered. One ditch runs across the hill following the line of the pair of late Iron Age ditches blocking the main w entrance: this Neolithic ditch would appear to enclose the s part of the hill. At the E Iron Age entrance, however, part of a second Neolithic ditch has been found. Both ditches were 6–7 ft. deep and flat-floored, in the Neolithic manner. A circular hut with wattle-and-daub walls was found near the w entrance: and post-holes were associated with both ditches. The Neolithic pottery is of interest because of its close stylistic ties with Brittany. This camp must have been built by a group of farmers and herdsmen c. 3,400–3,100 BC.

Membury Castle, hill-fort (ST/283028) 3¾ miles NNW of Axminster (A358, A373), E of Membury.

This hill-fort is roughly pear-shaped, its bank, ditch and counterscarp bank en-closing 2–3 acres. The hill on which the camp stands falls away steeply on all sides, making elaborate fortification unneces-sary. The main bank nowhere exceeds 4 ft. in ht. Part of its material has been derived from inside. The main entrance faces NE, though there may be a second original entrance at the sw. The former is elabor-ate: the N rampart turns outwards slightly while the s bank turns in and increases in ht. and size. Undated.

*Milber Down, hill-slope fort and Roman habitation site (SX/884699) 1½ miles SE of Newton Abbot, cut by road from latter to Watcombe Park and A379. Finds in Torquay Museum.

This is an example of a small specialised group of hill-forts built, it seems, by herds-men as cattle pens. Its situation on a hill-slope instead of on a hill-top rules out military defence as a main purpose, as do the wide spaces between its enclosing earthworks.

Milber Down had 4 roughly rectangular banks and ditches, each with an entrance near the centre of the NW side, facing down the valley to Aller Brook (the modern road passes through the 3 inner entrances; the outermost entrance lies to the N in the wood). The innermost enclosure contains an area of 3 acres. Its bank, ditch and counterscarp bank are 62 ft. wide. It is separated from the second earthwork by a space of 80–90 ft., which is crossed by 3 small banks, 2 on the NE side, one at the SE. The second earthwork is similar but only 40 ft. wide. The space between the second and third earthworks is about 90 ft. wide. The space between the second and third earthworks is about 90 ft. wide; the third earthwork is 40 ft. across but has no counterscarp bank. These 3 lines of banks and ditches could have served as a defence in the military sense. The innermost ditch was shown to be V-shaped and nearly 10 ft. deep. The outermost earthwork is quite different. It lies nearly 400 ft. outside the third bank and ditch and it is of very slight construction. Its N and E sides have been destroyed. A sunken track with a bank on each side forms a curved approach from its entrance to that of the third earthwork. No elaborate stone- or timberwork appears to have been used in the construction of these earthworks, nor have any Iron Age huts been found inside. Pottery suggests that the site was built in the 2nd century BC and went out of use before the Roman Conquest.

There is a small rectangular Romano-British enclosure about 50 ft. E of the outermost Iron Age earthwork, on the s side of the road. It is much ploughed down. Its own field system lies to the sw and overlies (and cuts through) the outermost Iron Age earthwork here. It is defined by a V-shaped ditch nearly 12 ft. deep and a bank inside, faced with stone. Traces of timber buildings were found within. This site had been built in the mid 1st century AD.

Visitors to Torquay Museum should note the Roman bronze models of a stag, a bird with detachable wings, a duck with a cake in its mouth, a ball and a ring, found high up in the ditch of the second Iron Age earthwork, but perhaps de-posited there by those living in the Roman settlement.

Musbury Castle, hill-fort (SY/283942) 3

miles SW of Axminster (A358, A373), $\frac{1}{2}$ mile SE of Musbury (A358).

An elongated camp of 6 acres occupies one end of a ridge commanding the River Axe. The very steep hillsides on the E and W have allowed the main defences to consist of a bank and ditch with traces of a counterscarp bank. On the NW side, however, where the ground is less helpful, the defences become triple. Two banks cut off the ridge here, the outer one being 8 ft. high, while a third bank lies astride the ridge about 400 ft. from the S end. The original entrance is probably at the NE. The oblique causeway through the earthworks at the SE may also be an original entrance. Excavation is necessary before these suggestions are confirmed. Until this happens, the short section of bank and ditch across the spur opposite the SE entrance, and the length of bank running down the hillside to the W cannot be explained. Undated.

Noss Camp, hill-slope fort (SX/888536) $2\frac{1}{2}$ miles SW of Brixham (B3203, B3205), $\frac{1}{4}$ mile N of A379 to Dartmouth.

This camp occupies the steeply sloping end of a spur. It is overlooked by higher ground (to the NE) and cannot have been primarily military. Noss Camp has a main enclosure oval in plan and containing 3 acres, strengthened by a curved length of earthwork immediately to the NE and by a second, longer structure 400 ft. up the hill. Original entrances to the enclosure cannot now be identified. Two streams can be found to the N and S. Undated.

Prestonbury Castle, hill-fort (SX/746900) $2\frac{1}{2}$ miles N of Moretonhampstead (A382, B3212), 1 mile SE of Drewsteignton.

This site has 3 ramparts, widely spaced, the innermost being continuous and roughly oval in plan. There is no ditch around the innermost rampart. A steep fall on the SW side makes the main rampart, $7\frac{1}{2}$ ft. high, sufficient protection here: E and N the other 2 earthworks were built to protect the site against more open ground, and to provide enclosed areas E of the innermost earthwork. The area within the main earthwork is 3 acres. There is an entrance through each earthwork facing NE or E. That through the outermost is a fine in-turned example. Undated.

The Rings, Loddiswell. Hill-fort. See

Blackdown Camp.
Shoulsbarrow Castle, hill-fort (SS/705391) $4\frac{1}{2}$ miles SE of junction of A39, A399, B3226, $1\frac{1}{2}$ miles SE of Challacombe (B3358). N of road from Five Cross Way to Mole's Chamber.

This camp is rectangular in shape, enclosing an area of 4 acres. Its S and SW sides are protected by the sharp fall of the land towards the River Bray. The banks defending this site are 4–7 ft. high, the ditches outside them being now almost silted up. They are widely spaced and the outer line is incomplete. There is a simple entrance through the W side and 1 hut inside. Undated.

Sidbury Castle, hill-fort (SY/128913) $2\frac{1}{2}$ miles N of Sidmouth (B3175 off A35), $\frac{3}{4}$ mile SW of Sidbury (A375).

An area of 11 acres is enclosed by the defences of this triangular hill-fort. There are 2 stout ramparts on all sides, with a ditch between them. The inner bank is still 4 ft. high and the ditch now about 8 ft. deep. There appears to be a ditch or quarry within the inner bank at the S corner of the camp. This would have provided additional material for the ramparts.

The main entrance is at the NW. The inner ramparts here run close together for nearly 200 ft., providing a narrow passage to the interior. In addition the N bank makes a bend N, forming an extra defensive platform. A hoard of slingstones has been found. Undated.

Stoke Hill Camp, hill-fort (SX/927957) $1\frac{1}{2}$ miles NNE of Exeter, $\frac{1}{2}$ mile N of Higher Duryard.

The top of the hill, an area of $6\frac{1}{2}$ acres, is enclosed by a bank and ditch with a counterscarp bank. The hill-fort is oval in plan. The earthworks on the N side are well preserved because they are covered by trees. The original entrance, a gap which may originally have been in-turned, is at the E end. Excavation has revealed that front and back of the rampart was faced with turf. Undated.

Woodbury Castle, hill-fort (SY/032873) $4\frac{1}{2}$ miles NE of Exmouth (A376, A377), $1\frac{1}{2}$ miles E of Woodbury (B3179), crossed by B3180.

This is an irregularly shaped fortification of about 5 acres, on the highest point of Woodbury Common. Its main defence consists of a powerful bank and ditch around the E side. Along the NW there are 2 main banks and ditches; here a smaller outermost bank continues S beyond the central, in-turned entrance in this side to form a wide-spaced outer line of defence around the SW and S. It is not continuous and was shown by excavation in 1971 to be unfinished. It has its own, out-turned entrance in the S side which gave access to the space between it and the inner rampart. There is also an entrance at the N end of the hill-fort, the B3138 crossing this and the W entrance. Excavation has established a pre-fort palisade enclosure and shown that the cross-ridge earthwork N of the fort had 2 phases, the second including a palisade along its crest. The hill-fort is a complex structure, containing several phases of timber buildings. Not yet closely dated, it was abandoned before c. 200 BC. The profile of these earthworks may have been 'improved' in Napoleonic times.

Wooston Castle, hill-slope fort (SX/765897) $2\frac{1}{4}$ miles NE of Moretonhampstead (A382, B3212), $\frac{1}{2}$ mile N of Wooston.

The steep N slope to the Teign River protects this fort on that side: but it is overlooked by higher ground to the S and must belong to the group of earthworks apparently more pastoral than military in purpose.

The main enclosure here, obscured by trees, is roughly rectangular, 6 acres in area. It has an entrance facing S. South of it a more massive earthwork cuts across this neck of land. There is an entrance through the centre of it, the bank knobbed up on the W side and in-turned on the E side.

There are 2 earthworks further to the S, each with a central entrance. They may originally have been extended with palisades running E and W. A hollow trackway joins the entrances of the middle and N of these 3 lengths of earthwork. Undated.

Dorset

NEOLITHIC

Culliford Tree, long barrows. See Bronze Age, **Came Wood.**

*****Dorset Cursus,** avenue and long barrows (ST/971123–SU/041188), parallel to, and on S side of A354; W end 1 mile NW of Gussage St Michael.

This is the longest and most remarkable example of a type of ceremonial earthwork peculiar to Gt Britain, called a cursus. These sites consist of a parallel pair of banks and ditches usually about 100 yds. apart, laid out straight and up to a mile in length. The Dorset Cursus, however, is 6 miles long; it encloses 220 acres. The volume of earth in its banks is about $6\frac{1}{2}$ million cubic feet.

The SW end of this site begins on Thickthorn Down, immediately W of one of 2 long barrows mentioned below. Here the bank and ditch curve around to form a squared-off end to the cursus. The earthwork runs NE across a valley and up to Gussage Hill. Here, where it is clearly visible, it appears to have been aligned on its builders on a long barrow which is across its path. The cursus encloses this barrow, which is 165 ft. long, 70 ft. wide and 11 ft. high. It has side-ditches now filled by the plough. After cutting across the corner of a rectangular tree plantation, the curses crosses lower ground and then rises towards Bottlebush Down. This is the most rewarding part of it. First, it is cut by Ackling Dyke, the well-defined causeway of a Roman road (see Bronze Age, **Oakley Down**); then the cursus skirts the NW side of a plantation and the end of its first section is reached $\frac{1}{4}$ mile S of the road to Cranborne. This cursus was built in 2 distinct sections, the S being $3\frac{1}{2}$ miles long. The N section appears to have been added later, continuing for a further 2½ miles.

The S end of the N section is well defined from where it begins. It runs under the road to Cranborne, down a gentle slope and into a wood ½ mile SE of the Oakley Down barrow cemetery (p. 106). In this wood another long barrow has been carefully incorporated, the mound being used to form part of the W side of the cursus. This long barrow is 140 ft. in length, 40 ft. in width and 7 ft. high at the NE end. Emerging from the NE side of the wood, the ceremonial earthwork has been ploughed out until its NE end is reached. This can be seen a few hundred yds. short of Bokerley Dyke (the Romano-British earthwork). Here, as on Thickthorn Down to the SW, 2 long barrows are to be found, the N one lying immediately E of the cursus end. Aerial photographs and probing on the ground suggest that these 2 mounds may originally have been 1 long barrow, as the ditch around them appears to be continuous. The N mound is 175 ft. long, the other is 300 ft. long. Both are about 70 ft. wide and 4–5 ft. high. Ploughing has filled their ditches. Just over ½ mile to the S, probing has revealed a gap across each ditch of the cursus, a feature found in several other examples of this type of monument.

This earthwork, product of religious beliefs in which the long barrow clearly played a part, belongs to native Neolithic culture in Britain and should be dated c. 2,500 BC.

*Eggardon, sacred site (SY/546946) 3¾ miles SW of Maiden Newton (A356); reached by minor roads off A35 and A356.

This site is a henge monument nearly 200 ft. in diam. with the remains of a small round barrow at its centre (probably the same date) and another overlying part of its bank and ditch on the SW side. The circle has its ditch on the inside and there are entrance gaps at the NW and SE. Its situation, on the side of a piece of rising ground and below the crest, is quite characteristic of henge monuments. Probable date, c. 2,500–1,700 BC.

*Grey Mare and her Colts, chambered long barrow (SY/583871) 1½ miles NW of Portesham (B3157), 1½ miles NNE of Abbotsbury (B3157).

This badly overgrown barrow is one of the simpler forms of communal tomb within a class which is concentrated in various areas around the Irish Sea, e.g. the Cotswolds. This one contains the remains of a single rectangular stone burial chamber of sarsen stones set at the SE end of a long barrow. The chamber, roofed by a capstone now fallen, opens directly on to a shallow, concave forecourt defined by upright stones placed at the end of the barrow mound. The barrow itself is about 75 ft. long, 40 ft. wide at the SE end and has a max. ht. of 4 ft. Originally, the mound would have covered the stones of the chamber. Probable date, c. 3,000 BC.

*Hambledon Hill, causewayed camp and long barrows (ST/848122) ¾ mile E of Child Oakford; 1¾ miles SW of Iwerne Minster (A350). Finds in Dorchester Museum.

Outside the SE entrance to the Iron Age hill-fort (p. 113) slight traces can be seen of a Neolithic causewayed camp. It follows the line of the 600 ft. contour at a point where three spurs meet. The main camp, roughly triangular in plan, encloses about 20 acres and comprises a bank and interrupted ditch, obliterated along the N. Extra defences were provided by pairs of causewayed banks and ditches (1) 40 yds. S, (2) 100 ft. E and (3) ¼ mile E, cutting across Steepleton Spur and Shroton Spur. Possibly the Iron Age hill-fort overlies a fourth cross-dyke facing NW. Windmill Hill pottery and stone, flint and bone tools, together with a C14 determination, suggest a date c. 2,900–2,700 BC.

The first long barrow lies between the main earthwork of the Neolithic site and its outer defences on Steepleton Spur. Orientated SE/NW, it is 84 ft. long, 41 ft. broad and 7 ft. high.

The second long barrow is to be found nearly at the centre of the Iron Age site. Lying parallel to this spur, nearly S/N, it has a length of 225 ft. a breadth of 55 ft. and is nearly 6 ft. high.

Nothing is known of the contents of either barrow but both must belong to the period 3,500–2,500 BC. It seems likely, from its position, that the smaller long barrow post-dates the Neolithic earthworks between which it lies.

Hell Stone, chambered long barrow (SY/ 605867) ½ mile N of Portesham (B3157).

These stones were restored in 1866 and it is impossible to reconstruct the original shape of the burial chamber which they constituted; their present arrangement is incorrect. There are traces of a barrow mound associated with the stones, at least 88 ft. long, c. 40 ft. wide and 5 ft. max. ht. This is probably another outlier of the series of family tombs found in the Cotswolds and elsewhere. The Dorset examples suggest connections with N France. Date, c. 3,000 BC.

The central circle lies 200 yds. to the N, beside the road to Gussage All Saints. It is slightly oval in plan, with a max. diam. of 350 ft. The well-defined ditch is inside the bank and there are entrances at the NE and SW. Close to the W entrance the bank is 12 ft. high and the ditch 35 ft. wide. The ruins of a Norman and later church stand at the centre of this circle, making the place one of the most unusual and romantic in Britain. The forthright siting of a Christian church at the centre of a pagan sanctuary here should be contrasted with the location of an even earlier

21   *Central Knowlton henge monument (with deserted church) and barrows. Note crop-
marked ditches around tree-covered barrow*

*Knowlton Circles, sacred sites and Bronze Age round barrows (SU/024100, S circle) 2¾ miles SW of Cranborne (B3078); S circle cut by B3078.

There are 3 sacred sites, or henge monuments, arranged almost in a straight line NW/SE, which are crossed by the Cranborne–Wimborne and Knowlton–Gussage All Saints roads (fig. 21).

The S circle is cut almost along its diam. by the main road, Knowlton Farm occupying the N part of the site. This earthwork is almost circular in plan. It has a diam. of 800 ft. Like all true henge monuments, its ditch is on the inside. In the well-preserved section behind the farm, there appears to be a flat space, or berm, between bank and ditch. Aerial photographs suggest that there were original entrances roughly E and W.

church immediately outside the circle at Avebury (Wilts., below).

The N Knowlton circle, unfortunately under the plough, is to be found 100 yds. further N and 250 ft. E of the road to Gussage All Saints. Aerial surveys have revealed that it is D-shaped, a broad entrance occurring at the S side where the straight arm of the D should be. The bank lies outside the ditch. The long axis of this site measures 275 ft.

There is another circle between the last and the road, called the Old Churchyard. Since it has an *outer* ditch and is markedly rectangular in plan, it is unlikely to be pre-Roman in date.

About 200 ft. E of the central circle an enormous round barrow can be seen, covered with trees. Its mound is 20 ft. high and 135 ft. in diam. It has a quarry ditch around its base and both are surrounded by an outer ditch having a diam of 385 ft. A badly damaged bowl-barrow can be seen close to the road between the central and s circles, while air photographs have revealed other barrows concentrated around the 3 circles. Clearly, in late Neolithic and Early Bronze Age times these circles possessed a sanctity akin to that of Stonehenge. The Knowlton Circles must have been in use during the period 2,500–1,700 BC.

*Litton Cheney, earth circles and stones (SY/558917) ¾ mile N of Litton Cheney and N of A35.

There are 2 circles within 150 ft. of each other on high ground here, both of unusual design. The w circle consists of a ditch and bank, the latter on the inside, with a possible entrance on the SE. This has a max. diam. of 125 ft. There are 4 depressions, 20 ft. apart, on top of the bank at the s and sw, with another at the NW. These suggest that originally stones had been set up in the bank of this site.

A second circle, of slight proportions, is to be found 136 ft. to the SE. It comprises a shallow (i.e. silted-up) ditch 70 ft. in diam., surrounding a flat space 47 ft. across. On the s side, close to the inner edge of the ditch, 1 small sarsen stands; it may be the remains of a circle of stones surrounded by a ditch. Three other sarsens lie scattered, 100 ft. to the s. Whether they have been removed from this circle, or constitute a circle or avenue on their own is at present problematical.

The construction and use of these sites is likely to fall within the period 2,200–1,400 BC.

*Long Barrow Hill, bank barrow and long barrow (SY/572912, bank barrow), 200 yds. s of A35, ¾ mile N of Long Bredy.

This fine example of a bank barrow, marked on the 1-in. O.S. as 'earthworks', is 645 ft. in length and 69 ft. in width. It is orientated NE/SW, and is higher at the NE. Its sides are roughly parallel and are flanked by quarry ditches which do not enclose either end. There is a gap, probably of recent origin, 60 yds. from the higher end. Date, c. 2,500 BC.

A normal long barrow can be seen 200 yds. to the SE. It is orientated SE/NW and is 116 ft. long. It has quarry ditches along its flanks but not enclosing its ends. At the SE, its mound is 5½ ft. high. Probable date 3,500–2,500 BC.

Maiden Castle, long mound and causewayed camp. See Iron Age.

*Maumbury Rings, sacred site and Roman amphitheatre (SY/690899) on s outskirts of Dorchester, on E side of A354. Finds in Dorchester Museum.

This site was used as an amphitheatre in Roman times and as a gun emplacement in the Civil Wars. Its bank was raised and fitted for seats by the Romano-Britons and the whole of its floor lowered several feet. The remains of the gun emplacement can be seen dug into the bank opposite the entrance. Originally, it was a Neolithic henge monument. It is nearly circular in plan, with a diam. of 330 ft. It consists of a massive bank more than 15 ft. high, made from chalk dug from a ditch on the inside. The way in which this ditch was dug recalls the method used in many other Neolithic sites – the tops of a series of contiguous pits being enlarged until a more or less continuous ditch had been achieved. Here, however, many of the pits were as much as 35 ft. deep, suggesting that at this site they were a feature on their own and not just a quarry for the bank. The single entrance through the earthwork is on the NE. In the 18th century an upright stone stood here, a feature frequently met with at the entrance to henge monuments.

A series of remarkable phallic carvings in chalk from the ditch points to the fertility rites which must have been performed here c. 2,500–1,700 BC.

*Mount Pleasant, sacred site and round barrow (SY/710899) 1¼ miles E of Dorchester, N of A352 and road to w Stafford. Finds in Dorchester Museum.

The much-ploughed bank and ditch of a henge monument, enclosing 12 acres, has been shown by recent excavations to have been built c. 2,000 BC, with entrances SE, SW, NW and NE. It superseded an open settlement c. 2,100 BC, which included a timber-framed building c. 115 ft. in diameter, within a ditch. The main earthwork was replaced, c. 1,700 BC, by a palisade of oak posts set side by side in a trench and standing c. 18 ft. above ground, with N and E entrances corresponding to those through the earthworks; the work of the Beaker Folk, it enclosed 11 acres. The timber building was also replaced by a stone cove with outlying monolith. A mound 9 ft. high and over 100 ft. across, Conquer Barrow, was built over the earthwork on the w, c. 1,600 BC. There is no record of its contents.

Nine Barrow Down, Corfe Castle, long barrow. See Bronze Age.

Pimperne, long barrow (ST/917104) 3 miles NE of Blandford Forum (A350, A354), on N side of A354.

Coming up the road from Salisbury to Blandford, the Pimperne long barrow will appear almost as conspicuously to the 20th-century visitor as it did to those whose kinsfolk lay buried beneath it, except that turf now hides its original whiteness. It is one of the largest in Dorset, having a length of about 350 ft. and a breadth of 90 ft. Like so many Dorset long barrows, it is parallel-sided rather than wedge-shaped and its ht. of 8 ft. is fairly constant from end to end. Its prominent side-ditches, which do not continue around either end, are separated from the mound by broad berms. Probably date, 3,500–2,500 BC.

Poor Lot, long barrows. See Bronze Age.

*Smacam Down, long barrow (SY/657994) 1¼ miles SSW of Cerne Abbas (A352).

About 30 yds. w of the enclosure of a Romano-British settlement a Neolithic long barrow has been found. It is orientated S/N and is wedge-shaped in the Wessex manner. It has a length of 98 ft. and is 40 ft. wide at the s end. Its max. ht. is 5 ft. The ditch appears to run all round the mound except at the s end, where one of the Roman 'Celtic' fields has damaged the barrow. Date, 3,500–2,500 BC.

*Thickthorn, long barrows (ST/972122) 1 mile NW of Gussage St Michael. Finds in Dorchester Museum.

There are 2 long barrows close together on the chalk ridge here, both lying immediately SE of the s end of the **Dorset Cursus** (above). The first and smaller long barrow is about 25 yds. SE of the Cursus.

Before excavation in 1933, and as now restored, this site consisted of a mound 7 ft. high and 90 ft. long, set within a horseshoe-shaped ditch 15 ft. wide and 7 ft. deep, the barrow being aligned SE/NW.

At the E end the ditch discontinues, leaving a causeway through to the area within nearly 60 ft. wide. Unusual features of this long barrow are its relative shortness and its mound, which is highest at the centre.

Excavation, which cleared the whole mound, failed to reveal any skeletons associated with the construction of the barrow. It showed that the mound of chalk covered a central structure of turf which must at some stage have contained corpses. Two post-holes were found on the causeway at the E end, one of them placed exactly on the long axis of the barrow. Finds of pottery on the bottom of the ditch showed that this site had been built by Windmill Hill people c. 3,500–2,500 BC.

At the end of the period, 3 inhumations of the Beaker people took place at the SW side of the mound. The remains of a young woman and a child had been placed crouched in a shallow grave; close by, a second inhumation was found, a female aged 17–18. Both graves contained beakers, the second accompanied by a copper awl. These burials were probably made c. 2,000–1,700 BC.

The second and larger long barrow on Thickthorn Down is close to the s end of the Dorset Cursus. Its mound, which is 153 ft. long, 67 ft. wide and 7 ft. high, is surrounded by a U-shaped quarry ditch, the open end facing SE. Like the other long barrow, this one is parallel to the ridge on which it stands. It has not been excavated but must be contemporary with the smaller long barrow.

*Wor Barrow, long barrow (SU/012173) ¾ mile E of Handley (B3081); ¼ mile NW of A354. Finds in Salisbury Museum.

This long barrow was excavated at the end of the last century by Gen. Pitt-Rivers (fig. 22). Originally appearing as an oval mound set within a ditch in the usual manner, today the visitor will find the ditch cleared out to its original depth and shape, the contents heaped around the outside, and the space within, where the mound stood formerly, now quite flat. This work, one of the few examples of the total excavation of a site in the 19th century, revealed that there were 2 distinct phases of building concealed beneath the barrow mound.

In phase 1 a rectangular wooden stockade, measuring 90 × 35 ft., with a funnel-shaped entrance at the SE end had been erected and surrounded by a slight ditch, dug as a series of separate sections in the Neolithic manner and enclosing an area roughly 140 × 90 ft. It also had an entrance at the SE. The spoil from the ditch was heaped up around the outside of the wooden structure it surrounded.

In phase 2, the ditch which the visitor sees was dug: in several places it removed all traces of the ditch of phase 1. The material derived from it was used to build a long mound, originally nearly 20 ft. high and 150 ft. in length, which covered completely the wooden structure and the area within the ditch of phase 1. Like the first ditch, the second was not continuous but dug in 4 separate sections.

We may suppose that the wooden enclosure was a place where corpses were preserved until the time for building a barrow was decreed. At least 6 bodies were placed there and provided, it seems, with the additional protection of some sort of 'mortuary house' made of turves. Just before the long barrow mound was heaped up, the remains of these skeletons were arranged in their final position; to Gen. Pitt-Rivers, it was clear that at least 3 of

the skeletons consisted of no more than bundles of loose bones when the last burial rites were performed. This site must have been started c. 3,500–2,500 BC.

BRONZE AGE

*Afflington Barrow, round barrow (SY/968788) 3½ miles W of Swanage, ¼ mile SW of B3069 and road to Worth Matravers. Finds in Dorchester Museum.

This bowl-barrow is about 58 ft. in diam. and 6 ft. high. It was opened in the last century and the main burial was found to be a cremation, placed on wood or bark and furnished with a shale ring. On the floor of the barrow there was also considerable evidence of burning. Perhaps the cremation had taken place on the spot. A skeleton was also found, in a crouched position, which may be contemporary with the cremation. Higher up, 9 skeletons had been buried in 2 rows of 3 and 4 graves, some lined with slabs (one of shale). Rings and other objects found with these suggest that they are Romano-British. The barrow must have been built c. 1,700–1,400 BC.

22   *Wor Barrow: A typical Long Barrow Ditch*

*Badbury Barrow, round barrows (ST/ 948035) 4¼ miles NW of Wimborne Minster (A31, A341), 1¼ miles ESE of Tarrant Keynston (B3082), on S side of B3082. Finds in British Museum.

There are 2 bowl-barrows close together, on either side of the track to Shapwick, and there is a third, Straw Barrow, 300 yds. to the S. One of these is the barrow from which, in 1845, a large block of sandstone was removed, bearing carvings of daggers and axes like those at **Stonehenge** (Wilts., below). This same barrow had at its centre a heap of sandstone blocks surrounded first by a ring of flints and then a stout wall of sandstone blocks. Chalk covered the mound. In or under the central stone heap were at least 3 skeletons, 2 furnished with food vessels (fig. 8). There were also more than 15 cremations, but not all these were contemporary with the inhumations. There were several collared urns with them.

The carvings of daggers and axes would date this barrow to the period 1,700–1,400 BC. Since Straw Barrow has many sandstone blocks scattered over it today, it is possible that the details described refer to it rather than to one of the others. One of the latter is also known to have contained a Middle Bronze Age urn with cremation, indicating a date of c. 1,250–1,000 BC. All are about 60 ft. across and 2–3 ft. high.

Bincombe Hill, barrow cemetery (SY/ 689846) 1½ miles NE of Broadway (A354), ¼ mile E of Bincombe.

There are about 7 well-preserved barrows in this cemetery, one a bell-barrow. This barrow has a mound about 11 ft. high and 92 ft. in diam.: there is a ditch around it, giving it an overall diam. of about 140 ft. One of the bowl-barrows is over 100 ft. in diam., with a mound 12½ ft. high. There is also a triple bowl-barrow, each mound being 64–67 ft. wide and 7–9 ft. high – all enclosed by one ditch. The cemetery would have accumulated c. 1,700–1,400 BC.

Bradford Barrow, round barrow (ST/ 981046) 3¼ miles NW of Wimborne Minster (A31, A341), 1½ miles NW of Hinton Parva (B3078); track from Witchampton.

This is perhaps the largest bowl-barrow in Dorset. It has a diam. of over 100 ft. and a ht. of 20 ft. There is a surrounding ditch. Its conical outline might suggest

that it is Roman. Otherwise, it would belong to the period 1,700–1,400 BC.

Came Wood, round barrows and Neolithic bank barrow (SY/695855–SY/ 705853) 1½ miles NW of Preston (A353), on N side of road to A354 and Ridgeway.

Together with a long barrow, there are bell-, bowl- and pond-borrows in this area. They form a spectacular cemetery in the Wessex style, probably associated with that on **Bincombe Hill** (above).

The bank barrow (SY/702853) is about 600 ft. in length, 57 ft. wide and 7 ft. high. It is orientated SE/NW and has a round barrow overlying its NW end. Date c. 2,500 BC.

Of the round barrows in this area, those at the ends of the bank barrow are both 11 ft. high, one 60 ft. in diam., the other about 90 ft. wide. North of the bank barrow there are 2 bowl-barrows and a pond-barrow (SY/703853). The latter is almost invisible, but appears to be about 50 ft. wide and less than 1 ft. deep. A second pond-barrow is close to the last (SY/703853), in only slightly better condition. It is 60 ft. across and 1 ft. deep: its surrounding bank is 15 ft. broad and 1 ft. high. There are 2 bell-barrows in Came Wood, close together (SY/696854). Both are about 9 ft. high. The E mound is 75 ft. wide, the w one 105 ft. Both have clear berms between the bases of their mounds and their ditches. There is another pond-barrow at SY/697854. This is 46 ft. wide and 9 ins. deep: its bank is 3 ft. high and there are possible traces of an outer ditch. The bowl at SY/699855 yielded 4 secondary inhumations, 1 with gold and amber beads and a cremation with incense cup and collared urn. Date, c. 1,700–1,400 BC.

Chalbury Camp, round barrows. See Iron Age.

*Clandon, round barrow (SY/656890) 2¼ miles SW of Dorchester, ¼ mile E of Winterborne St Martin and the B3159 from Upwey to the A35. Finds in Dorchester Museum.

This is a large bowl-barrow, over 80 ft. in diam. and nearly 20 ft. high. It contained one of the richest and finest groups of grave offerings in Wessex. The barrow was dug in 1882 and its main burial never reached. Above this, however, there was a pile of flints among which were a bronze

23   Clandon barrow: gold plate (6 × 4½ ins.), c. 1,700–1,400 BC

dagger, a lozenge-shaped gold plate (fig. 23), a shale mace-head with decorative gold studs, a cup carved from a lump of amber and a pottery incense cup. These belonged either to the primary burial or to a cremation added later. Above these there was another cremation deposited in a fine collared urn, and near the top there were 2 skeletons in stone-lined graves which may be Romano-British or pagan Saxon.

The gold lozenge plate should be compared with that from **Bush Barrow**, Normanton (Wilts.). Parallels in shale to the amber cup have been found in Wiltshire (in Salisbury Museum) and also in amber from the **Hove Barrow** (Brighton Museum). The mace-head is one of the most remarkable objects of this period in Britain. It is cushion-shaped, perforated to fit on to a wooden handle and with five gold-covered conical plugs let into it. It suggests that at least 1 burial in this barrow is that of a chief. Date, c. 1,700–1,400 BC.

Conquer Barrow. See Neolithic, **Mount Pleasant.**

Deverel Barrow, round barrow (SY/819990) 1 mile NE of Milborne (A354), between Dorchester and Blandford; between Bagber and Deverel Farms. Finds in Dorchester Museum and Bristol Museum.

This barrow has a modern wall built around it. It was a bowl-barrow, with a mound 3 ft. high and about 40 ft. in diam. It was excavated in 1824 by W.A. Miles (whose initials can be found carved on the two large stones on the mound). Near, but not at the centre, a cremation was found in a collared urn. This gives the barrow a date c. 1,700–1,400 BC. Later, c. 1,250 BC, over 20 cremations were added to the mound which may have been enlarged to receive them. Many of these had been deposited in Middle Bronze Age barrel- and bucket-shaped urns: most were found in pits, with stone slabs covering them (figs. 12, 13).

Eweleaze Barn, quadruple bell-barrow (SY/650871) 1 mile s of Winterborne St Martin, by track from B3159 sw to Friar Waddon.

Though still (1975) awaiting proof by excavation, this group of mounds appears to be the only quadruple bell-barrow in England. There is a fifth barrow, a bowl, a few yards further s and in the same alignment. All 4 bell-barrow mounds are 62–84 ft. in diam. and 7–8 ft. high. The ditch which appears to enclose all 4 is 15 ft. wide and separated from them by a berm 8–9 ft. broad. Date, c. 1,700–1,400 BC.

Five Marys, barrow cemetery (SY/790842) 2¾ miles ESE of A353/A352 junction, 1 mile w of Winfrith Newburgh.

There are 8 barrows in this group, arranged in a line E/W, following the ridge in the following order (E/W): bowl, pond, bell, bell, bowl, bowl, bowl, bell. The bowl-barrows have diams. of 20–70 ft. and hts. 1–7 ft. The mounds of the bells are 50–70 ft. wide and 8–9 ft. high, their overall diams. being about 90 ft. The pond-barrow is about 9 ft wide, with a slight outer bank giving it an overall diam. of about 20 ft. This cemetery, a good example of barrows accumulated in a straight line, must have been built in the period c. 1,700–1,400 BC.

Grim's Ditch, enclosure ditch. See Hampshire, p. 136.

*****Hampton Down,** stone circle (SY/596865) ½ mile NW of Portesham (B3157), on open downland at 680 ft.

Excavation, 1965, has shown that the present circle is a relatively recent re-arrangement of a circle of 9 stones (diam. c. 18 × 20 ft.) which lies under and to the w of the bank crossing the site. Date, c. 2,200–1,400 BC.

Hardy Monument, barrow. See **Ridgeway** (1) below.

Hengistbury Head. See Iron Age.

*Kingston Russell, stone circle (SY/577878) 1½ miles SSE of Long Bredy, on open downland at 620 ft.

This stone circle has a diam. of about 80 ft. Today it is slightly oval in plan, but some of its sarsens may have been moved from their original position. All the stones are now recumbent, though 1 was standing at the beginning of the 19th century. This circle was probably in use c. 2,200–1,400 BC.

Knowlton Circles, barrows. See Neolithic.

Nine Barrow Down, Corfe Castle, barrow cemetery and Neolithic long barrow (SY/993815) 2¼ miles ESE of Corfe Castle (A351, B3351), ¼ mile s of B3351. Close to **Rempstone Circle** (p. 107).

This cemetery, strung out along the s edge of Branscombe Hill, consists of 17 bowl-barrows and a Neolithic long barrow. The bowl-barrows have diams. ranging from 15–90 ft. Beginning at the w end, the second barrow, which is about 50 ft. across and 5½ ft. high, has a surrounding ditch interrupted by at least 4 causeways. The largest barrow in the cemetery (d. 90 ft., ht. 10 ft.) has a clear surrounding ditch still 2 ft. deep and over 10 ft. wide. No records exist indicating the contents of these mounds.

The long barrow, close to the largest bowl, is orientated E/W. Its length is 112 ft., its width 45 ft. and its ht. 6½ ft. Its ditch appears to have been dug as a series of pits never properly run together. Date, c. 3,500–2,500 BC.

This cemetery, like so many in Wessex, is grouped around an earlier long barrow. It is curiously devoid of the specialised barrow-types – bells, discs, saucers, ponds. It must have accumulated c. 1,700–1,400 BC.

*Nine Stones, stone circle (SY/611904) ½ mile w of Winterbourne Abbas (A35), on s side of A35.

This very small stone circle is on the s side of the Dorchester/Bridport road and is surrounded by an iron fence. It comprises 9 sarsen stones, though accounts written in the last century suggest that the large gap on the N side may have been filled by a tenth stone. The circle has a diam. of 25 ft.: 7 stones have hts. of 1–2½ ft. but 2 stones are 6 and 7 ft. high.

This sacred site, like the others in the Dorchester area, must belong to the period c. 2,200–1,400 BC.

*Oakley Down, barrow cemetery and Roman road Ackling Dyke (SU/007154) 1¼ miles SE of Handley (B3081), between Ackling Dyke and A354. Finds in Devizes Museum, Wiltshire.

This cemetery, one of the richest and most impressive in Wessex, contains at least 29 barrows arranged in one large group, with 5 outlying mounds to the NE. These barrows were excavated at their centres by Sir Richard Hoare in 1803 (fig. 10).

The 5 N barrows comprise 3 small bowl-barrows, cut by the Salisbury–Blandford road, a large bell-barrow and another bowl. The bell yielded a secondary crema-tion furnished with a handled pottery mug with four little feet, of continental origin, and a bronze dagger. A cremation was also found in the intact bowl-barrow.

The main part of the cemetery is 300 yds. to the SE. The 3 NE barrows are all discs, one with 3 mounds inside its ditch, another with 2 and the third, which is cut by the Roman road, 2 mounds within an oval ditch. Cremations, an urn and beads of shale and amber, were found in these – essentially women's things. Elements of an elaborate, crescent-shaped amber neck-lace were found in the oval disc, together with a miniature cup of 'Aldbourne' type.

Between these disc-barrows and the prominent bell-barrow to the sw, 5 bowl-barrows of varying sizes, a disc with 2 mounds and 3 small contiguous bowl-barrows can be found. One bowl, 50 yds. w of the oval disc-barrow, covered an inhumation with beaker, copper knife, a fine series of flint arrowheads and a button. Cremations and an incense cup were found in the others. Next we have the huge bell-barrow, in which no finds have yet been made. Immediately sw of it a small mound can be seen. In a low evening light a ditch is revealed surrounding it and showing that it is a disc-barrow. Beneath its mound remains of a funeral pyre were found, together with a cremation in one of the largest and finest collared urns in Britain. 8 bowl-barrows, 3 contiguous, lie to the s. Seven yielded cremations, 1 wrapped in cloth; the eighth covered an inhumation. The main cemetery is completed by a sixth disc-barrow cut by the Roman road and lying immediately to the E of it.

This cemetery must have accumulated here c. 1,700–1,400 BC.

Ackling Dyke, the Roman road from Old Sarum to Badbury Rings and to Dorchester (*Durnovaria*) skirts the barrow cemetery on the E side, overlying 2 of the disc-barrows. As elsewhere hereabouts, the road is very large and well preserved. In places its side-ditches are visible. Its *agger* is over 7 ft. high and the crown is about 10 ft. wide. It is metalled with flint beach pebbles brought from Pentridge Hill.

It should be noted how the Romans paid no regard to the barrow cemetery, their road cutting across 2 of the disc-barrows in arrogant fashion. This contrasts with the respect shown by natives for the burial mounds of their ancestors.

*Poor Lot, barrow cemetery and Neolithic long barrows (centre, SY/588907) $6\frac{1}{4}$ miles W of Dorchester, $\frac{1}{2}$ mile SE of Kingston Russell; mainly s of A35. Finds in Dorchester Museum.

This cemetery ranks with those around Stonehenge for the number and variety of its barrows. It may not be coincidental that immediately to the sw there are 2 long barrows (SY/580905). These are orientated SE/NW: one is 300 ft. long, the other 350 ft. Both are about 45 ft. wide and c. 6 ft. high at the E end. They decrease in height and width towards the w. They have side-ditches. Both mounds, particularly the N one, have been cut through at later times. Nothing is known of their contents, but they must be dated c. 3,500–2,500 BC.

The Bronze Age cemetery consists of at least 44 barrows. Of these, 24 are bowl-barrows, 7 are bell-barrows, 8 are disc-barrows and 5 are ponds. In addition, there is 1 which is a cairn of stones. Of the bowl-barrows, only 1 has a ditch which is clearly defined. Their diams. range from 20–100 ft. and their hts. from 1–13 ft. One (SY/588908) is slightly oval in plan, narrowing at the w end. There are 2 examples of 3 bowl-barrows arranged in a line touching each other.

The ditches around 2 of the bells are filled in, but all show the characteristic flat space around the base of the mound, in these examples appearing to be raised above the level of the surrounding land. The finest of them, its ditch quite plain, has a mound 11 ft. high and 90 ft. in diam.; its berm is 9 ft. broad and its ditch 12 ft. wide. There is one example of a twin bell-barrow (2 mounds within 1 ditch).

Four of the disc-barrows are a local version of the Wessex type in which the central mound has a slight ditch around its base, in turn enclosed within a bank and an outer ditch. The diams. of this type, which is restricted to S Dorset, are generally almost half that of a normal disc-barrow. Two of the normal disc-barrows in this cemetery have mounds sufficiently large (d. 38 ft., ht. $3\frac{1}{2}$ ft) to suggest they are intermediate between disc and bell in shape.

Two of the pond-barrows, close together, were excavated in 1952–3 (SY/587906). Each had an overall diam. of about 35 ft., their hollow centres being about 1 ft. deep and their surrounding banks about 1 ft. high. There was a causeway through the bank of each facing SE. Both central areas had a flint pavement extending as pathways out through the entrances. Each contained a circular setting of ritual pits, one group being covered by the flint pavement. No burials were found but fragments of collared urns were scattered in each. These barrows were probably ritual structures. Corpses may have been kept in them for the flesh to decay prior to cremation and burial elsewhere, or other ritual acts may have been carried out there during burial ceremonies.

This cemetery must have accumulated c. 1,700–1,400 BC. Nothing is known of the burials beneath the mounds.

*Rempstone, stone circle (SY/994821) $2\frac{1}{4}$ miles E of Corfe (A351, B3351); on s side of B3351 to Studland. Close to Rempstone Hall.

The remains of this circle are to be found in a thick wood. Only the N half of the site survives. It consists of 8 stones of sandstone from the local Bagshot Beds, grouped around the arc of a circle whose diam. must have been about 80 ft. Five of the stones still stand. The stones of this circle like those of the other Dorset circles, vary greatly in size, the largest here being about 4 ft. high. Probable date, 2,200–1,400 BC.

*Ridgeway, round barrows (SY/612875 to SY/663866) area of Hardy Monument, 1¼ miles NE of Portesham (B3157) extending E to A354 N of Upwey. Grave goods in Dorchester Museum.

This great chalk ridge, which looks out across the Channel to the S, and to the N deep into Wessex, was chosen by Bronze Age tribes as a burial ground for scores of their dead. It is here impossible to do more than pick out a few of the more notable barrows on this ridge, as good examples of types which are concentrated here more thickly than anywhere else in Dorset. When examining them one should remember that in the Bronze Age their mounds would have gleamed white beneath coverings of chalk, and reflect upon the impact which this burial area would have had upon the tribes whose ruling families lay buried there.

(1) Hardy Monument (SY/612875): S of the Monument there is a bell-barrow which has a mound 75 ft. in diam. and 6 ft. high, surrounded by a ditch with a total diam. of 114 ft. A section across this barrow can be seen exposed in the quarry to the W. This shows that there is a core of brown pebbly soil at the centre of the barrow, covered by 2 thin layers of soil, one grey, the other brown. The central feature is covered by an outer jacket of grey soil and pebbles, giving it a diam. of 55 ft. (excluding the berm) and a total ht. of about 5 ft. The old land surface beneath this barrow can be seen. Cut in gravel, the ditch around the barrow is U-shaped, nearly 5 ft. deep and of about the same width at ground level. Probable date, c. 1,700–1,400 BC.

(2) Ridgeway (SY/645864): just S of the crest of the hill. This bowl-barrow is about 60 ft. in diam. and 6 ft. high. It was excavated in the last century. The crouched skeletons of an adult and child were found in a pit at its base. These bodies were protected by large stones. Higher up there were 2 extended inhumations, each surrounded by stone slabs and provided with a pot, and a cremation in an urn. At the top of the mound there was the skeleton of a child, probably Romano-British. This barrow may have been built c. 2,000 BC, receiving additional burials until c. 1,250 BC, and the corpse of a child in the Christian era.

(3) Ridgeway (SY/657866), ¼ mile W of B3159. This bowl-barrow is about 80 ft. in diam. and at least 6 ft. high. It was opened in 1885 and yielded one of the richest series of grave-offerings yet found in Dorset. Just below the modern turf at the centre the first burial occurred – a heap of cremated bone placed in a pit dug after the barrow had been built. With the bones a series of burial offerings had been left: one was a small bronze axe-head, wrapped in cloth, of the type carved on the uprights at Stonehenge; there were 2 large bronze dagger-blades, perhaps of Breton origin, and a small bronze knife. One of the daggers had a pommel plated with gold sheet. At the base of the barrow the main burial was uncovered. It consisted of a massive stone cist made of a series of Portland stone slabs, the cover-stone weighing about a ton. The area of the coffin was 4 × 2 × 2 ft.: it lay N/S. Inside it were found the remains of a skeleton which appears to have decomposed before burial. Above the grave-pit a heap of stones had been piled to a ht. of 7 ft., and 13 ft. in diam. It contained a series of objects which may be interpreted as offerings to the dead man buried beneath it. They included a stone mace-head, a bone pin and pommel for a dagger (which does not seem to have been buried), a series of flint and chert scrapers and a polished flint axe. At the top of this pile of stones, and in it, there was a second inhumation protected by stone slabs. This skeleton, like the one at the base, was also incomplete. A fine bronze dagger-blade had been buried with it. At the same level, but separate, were the remains of a cremated skeleton.

The burial at the top with the gold dagger-pommel belongs to the period 1,700–1,400 BC. The barrow itself is earlier, and may be dated c. 2,000–1,700 BC.

(4) Ridgeway (SY/663866): on N side of B3159, where Ridgeway crosses road. This extraordinary site appears as a disc-barrow on an enormous scale. Its mound is about 80 ft. in diam. and 7 ft. high: it is surrounded by a flat space 40–50 ft. wide, with a ditch and outer bank around that. The latter has an overall diam. of 260 ft., the ditch and bank each being about 20 ft. wide. This site is so large that its bank and ditch have the proportions of a henge monument, with a burial mound at the centre. Its most likely date is c. 1,700–1,400 BC.

(5) See also **Eweleaze Barn**, quadruple bell-burrow.

Straw Barrow. See **Badbury Barrow.**

Upwey, disc-barrow. See **Ridgeway** (4).

IRON AGE

*Abbotsbury Castle, hill-fort and (?) Roman signal tower (SY/556865) 1½ miles NW of Abbotsbury (B3157), N of this road.

This hill-fort is triangular in plan, its defences enclosing 4½ acres. On the N, S and E sides the earthworks comprise 2 banks with a ditch between them. Here the natural fall of the ground necessitates nothing more. At the SE, more level ground has caused the building of 4 ramparts with ditches outside them. These have been laid out to provide a long entrance-passage flanked by banks N and S.

The innermost bank at the SE corner is very slight and the ditch outside it appears to have been partly filled by the next bank. This suggests that this fort may have been begun with a single bank and ditch and later enlarged to its present plan.

At the SW, the earthworks have been altered at some later stage, so that an almost square earthwork has been constructed in the angle of the innermost bank. It has been suggested, but never proved, that this may be the base of a Roman military signal tower. At its N and S corners, the small ditch surrounding it appears to cut the Iron Age ramparts.

Within the hill-fort, towards the SE, a group of about 9 circular depressions, roughly 20 ft. in diam., must represent the sites of huts. These may be contemporary

with the hill-fort. South-west of them there is the mound of a Bronze Age bowl-barrow. Not dated.

*Badbury Rings, hill-fort, Bronze Age barrows and Roman road (ST/964030) N of B3082, 3½ miles NW of Wimborne Minster (A31, A341).

A fairly conspicuous hill has been defended by 2 stout banks and ditches, with a much slighter, and possibly later bank and ditch surrounding these. There are original entrances E and W, the inner-most bank at the former being in-turned and outworks being added at the latter. There is an additional SW entrance through the outermost rampart, approached by a slight valley. These earthworks enclose 18 acres of mostly wooded ground and 100–200 ft. within the W entrance, the site of a hut – probably contemporary – can be seen as a depression in the ground.

Not dated by excavation, this fort must have had a lengthy development, perhaps including the Roman period.

In Roman times there was probably a large settlement either within the Iron Age ramparts or close to them. Here is the meeting place of 2 main roads, the Ackling Dyke from Old Sarum to Dorchester (p. 107) and one from Bath to Poole Harbour.

A superb length of Ackling Dyke impinges upon the outermost rampart of Badbury Ring at the NW. Here the road *agger* is 13 yds. wide and 4–6 ft. high; it is flanked by well-defined side-banks and ditches 40 yds. apart.

Five-hundred yds. W of the intersection with the Iron Age hill-fort, 3 conspicuous mounds are set immediately N of Ackling Dyke. A fourth mound of similar shape can be seen 400 ft. W of the intersection. Excavation (1959) has shown that these are Bronze Age bowl-barrows, the bank and ditch around the most W mound being recent.

*Bindon Hill, promontory fort (SY/835803 to centre) S of West Lulworth (B3070). Finds in Dorchester Museum.

This earthwork extends along the crest of a ridge, the E part of which is under an artillery range, for a distance of 2,600 yds. South of this ridge there is a coastal shelf cut into, on the W, by Lulworth Cove. Undoubtedly the earthworks were built to control this all-important natural harbour. The earthworks comprise a bank and ditch with a slight counterscarp bank. There is 1 main entrance, in-turned, 760 yds. from the w end of the ridge thus fortified. A bank and ditch cuts across Bindon Hill, facing E, 450 yds. w of the entrance. About 400 acres are enclosed.

Excavation in 1950 revealed how these earthworks had been built. A marking-out bank a few inches high had first been set up, the rampart being built exactly over this. This rampart consisted of a chalk rubble mound faced with vertical timbers (fig. 24) and revetted at the back by a line of widely spaced timbers with an earth ramp behind them. The lines of timbers were 12 ft. apart. It appears, however, that this plan was interrupted, or the rampart early thrown down; the outer facing was abandoned and the rearward revetment became the outer side of the rampart.

The material for the main rampart was produced from quarry-pits behind it; the small ditch outside it yielded enough for the counterscarp bank alone.

The cross bank towards the w end of the hill was never finished. On the ground it is still possible to see where its marking-out bank was never covered by the final earthwork. This is clear at the centre of the cross-bank and between its s end and the edge of Lulworth Cove (where a modern hedge-bank lies 25 ft. w of the marking-out bank).

These marking-out banks and the evident use of gangs of men during the building recall similar methods used at Ladle Hill (Hants.) and elsewhere.

Bindon Hill fort has been interpreted as a beach-head fortification set up hurriedly by early Iron Age invaders anxious to secure control of the harbour of Lulworth Cove. This is likely to have occurred c. 400 BC. Calculations, based on a practical experiment (seen in fig. 24), show that the entire earthwork could have been built by 60 men in 16 days.

*Buzbury Rings, hill-slope fort and boundary ditches (ST/918059) 2 miles ESE of Blandford Forum (A350, A354); cut by B3082.

24 *Bindon Hill Iron Age hill-fort: posts of rampart-facing restored in ancient post-holes*

This site is one of the most interesting forts in Wessex because it is the only example in the region of a hill-slope fort – the type of enclosure which was deliberately set on the side of a hill and below the highest ground, instead of enclosing the high ground like a normal hill-fort. Its E side is well below its W side and higher ground commands it from the N and W.

There are 2 main earthworks at Buzbury, an outer one kidney-shaped and enclosing 12 acres; and an inner one, roughly circular and not concentric with the other, surrounding $2\frac{1}{4}$ acres. Each consists of a bank and ditch, the former having an average ht. of 6 ft. There is also a ditch, established by excavation to be deep and V-shaped, on the *inside* of the outermost bank. Around the SW side there are segments of a third bank and ditch situated between the other two.

The main entrance appears to be on the SW where the ends of the banks are knobbed up and very slightly in-turned.

It appears that those who built this type of fort were primarily concerned with the herding of cattle rather than military defence. They are concentrated in Cornwall, Devon and South Wales. Date of Buzbury, c. 2nd–1st century BC.

A series of ditches radiates from the Rings. These may be boundary ditches of the later Bronze Age or, more likely, belong to the Iron Age or Romano-British 'Celtic' fields visible hereabouts. The W ditch is sufficiently wide and deep to suggest that it was a track leading to the river. It might be contemporary with the Rings and connected with the watering of cattle.

*Chalbury, hill-fort and Bronze Age round barrows (SY/695838) $3\frac{1}{2}$ miles NE of Weymouth; NW of Sutton Poyntz, off A353.

This camp commands a great sweep of country to the S, particularly the anchorage of Weymouth Bay. The strategical choice of this site is thus obvious. The hill on which this camp stands has steep sides, making elaborate fortification of the top unnecessary. The rampart is in fact single, enclosing a pear-shaped area of about $8\frac{1}{4}$ acres. In most places this rampart now stands only about 1 ft. above the present level of the quarry-ditch which can be seen

behind it. At the N end it reaches a height of 5 ft. This was the most vulnerable part of the camp because it is overlooked by Bincombe Hill to the NW. The original entrance is at the SE corner. It is approached by a terrace or causeway leading up the hillside from the N.

Excavation has revealed that the fortifications consist of a rampart with a steep-sided, flat-floored ditch outside it and a broad shallow quarry ditch within. There was a marked berm or space, between the rampart and the ditch outside it. The rampart had been faced with locally derived limestone blocks. These can still be seen sticking up through the turf along the SE side of the camp. Behind this revetment the mass of the rampart had been heaped until it reached a ht. of at least 6 ft. On the inside, and in fact covered by the uppermost layers of bank material, an inner retaining wall was found, built to give stability to the whole structure. No timbering appears to have been used. The outer ditch had an original depth of 15 ft. and a surface width of about 30 ft. The one entrance (the break in the rampart at the SW is modern) was not excavated but appears to be a simple break with an approach up a causeway and terrace. It is probably metalled and must have been used by wheeled traffic bringing supplies to the considerable population living within. The quarry ditch inside the rampart is about 30 ft. broad (though very irregular) and dug to an average depth of 6 ft.

Upwards of 70 shallow circular depressions and platforms scattered about in the area thus defended represent huts and other structures used by those living here. One has been excavated. It had an internal diam. of 33 ft. Its wall had a stone footing 3–4 ft. thick, on top of which a timber frame and thatched roof is likely to have been built. The floor of the hut had been cut to a depth of about 1 ft. into the underlying rock. The hut contained ample evidence of human occupation, including much pottery, burnt wheat, food bones and charcoal. Three more huts have been examined, with the same results. One other hut, of wood, was found overlying the quarry ditch. It was notable for the disarticulated remains of human skeletons which were scattered in it. The occupation debris covered them, showing what scant regard these early Iron Age peoples had for the dead.

This camp was built probably before the first fort at Maiden Castle. It could belong to the 6th or 5th century BC.

At the centre of the camp, towards the E side, 2 Bronze Age round barrows can be seen. The N mound is about 66 ft. in diam. and 5 ft. high. The s one is a little smaller and appears to be a stone heap. One was excavated in the last century and yielded a cremated burial with 2 broken urns. Probable date, c. 1,250 BC.

Chaldon Herring, field system (SY/793807) 9 miles sw of Wareham (A351, A352), on coast, called The Warren, 2 miles w of West Lulworth (B3070).

The map reference is at the centre of a typical group of 'Celtic' fields very probably of Iron Age origin. They cover 100 acres and are associated with settlements not now easy to see. There is a right of way along downs and across these fields from West Lulworth. Date, 1st millenium BC.

*Coney's Castle, hill-fort (SY/372975) 3¾ miles NE of Lyme Regis (A35, A3070), s of Marshwood (B3165).

The end of a ridge has been enclosed by earthworks of 2 periods. The earlier camp, which has an internal area of about 5 acres, consists of 2 banks with a ditch between them, well preserved on the N and E. On the w, the steep slope of the hillside has required the builders to make only a single bank. A modern road cuts across the camp and utilises what appears to be the only entrance, through the N side.

At a later date a small rectangular enclosure was added to the s end of the fort: its defences are likewise double on the E and s and single on the w. Not dated.

*Dungeon Hill, hill-fort (ST/689074) 4¼ miles NE of Cerne Abbas (A352), 1¼ miles N of Buckland Newton (B3143).

Originally the defences of this fort consisted of 2 banks with a ditch between them. Except on the E side, only the inner bank and the ditch are visible. These enclose an oval area of 9 acres. The main bank is large; in most places it rises 8 ft. above the plateau within. The entrances on the E and W sides are modern. An original entrance gap is at the s end. Not dated.

*Eggardun, hill-fort (SY/542947) 4¾ miles ENE of Bridport (A35, A3066); 1¼ miles SE of Powerstock.

This is one of the most spectacular and undamaged hill-forts in Dorset. It has an internal area of over 20 acres. Its main defences consist of 3 banks with ditches between them. Except at the E and NW, the land falls away sufficiently steeply to make this an adequate defence in the multi-rampart style. Original entrances at the E and NW face level ground. The innermost rampart at the E entrance is slightly in-turned and there is only 1 main bank and ditch beyond it. They are elaborately in-turned and there are minor earthworks between these 2 earthworks. A short section of bank and ditch runs south to the top of the hill-slope, immediately outside the entrance. The NW entrance is not in-turned; here the outer fort ramparts are set further out than elsewhere, creating defence in great depth along this flat ridge. The gaps through them are staggered. At a later stage an enclosure has been added by building a new earthwork further out.

In Iron Age times a landslide appears to have carried away the main defences in the middle of the s side. These were repaired by digging a wide ditch in the fallen material at the E end and rebuilding the outer bank and ditch. An additional bank and ditch was added at the base of the hill opposite the area of landslip: this has a gap in it for a track which leads up to the E entrance.

The whole area within the defences is covered with circular hollows which represent storage pits subsequently filled up with rubbish and with traces of hut circles, evidence that occupation here was permanent. Among them is a series of very small mounds which has not yet been explained, and also 2 barrows of the Bronze Age.

The outer ramparts with deep in-turned entrances must post-date the inner system, Eggardon developing over several centuries.

*Giant's Hill, settlement (ST/669023) ¾ mile NE of Cerne Abbas (A352).

There are well-preserved remains of a settlement with fields, perhaps of the Iron Age, about ¼ mile NE of the Giant. These are on top of Giant Hill. They lie 350 yds. NE of a stout bank and ditch which cut across Giant Hill, presumably a Bronze or Iron Age land boundary. The settlement itself incorporates 1 large cross-bank and ditch which may also belong to this boundary system.

The settlement comprises an oval enclosure with 2 entrances, 2 hut circles on its NW side, a third hut circle NE of it and beyond the incorporated cross-bank of the boundary system, and 2 other larger, rectangular enclosures; a droveway follows the SE sides of the latter. A bank and ditch lie NE of the settlement, perhaps protecting it, while further away in this direction the remains of 'Celtic' fields can be seen. Rubbish and storage pits can be found in the area of the hut circles. Date, Iron Age, or perhaps Romano-British.

Grim's Ditch, enclosure ditch. See Hampshire, p. 136.

*Grimston Down, settlement (SY/646955) 4½ miles NW of Dorchester, 1 mile NE of junction of A356 and A37.

The substantial remains of a farmstead set among the 'Celtic' fields its owners tilled can be found on this down. The fields can be traced over an area of 100 acres; roughly at the centre of these (map ref. above), several sunken tracks lead to a group of small banked enclosures which must mark the sites of farm buildings and paddocks for livestock. These features are immediately W of Grimston Down Plantation. Three such enclosures can be made out, a complete one on the W, with entrances E and W; a larger one NE of it, with an in-turned entrance facing N and a sunken track running through this, and a third enclosure, badly damaged by ploughing, to the S. Two small enclosures can just be traced some 100 yds. further to the S.

Undatable without excavation, this farmstead probably belongs to the Iron Age.

*Hambledon Hill, hill-fort (ST/845126) ¾ mile E of Child Okeford, 1¾ miles SW of Iwerne Minster (A350).

The ramparts of the Iron Age hill-fort encircle the N of 3 spurs which meet immediately to the S of it: the Neolithic camp at this junction has been described above (p. 99) together with 2 long barrows,

one of which lies at the centre of the earthworks now to be described. Two banks and ditches with counterscarp bank encircle the 31-acre bow-shaped top of the hill. Except at the SE, these are now little more than terraces in the steep hillsides. Behind the innermost rampart there is a broad quarry ditch or terrace around the N ⅔ of the hill-fort but becoming irregular round the SE end. There is an original entrance at the NE, damaged by a chalkquarry. It appears to have been a simple break in the ramparts giving access to the quarry scoop around the interior, but one end of the counterscarp bank is slightly out-turned here. The SW entrance, which has an elongated barbican of 2 banks and a ditch, has one side of the innermost bank in-turned. The SE entrance is the most elaborate and has developed as the defences here have been altered. Its passage through the innermost ramparts is in-turned. Once outside, outworks made it necessary to swing SE along the edge of the combe, following a ledge just below the highest point here. At the SE, the outworks are separated from the main defences by a space c. 50 yds. wide and comprise 2 pairs of massive banks and ditches; the inner of these changes direction and height at its NE end, perhaps suggesting a 2-stage development. The hill-fort has developed in 3 phases over several hundred years but awaits more precise dating. The earliest fort is at the N, enclosing about 12 acres. Its original S limit is marked by a now slight ditch (the bank has been removed). Next, a further 8 acres were enclosed by extending the innermost defences further S with a cross-bank S of the long barrow. It may have had an entrance at its SE corner. This cross-bank is well preserved although a hut platform has been built into its E end. Finally, the S ⅓ was enclosed, perhaps including the outermost ditch and bank around the whole fort, including the SE outworks at this time.

Within, over 200 hut platforms can be counted: their floors are 15–45 ft. in diam. The juxtaposition of major hill-forts like Hambledon and **Hod** (below) is matched in many parts of Britain.

*Hengistbury Head, promontory fort and Bronze Age round barrows (SZ/164910) on coast S of Christ Church. Best approached from Southbourne. Finds in Red House Museum, Christ Church.

Hengistbury Head is a long narrow peninsula forming the s side of Christ Church harbour. It is composed of gravel with sand on top, and since Bronze Age times has attracted settlers from inland, and traders from the continent seeking a landfall.

Sites of the Bronze Age consist of a series of bowl-barrows, 7 on the head and 2 on the low ground to the NW. One of the latter, the nearest to the Iron Age earthworks cutting off the peninsula (below), yielded a grave group of unusual richness. A large collared urn was found inverted over a cremation close to the centre of the barrow and nearly at its base. Together with bones in the urn, there was an incense cup, 3 amber beads, 2 hemispherical sheet-gold covers for a button and a halberd pendant of amber with a little blade of bronze. The last 2 are characteristic Wessex pieces; their discovery here must indicate one of the trade routes from the chalk lands of Wiltshire and Dorset to the continent and ultimately to the Mediterranean. Before excavation, this barrow was 100 ft. in diam. and 7 ft. high.

Two other barrows, at the w end of Warren Hill, were also excavated in 1911–12. They were found to cover cremations in urns of the Wessex Bronze Age. All these barrows must be dated c. 1,700–1,400 BC.

The Iron Age earthworks lie across the peninsula, their N ends curving E at Wick Hams, their s ends disappearing over the slight cliff edge above the beach – where good cross sections of banks and ditches can be seen. The area of Hengistbury Head which they cut off is nearly 1 square mile.

These earthworks extend for a distance of some 1,500 ft. They consist of 2 banks, the inner being the more massive, with a ditch in front of each. There is a simple entrance gap 18 ft. wide through the centre, which must be considered original. At the N end these defences curved round E to cover the low ground facing the harbour; 18th-century maps show that this happened also at the other end.

The inner rampart, which appears to have been heightened after its original construction once or twice in the Iron Age,

has an average ht. of 12 ft. above level ground. The outer bank is nowhere more than half this ht. No wooden revetting or internal strengthening has so far been found in either bank. The inner ditch was originally about 40 ft. wide and 12 ft. deep. The outer ditch, today only visible in the section exposed by the cliff at the s end, has a width of 20 ft. and a depth of 6½ ft.

On the land thus protected, evidence of extensive occupation from c. 500 BC to the Roman period has been found. Despite extensive excavation, the earthworks remain undated. A feature of the last Iron Age occupation is the 3,000 locally minted coins of the type now known as 'Hengistbury Head'.

*Hod Hill, hill-fort and Roman fort (ST/ 856106) 3¼ miles NW of Blandford Forum, immediately SW of junction of B-road to Child Okeford and A350. Finds in the British Museum.

This hill-fort is roughly rectangular in plan and encloses 54 acres. Along the N, E and s the defences comprise 2 massive banks and ditches, with a counterscarp and an irregular quarry ditch behind the innermost bank. Along the steep w side there is a slighter bank, ditch and counterscarp bank. There are 2 original entrances, at the NE corner, Steepleton Gate and at the SW, West Gate. The NW and central E gates are Roman and the SE gate recent. Excavations (1951–8) have revealed that the NE gate was inserted as an addition to the original plan; it has an outwork of 2 banks and medial ditch which enforced entry along a narrow passage from the s: the main banks are in-turned. It was shown that the entrance arrangements here were evolved over a long period. West Gate is also in-turned and is original. It has outworks which appear to be unfinished. At the NW corner of the hill-fort there are traces of an outwork, evidently an unfinished addition, intended to enclose level ground here. The platform it encloses is divided by a slight bank, probably Roman. Originally the interior of the hill-fort was covered with the huts, storage pits and other structures of a rich, thriving community living permanently within the ramparts. The quadrant in the SE corner of the hill-fort which has never been ploughed has traces of over 240 structures of various kinds, mainly circular huts with an average diam. of 30 ft. Some include additional curved extensions enclosing stables or other features; certain huts are noticeably larger than others, suggesting that there were differences in wealth and position among these Celts. This hill-top was first fortified with ramparts about 400 BC, though occupation probably began earlier. Evidence for a final attack by the Romans has been found.

The site is of exceptional interest because an early Roman fort was constructed in the NW corner soon after the Conquest. Units of a legion and some cavalry were stationed here, probably to act as a police force over the large farming population in Cranborne Chase while it was being subjected to serfdom.

The fort has been excavated from 1951–7. Its fortifications consist of an outermost ditch with vertical outer face and sloping inner face, separated from 2 inner ditches and a rampart by a flat space 40 ft. wide. With this arrangement an enemy, once across the first ditch, would find his retreat cut off by its vertical outer face and himself fired on by those on the rampart. The middle and inner ditches were cut originally to depths of $4\frac{1}{2}$ ft. and $6\frac{1}{2}$ ft., and widths of $7\frac{1}{2}$ ft. and 11 ft. respectively. The first was narrow and steep-sided, with a narrow slot at the bottom; the innermost was wider, with a steep outer face. The rampart behind all these works was of turf and chalk, on a foundation of logs, with a vertical back. Of the gates, the E (*porta praetoria*) was double and wooden, set between flanking towers. The S gate (*porta principalis dextra*) was single and rebuilt once. It was found to overlie an Iron Age hut dismantled to allow this. There is a third gate at the NW – Hanford Gate. This was made by cutting a gap through the Iron Age ramparts and lining it with timbers. At some stage during the Roman occupation this gate was deliberately demolished.

Causeways from the E and S gates lead to the headquarters building (*principia*) which has been identified at the centre of the fort. Behind it lay the commandant's house. Barracks and latrines for the legionaries, stables for the horses, a granary, sheds and a chalk-cut water cistern with a capacity of 1,900 gallons have been found arranged neatly within the fort. The stables were near Hanford Gate, making it easy to lead the horses down to water. All the buildings were of timber, and wattle-and-daub. At some stage the S part of the fort was destroyed by fire.

*Maiden Castle, hill-fort, Neolithic long barrow, Romano-British temple (SY/ 668885) $1\frac{3}{4}$ miles SW of Dorchester, reached best by road to Winterborne Monkton. Finds in Dorchester Museum.

The hill on which Maiden Castle stands was first selected for habitation by a group of early Neolithic farmers from W Europe who built a causewayed camp of 2 ramparts on the line followed by the first Iron Age hill-fort – and for that reason hidden from our view. This Neolithic camp set at the E end of the hill enclosed an area of some 10 acres and would have been in use about 3,500 BC.

Generations – perhaps centuries – later, a long barrow of unusual length and shape was erected along the top of the hill. It had a length of 1,790 ft., runs nearly E/W and bends sharply S where it runs over the ditches of the earlier causewayed camp: its E end reaches nearly to the centre of the latter. Its quarry ditches are about 65 ft. apart and originally there would have been a substantial mound between them. The mound was laid out to follow the highest contour of the hill. At the E end, on the central axis of the site, a ritual pit filled with early Neolithic (Windmill Hill) pottery, limpet shells and animal bones was found. Seventy ft. further W, also on the central axis, the excavators of 1934–7 discovered the bones of a man of 25–35, who had been killed, hacked to pieces and his brain removed, a hideous form of foundation burial. Ten yds. to the SE, and also probably contemporary with the mound, the skeletons of 2 children had been buried, furnished with a tiny Neolithic pot.

This site, its architecture inspired by that of the long barrows and bank barrows, is now only revealed to the visitor by the outlines of the archaeologist's trenches dug at regular intervals along its N ditch. Its E end is 125 ft. SE of the Romano-British temple. Its S ditch passes 10 ft. N of the modern dew-pond which lies immediately

25   *Maiden Castle Iron Age hill-fort: hut foundation, hoard of slingstone ammunition in foreground, right*

outside the w side of the partly demolished rampart of the earliest Iron Age hill-fort (see below). If you stand on this rampart and look w, the Neolithic mound is just visible. It was probably built c. 3,000–2,500 BC.

In the ?6th century BC, the first Iron Age ramparts were erected here, enclosing 16 acres at the E end of the hill. The w side of this fort lies to the E of the modern dew-pond mentioned above; the Romano-British temple lies 350 ft. further E. There were entrances through the E and w sides, the former being double.

All but the w side of this small fort was incorporated in the later earthworks which confront the visitor. The w side, however, was partly levelled in Iron Age times when the ramparts were extended to enclose the whole hill (below).

This first rampart was revetted back and front with stout timbers: it was 12 ft. wide and originally probably 10 ft. high. Outside it, separated from it by a 10 ft. berm, was a ditch 50 ft. in width and dug to a depth of 20 ft. Outside the E entrance there

had been a cobbled surface perhaps used as a cattle market.

Early in the 4th century BC the rampart of phase 1 was extended w to fortify the whole hill. It enclosed about 47 acres of land. Its rampart differed from that of the first phase in that there was no berm or gap between bank and ditch; the new bank was not revetted. The earliest w entrance was double, like that at the E end of the hill. Soon after this extension, however, both entrances were furnished with simple outworks revetted with timber and stone. All this work is hidden beneath the ramparts of the hill-fort in its final form. The skeleton of a woman in a pit (fig. 27) was found at the junction of periods 1 and 2 on the N side of the hill-fort. This must represent a foundation burial dedicating the enlarged fort.

Within these earthworks, a large population lived permanently in wood and stone huts connected by roughly metalled tracks. Pits for storage and rubbish were dug everywhere (figs. 25, 26).

Early in the 2nd century BC new im-

26   *Maiden Castle Iron Age hill-fort: storage pits*

migrants from France came to this site and rebuilt it, heightening the main rampart, revetting it with timber and limestone (from Upwey, 2 miles distant), adding an outer line of bank and ditch and making the outworks of both entrances more elaborate. These people depended on the sling as their chief weapon: defence in depth was therefore sought. Towards the end of the 1st century BC the defences of the fort were brought to their present form. In particular, the entrances were remodelled to prevent easy passage to the actual gates through the innermost rampart: fighting platforms and hoards of slingstones were placed outside the E gateways; these themselves were revetted with stone and sentry boxes were built at their inner ends.

The last pre-Roman period of occupation at Maiden Castle began c. 25 AD, when people using wheel-thrown pottery, some Roman pots obtained by trade, and casting their own coinage appeared on the site and repaired the defences which had

27   *Maiden Castle hill-fort: Iron Age foundation burial at junction of periods 1 and 2*

once again fallen into decay. The whole of
the interior appears to have been cleaned
up, rubbish pits being filled in and roads
remetalled.

Between 43 and 44 AD, Maiden Castle
was stormed and sacked by Vespasian's
legion in the course of its advance west-
wards. The main attack was launched on
the E gate which was itself demolished.
Immediately outside it a cemetery containing the bodies of those inhabitants
slain in the fight was uncovered during the
excavations (fig. 28).

In the Romano-British period the local
population was shifted into the valley – to
Durnovaria, the earliest Dorchester. The
area within the ramparts of Maiden Castle
came under the plough. Between 47 and
350 AD the Neolithic long mound was
almost levelled. Between AD 350 and 370 3
buildings were erected at the E end of the
hill, an oval hut, a Celtic temple and a
small adjoining house of 2 rooms. The
foundations of the temple and house are
still visible. The temple building consisted

of a *cella*, 16 ft. square, surrounded by a
veranda whose low outer wall perhaps
originally supported short pillars. The
walls of the latter were plastered inside and
out and it had a floor of brick *tesserae*. A
wooden fence surrounded the temple and
a well-made path led to its entrance which
faces E. Among the fragments representing
a variety of cult objects found in the
vicinity of the temple, a three-horned bull
and figures of Diana and Minerva should
be mentioned.

The small two-roomed house on the N
side of the temple probably belonged to a
resident priest.

Mortared walls were erected across the
E gateways of the Iron Age hill-fort: a 10 ft.
gap was left through the N wall and a
metalled track led through to the temple.
Nettlecombe Tout, promontory fort (ST/
737032) 5½ miles NNW of Puddletown
(A35, A354), 1¾ miles S of Mappowder.

This may be an unfinished fort. Protected by steep hillsides NE and NW, the
spur is cut across at the SE by a bank and

28   *Maiden Castle Iron Age hill-fort: early east entrance and roadway, this part later
blocked; war cemetery in foreground*

ditch. About 14 acres are enclosed. There may be an original entrance at the sw end of the rampart. Here there are traces of an extra earthwork outside it. Not dated.

*Pilsdon Pen Camp,** hill-fort (ST/413013) 1¾ miles sw of Broadwindsor (B3162, B3163, B3164); n of B3164. Finds in Dorchester Museum.

This camp encloses 7¾ acres. It occupies the end of a spur, with steep natural slopes aiding defence everywhere but on the NW. The earthworks comprise 2 banks and ditches with a counterscarp bank. Modern hedge-banks obscure the inner ditch on the NE and the outer ditch on the sw. At the NW there is a space between the 2 main banks.

Three entrances appear to be original;

29   Poundbury: Iron Age hill-fort, cutting across bank and ditch

these face SE, SW and N. At the first, the 2 outer banks stop short so as to form an oblique line of approach. There is a platform between the 2 main ramparts on the SE side of the second entrance.

Recent excavation of low mounds in the centre has shown a sequence of occupation beginning with huts, c. 26 ft. in diam., with traces of other structures: later, an area 160 ft. wide and of unknown length, defined by a straight bedding trench with buttress offsets (the NW side comprised 2 bedding trenches) was built over the huts. It had an entrance at its N corner but its purpose is unexplained. It was replaced by low banks before AD 43.

*Poundbury, lowland fort and Romano-British aqueduct (SY/683912) ¾ mile NW of Dorchester on N side of minor road to Bradford Peverell. Finds in Dorchester Museum.

The earthworks of this camp are roughly rectangular in plan and enclose an area of 15 acres. There are 2 lines of ramparts on all sides except the N, where the presence of the River Frome called only for 1 (though it has 2 ditches). The original entrance was through the E inner rampart, close to the mouth of the modern railway tunnel. The inner rampart was built of chalk heaped behind a vertical timber revetment and separated from the ditch by a berm. The bank would have been originally about 13 ft. high, and the V-shaped ditch in front of it the same in depth (fig. 29). This work was carried out in ?c. 6th century BC, contemporary with or slightly earlier than the first phase of Maiden Castle. Then, shortly before the Roman Conquest, the outer ditch and bank were added and the inner bank widened and heightened: a limestone parapet was built on its crest. Those responsible for this reconstruction probably belonged to the tribe which had seized Maiden Castle; Poundbury commanded a ford across the river and an approach to the great hill-fort.

A flat platform on the side of the Frome valley approaching the NW corner of the Iron Age camp marks the course of an aqueduct channel, originally 5 ft. deep and about 10 ft. wide, its cross section being rectangular. In places it was lined with puddled clay. It brought a stream of water from higher up the Frome (beginning 6½ miles to the SW, in Foxleaze withy bed), to *Durnovaria*. It may have been built in the late 1st century AD: in view of the proximity of the town to the river its construction appears never to have been justified.

Rawlsbury Camp, hill-fort (ST/767058) 5 miles SSW of Sturminster Newton (A357, B3091, B3092), 2 miles SE of Haselbury Bryan.

Roughly pear-shaped, this powerful hill-fort encloses over 5½ acres. Its defences comprise 2 main banks with a medial ditch but these vary with the terrain. At the W there is an outer ditch. The N side of the fort has been mutilated by trackways. The entrance is at the E. Here the banks turn outwards and the inner rampart on the S side bends sharply S to overlook the butt-end of the medial ditch here. A lengthy, well-covered passage to the interior is thus defined. Not dated.

*Spettisbury Rings,** hill-fort (ST/915019) 3¼ miles SE of Blandford Forum (A350, A354), SE of Spettisbury railway station, on S side of A350. Finds in British Museum.

A small, roughly oval hill-fort overlooking the River Stour and enclosing 4 acres, this site is situated in a sheltered position on a hill-slope and below its crest. The E defences have been destroyed by the railway cutting of 1857. At the N, near the cutting, the defensive bank and ditch is slight. Elsewhere along the circuit there are notable changes in the strength of the earthwork (in places it is 20 ft. above the original land surface) which suggest strongly that it was never finished. The entrance at the NW is original. Along the N it is possible to see that 'Celtic' field banks are linked to the defences.

When the railway cutting was built, a great hoard of Iron Age tools, weapons and ornaments was found in a pit dug into the hill-fort ditch, dating from the Roman Conquest period (c. AD 43–44). With it there were about 130 skeletons, many bearing evidence of a violent death and also Roman weapons. Probably we have here the farmstead of a rich Celtic princeling, hastily fortified by earthworks against the advancing Romans but the work overtaken and the chief and his retainers slaughtered by the Roman legionaries.

Durham

BRONZE AGE

*Batter Law, round barrow (NZ/406460) 1¾ miles NNW of Easington (A19, A182, B1283), ½ mile SE of Hesledon Moor East. Grave goods in Sunderland Museum.

Damaged by the plough and mutilated by ditches dug across it recently, this barrow is about 60 ft. in diam. and 5–6 ft. high. Its primary burial has not yet been found, but a secondary inhumation was uncovered in 1911. It was crouched and protected by some large stone slabs. The bones were those of a middle-aged male. A fine flint knife had been put in the grave. Date, c. 1,700–1,400 BC.

Hempstone Knoll, round barrow (NY/984251), 2¼ miles E of Middleton-in-Teesdale (B6277, B6278, B6282), ½ mile N of B6282, SE of Foggerthwaite House Farm.

This barrow, diam. c. 100 ft., ht. c. 7 ft., lies in the valley of the Bell Sike and commands a view of its confluence with the Eggleston Burn to the SE. It is possible that the growth of rushes around the E side may represent the site of a surrounding ditch: the mound is of earth and stones. Date, c. 1,700–1,400 BC.

*Murton Moor, round barrow (NZ/382460) 2¾ miles NW of Easington A19, A182, B1283), ½ mile NNE of South Hetton (A182, B1280). Grave goods in Sunderland Museum.

This round barrow, now under plough, is about 150 ft. in diam. and 4 ft. high. There is no trace of a surrounding ditch. A cremation burial was found 3 ft. s of the centre, placed in a hole just above the old land surface. A flint knife and scraper, both burnt, were with it. The primary burial may not have been found. Date, c. 2,200–1,400 BC.

Rantherley Hill, round barrow (NY/950379), 2½ miles WSW of Stanhope (B6278, B6293), ½ mile s of Eastgate (B6293), ¼ mile s of Billing Shield Farm.

Its prehistoric origin doubted by some, this appears to be a round cairn, lacking a surrounding ditch and evidently made from the local limestone, perhaps quarried from the hollow in the ridge above the mound. Its diam. is c. 70 ft. and ht. c. 12 ft. It has a commanding position, overlooking the river Wear, with views E and W. Date, c. 1,700–1,400 BC.

Swinkley Knoll, round barrow (NY/983242), 6¼ miles NW of Barnard Castle (A66, A67, A688), 2¼ miles ESE of Middleton-in-Teesdale (B6277, B6278, B6282), ¼ mile s of B6282.

A good example of a valley-sited barrow, this mound is situated at the w end of a natural sandhill which overlooks the river. The barrow is c. 50 ft. in diam. and c. 4 ft. high. It is composed, apparently, of river-worn stones and soil; around the SW side stones protrude which suggest the presence of a retaining kerb. Date, c. 1,700–1,400 BC.

Cultivation terraces, probably medieval, can be seen on the w side of the hill.

IRON AGE

Maiden Castle, promontory fort (NZ/283417) on SE edge of Durham, N of A177.

This roughly rectangular fort is protected on all but the w side by steep natural slopes. There are slight traces of a bank around the camp on the N, E and S sides. On the w side there is 1 rampart across the promontory, 18 ft. wide and 7 ft. high, with a ditch outside, still 4 ft. deep and the remains of a slight inner bank at the s end. There may have been an original entrance (followed by the footpath) near the N end of this side, where there is a break in the outer ditch. About 2 acres are thus enclosed. Undated.

Essex

Ambresbury Banks, hill-fort (TL/438004) 1¾ miles sw of Epping (A11) on s side of A11. N end of Epping Forest.

The plan of this camp is roughly rectangular and it encloses 11–12 acres. The defences consist of a bank, still 7 ft. high above the interior, a ditch and a counter-scarp bank (not everywhere visible). Excavation revealed that the ditch was V-shaped, 22 ft. wide at the top and dug to a depth of 10 ft. The well-developed in-turned entrance in the se side has been recently shown to be medieval. The only original entrance is a simple stone-lined gap at the centre of the w side. Undated.

Berechurch Dyke, see **Colchester.**

***Colchester** (*Camulodunum*). Belgic tribal capital and barrow. Finds in town museum; detailed guide sold there.

Before the Roman provincial capital was set up at the centre of modern Colchester, a late Iron Age Belgic tribe, the Trinovantes (fig.14), had their capital in the area of Lexden Park. During the 100 years prior to the Roman conquest this tribe had suffered much at the hands of its neighbours, the Catuvellauni from Hertfordshire and others from Kent. Indeed its appeal to Rome for help led to Julius Caesar's 2 campaigns in England in 55 and 54 BC. By AD 10 the Trinovantes had been absorbed by the greatest of Belgic chiefs, Cunobelinus, a Catuvellaunian, who became styled *Rex Britannorum*, for he also conquered Kent. He left Hertfordshire and set up his capital at Colchester, calling it *Camulodunum* on the fine series of gold, silver and bronze coins which he struck there. When Cunobelinus died c. AD 40 the jealousy of his neighbours and the rivalry of his sons opened the way for a third campaign by the Romans, this time a full-scale invasion with *Camulodunum* as its first objective. Since the se Belgae fought and were defeated s of the Thames, *Camulodunum* fell to Rome within a few days of the invasion in AD 43.

The late Iron Age tribes in Britain, particularly those of Belgic culture, protected their settlements with far flung earthworks quite unlike the more compact hill-forts of their neighbours. The straggling entrenchments w of Colchester are typical defensive works of these people.

The area of Colchester forms a great peninsula of 12 square miles, bounded on the N by the River Colne and by the Roman River on the s. The Iron Age earthworks to the w of the modern town cut off this peninsula and protect the only easy line of approach – from the w. Recent excavations have suggested that the earliest Belgic stronghold here was the area NW of Oliver's Farm and s of the B1022 (about TL/965220). It is defended by an earthwork following the contours and visible in places between Oliver's Thicks (wood) and Chest Wood, where it crosses the Roman River. Later, more elaborate earthworks were built to cut off the land between the 2 rivers. The westernmost of these is **Gryme's Dyke** (TL/956267 to TL/956214); behind it is **Triple Dyke** (TL/963260, Mott's Farm, to Gosbeck's Farm, TL/974229) and further to the E there is **Lexden Dyke** (TL/978270 to TL/974245). Unlike the earliest enclosure, these earthworks are laid out in a series of straight sections facing w. They protected a settlement which was concentrated behind Lexden Dyke and at its s end. It is likely that **Berechurch Dyke** belongs to this system (TM/003233 to TL/997203).

Finally, the capital of Cunobelinus seems to have been concentrated behind a fourth Dyke, not now visible, **Sheepen Dyke,** w of Sheepen Farm and mainly s of A12 (about TL/985257). This happened about AD 10.

Except for Triple Dyke, these earthworks consist of a single stout bank and ditch, the former faced with turf and often 12 ft. high. In places the ditch was 70 ft. wide at ground level and nearly 12 ft. deep.

The area protected by the dykes was never completely built over in Iron Age times. It included arable and pasture for the whole tribe, whose houses and temples were scattered about among the fields. But under Cunobelinus the Sheepen Farm area, about a ¼ square mile, saw a concentration of dwellings particularly on the low ground near the river. These were so flimsy that very little was found during extensive excavation: they must have been of wattle-and-daub, providing a standard of comfort as squalid as the material culture of those living in them was high. The wealth which these Belgae possessed, suggested by their household equipment and their trade even across the channel, can be appreciated by studying the collections in Colchester Museum.

Lexden Tumulus (TL/975247), c. 75 ft. in diam., was probably the burial mound of Addedomarus or one of his family. It contained one of the richest Belgic grave groups in England, deposited with a cremation in a large pit beneath the mound. Most of the objects had been ritually smashed or mutilated before being deposited with the bones of this prince at the end of the 1st century BC. They are displayed in Colchester Museum.

A series of flat graves has been found close to this barrow, all containing rich deposits. Clearly this was the cemetery of the tribal aristocracy.

When Roman Colchester was set up to the E, the Belgic areas of habitation were levelled and used as working quarters.

Danbury, hill-fort (TL/779052) 4½ miles E of Chelmsford, on S side of A414. Surrounds St John's Church. Finds in Colchester Museum.

A denuded bank and ditch surround the churchyard, originally enclosing c. 8 acres in an oval plan. The N side has been destroyed by the church and rectory; the entrance cannot now be traced. Not dated.

Gryme's Dyke, see **Colchester.**

Lexden Dyke and barrow, see **Colchester.**

Lexden Park, Belgic tribal capital and barrow. See **Colchester.**

Loughton Camp, hill-fort (TQ/418975) 3¾ miles SW of Epping (A11), ¾ mile NNW of Loughton (A121). In Epping Forest.

This camp is sub-rectangular in plan

and encloses about 6½ acres. The defences consist of a single bank and ditch, augmented by steep natural slopes on the W side. Without excavation it is not possible to say which gap in the earthworks is an original entrance. A stream rises in the SE corner. Undated.

Pitchbury Ramparts, hill-fort (TL/966290) 3 miles NW of Colchester, ½ mile NE of West Bergholt (A133).

The NW part of this hill-fort survives, protected by the wood. It was oval in plan and enclosed about 4½ acres. The defences consist of a bank, ditch and counterscarp bank. There is a simple gap in these facing NW, which may be an original entrance. Undated.

Ring Hill, hill-fort (TL/515382) 1½ miles W of Saffron Walden (A130, B1052, B1053), between A11 and railway.

Oval in plan, this fort follows the contour of the hill it encloses, protecting about 16½ acres. It overlooks the River Cam. Denuded and planted with trees, the defences consist of a bank, ditch and counterscarp bank, of which only the ditch is well preserved. Only excavation can establish which of the gaps in the earthworks are original entrances. Undated.

Sheepen Farm, Belgic tribal capital. See **Colchester.**

Triple Dyke, see **Colchester.**

Wallbury Camp, hill-fort (TL/492178) 2¼ miles S of Bishop's Stortford (A11, A119, A120); between A11 and Little Hallingbury.

The River Stort is overlooked by this camp which is set at the end of a spur. It is roughly D-shaped, the straight side on the W, and encloses about 31 acres. The defences consist of 2 banks and ditches and traces on the SE of a counterscarp bank. In places the inner bank rises 7 ft. above the interior. These earthworks are incomplete on the W side where the steep hill-slope makes elaborate fortification unnecessary. Of the several gaps in the defences, one facing NE and another near the middle of the W side may be prehistoric. Undated.

Gloucestershire

*NEOLITHIC

*Avening, long barrow burial chambers (ST/880983) 300 yds. N of Avening Church, E of A434.

There are 3 stone burial chambers set close together at the foot of a bank. They were erected there in 1806, having been removed from a long barrow nearby, perhaps that at ST/895978. It is said that they have the same relationship to each other now as they originally had in the barrow. The E chamber is about 6 ft. square, with 1 large capstone and an entrance of the port-hole type with a short approach passage. The middle chamber is rectangular, 5 ft. by 3 ft., with 1 capstone; its approach passage leads to a stone with a notch cut in its upper edge – half of another port-hole entrance. The W chamber is of similar size but lacks a capstone, passage or any form of blocking stone.

These port-hole entrances should be compared with those in the Rodmarton long barrow (p. 127); similar entrances are to be found in Spain, Portugal, N France and S Sweden. Date, c. 3,500–2,500 BC.

*Belas Knap, chambered long barrow (SP/ 022254) 1¾ miles s of Winchcombe (A46, B4078), W of road to Charlton Abbots. Finds in Cheltenham Museum.

Orientated N/S, Belas Knap is 174 ft. long and 60 ft. wide at its broader end. Here, at the N, 2 horn-like extensions of the barrow define a deep forecourt with a blind entrance at its centre (fig. 30). Burial chambers are to be found, 1 midway along the W side, 1 opposite it on the other side, a third between the latter and the S end and the fourth running N from the squared-off S end of the barrow. Each chamber is approached by a short passage. The mound comprises a core of oolitic limestone rubble with a carefully built revetting wall around it (restored by the Dept. of the Environment). At least 38 skeletons have been found in the chambers; several skulls appear to have been dealt a heavy blow just before, or soon after death. Among the small number of objects found with the bones, there were fragments of a perforated boar's tusk pendant, flint saw and sickleblades and hammer stones. Belas Knap may be dated 3,500–2,500 BC.

Bown Hill, chambered long barrow (SO/ 823018) ¼ mile s of B4066, 1¼ miles SW of Woodchester church (A46). Finds in

30   *Belas Knap: blind entrance to Neolithic chambered long barrow*

Cheltenham Museum.

This barrow, set E/W, is 180 ft. long and 60 ft. broad at the E end. In 1863 a rectangular chamber was found (already rifled) at the E end, approached by a forecourt. It contained the remains of at least 6 people. Quarrying has removed the E end. Fragments of pottery and the general layout suggest a date c. 3,500–2,500 BC for this tomb.

Colnpen, long barrow (SP/068084) ½ mile E of A429, 5 miles NE of Cirencester (A417, A419, A429).

It is likely that this unexcavated barrow contains stone burial chambers beneath its mound, like most Cotswold long barrows. Orientated E/W, it is about 300 ft. in length. Date, c. 3,500–2,500 BC.

Crickley Hill, causewayed camp. See Iron Age.

Eyford, chambered long barrow (SP/143257) 3 miles W of Stow-on-the-Wold (A424, A429, A436), 1¾ miles N of A436, ¾ mile N of Eyford Park. Grave goods in the British Museum.

This Cotswold tomb measures at least 110 ft. in length and is 45 ft. wide at the NE end where a U-shaped forecourt leads neither to chamber nor blind entrance. Four small, isolated chambers have been found in the mound, 1 on the N side towards the NE corner, 1 central near the SW end, another just N of this and a fourth S of it. Two were buried in the first; 2 adults, 3 children, an infant and a dog were found in the second; in the third there were 10 skeletons, 1 with a shale bead, while the fourth yielded 1 skeleton, that of a youth provided with a pottery bowl of Windmill Hill ware. Date, c. 3,500–2,500 BC.

Gatcombe Lodge, chambered long barrow (ST/884997) 1 mile N of Avening Church (A434), at N tip of Gatcombe Park.

This long barrow lies NE/SW, its dimensions being about 190 ft. by 70 ft. At the NE end there are the remains of a blind entrance. The only burial chamber so far discovered is on the N side, near the E end. This is built of 5 uprights with 2 more defining an entrance. A capstone roofs it and there is much fine drystone walling inside. One skeleton was found here in 1871. A large, partly buried stone on the N side, nearer the W end, may belong to another chamber. Date, c. 3,500–2,500 BC.

A standing stone, the Long Stone, is to be seen in an adjoining field (p. 126).

Hetty Pegler's Tump, chambered long barrow (SO/789001) W of B4066, 1 mile N of Uley church (B4066). Finds in Guy's Hospital Museum. Entry key at nearby farm. Torch necessary.

Orientated E/W and in a commanding position, this mound is 120 ft. long and 85 ft. broad at its E end, where a deep forecourt gives access to a parallel-sided gallery from which 2 pairs of side chambers lead off. The end of the gallery forms a fifth chamber, the general arrangement resembling **West Kennet** (p. 220). Only the side chambers on the S side are now visible. At least 15 skeletons were found here in 1854; among the objects with them was part of a perforated boar's tusk.

In layout this tomb should be early in the Cotswold series, c. 3,500–3,000 BC.

Lamborough Banks, chambered long barrow (SP/107094) 1¾ miles N of Bibury (A433), 1 mile N of Ablington, in Lamborough Banks covert.

This is a badly damaged mound 280 ft. long and with a max. width of 100 ft. It is orientated SE/NW. A large upright stone can be seen at the S end, between horns defining a forecourt, together with traces of 2 internal drystone walls edging the mound, which were recorded by excavators in 1854. At this time a stone chamber was found near the slab, containing 1 skeleton. Date, c. 3,500–2,500 BC.

Leighterton, chambered long barrow (ST/819913), between Leighterton and the A46 to the W; 5½ miles S of Nailsworth (A46, A434).

This huge barrow is orientated E/W; it is 270 ft. long and 20 ft. high at the E end. In the 17th century a stone was said to stand at the E end and in 1700 3 burial chambers were excavated. They contained inhumations and it seems that there were urns filled with burnt human bones at their entrances. Date, c. 3,500–2,500 BC.

Lodge Park, Eastington, chambered long barrow (SP/143125) near the NE corner of Lodge Park, between Aldsworth (A433) and Northleach (A10, A429).

One of the few unexcavated long barrows in Britain, this one is 150 ft. in length and aligned SE/NW. Two uprights and a capstone at the E end, with traces of stones behind them, suggest chambers or blind entrance here where the barrow attains its maximum width of 75 ft. Rabbits active around the foot of the mound suggest that a ditch surrounds it. Date, c. 3,500–2,500 BC.

Long Stone, Minchinhampton, standing stones (ST/884999) about 300 yds. N of Gatcombe Park long barrow (above) on N side of road to Minchinhampton.

An oolite upright stands 7 ft. 9 ins. above the top of a slight mound. Another, 3 ft. 2 ins. high, is set in a wall 34 ft. away. Both stones are probably *in situ* and are perhaps the remains of a portal dolmen whose long mound may have been visible early in the 19th century. Date c. 3,500–3,000 BC.

*Notgrove, chambered long barrow (SP/096212) 4¼ miles W of Bourton-on-the-Water (A429, B4068), immediately S of B4068. Finds in Cheltenham Museum.

Notgrove long barrow is 160 ft. in length and has a max. width of 83 ft. It lies E/W, a well-defined forecourt giving access to an ante-chamber and gallery, with 2 pairs of side chambers leading off the latter. There is also an end chamber. The roof of this structure no longer exists. Behind these chambers the excavators found a polygonal closed chamber surrounded by its own circular drystone wall, the whole covered by the barrow mound. This can not now be seen. Much drystone walling was used in the construction of the barrow; the mound itself incorporated 2 surrounding walls, one set a few feet behind the other and both, it seems, covered by the rubble of the mound. No surrounding ditch has been discovered. Fires and other deposits found in the forecourt suggest elaborate burial rituals.

Human bones represent about 11 corpses including 3 children. Finds comprised early Neolithic Windmill Hill pottery, later Neolithic Peterborough and Beaker wares, a leaf-shaped flint arrowhead, bone tools and amulet and a large shale bead. This barrow was built c. 3,000 BC and remained in use for several generations.

*Nympsfield, chambered long barrow (SO/794013) 4¼ miles SW of Stroud (A46, A419), immediately W of B4066 to Dursley (A4135, B4066). Finds in Stroud Museum.

This cairn is at least 90 ft. long and has a max. width of 60 ft. It lies E/W. A deep forecourt at the E end leads into an ante-chamber behind which is a pair of side chambers and an end chamber. The roof is now missing. A drystone wall runs around the mound, hidden by barrow material as at Notgrove: at the E end the horns defining the forecourt cover 2 such revetting walls; at the W end this surrounding wall is concave and the open area beyond it provided evidence of fires and post-holes. There was also a hearth and a pit in the forecourt at the E end. The burial chambers were all enclosed by another wall, oval in plan, recalling, perhaps, the circular cist behind the main structure at Notgrove. There was no surrounding ditch.

The remains of some 20 burials have been found here, together with pottery of Windmill Hill and Peterborough types, a leaf-shaped flint arrowhead and a dog-whelk shell perforated for suspension. Some of the human bones had been charred by fire but not properly cremated. This barrow must have been built c. 3,000 BC and remained in use for a long time.

Pole's Wood, South, chambered long barrow (SP/167264) 1½ miles W of Stow-on-the-Wold (A424, A429, A436), 1,100 yds. SW of Upper Swell (B4077). Pottery in the British Museum.

The mound of this barrow, today sadly damaged, is 180 ft. long and orientated E/W. Max. width at the E end is 70 ft. Here a forecourt was visible in 1874, but it had neither entrance nor blind entrance. There is 1 visible burial chamber with approach passage on the N side, near the W end. Nine or 10 skeletons were found in the chamber, with 3 more in the passage outside. A bowl of Peterborough ware was found near the surface in the N horn at the E end. Date of barrow, c. 2,500 BC.

Pole's Wood, East, a similar long barrow, will be found 500 yds. NE.

Randwick, chambered long barrow (SO/825069) 2 miles NW of Stroud (A46, A419) on Randwick Hill, ¼ mile NW of church. Finds in Gloucester Museum.

Orientated NE/SW, this damaged barrow at one time had a length of 185 ft. and a max. width at the E end of 86 ft. The forecourt defined by horns gives access to a simple rectangular burial chamber, one of the 3 main designs in the layout of Cotswold chambered tombs (p. 16). Excavation in 1883 revealed that the material composing the mound incorporates a wall with offsets running down its centre. At least 4 skeletons have been found here. Date, c. 3,000 BC.

This barrow, orientated N/S is 130 ft. long and is highest at the N end where it is 70 ft. wide. Here there is set an upright stone 6 ft. high. No chambers have yet been found in Tinglestone. Date, c. 3,500–2,500 BC.

31 *Rodmarton: Neolithic chambered long barrow. Steps down to chamber entrance*

*Rodmarton (Windmill Tump), chambered long barrow (ST/933973) 3¾ miles NE of Tetbury (A433, A434, A4135), ½ mile N of A433. Finds in the British Museum.

This mound is about 180 ft. long and 70 ft. wide at its E end. Here a fine blind entrance lies at the centre of a forecourt. Nearly 40 ft. to the W there are 2 burial chambers approached by passages and short flights of steps from the N and S sides of the mound (fig. 31). Each had a porthole entrance, formed by pairs of uprights with semicircular notches cut in each. These features cannot now be seen. Remains of 13–18 individuals have been found here together with 2 fine leaf-shaped flint arrowheads. Date, c. 3,000 BC.

Swell, long barrow. See **Pole's Wood, South.**

Tinglestone, long barrow (ST/882989) ¾ mile N of Avening (A434), at the SE corner of Gatcombe Park. Surface finds in Gloucester Museum.

Uley, long barrow. See **Hetty Pegler's Tump.**

West Barrow, long barrow. See **Leighterton.**

West Tump, chambered long barrow (SO/912132) 1 mile S of Birdlip (A417, B4070), in Buckle Wood, W of B4070 to Stroud. Finds in Cheltenham Museum.

There is a blind entrance at the E end of this barrow; it has a length of 150 ft. and a width of 76 ft. At the W end a passage was found in 1880, leading in from the S side and giving access to a chamber. The remains of 20 were found scattered in the 2; the carefully disposed skeleton of a girl at the back of the chamber was the only one not in disorder. The bones of an infant were close to her. Four more skeletons appear to have been found in the forecourt at the E end. Date of erection, c. 3,000 BC.

Windmill Tump, chambered long barrow. See **Rodmarton.**

BRONZE AGE

Air Balloon Inn, barrow cemetery (SO/935159) 4¼ miles s of Cheltenham, in wood s of A436/B4070 junction.

This is a small cemetery of presumed early Bronze Age date – c. 1,700 BC, in the Wessex tradition. It consists of 1 very large and 2 small bowl-barrows situated so as to take advantage of the superb view towards the River Severn. Nothing is known of their contents.

*Snowshill, barrow cemetery (SP/092333) ½ mile sw of Snowshill, 2¾ miles s of Broadway (A44, A46). Grave goods in British Museum.

There are 6 bowl-barrows in this cemetery. One of them, 66 ft. in diam. and, in 1881, 5½ ft. high, covered a rectangular cist (4 ft. by 3 ft. by 2½ ft.) consisting of 4 slabs of oolite sunk partly into the subsoil and covered by a fifth slab. In it were found the bones of an adult, furnished with a large bronze dagger, a bronze spearhead of the earliest type, a bronze T-headed pin of central European inspiration and a stone battle-axe. This grave group should be compared with the even richer Wessex examples. It may be dated c. 1,700–1,400 BC.

*Soldier's Grave, round barrow (SO/794015) 230 yds. N of Nympsfield chambered long barrow (above); in wood. Finds in Stroud Museum.

This round barrow, 56 ft. in diam., originally about 8 ft. high and made of oolite rubble, contained a rock-cut, boat-shaped burial pit 11 ft. long, 4½ ft. wide and 3½ ft. deep (fig. 32; no longer visible); the pointed end faced due S. This pit was neatly lined with drystone walling; at the N end the bones of more than 28 people lay in a disordered heap, together with pottery. Animal bones and those of another adult human were found scattered in the material of the barrow-mound.

Here we have an example of the fusion of Neolithic and Bronze Age funeral customs – collective burial of the Stone Age under a circular mound of the succeeding Bronze Age tradition. Soldier's Grave may be dated c. 2,000–1,400 BC.

IRON AGE

*Bagendon, enclosure (SP/017060 – excavated area) 2½ miles NNW of Cirencester (A417, A429), w of A435. Finds in Cirencester Museum.

Recent excavation (at map ref.) has established that the area protected by the

32   *Soldier's grave: Bronze Age boat-shaped tomb, human bones piled in 'bow' end*

Bagendon earthworks was the tribal capital of the Dobunni (fig. 14) after they had come under the influence of the powerful Belgic Catuvellauni from Essex and Hertfordshire before AD 10. A mint was established at Bagendon and the community thrived – imported red wares from Italy and bronze and iron brooches and other ornaments made at the site by continental blacksmiths attest their prosperity.

Earthworks enclose about 200 acres, an area well provided with water and the natural protection of forests and surrounding hill-slopes. Along the N side the bank of **Scrubditch** (SP/010077 centre) still stands nearly 10 ft. high: its ditch faces s but it must nevertheless belong to the system of defensive earthworks round the Dubunnic capital. Along the E side a bank and ditch facing E follows the w side of the road from Woodmancote to Perrott's Brook (called Dykes on 1-in. O.S.). The bank stands 5 ft. towards the s end. There are traces of other banks and ditches E of this road but these are now levelled by cultivation and cannot be interpreted without excavation. The s side of the area is defined by a bank and ditch facing s, following the road called Welsh Way and on the s side of it. Though the ditch is almost silted up, the bank along this side is still clear. It may have been the citadel of the site.

Beckbury Camp, hill-fort (SP/064299) 1 mile E of Hailes Abbey, $\frac{1}{4}$ mile E of Hailes Wood; $2\frac{1}{2}$ miles NE of Winchcombe (A46, B4078).

This small camp is rectangular in plan and encloses $4\frac{1}{2}$ acres. It has a single bank and ditch. The latter is now almost filled but the bank is well preserved on the E and s. Possible entrances may have been at the NE and sw. Not dated.

Bloody Acre Camp, promontory fort (ST/689915) $4\frac{1}{4}$ miles w of Wotton-under-Edge (B4058, B4060), $\frac{3}{4}$ mile N of Cromhall, off B4058.

This may be considered a promontory fort, its main artificial defences facing w and enclosing roughly 10 acres. Triangular in plan, its NE and SE sides are protected by steep natural hill-slopes. On the sw there are 3 massive banks with silted-up ditches between them. The innermost bank and

part of the middle earthwork can also be seen on the NW. It is possible that an original entrance was at the N end of the line of earthworks cutting off the promontory. The inner of the 2 ramparts here bends E to follow the edge of the hillside for a short distance – forming in effect an in-turned entrance. Other gaps in the innermost bank further s are probably not prehistoric. Not dated.

Brackenbury Camp, promontory fort (ST/747948) 1 mile NW of Wotton-under-Edge (B4058, B4060); at w edge of Westridge Wood, E of B4060.

This is a triangular promontory fort protected on the s and w sides by a bank and ditch and by the natural slope of the hillside, and on the E by 2 stout widely spaced banks and ditches. The area thus defined is 8 acres. There is an entrance through the s side, approached from the s by a hollow way. Though overgrown with trees, the defensive arrangement of this fort shows how these military engineers of the Iron Age utilised land and added to natural fortification only where necessary. Not dated.

The Bulwarks, Minchinhampton. See **Minchinhampton.**

Cleeve Hill, Promontory fort (SO/985255) $2\frac{3}{4}$ miles NE of Cheltenham, E of A46, s of Cleeve Hill. Finds in Cheltenham Museum.

These widely spaced earthworks at the w edge of Cleeve Common cut off a slight promontory of about 2 acres. Precipitous land provides a natural defence on the w. The E sides are defended by 2 well-defined banks with a ditch outside each. There is no entrance gap through these; access may originally have been obtained around the ends of the earthworks. Not dated.

*Crickley Hill, promontory fort and Neolithic camp (SO/928161) $4\frac{1}{4}$ miles s of Cheltenham, $\frac{1}{2}$ mile w of junction of A417, A436 and B4070.

A triangular area of 9 acres, protected by steep hill-slopes N and s, is defended along the E by a convex-curving rampart comprising bank, ditch and traces of an outer bank. This hill-fort, dated by excavations (1969, continuing) to the 6th–5th century BC, had an entrance near the N end, in whose 3rd phase the curved outwork was added. The 1st rampart was drystone-faced, the front vertical and rear stepped and strengthened by a frame of vertical and horizontal timbers. This was incorporated in a slightly larger, dumped rampart with vertical drystone front, and finally replaced by a widened rampart whose front was stepped, and a broader ditch. The entrance had undergone many changes, including bastions back and front, gates with bridge over and ending with the outwork which had a gate at its outer end. The first phase hill-fort had been destroyed by fire and the site was abandoned early in the Iron Age (but re-occupied c. 6th century AD).

A roadway led from the first hill-fort gate to a group of at least 6 timber-framed long houses, their lengths c. 25–75 ft. and a series of store huts with raised floor, c. 12 ft. square. These houses were burnt, to be replaced in the next hill-fort phase by one large round house with porch facing W, diam. 50 ft., and at least 5 other huts with diams. c. 16–25 ft. and porches facing SE.

A slight bank and ditch 450 ft. to the W incorporating 2 periods, is Neolithic, c. 3,000 BC, part of a causewayed camp which included a second bank and ditch not now visible. Pottery including Abingdon ware, stone and flint tools and other material have been found in association.

Haresfield Beacon, hill-fort (SO/825090) 3 miles NW of Stroud (A46, A419), 1½ miles E of Little Haresfield and A419.

This elaborate fort appears to have been built in 2 stages. A single bank and ditch enclosed the top of Ring Hill (with Haresfield Beacon) and at a later period this defended area of some 16 acres was more than doubled by an E extension taking in Haresfield Hill. Both earthworks follow the natural contours. Of the gaps in the bank and ditch on Ring Hill, one in the S side, halfway between the E end of the Hill and the trig. point, may be an original entrance. Here the bank on the W side runs behind that on the E; it is approached by a track up the hillside from the W. Entrances to this and to the extension may also have been where the modern road now crosses the hill-fort. This camp is undated. It was certainly occupied during the Roman period.

Horton, promontory fort (ST/765844) 2¾

miles NE of Chipping Sodbury (A432, B4060), ¼ mile S of church.

Steep hillsides protect this fort on the W and S. The area of about 8 acres which is enclosed is nearly rectangular in plan. It is protected by a bank and ditch, the latter now silted up. The original entrance is no longer clear. It is possible that this site may have belonged to the same defensive system as **Sodbury** (p. 47). Not dated.

*Leckhampton Hill, promontory fort and barrow (SO/948184) 2½ miles S of Cheltenham, E of B4070. Finds in Cheltenham Museum.

This promontory fort is protected by steep hill-slopes along the N and W and by a rampart and ditch along the E and S. Over 6 acres are enclosed. There are traces of a bank about 350 yds. outside this earthwork but its Iron Age date has not yet been established. The original entrance is through the E side. Excavation (1969–70) has shown that the rampart comprises a rubble core resting on, and interlaced with, brushwood and timbers most of which has been burnt until, with the subsequent addition of rainwater, it has become slaked lime (produced by a temperature of at least 1,000°C.). At the front and back are the remains of a vertical drystone wall giving an average width of c. 18 ft. and original ht. of c. 9–12 ft. The rock-cut ditch in front, separated by a berm c. 3–4 ft. wide, is irregular, c. 9–12 ft. wide and c. 4–9 ft. deep. At the entrance, the rampart ends turn inwards slightly and contain semicircular guard chambers, with a 10 ft. roadway in between. Date, c. 4th–3rd century BC.

Outside the fort, close to the entrance, there stands a round barrow (mound 4 ft. high, 36 ft. diam.) set within a bank and ditch square in plan (90 × 90 ft.). This site has not yet been dated but it may possibly be contemporary with the fort.

*Lydney, promontory fort, Romano-British iron mine and temple with guest-house etc. (SO/616026), in Lydney Park, 1 mile SW of Lydney (A48, B4231, B4234), N of A 48. Finds in Lydney Park private museum.

The earliest visible remains at the S end of this great spur which looks S to the Severn is an earthwork cutting across the spur to defend 5 acres of ground elsewhere protected by the steep hillsides. This earthwork, built probably in the 1st century BC, consists of a bank 5 ft. high, dug from a V-shaped ditch 8 ft. in depth. Late in the Roman period the ht. of the bank was nearly doubled and another bank and ditch dug just outside. A rock-cut, entrance gully at the SE corner of the prehistoric enclosure may have originated in the pre-Roman period. In Roman times it became the main entrance to the area of the temple and its outbuildings.

In the 2nd and 3rd centuries AD the site first attained importance because of the

This sanctuary clearly catered for the well-to-do who would pay for healing and help. In the 5th century a wall was built around the SW and SE sides of the sanctuary and across the space between the guest-house and the baths; a gate was set up here. It was probably at this time that the prehistoric earthworks were reinforced and the outer bank and ditch dug.

Of the many votive offerings from the temple area now in the museum at the foot of the spur, the exquisite bronze of a wolf-hound with its head turned back should be seen (copy in Bristol City Museum).

33   *Minchinhampton: section across ditch and drystone-faced rampart, late Iron Age*

iron ore that could be obtained there. A mining community flourished. The gallery of 1 such mine, dug out later than the 3rd century, can be explored: its walls still bear the marks of Roman picks. The shaft had been covered by a later hut-floor and was itself cut through part of the Iron Age rampart.

In the middle of the 4th century a temple dedicated to the hunting god Nodens was built close to the s point of the spur; NE and NW of it were erected an imposing guest-house, a long dormitory (where the sick lay awaiting healing, and other divine counsel) and a suite of baths.

*Minchinhampton, enclosure (SO/858010) 1 mile NW of Minchinhampton, on Minchinhampton Common, $2\frac{3}{4}$ miles s of Stroud (A46, A419). Finds in Stroud Museum, British Museum (decorated bronze).

This site, known as The Bulwarks, consists of a bank and ditch over a mile long, cutting off a spur to the N and defended on the E and W by steep hillsides. Some 600 acres are thus enclosed. Excavation has shown that the ditch had a flat floor and was cut into the rock to a depth of 6 ft. (fig. 33). It was 12 ft. wide. The material from it had been used to form a bank today 30 ft. wide and 5 ft. high; in Iron Age times the width would have been about 16 ft. The bank was faced on the s side by a vertical drystone wall. There was a space of 8 ft. between bank and ditch. Perhaps built by Caratacus, AD 43–7, after his defeat by the Romans.

Nottingham Hill, hill-fort (SO/983283) $4\frac{1}{4}$ miles NE of Cheltenham, $\frac{3}{4}$ mile N of Woodmancote (A46). Finds in Cheltenham Museum.

This fort encloses the top of a naturally defended spur extending NW. Southeast of it a saddle (crossed by A46) joins it to Cleeve Hill and the mass of the Cotswolds.

berm on the s side of the fort, and with a large counterscarp bank here. The interior of the camp has been cut up by quarrying; the defences around the N side have also been obscured but appear to have resembled those on the s side. At the w, NE and SE corners the main rampart projects as a horn. The purpose of these structures must remain obscure without excavation, but they may have been a device to cover dangerously flat ground at these points. No original entrances can now be identified; a break just SE of the trig. point may have been made by those working the quarry. Date, c. 3rd–1st century BC.

34   *Painswick Beacon: Iron Age hill-fort. In-turned entrance centre right*

The area within its defences is about 120 acres. The earthworks are best preserved on the SE side, where they comprise 2 banks and ditches with a possible entrance at the s end. On the other sides the natural fall of the land has been accentuated by a bank and ditch with a second bank on the N side. An original entrance may have existed at the northernmost point of the fort. Not dated.

*Oxenton Hill, hill-fort (SO/973313) $5\frac{3}{4}$ miles N of Cheltenham, E of A435 and Oxenton village. Best reached by Dixton. Finds in Cheltenham Museum.

This earthwork crowns a hill which rises nearly isolated to 734 ft. O.D. In plan it is roughly triangular, the area within its defences about 7 acres. The earthworks consist of a bank and ditch separated by a

Painswick Beacon, hill-fort (SO/868118) $1\frac{1}{4}$ miles N of Painswick (A46), N of minor road linking A46 and B4073.

Though badly obscured inside by old quarries and a golf course, it is still possible to trace the defences of this fort which enclose an area of about 7 acres (fig. 34). In plan it is triangular. On its N side the remains of at least 1 bank and ditch can be found, while the defences on the other 2 sides consist of 3 closely set banks with 2 ditches. There is an in-turned entrance at the SE.

Ring Hill, hill-fort. See **Haresfield Beacon.**

*Salmonsbury Camp, lowland fort (SP/175208), $\frac{1}{4}$ mile E of Bourton-on-the-Water (A429, B4068); finds in Ashmolean (Oxford), Cheltenham and Gloucester Museums.

This camp lies between the Rivers Dickler and Windrush, on a patch of gravel. It is square, enclosing about 56 acres. Swamps would have protected at least 2 sides. On the E 2 curved ramparts extending from the main defences appear to be causeways running out into the marshes and towards the Dickler. The main earthwork consists of an inner bank, today 60 ft. wide and 2½ ft. high, erected from a V-shaped quarry ditch 34 ft. wide and 12 ft. deep; immediately beyond, there is also an outer bank, 40 ft. wide and somewhat levelled by ploughing, with an outer ditch originally 19 ft. wide and 9 ft. deep.

A drystone wall of oolite faced the main rampart, still visible below the field-wall cresting the rampart along the N side, near its centre. There was an entrance near the centre of the N side and another at the SW corner (partly under Camp House), both originally in-turned.

Within, circular wooden huts have been excavated and in 1860 a hoard of currency bars was found near the N side. Two crouched inhumation burials have been discovered close to the area of the currency bars. Pits c. 3rd century BC have been found sealed beneath the hill-fort ramparts which were built c. 2nd century BC.

Scrubditch, earthwork. See **Bagendon.**
Uley Bury, hill-fort (ST/784989) ½ mile NW of Uley (B4066) skirted on NE by B4066 from Dursley (A4135, B4066). Gold coin of the Dobunni in Gloucester Museum.

One of the most powerful hill-forts in the county, Uley Bury consists of a bank and ditch, roughly rectangular in plan, enclosing 32 acres. It is strategically situated at the S end of a steep-sided spur. One entrance is at the N corner of the camp where the old quarries have damaged the extra banks and ditches placed across this neck of land to defend it. There is a less certainly original entrance at the S corner of the camp. Not dated.
Windrush Camp, lowland fort (SP/181123) ¾ mile SW of Windrush, S of A40 from Burford (A40, A361, A424) to Northleach (A40, A429).

This is an almost circular fort enclosing about 6½ acres. Originally it had a single bank and ditch, the latter now silted up. They have been laid out in a series of almost straight sections, perhaps representing gang-work. There may have been an original entrance facing W. This is one of a number of small E Cotswold/Oxfordshire forts which were probably designed as cattle enclosures. Not dated.

Greater London

IRON AGE

Caesar's Camp, Keston. See **Keston.**
*****Caesar's Camp,** hill-fort (TQ/224711) on Wimbledon Common, ¾ mile NE of junction of A3 and A238.

Caesar's Camp is circular in shape, but a section of the earthwork on the N side is straight, following the contour of the ground. This fort has a single bank and ditch which enclose about 11 acres. An original entrance may have existed on the W side, 100 ft. N of the footpath. Towards the end of the last century the earthwork

was reduced by a local builder who planned to erect houses on it.

Excavation has shown that when first dug the camp ditch was 30–40 ft. wide and over 12 ft. deep. Behind it a bank had been piled, 30 ft. broad at its base and faced front and back with vertical walls of stout timbers. Those on the ditch-side would probably have been carried up to give protection to people on top of the bank. A berm of about 10 ft. separated the bank from its ditch. Pottery found in the ditch and under the bank suggests that Caesar's Camp must have been built in the 5th century BC.

*Keston, hill-forts (TQ/422639) 3¾ miles SSE of Bromley, ¾ mile S of Keston Mark (A232, A233), N of Holwood House. Finds in Maidstone Museum.

This roughly oval hill-fort originally enclosed c. 43 acres: much of it has been levelled but it remains upstanding around the N and W and can be traced around the S. Everywhere the defences comprise a bank, ditch and counterscarp, but there are 3 banks along the W. The original entrance, slightly in-turned, is at the NW. Excavation has shown that the inner bank was enlarged twice and the inner V-shaped ditch was c. 15 ft. deep. At the NW entrance, timbers and flints revetted a simple 1st period entrance. Later the entrance was narrowed and was in-turned

on the N side. A well-worn roadway with a drain was found, but no clear evidence for a gate. Not dated.

Immediately to the NW, centred on TQ/418642 on Keston Common, a second earthwork can be seen. With a weak single bank and ditch along its S side, it cuts off about 15 acres of land defended on the NE and NW by low swampy ground. This earthwork, the bank of which does not now exceed 3 ft. in ht. anywhere, is laid out in 3 straight sections. There is a gap, probably an original entrance, almost midway along the rampart. It provides a passageway across the ditch about 6 ft. wide. This site may have been used as a cattle pound for those living in the larger camp in Holwood Park.

Greater Manchester

BRONZE AGE

Chapeltown, stone circles (SD/716159) 4¼ miles SSE of Darwen, 1 mile W of Chapeltown (B6391).

There are 2 circles here. The first is a ring of 6–7 stones, originally 11–12, with a diam. of about 50 ft. Their hts. are 1–4 ft. There is an outlying stone about 40 ft. to

the SW.

About 60 ft. SW of the latter, close to the hill-top, there are the remains of a second circle. This is about 36 ft. across. Its wall consists of 2 rings of closely set stones 4 ft. apart, the space between filled with rubble. A concentration of stones at the centre suggests the site of a burial. Date of both, c. 1,700–1,400 BC.

Hampshire

(See also Isle of Wight)

*NEOLITHIC

Danebury, long barrows (SU/320383, central barrow) 2¼ miles E of Over Wallop (A343, B3084), reached by track SE off A343. Surface find in Winchester Museum.

Three good examples of Wessex long barrows are situated close together ½ mile N of Danebury Hill. The W barrow has a mound 210 ft. long, 72 ft. wide and 6 ft. high. It is orientated E/W. There are prominent side-ditches about 27 ft. wide and there appear to be berms between these ditches and the base of the mound – an unusual feature. A fragment of late Neolithic pottery has been found in a rabbit-scrape at the E end of the N ditch.

The central barrow is about 170 ft. in length, 70 ft. in width and 4 ft. in ht. It lies E/W, its E end being the higher. Its flanking ditches are about 15 ft. wide.

The third long barrow, about ¼ mile NE of the last, is a 'short' long barrow, 85 ft. long and nearly as wide, with a ht. of 4½ ft. Its surrounding ditch is plainer on the N than on the S and clearly does not continue around the ends of the mound. These barrows may be dated 3,500–2,500 BC.

Duck's Nest, long barrow (SU/104204) 1¼ miles NW of Rockbourne, ¼ mile E of road joining latter to A354.

This is one of the highest long barrows in the county, having an elevation of about 12–15 ft. Orientated N/S, it is about 150 ft. long and 75 ft. wide. Its side-ditches have a width of about 15 ft. It must have been built c. 3,500–2,500 BC.

Giant's Grave, long barrow (SU/139200) 1¾ miles NW of Breamore (A338), SW of Miz Maze Wood.

Originally a large example of a long barrow, the W end of this has been badly damaged. It has a length of some 180 ft. and a width of 84 ft., its long axis being nearly E/W. Its E (higher) end stands nearly 11 ft. high. There are side-ditches. Date, c. 3,500–2,500 BC.

Grans Barrow, long barrow (SU/090198) 1¼ miles E of Martin, 1¾ miles NW of Rockbourne.

This mound is orientated SE/NW. It is large, being nearly 200 ft. in length, 60 ft. in width and in ht. 9 ft. at the S end, 6½ ft. at the N. Ditches around the sides cannot be seen clearly on the surface. Probable date, 3,500–2,500 BC.

Houghton Down, long barrow (SU/330357) 2 miles W of Stockbridge (A30, A272, A3057), ¼ mile N of A30.

For some reason the mound of this barrow today is only 1 ft. high, although its other dimensions are large – a length of 180 ft. and a width of 40 ft. There are traces of flanking ditches about 15 ft. wide. Excavations were carried out here at the end of the last century, when several skeletons were found, buried in the contracted position. A secondary cremation, probably of the Bronze Age, was also found somewhere in the mound. This barrow was built c. 3,500–2,500 BC.

Knap Barrow, long barrow (SU/089199) 2 miles NW of Rockbourne, 200 yds. NW of Grans Barrow (above).

Although part of the mound of this barrow has long been under cultivation, it remains a fine example, 320 ft. long – the largest in the county. It may originally have been 100 ft. wide. Lying SE/NW, its S end is about 6 ft. high, its N end 4 ft. Side-ditches are not visible but probably exist. Date, c. 3,500–2,500 BC.

Lamborough, long barrow (SU/593284) ¾ mile E of Cheriton (B3046), ½ mile NW of Hinton Ampner (S of A272). Pottery in Winchester Museum.

This long barrow, orientated E/W, measures 220 × 118 ft.; it is 7 ft. high at the E end and nearly 2 ft. lower at the W end. Flanking ditches can be seen.

Trenches were cut across the ditches in 1932. They were shown to measure 18–20 ft. in width at the surface of the chalk and 8–12 ft. in depth. The ditches appeared to be narrowing towards the E end and to stop at the extreme E end, as is usual among long barrows in Wessex. A fragment of pottery low down in the ditch suggests that this barrow was built c. 3,000–2,500 BC.

Martins Farm, long barrow (SU/251385) 1¾ miles N of A343/A30 junction, 5¼ miles SE of Amesbury (A303, A345).

This mound lies E/W. It is nearly 100 ft. long and 50 ft. wide. Its E end is 5 ft. high. There are distinct flanking ditches about 13 ft. wide and sinking 2½ ft. at their centres. This mound was probably built c. 3,500–2,500 BC.

Moody's Down, long barrows (SU/435388, E mound) between Stockbridge (A30, A272, A3057) and Sutton Scotney (A30, A34), ¼ mile N of crossing of B3420 and A30. Pottery in Winchester Museum.

There are 3 long barrows within ¾ mile of each other; one is E of Moody's Down Farm, the second lying just w of the farm and on the s side of B3420 to Andover. The third is sw of the last, at SU/417383. The first is 220 ft. long, 75 ft. wide and 4 ft. high. Ploughing may account for the uniform ht. of this mound along its entire length. There are clear flanking ditches 27 ft. wide and the barrow is orientated SE/NW. This site is quite rectangular in overall plan. A fragment of pottery from a rabbit-scrape is Windmill Hill ware and suggests that this, like the other long barrows close to it, was built between 3,500 and 2,500 BC.

The middle mound is almost certainly a long barrow although today it appears nearly as wide as it is long. It measures 125 ft. by 93 ft., being orientated E/W, the larger end to the E. It is about 4½ ft. high. Side-ditches are not visible but doubtless exist.

The SW mound lies SE/NW. Under the plough, it is about 150 ft. long, 90 ft. wide and 4 ft. high. Nothing is known of the burials beneath these long barrows.

*BRONZE AGE

Burghclere Seven Barrows, barrow cemetery (SU/462553, s end) midway between Whitchurch (A34, B3400) and Burghclere, ¾ mile N of Litchfield (A34); close to A34.

There are at least 10 barrows in the cemetery. Seven at the s end lie immediately w of the A34 or are just overlapped by it; 2 others are between the road and the railway while the tenth is overlapped on its w side by the railway embankment. All the mounds have had their type features obscured by ploughing. Beginning at the s end, the first barrow is probably a bell; it has a diam. of 160 ft. and a ht. of 10 ft. The next 4 are bowl-barrows, with hts. ranging from 1–8 ft. and diams. from 40–80 ft. The barrow w of the junction of the A34 and a footpath leading to Chapman's Dell is a disc; though almost ploughed flat, it can be seen to have a mound 28 ft. across and 6 ins. high, placed at the centre of a platform 63 ft. in diam. and defined by a ditch 16 ft. wide. There are traces of a bank outside the ditch, giving an overall diam. of 131 ft. East of this and bisected by the A34 there is a second barrow which is also probably a disc. Unfortunately it can only be seen under special conditions (e.g. when it is under a suitable crop). The 3 N barrows are bowls, 4–9 ft. high and 60–100 ft. across.

This cemetery is laid out in a line (orientated N/S) in the manner of some of the famous groups around Stonehenge. It can be considered broadly contemporary with that sacred site, c. 1,700–1,400 BC.

Flower Down, disc-barrow (SU/459319) 2 miles NW of Winchester, just behind Flowerdown omnibus shelter.

This has been described as the finest disc-barrow in Hampshire. It has a max. diam. of 178 ft. and there are 2 mounds on the circular platform defined by the ditch with outer bank. The surrounding bank is 23 ft. broad and 2 ft. high. The ditch within it is 19 ft. wide. The central platform is 98 ft. across. At its centre stands 1 mound, having a diam. of 26 ft. and a ht. of 2 ft. South-west of this there is a second mound, slightly smaller and lower. Both mounds are probably contemporary and the barrow must have been built c. 1,700–1,400 BC.

*Grim's Ditch, enclosure ditch, centre 6½ miles sw of Salisbury. Overlies parts of Wilts, Dorset, Hants.

Grim's Ditch encloses a roughly rectangular area of about 16 square miles. Its

N side runs nearly E/W from Middle Chase Farm (Wilts., SU/005207), through Vernditch Chase and Knighton Wood, across A354 at SU/070222, past Great Yews to just beyond Down Farm (SU/143232). Between Vernditch Chase and Knighton Wood the Ditch must lie beneath the Roman road. At Down Farm it turns SW to Breamore Down (SU/131208). It probably continued to Whitsbury Castle Ditches hill-fort (p. 143) then swung W. It can be seen again NW of Damerham Knoll (SU/094189) and runs W to where the Roman Bokerley Dyke crosses it (SU/055181). It then runs NW, behind (i.e. W of) the latter, probably runs under it again at SU/034198 and then stops. Another and probably earlier section of Grim's Ditch runs N towards Vernditch Chase from SU/049188. This passes E of the Martin Down late Bronze Age enclosure (below) but overlies 'Celtic' fields which are contemporary. This stretch joins the northerly E/W length of the Ditch in Vernditch Chase at SU/040211 (not shown on 1-in O.S but clear on ground) and both must be broadly contemporary. It seems likely that the southerly E/W section is the latest but that all belong to one prehistoric system of land enclosure started c. 1,000 BC and continued into Iron Age times. The land so defined was perhaps a great stock ranch owned by one tribe. Everywhere the earthwork consists of 2 banks 50–60 ft. wide, with a V-shaped ditch 5–6 ft. deep between them. One bank is usually higher than the other but no rule appears to govern this. The ditch has many sharp twists in it, perhaps caused by large trees obstructing its path during building.

Hengistbury Head, round barrows. See Iron Age.

Ibsley Common, saucer-barrow (SU/176105) 2¾ miles SE of Fordingbridge (A338, B3078), nearly 1 mile E of South Gorley. Grave goods in Salisbury Museum.

Not marked on the 1-in. O.S., this barrow was discovered in 1917 and excavated. It has a central mound 16 ft. in diam. and 1 ft. in ht., surrounded by a ditch 5 ft. wide. Outside this there is a bank 12 ft. broad and 1 ft. high, composed of material derived from the ditch. At the centre of the mound a pit was discovered

dug into the subsoil, containing an inverted Bronze Age cinerary urn. Although much wood ash was found in and around the urn there were no traces of cremated bone. This barrow may be dated c. 1,700–1,400 BC.

Ladle Hill, disc, bell- and saucer-barrows. See Iron Age.

*Martin Down, enclosure and 'Celtic' fields (SU/043201) 9 miles SW of Salisbury, ¼ mile S of A354, ½ mile ENE of Bokerley Junction. Finds in Salisbury Museum.

This Middle–Late Bronze Age enclosure (c. 1,200 BC) is rectangular in plan and encloses 2 acres. There is a very broad gap in the NW side. The earthwork comprises a bank today 2 ft. high and a ditch shown by excavation to be V-shaped, 7–10 ft. deep. There are entrance gaps 90 ft. NE and SE of the E corner. It has been reconstructed by Gen. Pitt-Rivers after he had excavated it. This enclosure, probably intended for the pounding of flocks and herds (the large gap at the NW could have been blocked by hurdles or hedges), may be associated with the system of 'Celtic' fields which surrounds it and is certainly contemporary with part of Grim's Ditch (p. 136).

Petersfield Heath, barrow cemetery (SU/758232, bell-barrow) ¾ mile SE of Petersfield (A3, A272).

Although fairly widely scattered, there are sufficient barrows within an area 2,600 × 900 ft. (the E half of the heath) to warrant their description as a cemetery in something approaching the Wessex manner.

The northernmost barrow, in part cut by the road which bounds this part of the heath, is a bell, its mound 120 ft. across, 8 ft. high and tree-covered. It has a berm about 12 ft. wide, surrounded by a ditch a little less in width.

There is a disc-barrow 250 ft. to the S. It is unusual because it appears to have a ditch *outside* its bank, and neither of the 2 mounds on the plateau so defined are in the centre of it. These mounds, 30 and 25 ft. in diam., 2 and 1 ft. in ht., lie in the SW half of an area 70 ft. across. A bank 25 ft. broad surrounds this plateau and there is a ditch outside, 10 ft. wide on the SW side.

There are 15 bowl-barrows on the

heath, ranging in ht. from 10 to 1½ ft. and in diam. from 40–20 ft. In addition there are 4 saucer-barrows, one 750 ft. s of the golf clubhouse (with a bowl 200 ft. N of it), another is 550 ft. sw of the first (with bowls N and E of it) and 2 more are 650 ft. ESE of the last, close together and just NE of a bowl-barrow. These 4 are slight in elevation and have overall diams. of (N/S) 44, 88, 30 and 30 ft.

There are no excavation records for this group of round barrows although most of them have probably been opened in the past. They must have accumulated here c. 1,700–1,400 BC.

Popham Beacons, barrow cemetery (SU/ 525439) ¾ mile NE of Micheldever Railway Station (B3049), on N side of A30.

This is a small cemetery in the Wessex manner and it must have been built up in the period 1,700–1,400 BC. It comprises 5 barrows in a straight line NE/SW.

At the N end there is a bowl-barrow about 90 ft. in diam. and 6 ft. in ht., with a visible surrounding ditch. About 45 ft. to the s there is a bell-barrow and a bowl-barrow each impinging upon a saucer-barrow placed between them. The bell, tree-grown and damaged by rabbits so that its specialised form is obscured, appears to be nearly 140 ft. across and 8 ft. high, with a surrounding ditch 14 ft. in width. The bowl is nearly 120 ft. in diam. and is 6 ft. high. Between these barrows the remains of an earlier saucer-barrow can be seen. Originally it would have had an overall diam. of 160 ft. – rather large for a true saucer. Its mound is 2 ft. high and 88 ft. across, and there is a surrounding ditch 18 ft. wide with a bank outside it the same in breadth.

The second bell in this group lies less than 30 ft. s of the middle bowl. Its total diam. is 130 ft. and its mound stands 7 ft. high. The berm between mound and ditch is now overspread with mound material, but probably originally existed.

Roundwood, barrow cemetery (SU/507444) 1¼ miles NW of Micheldever Railway Station (B3049), 1¼ miles WNW of Popham Beacons barrows (above). Finds in Winchester Museum.

This group of 4 barrows is arranged in a line E/W. From E to W, it consists of a single bell-barrow, a twin barrow and 2

possible disc-barrows, both almost levelled by cultivation.

The single bell has a mound 70 ft. across and 9 ft. high, separated from its now almost invisible ditch by a berm 12 ft. wide – a feature only exposed by excavation in 1920. The corpse of a man had been cremated at the centre of the barrow and his ashes placed in a pit dug through ground burnt red by the heat of the pyre. Soil had been scraped up and heaped over the central area, after which the surrounding ditch was dug to provide chalk for a capping to the barrow, a sequence of building found in most round barrows with ditches in chalk country.

The twin barrow lies immediately to the w. Two mounds were revealed by excavation to be surrounded by an oval ditch. It was not possible to say whether this was a twin bell or a twin bowl-barrow. Neither burial nor any other feature were revealed in the w mound; at the centre of the E mound a great pile of flints had been heaped over the original burial. This had been robbed without record before 1920 and only scattered wood-ash was encountered.

Just beyond the hedge which lies to the w of the twin barrow there are the ploughed-out remains of what are probably 2 disc-barrows. Excavation of the E one revealed a flat-floored circular surrounding ditch, 6 ft. wide and 4 ft. deep, with an outer bank. No burials were found during the small-scale excavations at the centre. The w disc has not been examined by excavation. This cemetery may be dated c. 1,700–1,400 BC.

Setley Plain, overlapping disc-barrows (SU/296000) 1¼ miles s of Brockenhurst (A337, B3055), between A337 and B3055.

There are only 2 known examples of disc-barrows which overlap – Grafton (Wilts., p. 224) and this pair on Setley Plain. The earlier of the 2 discs is the NW; it has a mound 48 ft. across and 4 ft. high, set at the centre of a plateau 72 ft. in diam. This is surrounded by a ditch 11 ft. wide and with a bank outside, 13 ft. broad. It is overlapped at the SE by the second disc. This one is larger, having an overall diam. of 140 ft. Its mound is 46 ft. in diam. and 3½ ft. high, standing at the centre of a plateau 92 ft. across.

These mounds were dug in 1793 and ample traces of cremation *in situ* were found, but no grave-goods. Date, c. 1,700–1,400 BC.

Another presumably contemporary disc-barrow can be found less than 500 yds. away to the SE; it is an unusually small example.

*Stockbridge Down, round barrows (SU/375347, centre of group) 1 mile E of Stockbridge (A30, A272, A3057), immediately N of A272. Grave goods in British Museum.

There is a scattered group of 14 bowl-barrows on the SE side of the spur which extends from Woolbury Ring hill-fort (p. 143) to where the A30 is met by the minor road to Little Somborne. Outwardly there is nothing exceptional about these barrows, which have diams. ranging from 50 to 20 ft. and hts. from 3 ft. to 9 ins. One, however, was scientifically excavated in 1938 with important results. It lies 2,400 ft. ENE of the road junction referred to above, 800 ft. SW of the W entrance to Woolbury Ring. It is only 25 ft. in diam. and 1½ ft. high. Its ditch was not a continuous ring, but made up of 5 elongated pits with broad gaps between them. The mound was composed of large flints and soil. At the centre an oval grave pit contained a crouched skeleton with a bell-beaker and a copper awl. There were 2 cremations near the top of the grave. This burial must have been deposited about 2,000 BC. In the Bronze Age, about 1,500 BC, a collared urn containing a cremation had been put upside down in a pit dug into the outer side of a ditch segment on the W side of the barrow. These bones were those of a child of about 15. With them there was a necklace of beads made of shale, amber and faience – the latter perhaps Near Eastern – and a bronze awl.

Whiteshoot Plantation, bell and saucer-barrows (SU/290330) 4½ miles SW of Stockbridge (A30, A272, A3057), 1 mile W of Broughton (B3084).

This group consists of a bell-barrow, with a saucer on its E and W sides. The bell has a mound 60 ft. across and 6 ft. high, with evidence of robbing at its centre. It is surrounded by a berm 15 ft. broad, separating it from a ditch 18 ft. wide.

The W saucer-barrow has a very low

mound 23 ft. across, with a surrounding ditch 10 ft. wide and an outer bank 18 ft. broad and a little higher than the mound within. The other saucer is only slightly larger. This group, typical examples of specialised Wessex forms, must have been built c. 1,700–1,400 BC.

IRON AGE

Beacon Hill, hill-fort (SU/458573) 2 miles N of Litchfield (A34), ¼ mile W of A34.

This superb hill-fort, hour-glass in plan, has defences consisting of a bank, ditch and counterscarp bank, enclosing an area of about 12 acres. There is an original entrance facing S. The inner bank stands to a ht. of 7 ft. with a V-shaped ditch outside it still about 10 ft. deep. The counterscarp bank is slight, the steep slope of the hill requiring nothing more elaborate. At the entrance the ends of both banks and the ditch are in-turned, and there are also outworks. Dotted about within the camp, the remains of contemporary hut circles can be seen, ranging in diam. from 20–30 ft. They suggest that this camp was occupied permanently. Though still unexcavated, it is likely to have been built in the 1st or 2nd century BC.

*Buckland Rings, lowland fort (SZ/315968) 3¼ miles SE of Brockenhurst (A337, B3055), on W side of A337 and S side of railway crossing over road. Finds in Winchester Museum.

This hill-fort occupies a flat-topped knoll 90 ft. above sea level. The camp is roughly rectangular in plan. It is defended by 3 lines of banks with 2 ditches, and entered by a gap through the E side. The area thus enclosed is 7 acres. The innermost bank is everywhere about 8 ft. high and 30 ft. broad at its base. The middle bank is about half this ht. and has an unusually broad, flat top. The outer bank is even lower. The ditches vary in width from 40–25 ft. and in depth from 12–6 ft. The ramparts were originally faced and backed with vertical timbers. At the entrance, the innermost rampart is in-turned, forming a long, funnel-like passage, with a pair of stout gates at the W end. Excavation revealed that this passage had been hollowed by constant traffic in Iron Age times.

Buckland Rings was built probably in the 1st century BC. Evidence was found to suggest that its defences had been deliberately dismantled, possibly at the behest of the Roman authorities after they had conquered the area about 44–5 AD.

Bullsdown, hill-fort (SU/671584) 4¼ miles NE of Basingstoke, ½ mile NW of Sherfield Green (A33).

These earthworks are oval in plan and enclose an area of 10 acres. The entrance, which would have been at the NE, is now destroyed. There are 3 banks and ditches, the middle bank having an unusually broad and flat top. Today the banks stand to no great ht.; in places the inner and middle ditches are still 5 ft. deep. Not dated.

*Bury Hill, hill-fort (SU/345435) 1½ miles SW of Andover (A303, A343, A3057), ¼ mile SE of A343. Finds in Winchester Museum.

The earthworks of this three-period hill-fort crown a hill which rises sharply out of its surroundings to attain a ht. of 300 ft. The earliest fortification here is an irregular oval in plan, enclosing 22 acres and consisting of a single bank with ditch outside and an entrance at the SE. It fortifies most of the hill along the 300-ft. contour but the E half of its circumference is incorporated in the defences of the smaller fort of period 2. The original bank (which reaches as far N as the chalk pit and wood) was about 25 ft. broad at its base and was originally 8 ft. high. It had no timber facings or supports. The U-shaped ditch outside it was dug to a depth of 11 ft. and was about 12 ft. wide at ground level. This camp was built c. 6th–5th centuries BC.

In period 2 the camp defences were altered and the area fortified was contracted to 11¾ acres. There are 2 ramparts and ditches and the entrance of period 1 was retained. Where preserved from the plough, both period 2 ramparts are in places 8 ft. high. The ditches outside them were originally V-shaped; the inner one was 20 ft. deep, the outer one 5–10 ft. deep. No traces of timbering in the ramparts were found in the excavations of 1939. The entrance-passage is about 30 ft. wide. The ramparts and ditches end here without being turned in. Period 2 can be dated

about 100 BC.

At the end of the 1st century BC Belgic tribes pushing W occupied this fort, and restored it to its original size. It appears to have been dismantled and abandoned at the end of the 1st century AD.

*Butser Hill, plateau enclosure (SU/712201) and 'Celtic' fields (SU/720200), 2¾ miles SW of Petersfield (A3, A272), W of A3.

Butser is an irregularly shaped hill over 800 ft. high. It is flat-topped. To the SW a very narrow neck joins it to a second, elongated hill only a little less in ht. Earthworks erected across this neck appear to have been intended to isolate and fortify Butser Hill, whose plateau-like top has an area of about 100 acres.

There are 3 lines of earthworks cutting off the hill. The most S runs across the N end of the long hill to the S and consists of a bank and ditch (facing S) with a slight counterscarp bank. The inner bank is today less than 6 ft. high. It is not shown on the 1-in. O.S. Five hundred and fifty yards to the N occurs the S of the 2 earthworks shown on the map, both straddling the narrow neck connecting these 2 hills. It consists of a bank and ditch with counterscarp bank running straight, NW/SE. Its dimensions are slightly less than those of the earthwork described above. Two hundred yards N there is the third earthwork, facing S and concave in plan. It has a bank 30 ft. broad and 5 ft. high, separated from its ditch by a flat berm in places 12 ft. broad. Breaks in the bank and causeways across the ditch suggest that this earthwork is unfinished.

Additional earthworks, of slighter proportions, cut across the NE and SE spurs of Butser Hill. Undated; Late Bronze or Early Iron Age.

The British Association has (1972) established a centre for practical research into prehistoric, and especially Iron Age methods of agriculture on Little Butser, about SU/719212.

On the SE slopes of Butser Hill there is a fine series of lynchets marking out small rectangular fields; they reach almost to the main Portsmouth road. Their original S boundary is still visible in places.

Romano-British pottery exposed by rabbits and the plough hereabouts suggests that the fields were cultivated in Roman times; but they may have been begun in the Iron Age and tilled by those using Butser Hill as a refuge in time of scare.

Castle Ditches, hill-fort. See **Whitsbury Camp.**

Damerham Knoll, hill-fort. See **Rockbourne Knoll.**

*Danebury, hill-fort (SU/323377) $2\frac{3}{4}$ miles NW of Stockbridge (A30, A272, A3057), between A30 and A343. Location of finds not yet decided.

This superb hill-fort, currently under excavation, comprises a main, inner bank, ditch and counterscarp of roughly oval plan, enclosing 13 acres, with a middle bank, ditch and counterscarp around the S side and the whole surrounded by a slight, outer earthwork of similar composition, associated with a parallel pair of banks and ditches 50 yds. apart, leading SE for over 1 mile. The main entrance to the inner and middle earthworks is on the E side: a slightly less elaborate entrance through these is at the SW but this has been blocked by an extension of the inner rampart – a most unusual feature in a hill-fort. Both entrances are reflected in less elaborate entrances through the outer earthwork. Wide gaps between the three sets of earthworks would have allowed space for penning livestock.

Excavation has revealed a series of ritual pits containing posts beneath the E entrance, which may be Late Bronze Age, c. 1,000–800 BC. The earliest hill-fort, which followed, comprised the inner earthworks. At first the inner rampart was timber-faced and about 15 ft. high. Next, its timbering was removed and the rampart was given a steeply sloping front, a flint breastwork and a new V-shaped ditch (c. 50 ft. from ditch floor to rampart crest). The middle earthwork was added at this time. After a long lapse, the rampart was heightened and the ditch was re-shaped to a broad, flat profile, c. 34 ft. wide and under 6 ft. in depth. The outer earthwork was now added.

So far 7 main phases of development have been unearthed at the E entrance. It began as a simple break in the earthworks, with single, then double gates, and guard chambers. In phase 5a the outworks were added and then elaborated, the long out-

curving arm along the N side of the entrance-passage acting as a command point from which the main gate, the outer gate (closing the gap in the outermost outworks) and all other areas of the E entrance could be controlled. The first hill-fort was built c. 4th century BC. Phase 2 is 3rd–2nd century BC and the outer defences were added in the 1st century BC. The main rampart was refurbished against the Roman advance c. 43–4 AD.

Within, traces of an extensive settlement of huts, storage pits and other features is being found.

*Ladle Hill, hill-fort and Bronze Age round barrows (SU/478568) 3 miles SW of Kingsclere (A339, B3051), 2 miles NE of Litchfield (A34).

This is one of several hill-forts in Britain which demonstrate clearly how the defences of these sites were planned and built, for it was itself never finished.

The Iron Age designers set out to build a fortress enclosing 7 acres of ground within a single bank and ditch, oval in plan and with simple entrances E and W. They began by utilising the Late Bronze Age boundary ditch which comes up from the SW: it was incorporated in the NW side of their camp. Around the rest of the circuit to be fortified they dug a marking-out ditch, a very slight trench still visible for 100 ft. a short distance N of the E entrance. After this, the digging of the main ditch was begun, following (and destroying) the marking-out trench. The labour was done by gangs whose efforts, in sections of unfinished ditch varying from 50–270 ft. in length, can be clearly distinguished. The rampart was to be piled behind each section of ditch but first the turf and top-soil had been scraped up and dumped behind the site of the rampart. These heaps of humus are still visible, symbols of the frantic energy with which this fort must have been begun. The core of the mound was to be of chalk rubble. Without excavation we cannot say whether at this early stage posts for a timber facing or for internal strengthening had been set up.

Not yet dated, this fort probably replaced the Middle or Late Bronze Age settlement consisting of the 2 small enclosures 500 yds. SW, the 'Celtic' fields further sw and the boundary ditches incorporated in the hill-fort – a good example of continuity from Bronze to Iron Age.

From N to s the first Bronze Age barrow on Ladle Hill lies just to the N of the Iron Age hill-fort. It is a disc-barrow of large proportions, an outer bank 18 ft. broad and a ditch within 12 ft. wide, defining a circular plateau 76 ft. across. At the centre of this there is a mound 28 ft. in diam. and 1 ft. high.

There is a bell-barrow overlapping a saucer-barrow 600 yds. SE of the disc. It has a mound 56 ft. in diam. and $5\frac{1}{2}$ ft. high, separated from its ditch by a berm 10 ft. wide. There is a surrounding ditch 15 ft. across. A prominent hollow at the centre of the mound of this barrow indicates that it has been opened in the past – with no known result.

The bell-barrow ditch cuts through the bank of a saucer-barrow which must therefore be earlier in date. The mound of the latter is about 1 ft. high and is 47 ft. across. It has a surrounding ditch 10 ft. wide and a low bank outside that, 11 ft. broad.

These barrows, all typical examples of specialised Wessex forms, must be broadly contemporary with the final phase of building at Stonehenge, c. 1,700–1,400 BC.

Old Winchester Hill, hill-fort and Bronze Age round barrows (SU/641206), $2\frac{1}{4}$ miles s of West Meon (A32) and approached by track s from West Meon or NE from Meonstoke (A32).

The camp on this hill has a fine command of the country around it. Its earthwork, which consists of a bank, ditch and counterscarp bank, with entrances E and w encloses about 14 acres. In plan it is an irregular oval. In most places the main bank has a ht. of 4–5 ft. above level ground; it is nearly twice as high at the E entrance. The main ditch is today nearly silted up. When first dug, it would have been V-shaped, with a depth of at least 12 ft. in the chalk. Both entrances are inturned, that on the E being defended by additional outworks. This camp has not yet been dated by excavation.

There are Bronze Age bowl-barrows, some of them fine and large, outside both entrances and on top of the hill within the camp. These probably belong to the period 1,700–1,400 BC.

*Quarley Hill, hill-fort (SU/262423) $4\frac{1}{2}$ miles SE of Tidworth (A338, A3026), 1 mile NW of Grateley; close to B3084. Finds in Winchester Museum.

Like the hill-fort on Ladle Hill, this one can be shown to be later than boundary ditches of the Late Bronze Age. At Ladle Hill, one of these was incorporated in the laying out of the camp. At Quarley, a network of similar ditches is overlain by the earthwork defences of an Iron Age community who probably still recognised them as boundaries.

During excavations in 1938, the remains of a timber stockade were found running across the sw entrance-causeway, suggesting that the earthworks of the later Iron Age replaced a timber defence of the 6th or 5th century BC.

The earthworks visible today consist of a bank, ditch and counterscarp bank. They are oval in plan and enclose about $8\frac{1}{2}$ acres. There are entrances opposite each other, NE and sw. The gaps on the N and s sides were intended to be filled up, but excavation revealed that the camp was never finished. Neither main entrance has outworks. The Late Bronze Age ditches referred to can be seen running under the Iron Age defences N and s of the NE entrance; they make a right-angled bend within the camp.

The main bank was originally about 27 ft. broad at its base and stood to a ht. of at least 7 ft. It had no timber facings or supports but its outer side and core were composed of solid chalk blocks, earth and loose chalk being heaped on the inner side. The ditch in front of it must have been about 25 ft. wide at ground level and 12 ft. deep. It was V-shaped. The counterscarp bank was a slight affair, about 10 ft. wide and 2–3 ft. high.

Only the NE entrance has been excavated. It was shown that a complicated timber structure involving gates with a bridge over the top was intended. Post-holes were dug but the work was stopped before timbers were set up in them.

The great period of fortification on Quarley Hill must belong to the 4th century BC; those who built it and abandoned it before their work was quite done evidently followed closely upon the people who set up a timber stockade here at the beginning of the Iron Age.

Rockbourne Knoll, hill-fort (SU/099185) 4 miles sw of Fordingbridge (A338, B3078), 1 mile NW of Rockbourne.

This hill-fort is roughly oval in plan, enclosing c. 4 acres. Tree-covered, its earthworks comprise a bank, ditch and traces of a counterscarp. The main entrance appears to have been at the NW; here, the N end of the counterscarp bank has been developed into a triangular space and raised in ht. where it forms part of the entrance passage. It is not known whether the corresponding but simple break in the defences at the SE is an original entrance.

The N arc of the earthworks abut upon a linear ditch which extends to the W end of the hill-top in one direction and dies out a short distance to the SE of the hill-fort. In all probability this bank and ditch is part of an earlier, possibly Middle–Late Bronze Age boundary system defining tracts of land associated with open farming settlements of a type well-known in the chalk country of s England. So often, as here, Iron Age hill-forts are physically associated with these earlier land divisions, suggesting a continuity in land usage which is such a compelling aspect of this period in prehistory. The hill-fort not dated.

*St Catherine's Hill, hill-fort (SU/484276) 1¼ miles s of Winchester, on E side of A33. Finds in Winchester Museum.

The earthworks of this camp crown a gently rounded hill named after the medieval chapel built on top and dedicated to St Catherine. They comprise a bank and ditch with a counterscarp bank. There is an original in-turned entrance on the NE. The area of this camp is 23 acres.

The main bank, composed of chalk rubble and soil without any timbering, was originally about 40 ft. wide and about 8 ft. high. The ditch would have been about 25 ft. wide at ground level and was dug to a depth of 11–12 ft. The entrance gap through this bank at the NE is deliberately set slightly askew to that through the ditch outside it. The in-turned ends of the bank here were found to be revetted with timbers and, at a later date, with chalk blocks. The inner half of the entrance

passage was a little wider than the outer half, allowing for 2 sentry posts; there were gates crossing the passage at the junction of the 2 widths. Subsequently, the outer half of this passage was narrowed and revetted with flint walling and the sentry posts dismantled.

These earthworks were first erected c. 6th–5th century BC. A period followed in which the defences were allowed to fall into decay – a period of peace. Late in the 2nd century BC a local scare saw the repair and heightening of the earthworks, especially at the entrance, which was narrowed at this period. These troubled times passed. Once more the ramparts were allowed to fall into decay – in part, even, being dismantled. In the mid 1st century BC the hill-fort was taken, sacked and left deserted. Those responsible for this were probably Late Iron Age Belgic people pushing into Wessex. It saw no further permanent occupation until the construction of the chapel in medieval times.

Whitsbury Camp, hill-fort (SU/128196) 3½ miles NNW of Fordingbridge (A338, B3078), 1½ miles NE of Rockbourne.

This fort has defences consisting of 3 lines of banks, with ditches between them. They enclose about 16 acres. The site is roughly oval in plan. Stables and other buildings now occupy the position of the entrance which has been destroyed. The banks are graded down in size, the innermost and highest standing 10 ft. above level ground. Not dated.

Winklebury Camp, hill-fort (SU/613529) 1½ miles ENE of Basingstoke, s of A339. Finds in Salisbury Museum (Wilts.) and Chilcomb House, Winchester (County Museum Service).

This fort encloses 19 acres. Though sadly mutilated, it is of importance because it must be one of the earliest hill-forts in the country. Pottery sealed beneath its bank suggests that it was erected in the 6th or 5th century BC. It is roughly oval, having sides laid out in a series of straight sections. On the s side its ditch is still 15 ft. deep in places; on the E, remains of the bank stand 5 ft. above the flat ground within. The entrance was probably hereabouts.

Woolbury, hill-fort (SU/381353) 1½ miles E of Stockbridge (A30, A272, A3057), between A30 and A272.

This is a large camp, enclosing 20 acres. It is roughly circular in plan, having sides laid out in straight sections. It comprises a single bank and ditch, with a simple entrance at the sw. Ploughing has removed the E side. In places, the main bank is 10 ft. high; the ditch is still 6 ft. deep. Slight earthworks joining it from the sw may correspond to the earlier ditches underlying Quarley Hill fort (above, p. 142) and

those incorporated at Ladle Hill (p. 141). One of these runs SE for c. 200 yds., another sw for c 100 yds. They are associated with 'Celtic' fields occurring extensively on their NE and NW sides, but which cannot be seen in the angle formed by these boundary ditches. It would appear that the ditches separated arable from pasture for those inhabiting the hill-fort. Undated.

Hereford and Worcester

PALAEOLITHIC

*King Arthur's Cave, inhabited cave (SO/545155) 2½ miles NE of Monmouth (A40, A466, A4136), ¾ mile sw of Gt Doward. Finds in Cheltenham Museum, Gloucester Museum, University of Bristol Spelaeological Society Museum. Torch needed.

The cave has 2 chambers. Each is approached by a short passage leading in from a broad entrance divided by a thick pillar of natural rock. Excavation has shown that the cave was inhabited from late Ice Age times until the Roman occupation. Its earliest users, hunters of the Upper Palaeolithic and Mesolithic ages (c. 12,000–4,000 BC) were the most frequent. At first they appear to have lived inside the cave; later they worked just outside and within its mouth, lighting fires and remaining for relatively short periods during hunting expeditions. An extensive series of flint tools and some bone implements have been found.

*NEOLITHIC

Arthur's Stone, chambered long barrow (SO/318431) 2¾ miles S of Willersley (A438, A4111), 1 mile N of Dorstone (B4348), S of road to Pen-y-Moor Farm.

This barrow appears to consist of a

mound orientated N/S, with a chamber and passage at the S end. This passage is unusual because it changes direction from N to NW. There are 2 other stones s of the chamber. The mound is at least 85 ft. long. It is likely that excavation would reveal an original ground plan very different from the puzzling shape which the chamber and passage now appear to have had.

The burial chamber itself is oval, 18 × 7 ft., a huge roofing stone being supported by 9 uprights. To the N of it, 3 stones suggest that there was an ante-chamber, approached by the passage. The 2 isolated stones to the S may be the remains of an edging to the barrow mound. No details of burials have been recorded. The rock here is Old Red Sandstone. Date, c. 3,500–2,500 BC.

BRONZE AGE

Little Doward, round barrows. See Iron Age.

*IRON AGE

*Aconbury, hill-fort (SO/504331) 4¼ miles S of Hereford, ½ mile NE of A466/A49 junction. Finds in Hereford Museum.

The plan of this camp is roughly rectangular, its outline following the shape of the hill. The ground around it is nowhere exceptionally steep but its artificial defences consist only of a bank, ditch and a counterscarp bank, enclosing 17½ acres. Slight excavation has suggested that the bank contains internal revetments and that the site was permanently occupied in the 2nd century BC and after the Roman Conquest. There are in-turned entrances at the SE and SW. The latter has an outwork.

Aymestrey–Pyon Wood Camp, hill-fort (SO/424664) 6 miles NW of Leominster, ¾ mile N of Aymestrey (A4110), S of track to Ballsgate Common.

The main protection for this camp is the steepness of the hill which it crowns. It is now covered by trees. It is roughly triangular, its earthworks consisting of a bank, ditch and counterscarp bank. There are traces of a quarry-ditch within the inner rampart. An area of 9 acres is enclosed. There is an in-turned entrance facing SE, approached by a hollow way with a bank on the E side. This site looks across the valley E towards **Croft Ambrey** (below). Not dated.

Bach Camp, hill-fort (SO/547603) 3¼ miles ENE of Leominster (A44, A49), 1¾ miles SE of Kimbolton (B4553).

Though small (area 6¼ acres), the defences of this camp are stout and elaborate. Steep slopes on all sides are augmented by a bank, ditch and counterscarp bank. Everywhere the innermost bank is very denuded. Between it and the second bank on the NW side there is a very wide, shallow ditch or scoop. There is an in-turned entrance at the S end, and others at the NW and N: of these the former may be modern. Not dated.

*Bredon Hill, promontory fort (SO/958402) 6 miles NE of Tewkesbury, 2¼ miles SE of Eckington, off B4080. Finds in Birmingham City Museum.

Two lines of ramparts, the inner pierced by a central entrance, here cut off one of the N spurs of Bredon Hill, fortifying an area of 22 acres. North and W the natural fall of the ground was a sufficient protection. The inner rampart is earlier than the outer: it cut off 11 acres of land. Its ditch was dug 8 ft. into solid rock and the spoil piled inside to form a bank 8–11 ft. high. The main and only entrance was a 12 ft.

wide diagonal passage-way formed by staggering the ends of bank and ditch at this point. One circular hut found inside belongs to this period, c. 200 BC. It was 12 ft. in diam., had wattle-and-daub walls and enclosed a storage pit. There was also a water sump, connected by a drainage gully to a water catchment outside. The builders of this phase had trade and cultural connections with Cornwall and the SW.

Later in the 1st century BC the outer rampart was added, doubling the area of the camp. It still stands to a ht. of 6–8 ft. Its ditch, V-shaped, was 6 ft. deep. The outer face of the rampart had a stone facing and there was a flat space, or berm, between it and the inner edge of the ditch. The central gaps through this earthwork are probably modern, for access was obtained through 2 side entrances, made by turning back, northwards, its extreme ends to provide narrow passage-ways, each about 140 ft. long. These lead into the area between the 2 main ramparts. At these entrances of phase 2, the bank has a core of rubble and earth faced, on the inside, with drystone.

In phase 2, the entrance through the earthwork of phase 1 was redesigned: a corridor 25 ft. wide and over 100 ft. long was built straight through the bank and ditch, levelling the tip of the former and filling in the butt-end of the latter to do so. This is the entrance visible today.

This camp was deserted before the Romans reached it. It seems to have been sacked either by a band of marauders or, more likely, by a Belgic tribe from the SE. The main inner gateway had been burnt down, bringing with it a series of trophies in the form of human skulls set on poles over it. Around it over 50 skeletons, mainly of young males, were found hacked to pieces, scene of a last stand by the inhabitants at their inner gate.

Capler Camp, hill-fort (SO/593329) 7 miles SE of Hereford, 1¼ miles SE of Fownhope (B4224).

Capler is triangular in plan, its earthworks enclosing the long, narrow top of a hill commanding the River Wye. An area of about 10 acres is thus fortified. The defences consist of 2 banks and ditches on the S, with a scarped hillside facing N.

Here the crest of the scarp is likely to have been protected in addition by a stockade or slight bank. The entrance is at the E end, where the S rampart ends in a large mound and the rampart N of it continues E to make a well-protected approach. Not dated.

Conderton Camp, hill-fort (SO/972384) 6 miles NE of Tewkesbury (A38, A438, B4080), 2 miles NNW of Beckford and A438. Finds in Birmingham City Museum.

Roughly triangular in shape (fig. 35), this hill-fort is set on a spur and protected by steep hillsides on all but the N side. About 3 acres are enclosed. Extensive excavation, 1958–9, has shown that the site was built in 2 phases. In period 1 (c. 100 BC) the outer earthwork was completed, with a simple entrance at the S end and another in the middle of the N side. The defence was a bank and V-shaped ditch, with a slight counterscarp bank along the E and W sides. This site was a weak cattle enclosure.

In the 1st century BC a new earthwork was built across the spur within the hill-fort, cutting off about 2 acres to the N. This earthwork was a bank of soil and rubble faced on the S with drystone walling. There was no ditch in front of it. It had a central in-turned entrance. Within, a village of circular huts, working hollows and storage pits (fig. 36) was built. Rises and hollows all over this area can still be seen clearly. To the S the remainder of the phase 1 hill-fort was probably used to stall livestock.

At this time the in-turned entrance through the N side of the hill-fort was reconstructed. Excavation has shown that its in-turns were lined with drystone walling and with apse-like inner ends. This passage-way was altered at least once before it was finally blocked off by a dry-stone cross-wall and the entrance put out of use.

Pottery from the interior indicates contacts with the Cotswolds and the SW, habitation ceasing before the Roman conquest. Conderton Camp and Bredon Hill hill-fort must have been used by the same group of people.

Coxall Knoll, hill-fort (SO/366734) 2½ miles W of Leintwardine (A4113), ½ mile NE of junction of A4113 and B4367.

The W half of the area of 12 acres

enclosed by these ramparts is an oval hill-fort to which the 2 E enclosures must be regarded as additions. It is defended on the N by 3 banks and ditches, on the E by 2 and on the S by 1; on this side the steep hill renders elaborate fortification unnecessary. There is an entrance at the W end, where the innermost bank is in-turned and the outermost bank on the N side runs outwards for 300 yds. There is an additional outwork on the S side here. There is also a probable entrance in the E side.

The first additional enclosure on the E side was originally protected by a bank, ditch and counterscarp bank, but the latter has now almost disappeared. Within the main bank here there is a wide, deep quarry ditch from which extra material was provided for the bank. There is an entrance to this enclosure at its S junction with the original fort to the W: the W side of the rampart here is in-turned. A break in the N side of this allows access to the second enclosure.

The second enclosure is smaller, and likewise protected by a bank, ditch and counterscarp bank. The latter is damaged, but can be seen at the N end and at the E junction with the enclosure to the S. One original entrance to the second enclosure is a simple break in its ramparts facing N: there may be a second entrance where its defences join those of the S enclosure, at the W end. Not dated.

*Credenhill, hill-fort (SO/451445) 4½ miles NW of Hereford, ½ mile N of Credenhill and A480. Finds in Hereford Museum.

The defences of this very large hill-fort follow the 600 ft. contour and enclose nearly 50 acres. They comprise a bank and ditch with a slight counterscarp bank. There are traces of a quarry-ditch inside the main rampart around most of the circuit. Original in-turned entrances are at the centre of the E side and at the SE corner, each approached by a hollow way cut deeply into the hillside. Trial excavation has shown that the internal quarry ditch is 5–10 ft. deep. Its gradual in-filling was found to include various occupation layers associated with rectangular wooden buildings with 4 corner posts, measuring c. 12 × 8 ft., which had been rebuilt several times in the same place. There were also storage

35   *Conderton Camp, from the air*

36   *Conderton Camp: drystone footings of Iron Age hut (diam. 20 ft.), overlying earlier storage pits. Paved porch and entrance in front of kneeling figure. Footing restored to near original height on left, by pole (Graded in feet)*

pits and other remains of occupation including pottery with stamped and incised patterns typical of the West Midland Iron Age. Date, c. 400 BC; occupied continuously until c. AD 75.

*Croft Ambry, hill-fort (SO/444668) 6½ miles SW of Ludlow (A49, A4117), 2¼ miles NE of Mortimer's Cross, 1 mile E of A4110 and Yatton. Finds in Hereford and Birmingham City Museums.

This hill-fort, triangular in plan and its defences covering a total area of 32 acres, is protected along the N by a steep slope. It has been extensively excavated, 1960–6. The earliest fort occupied the level plateau of 5½ acres at the highest point of the hill. Its rampart has gone but its ditch is the great half-filled hollow lying within the innermost visible rampart. On this plateau rows of rectangular wooden timber buildings have been found, dating perhaps from the later 6th century BC. Entrances were at the E and W ends and at least 5 periods of construction are recorded. The fort was enlarged to 8¾ acres by a massive reconstruction of its defences about 390 BC. These comprised the present innermost rampart with its 2 outer banks separated by 2 ditches. The original E entrance was remodelled and the W entrance may have continued as a postern: a new SW gate was added and here 15 periods of construction have been uncovered. Both incorporated guard chambers and metalled roadways. The plateau within and especially the innermost ditch (of the 1st hill-fort) were used for intensive occupation until the Roman Conquest (hereabouts, AD 49), including wooden granaries and storage pits. The many burnt huts found suggest a final destruction, perhaps by the Romans. There was much pottery (imported from the Malverns) and excellent metalwork. Finally, the 2 outermost banks and ditches forming a lightly defended annexe of 12 acres, with entrances E and SW were added at an unknown period. It contains a mound of the late 2nd century AD, perhaps the site of a sanctuary.

*Dinedor, hill-fort (SO/524364) 2½ miles S of Hereford, ¾ mile SW of Dinedor (off B4399).

Ramparts here crown a roughly rectangular hill-top, being built where its sides begin to drop steeply. Twelve acres

are fortified by a bank and ditch. For most of the circuit the bank is flattened and the ditch shows as a terrace in the hill-side. But on the NE, the bank stands up clearly. There is 1 entrance, through the E side. It is not in-turned but there appears to have been an extra bank outside it. Excavation has shown that there had been permanent and dense occupation in the area immediately behind the rampart, probably all round the camp. Both sides of the rampart may have been faced with stone. Not yet closely dated, but at latest 2nd century BC.

St Ethelbert's Camp, hill-fort (SO/587388) 4¾ miles E of Hereford, 1¼ miles NE of Mordiford (B4224): on Backbury Hill.

This camp stands at 700 ft. O.D., commanding the confluence of the Rivers Frome, Lugg and Wye. It is roughly triangular in plan and encloses an area of about 5 acres. Steep slopes protect the W and E sides; here there is a bank, ditch and counterscarp bank, but the defences on the E have been obscured by landslides. To the NW there are 2 banks and ditches with a counterscarp bank. There appears to be an original entrance facing NE: the inner bank on the N turns inwards and there is an isolated bank on the E side which also turns in, making a well-defended approach. It is not known if the break in the W side is original. Not dated.

Gadbury Bank, hill-fort (SO/793316) 1¼ miles N of Staunton (A417, B4208, B4213), E of B4208.

An isolated flat-topped knoll of about 10 acres is defended by a single bank and ditch. There appears to be an original in-turned entrance at the NE. The bank is nowhere high above the interior; the ditch appears as a ledge around the camp, a short distance below the crest. Not dated.

Garmsley Camp, hill-fort (SO/620618) 4¾ miles SSW of Newnham (A443, A456), 1¼ miles SW of Kyre Magna and B4214.

This camp, which stands on a spur, has an area of 9 acres. Its defences consist of a bank, ditch and counterscarp bank. There is an in-turned entrance facing W, where the main bank is very impressive. Towards the NE there are traces of a second in-turned entrance which may be original, and a simple gap which is perhaps fairly modern. Not dated.

Herefordshire Beacon, hill-fort (SO/

760399) 3¼ miles NE of Ledbury (A417, A438, A449), ¾ mile sw of Little Malvern, on s side of A449. Some surface finds in Hereford Museum.

This great earthwork encloses an upstanding ridge on the Malvern hills. It is of unusual interest because of substantial additions made in medieval times.

The hill-fort is best understood by going first to the earthwork which surrounds the central part of this ridge. This is the earliest hill-fort on the site and encloses about 8 acres. The defences consisted of a single bank and ditch, with a counterscarp bank facing NE, the position of 1 entrance. A second entrance faced sw. Some of the material for the bank has been derived from immediately behind. This first fort is now confused by a medieval castle enclosure of the 11th–12th centuries, which stands at its centre.

In the next phase, the whole of the ridge was enclosed by additional earthworks, the area involved being over 32 acres. The new fortification consisted of a bank, ditch and counterscarp bank. In some places the inner bank has been augmented by material dug out from behind it.

Where the new work passes the w side of the period 1 fort, the earthwork of the latter is incorporated and cannot now be seen; but on the E side the new rampart lies outside this, providing 2 banks and ditches and a counterscarp bank. There were now 4 entrances, the banks and ditches overlapping slightly at each: one is at the NE corner, 2 others face E and w just s of the period 1 fort and the fourth is in the SE corner. A contemporary trackway runs up the hill-side to enter the w entrance. Not dated, but unlikely to have been started later than the 2nd century BC.

Hollybush Hill, hill-fort. See **Midsummer Hill.**

Ivington Camp, hill-fort (SO/485547) 2 miles NW of Hope-under-Dinmore (A49, A417), track from Ivington, via Ivington Park.

Roughly triangular defences comprising 2 banks and 2 ditches defend the flat-topped end of ground whose NW and SE sides are protected in addition by steep hill-slopes. Twenty acres are thus enclosed. There is an original entrance at the NE, where the inner rampart on the s side

is turned in and its N counterpart is out-turned. Here there are outworks, some almost ploughed flat, not yet fully explained. The main entrance was at the SE, where the inner ramparts are in-turned and 2 extra banks protect a contemporary approach road coming up the hill from the sw. Immediately SE of the entrance between the 2 main ramparts, there is a cruciform structure, presumably a strategic command point connected with the protection of this entrance. The gap in the w side used by the farm is probably modern. An unexplained feature of the inner rampart around its SE and sw sides is a terrace behind the crest. It may be original but has been accentuated by interior ploughing. In the NW corner of the camp, there is an enclosure of 8 acres, defended by a bank with traces of a ditch, which may be the earliest phase of this elaborate hill-fort. The gap in its E side is probably modern. Undated.

Little Doward, hill-fort and Bronze Age barrows (SO/539160) 2¾ miles NE of Monmouth (A40, A466, A4136), s of Little Doward (A40).

This camp is roughly oval and encloses 14 acres; it has an extension to the SE which contains a further 6 acres. Today the defences comprise a bank and ditch with a counterscarp bank, but reports of the last century suggest that there has been a second bank and ditch facing N and w. The s side is so protected by the steep hillside that only a small additional bank was required. One entrance faced NW, where the outer rampart runs outwards. The extension to the camp had precipitous hillsides as its main protection, though originally there is likely to have been a bank or palisade around it. There is a second entrance at the N junction of the main camp and this annexe, where the bank of the former is in-turned on the E side. Not dated.

Within the main camp there are 5 barrow mounds which probably belong to the period c. 1,700–1,400 BC. Some have traces of surrounding ditches and at least 2 appear to be rectangular in plan.

Midsummer and Holybush Hills, hill-fort (SO/761375) 2 miles ssw of Little Malvern (A449, A4104), N of A438 and Hollybush. Finds in Birmingham City Museum.

An area of 19 acres is enclosed by the bank and ditch of a hill-fort: two hills lie within these defences. In places there are traces of an outer bank, while a shallow quarry ditch also lies inside the main bank. One entrance is at the sw, in the valley between Midsummer and Hollybush hills. It is deeply in-turned, its NW area also enclosing a natural spring and marshy ground. There is a second entrance, its s side in-turned, at the N end of the hill-fort. Nearly 250 scoops into the hillsides have been plotted at various points in the interior and many of these represent emplacements for Iron Age huts. The long mound between the 2 hills is a pillow-mound, of recent origin, and other slight earthworks within the defences are also probably historic.

This hill-fort has been excavated (chiefly at the sw entrance) from 1965–70. The main rampart had a drystone-faced outer side, the stone brought from over a mile away. The sw entrance was shown to have had a sequence of 17 timber gates, some incorporating guard chambers, all set in various layouts at the inner end of a stone-faced corridor formed by the in-turned rampart-ends, c. 25–35 ft. long and c. 17 ft. wide. Most gate phases included a re-metalled roadway. Within, there is evidence for dense occupation, including rows of rectangular (c. 12–15 ft. × 8–12 ft.) wooden houses. Much pottery and metalwork was found, of a type linking this fort with Croft Ambrey, Credon Hill, Sutton Walls and the forts on Bredon Hill. Date, c. 450 BC, perhaps destroyed by the Romans.

Red Earl's Dyke, s of the hill-fort on Hollybush Hill, is medieval.

Oyster Hill, hill-fort. See **Dinedor.**

Pyon Wood Camp, hill-fort. See **Aymestrey.**

Risbury Camp, hill-fort (SO/542553) 3¾ miles SE of Leominster (A44, A49), reached by road to Risbury via Stoke Prior.

This camp occupies a low spur in the angle of 2 streams. Nine acres are enclosed (the earthworks cover 26). Along the N and w there are 2–3 ramparts and ditches, with the main entrance near the centre of the w side (the break in the E side is probably modern). Along the E side there are 4

ramparts; here and at the s the defences are more widespread, forming a zone about 300 ft. wide. Everywhere the inner-most bank is exceptionally large. On the SE and SW there is a series of cross-banks between the ramparts which recalls the enclosures at Old Oswestry (Shropshire). The central bank along the s and E sides is denuded and may represent an earlier phase: it appears to have an original entrance midway along the s side. The ramparts seem to be of dump construction, but 19th-century reports suggest that in places there may have been stone facings. Undated, but clearly a long history.

37 *Sutton Walls Iron Age hill-fort: slaughtered inhabitants in ditch at west entrance*

*Sutton Walls, hill-fort (SO/525464) 4 miles N of Hereford, reached by track N from Sutton St Michael. Finds in Hereford Museum.

This hill-fort is an elongated oval in plan, its defended area being about 29 acres. Fortification consists of a single massive bank and ditch, further protection being afforded by the steep sides of this hill. There are original entrances at the E and W ends. The former is a simple break in the earthworks. The latter, slightly narrower, is better protected because the s bank of the hill-fort extends W to cover the approach to it. This extension is not now obvious because it has been cut through by a modern path. The passage through each entrance has been hollowed out with use. The gaps through the N and s sides of the camp are modern.

Excavation has shown that the hill was occupied before the hill-fort was built. By about the 4th or 3rd century the rampart was erected, material being provided by a ditch outside and from wide shallow scoops within. Huts were built in these. The ditch was V-shaped and nearly 15 ft. deep. Before the Roman Conquest the rampart was heightened and the ditch widened. The W entrance, and probably the whole rampart, were faced either with timber or stone.

Soon after the ditch had been widened, a slaughter of the camp's inmates occurred. This was probably carried out by Roman troops passing into this part of England about 48 AD. The skeletons of 24 victims were found thrown into the ditch at the W entrance. Some had been killed in battle, others captured and decapitated (fig. 37).

During the Roman period the defences were doubtless dismantled, but the site continued to be occupied. Circular huts containing much Romano-British domestic rubbish have been uncovered. Some were in use down to the 3rd century AD. A T-shaped corn-drying furnace has also been found. Among the interesting material to be seen in Hereford Museum, the large iron anvil, one of the largest pre-Roman iron objects in Britain, should not be missed.

Wall Hills, hill-fort (SO/690380) 1¼ miles W of Ledbury (A417, A438, A449).

This fort consists of a main enclosure with a large extension to the NE. The defences cover an area of 36 acres. The main and probably the original hill-fort is roughly rectangular and is protected by a bank, ditch and counterscarp bank. The extension now shows only a ditch and outer bank, but originally it is likely to have had either an inner bank or stockade.

The 2 contemporary entrances to the main camp are (1) near the middle of its N side, immediately E of its junction with the extension and (2) at the SE corner, where there is the second junction of main camp and extension. The latter has a slightly in-turned N rampart. The extension also has 2 Iron Age entrances, one at the NE corner, the other to the W of it, in a re-entrant in the N side. Both are in-turned. Not dated.

Wall Hills, hill-fort (SO/630598) 4¾ miles NW of Bromyard (A44, A465), between Collington (B4214) and Thornbury.

This hill-fort occupies the top of a hill, the steep sides of which add to its strength on the W and part of the E. An area of about 25 acres is protected by a single bank and ditch with traces of a counter-scarp bank; in plan the camp is roughly pear-shaped. An original entrance appears to face SE: here, the s bank forks to run outwards and inwards and the N bank runs inwards. A second entrance can be seen at the N end of the W side, the N bank turning inwards; the end of the s bank is now destroyed. All other gaps are modern. Not dated.

Walterstone Camp, hill-fort (SO/348251) 3¼ miles SW of Pontrilas (A465, B4347), ½ mile E of Walterstone.

This hill-fort is roughly oval in plan, enclosing an area of about 4 acres. It is defended all around by 3 banks and ditches. There is an entrance at the SW and originally another at the NE. Both are simple. The earthworks and mounds outside the latter may be medieval. This fort must have been built here to control the River Monnow. Not dated.

Wapley Hill, hill-fort and barrows (SO/ 345625) 2¼ miles SE of Presteigne (B4355, B4362), reached by track N from road joining Stansbatch and Combe Moor (B4362).

This site stands on top of a hill which rises 600 ft. above, and commands, the River Lugg. It covers an area of 25 acres. The N side of the hill-fort is protected by a precipitous hillside. The other 2 sides of this triangular fortress are formed, on the s, by 4 banks and ditches, and on the E by 5. Of the latter, the outer 2 are separated from the inner banks by a flat space. The entrance is in the middle of the s side and is elaborately in-turned – particularly the innermost bank on the E side. The outermost bank on this side, which, like that on the W side of the entrance, has been brought forward nearly 50 yds., curves N to block the space between it and the inner banks. This passage-way to the interior is oblique to the line of the earthworks and is 125 yds. long. The defences on the N side appear now as a very slight bank, the steep hillside making unnecessary anything more. There may have been another original entrance at the N apex of the camp. Not dated.

Woodbury Hill, hill-fort (SO/749645) 5¾ miles SW of Stourport on Severn (A451, A4025, B4193, B4195), 1 mile S of Gt Witley; W of B4157.

This camp encloses about 26 acres. It is hour-glass in plan and is protected by a bank, ditch and counterscarp bank, well preserved on the S and NW sides. At the NW, where the footpath crosses the earthworks, there appears to be an in-turned entrance. Here the ends of the main bank enter the camp and curve SW for an unusual distance. Not dated.

Wychbury Hill Camp, hill-fort (SO/920818) 2 miles SE of Stourbridge (A451, A458, A491), ½ mile NE of Hagley. Reached by track N from A456.

Steep hill-slopes on the N and W sides

are an added protection to this large and powerful hill-fort. It is roughly triangular in plan, its main ramparts enclosing 7½ acres. An additional earthwork on the SW side almost doubles the fortified area and suggests that the site was developed in at least 2 stages.

The hill-fort is protected on the N side by 1 slight bank, probably supporting a palisade; the fall of the hill renders further fortification unnecessary. Around the S side there are 2 banks and a counterscarp bank, the innermost bank being much the stoutest. There are well-developed in-turned entrances at the E and W ends.

The W entrance is approached by a long causeway with a bank and ditch on either side of it. On the surface it appears that this feature is an addition and that the entrance itself was made after the banks and ditches had been built around this side of the hill – the ditches being filled in to provide a causeway through to the interior. The causeway runs S from the entrance for about 300 ft. to meet a ditch and bank which runs out from the S side of the hill-fort near its E end – an annexe of late date in the history of the site. The modern Wychbury Cottage lies across this secondary feature. Not dated.

Hertfordshire

NEOLITHIC

Therfield Heath, long barrow. See Bronze Age.

BRONZE AGE

*Therfield Heath, barrow cemetery and Neolithic long barrow (TL/342402) 1 mile W of Royston (A10, A14, A505), S of A505. Finds in Museum of Archaeology and Ethnology, Cambridge.

There are 8 bowl-barrows in this Bronze Age cemetery, an accumulation reminiscent of the cemeteries in Wessex. They have diams. of 20–70 ft. and hts. of 3–12 ft. Cremations and inhumations have been recorded from them, 9 disarticulated skeletons being recorded from one mound. Period, c. 1,700–1,400 BC.

The round barrows lie immediately N of a long barrow of earlier date (c. 3,000 BC). This is 125 ft. in length and 5–8 ft. high, orientated E/W. It has a continuous ditch around it and its mound has been shown to be a chalk-covered stack of turves. Its main burials have not yet been located but 1 skeleton, buried as a group of disarticulated bones, has been found at the w end.

IRON AGE

Arbury Banks, lowland-fort (TL/262387) 3 miles NNE of Baldock A1, A505, A507), ¾ mile sw of Ashwell. Finds in Ashwell Museum.

About 12½ acres are enclosed by an oval bank and ditch, originally having a counterscarp bank and entrances at the NW and SE. Within, aerial survey has revealed traces of a circular hut and other buildings, while 19th-century excavation exposed storage pits and other remains of permanent occupation, c. 3rd–1st century BC. The ditch was shown to be V-shaped and over 12 ft. deep. Though large in area, this fort may have housed only one family group.

The Aubreys, lowland fort (TL/095112) 1 mile sw of Redbourn (A5), on N side of B487.

This fort commands the River Ver. Nearly 17½ acres are enclosed by an oval earthwork. The defences consist of 2 banks and ditches on all except the NW side, where there is a single bank and ditch. There are also traces of a counterscarp bank, visible at the sw, w of Foster's Farm. There appear to be 2 original entrances, both simple: the main one faces w, at the s end of the length of single bank and ditch. A smaller entrance faces NW, at the N end of the same length of the earthwork. Not dated.

Beech Bottom Dyke, Belgic earthwork. See **St Albans.**

Devil's Dyke, Belgic earthwork. See **St Albans.**

Prae Wood, Belgic settlement. See **St Albans.**

Ravensburgh Castle, hill-fort (TL/099295) 5¼ miles N of Luton, ¾ mile s of Hexton (B655). Private estate. Finds in Letchworth Museum.

Though overgrown and in part tree-covered, this fort is sufficiently well preserved to be described and visited. It is roughly rectangular in plan and encloses 22 acres. It is set on top of a hill and commands much country, including the Icknield Way. Steep hillsides protect it on the N, s and w. Its defences consist of a stout bank and ditch with a slight counterscarp bank and a second ditch and bank on the w side. These are easily seen everywhere except on the E and NE sides. Recent excavation has shown that the rampart was faced on both sides by vertical timbers, tied together by cross-members. There are 2 simple gaps in the earthworks on the E side, that at the SE corner being an original entrance. The main entrance appears to be at the NW corner. Here the s bank runs out and the N bank turns in to form an oblique passage-way through to the interior. At this point there are traces of the outer ditch but these features at the entrance have been damaged by ploughing. Date, c. 400 BC, refortified c. 1st century BC, possibly by Cassivellaunus, whom Caesar may have attacked here, in 54 BC.

*St Albans, Iron Age earthworks. See below for map refs. Finds in Verulamium Museum, **St Albans.**

The NW corner of the late Iron Age town can be seen in Prae Wood (TL/ 123068), 1½ miles w of St Albans, N of A414. The area of this Belgic settlement, perhaps the capital of Tasciovanus (c. 15 BC–AD 10), King of the Catuvellauni (fig. 14), extended s towards A412. This site dominated the ford across the Ver at St Michael's and commanded the surrounding country. There is little to be seen now, Prae Wood containing many slight earthworks, some of which belong to this site, others being later. Excavation has shown that this was a lightly defended capital. Its fortifications, which included a stockade, were rebuilt against the Roman legions about AD 43. The settlement flourished, a royal mint being established there. In the second quarter of the 1st century AD the tribal capital was moved to Colchester; the Prae Wood settlement continued to thrive, however.

To the N of this site, between A5 and Gorhambury Park (TL/124085), is Devil's Dyke. Its purpose was to block open country between the river and wooded ground to the w, marking the N limit of the territory directly associated with the tribal capital. The ditch is at least 50 ft. wide, but of unknown depth. It was probably built towards the end of the 1st century BC.

Beech Bottom Dyke (TL/155093 to centre. Well seen at TL/150088) lies between A6 and B651. Its w end is 1 mile N of St Albans centre. It is crossed by the railway. Like Devil's Dyke, it covered open ground between the Rivers Ver and Lea. Of unusual strength, its ditch today is 29 ft. deep and 90 ft. wide. The original depth is not known. It has a main bank on its s side and a slight one on the N side. This boundary dyke should be associated with the earlier Belgic settlement at Wheathampstead (below). The Devil's Dyke N of Prae Wood would be its subsequent extension.

Wheathampstead (TL/184135, TL/ 188134): on the E side of this town there are 2 stretches of a bank and ditch, the w called Devil's Dyke, the E called The Slad. Each appears to be part of 1 earthwork enclosing 90–100 acres. Excavation has shown that the Devil's Dyke is up to 40 ft. deep and nearly 90 ft. wide at the surface. There is a bank 9 ft. high on its E side and another, 6 ft. high, on its w side. These earthworks may be part of the defences of the tribal capital of King Cassivellaunus (flourishing 54 BC, died c. 40–35 BC). They would have commanded a ford across the River Lea. Wheathampstead may have been the place where, in 54 BC, Julius Caesar inflicted a defeat on the Catuvellaunian forces.

Humberside

NEOLITHIC

*Kilham, long barrow (TA/056674) 2½ miles w of Rudstone (B1253), w of road from Sheep Rake Lane to Dotterill Park. Grave goods in British Museum.

Now heavily ploughed, the mound lies NE/SW and was 170 ft. long and 60 ft. wide at the NE. A Bronze Age mound had been added to the sw end, covering a food vessel burial (c. 2,000–1,400 BC), with other burials of this period added to the long barrow. Recent excavation has shown that after an initial phase comprising an enigmatic pair of parallel ditches c. 140 ft. long and 21 ft. apart, a rectangular enclosure of timbers set in a bedding trench was constructed, c. 180 ft. long and 25–30 ft. wide, with squared ends and an entrance (with a ritual pit) at each end and another in the N corner. Within this enclosure there had been a timber and earth burial chamber, yielding 2 burials in the 19th century and other features including a forecourt to the chamber. An avenue of timber uprights extended from the NE end of the enclosure for an unknown distance. Quarry ditches had been dug outside the N and s sides of the enclosure in 2 stages: first, the w ¾ of the enclosure was filled with chalk from ditches of corresponding length. Then, perhaps after the E quarter with its burial chamber had been burnt, further lengths of ditch were dug to provide chalk to cover it. Date, c. 2,880 BC (C14).

*Willy Howe, round barrow (TA/063724) 3½ miles NW of Rudston (B1253), 1 mile ESE of Wold Newton.

This resembles **Duggleby Howe** (p. 241) in size and situation, being 24 ft. high and about 130 ft. in diam. No burials have yet been found in it (although a large deep grave-pit was revealed), nor evidence for date – but perhaps c. 2,200–1,700 BC.

BRONZE AGE

*Callis Wold, round barrows (around SE/830555) 4½ miles NE of Pocklington (B1246, B1247), between A166 and Millington Heights. Grave goods in Transport Museum, Hull.

There are at least 16 barrows in this group, most now damaged by the plough and none close enough to constitute a true barrow cemetery. The mound at SE/ 829556 was found to have covered an elaborate double circle of stakes 21 ft. and 28 ft. in diam.; at the centre there was an oval grave containing a crouched inhumation burial with a food vessel and a stone battle-axe. A ditch 100 ft. in diam. surrounded the mound. It is possible that the stakes had originally supported the walls of an enclosure or even a large hut. The mound at SE/825569, on the N side of A166, contained cremations in collared urns and beads of jet, with 2 of Near Eastern blue faience. Other mounds in this area covered cremations and a few inhumations (one buried with 2 goats and a pig), with collared urns, food vessels, flint and bone tools. Date, c. 1,700–1,400 BC.

Rudstone, standing stone (TA/097677) 5¼ miles W of Bridlington (A165, A166, B1253), in Rudstone churchyard, on B1253.

This block of stone, 25½ ft. high, 6 ft. wide and 2¼ ft. thick, is perhaps the largest monolith in Britain. It is of grit brought from Cayton or Carnelian Bays, over 10 miles to the N. The stone is likely to have been erected c. 2,200–1,400 BC.

South Side Mount, round barrow (TA/ 107665) 1 mile SE of Rudstone (B1253), 4½ miles W of Bridlington (A165, A166, B1255). Grave goods in British Museum.

This chalk mound now being ploughed out was originally 100 ft. in diam. and 9 ft. high. Skeletons of 17 men, women and children were found in the mound, all evidently secondary burials. They were accompanied by food vessels and beakers, with many flint tools. The primary burial has not yet been uncovered. Recent aerial photographs show the mound to be surrounded by a circular ditch with a causeway and by a square ditch a little further out. Date, c. 1,700–1,400 BC.

*Towthorpe, round barrows (around SE/ 879638) 7½ miles SE of Malton (A64, A169, B1248, B1257), along green road from Aldro to Sledmere (B1251, B1252, B1253). Grave goods in Transport Museum, Hull.

Barrows occur at intervals along this lane which may mark the line of a prehistoric track. At SE/879638, beside B1248 and at W end of Towthorpe Plantation, there is a mound which was 12½ ft. high in 1870 and 132 ft. in diam. At its base and central, a grave was found, containing an extended skeleton of an adult. A fine bronze dagger of Wessex or Breton origin, a stone hammer head with shaft hole and a flint knife were with the corpse. Higher in the mound there were the cremated bones of a child, deposited in a wooden box. At SE/885641, a mound originally over 8 ft. high covered several burials and included internal wooden structures. Near the centre a grave contained a contracted skeleton furnished with a stout bronze dagger also of Wessex or Breton origin. A large number of inhumations have been found in this line of barrows, with food vessels, beakers, flint tools and ornaments of bone. Date, c. 2,000–1,400 BC.

Willy Howe, round barrow. See Neolithic.

IRON AGE

Dane's Dyke, defensive earthwork (TA/ 216694, S end) 2¾ miles NE of Bridlington (A165, B1253, B1255), ¾ mile W of Flamborough (B1229, B1255).

Of the many lines of earthworks in this area, Dane's Dyke seems likely to be pre-Roman. Future excavations may also show that many of the other ditch systems hereabouts also belong to the Iron Age. Cutting off a peninsula of 5 square miles, it extends N from coast to coast, from Dane's Dyke House. It is much more massive than most of these earthworks, consisting of a bank up to 18 ft. high, a ditch 60 ft. wide in places, facing W, and a counterscarp bank.

*Dane's Graves, barrow cemetery (TA/ 018633) 3½ miles N of Driffield (A164, A166, B1249), ½ mile E of B1249. Grave goods in British Museum.

On these gentle slopes over 200 round barrows, 10–30 ft. in diam. and 1–4 ft. high, can be found; some have a surrounding ditch. They are the survivors of a larger cemetery. They belong to the mid 2nd century BC and may represent a movement of people direct to the Yorkshire Wolds from N France. The corpses buried here were placed, crouched and unburnt, in oblong graves beneath the barrows. Several had been furnished with grave goods, pots containing food offerings including joints of pork, iron and bronze

brooches, pins, armlets and beads. One burial consisted of 2 men buried with their 2-wheeled chariot. Though the horses had not been buried, their snafflebits and other items of harness had been put in the grave.

Isle of Wight

NEOLITHIC

Afton Down, long barrow. See Bronze Age.
***Long Stone,** long barrow (SZ/408843) 3 miles NNW of Shorwell (B3323, B3399), ½ mile N of Mottistone (B3399).

This long barrow has a mound 100 ft. in length and about 30 ft. wide at the E end (it is orientated E/W). Here it is 4 ft. high. At the E end there are 2 blocks of locally derived sandstone, one recumbent, the other standing 13 ft. above ground. Excavation has failed to reveal flanking ditches or burials, but showed that there is a kerb of stones along the N side of the barrow, which doubtless enclosed the whole mound. The 2 monoliths at the E were probably always free-standing uprights, a feature found in some other long barrows. They are not the remains of a burial chamber. Date, 3,500–2,500 BC.

*BRONZE AGE

Afton Down, barrow cemetery and Neolithic long barrow (SZ/352857) 1 mile SE of Freshwater (A3055), at W end of golf course. Grave goods in Carisbrooke Castle Museum.

This cemetery extends in a ragged line for nearly ¼ mile. It comprises 2 bell-barrows, a disc-barrow and 11 bowl-barrows. Several have been opened in the last century and yielded burials after cremation. The bowl-barrow at the W end is the tallest, 8 ft. high. Moving E, the next mound is a Neolithic long barrow, 3 ft. high at the E end and over 120 ft. in length.

To the E there are the remains of a disc-barrow 103 ft. in diam., converted into a tee green. After 2 bowls, one 6 ft. high, there is a bell-barrow, nearly 100 ft. in diam. and 5 ft. in ht. A bowl 6 ft. high separates it from a second bell-barrow 4 ft. high, which had an unaccompanied cremation at its centre.

The last site in this group comprises 3 small bowls touching each other. Each is about 1 ft. high and cremations have been found in them. Date of long barrow, 3,500–2,500 BC: cemetery c. 1,700–1,400 BC.

Devil's Punchbowl, round barrow (SZ/597869) 1¾ miles N of Sandown (A3055, B3395), ½ mile W of Brading (A3055), on N side of minor road W to Askey Down. Grave goods in British Museum.

This bowl-barrow is over 60 ft. in diam. and 5 ft. high. Its primary burial has not been found but higher up in the mound there was a crouched inhumation, provided with a hammer head of antler. Date, c. 2,000–1,400 BC.

Five Barrows, barrow cemetery (SZ/390852) 1 mile N of Brook (bet. B3399 and A3055).

This cemetery is irregularly planned but extends W/E, a bell-barrow at its W end. There are 8 mounds in the cemetery, the bell being 8 ft. high. Of the others, 6 are bowls (hts. 1½–6½ ft.) and 1, at the E end, is a disc-barrow 116 ft. across. The tallest bowl at the E end has an apparent causeway across its ditch at the NE. There are no burial records, though hollows at the centre of most indicate past excavations. Date, c. 1,700–1,400 BC.

Gallibury Hump, round barrow (SZ/ 443842) 1¼ miles NW of Shorwell (B3323, B3399).

This barrow is of note as being perhaps the largest on the mainland of Britain. It is 10 ft. high and nearly 100 ft. in diam. It has a large excavation hollow at the centre but nothing is known of its contents. The mound appears to be a heap of flints. Date, c. 1,700–1,400 BC.

Micah Morey's Tump, round barrows (SZ/536876) 2½ miles SE of Newport, ½ mile N of Arreton (A3056), E of Downend.

This bowl-barrow is the last survivor of a group of 3–4 mounds. It is nearly 60 ft. in diam. and 6½ ft. high. Nothing is known of its primary burial, but Saxon interments have been found high in the mound. Morey was hanged from a gibbet here about 1730. The socket for this post was found in 1815 when the Saxon burials were uncovered. Date, c. 1,700–1,400 BC.

Shalcombe, barrow cemetery (SZ/391855) 1 mile N of Brook (between B3399, A3055). In plantation N of **Five Barrows** cemetery (above). Grave goods in Carisbrooke Castle Museum.

This cemetery has 5 bowl-barrows and a bell. Now obscured by firs, the bowls are insignificant in size but from 1 of them came the most important grave goods in the Island – a bronze knife with bone handle-pommel, a small bronze chisel and 2 boar's tusks, an assemblage reminiscent of the grave goods from barrows around Stonehenge. There is a bell-barrow in this group, perhaps the finest in the Island. It is 7 ft. high and 143 ft. in diam. Date, c. 1,700–1,400 BC.

IRON AGE

*Chillerton Down Camp, promontory fort (SZ/483842) 3¼ miles SSW of Newport (A3020, A3054), ½ mile W of Chillerton Street.

A roughly rectangular spur is cut off at the SW by a massive bank and ditch, 25 acres being thus protected. Steep slopes on N, S and E make further earthworks unnecessary. The rampart, still 10 ft. high, appears to have been built by 5 gangs, each raising a mound of chalk rubble from the ditch. A gap between the NW end of the rampart and the edge of the spur formed the entrance: it was approached by an embanked track from the SW, now ploughed out. It is possible that this fort is unfinished. Not yet dated.

Five Barrows Camp, promontory fort. See Chillerton Down Camp, above.

Kent

PALAEOLITHIC

*Oldbury Hill, rock shelters (TQ/586565) on E side of Oldbury hill-fort, ¾ mile SW of Ightham (A25, A227). Finds in Maidstone Museum.

On the E side of Oldbury Hill, 400 yds. S of the NE gate of the Iron Age hill-fort (p. 159), the remains of rock-shelters apparently used by Old Stone Age hunters are to be seen. They are formed by the natural hollowing-out of soft sandstone which here underlies the hard upper layers of Greensand. Large numbers of flint implements, suggesting a workshop, were found here late in the last century. These shelters may have been used thus, c. 35,000 BC, by hunters of Mousterian culture.

NEOLITHIC

Addington Park, chambered long barrow (TQ/654592) 2¼ miles E of Wrotham (A20, A227), cut by road into Addington from Trottiscliffe. Close to the Chestnuts burial chamber and to Addington Church.

This burial mound, orientated NE/SW, is about 200 ft. in length and 40 ft. in breadth. In plan it is conspicuously rectangular. At the NE end a jumble of stones represents either a blind entrance or, more likely, a burial chamber. There is a curb of stone slabs on both sides of the mound. No burials or other discoveries have been recorded from this barrow. Likely date, c. 3,500–2,500 BC, but its resemblance, in plan, to N German and Dutch tombs of slightly later date should be noted.

*Chestnuts, burial chamber (TQ/652592) 2½ miles E of Wrotham (A20, A227), ¼ mile NW of Addington, off A20. Finds in Maidstone Museum.

Excavated in 1957, this chambered tomb comprises a D-shaped mound of scraped-up topsoil, originally about 64 ft. wide, 50 ft. long and never very high. There was no evidence for a surrounding ditch or stone kerb. At the E end a convex facade of massive sarsen slabs gave access to a slightly wedge-shaped chamber, c. 12 ft. long, 7½ ft. at its widest and c. 10 ft. high, divided into 2 at its centre by an upright stone. Cremated remains of at least 9 people, with 2 or more infants, were found, with Windmill Hill pottery, apparently thrown into the forecourt when more burials with later Neolithic pottery were added. Date, c. 3,500–2,500 BC.

*Coldrum, chambered long barrow and alignment (TQ/654607) 2¾ miles NE of Wrotham (A20, A227), 1 mile NE of Trottiscliffe. Close to Chestnuts burial chamber and Addington Park long barrow. Finds in Maidstone Museum.

Coldrum is unusually short for its width, being 70 × 50 ft. An elaborate retaining wall of sarsen slabs defines the mound. Orientated E/W, a rectangular stone burial chamber is situated at the E end. Excavations carried out here in 1910 and again in 1922 showed that at least 22, including infants as well as the aged, had been buried at different times in this communal tomb. Certain skeletal like-nesses made it probable that they were all members of one family. One skull seems to have been accorded special attention; it was found placed on a carefully made stone shelf in the chamber. Flints and early Neolithic pottery were found here in 1910. This barrow may have been in use c. 3,000 BC.

Countless Stones, see **Lower Kits Coty.**

*Jullieberrie's Grave, long barrow (TR/077532) ¼ mile SE of junction of A252 from Chilham and A28 from Ashford. Finds in Chilham Castle.

This is an outlying specimen of the unchambered long barrow more familiar in Wessex and elsewhere on the chalk. A quarry has removed its N end, with any burials that it may have covered; we are left with a mound 144 ft. in length, 48 ft. in width at the N end and tapering to 42 ft. in width at the opposite end. Its greatest ht. is 7 ft. An irregularly planned ditch, no longer visible, runs around the mound as it survives, but may originally have been open at the N end. Roughly U-shaped, the ditch was dug 5 ft. into the chalk and had a width of 15–20 ft. The mound is composed of chalk from this ditch.

During excavations in 1937, 4 Romano-British burials were found in the upper ditch-filling at the S end. The quarry having destroyed all Neolithic burials, these are the only skeletons so far found in this barrow.

The most important object discovered during the excavations was a polished flint axe of specifically Nordic type – probably an import from Scandinavia or North Germany where such tools were current about 2,500 BC. Julliberrie's Grave must have been built about this time.

Kits Coty, chambered long barrow (TQ/745608) 5¼ miles s of Rochester (A2, A228, A229), ¼ mile NW of Junction of A229 and B road from Aylesford.

The mound of this barrow has been so denuded by the plough that its original dimensions cannot be given. Eighteenth-century sketches by Stukeley, however, establish that it was elongated, and orientated E/W. At its E end there was a rectangular burial chamber, of which 3 uprights and a capstone survive (it is likely that these stones are part of a chamber and not a blind entrance). Stukeley's sketch suggests that there was a megalithic structure at the w end also – unless the stone he showed represents the remains of a retaining wall. Date, c. 3,000 BC.

Lower Kits Coty, burial chamber (TQ/ 744604) ¼ mile s of Kits Coty, off s side of road to Aylesford (B2011) from Lower Bell Inn.

Today, a jumbled heap of about 20 sarsen stones is all that remains here of a burial chamber. In the 18th century these stones were less ruined and Stukeley shows them as a D-shaped setting. Date, c. 3,000 BC.

BRONZE AGE

*Ringwould, round barrows (TR/365471) 4¼ miles NE of Dover harbour, ¾ mile SE of Ringwould (A258, B2057), off A258; on Free Down. Grave goods in Maidstone Museum.

Two bowl-barrows are situated close together here. The w mound, slightly oval in plan, about 75 ft. in diam. and 4½ ft. high, was excavated in 1872. Beneath it 4 pits were found, dug into the native chalk and evidently all primary. They were covered first by chalk, then soil, a heap of flints next and finally an outer jacket of earth. In every pit there was a cremation, each in a cinerary urn; all the urns were inverted. There was also an incense cup with 1 urn and 2 more with another, together with faience beads, 3 segmented and 1 oblate. The urns are late in the British series and must have been deposited here c. 1,400 BC. The faience beads, like those from Wessex and Sussex, would have been traded to Britain from the Near East about the same time.

The E barrow, of roughly the same dimensions, was also excavated in 1872, but no burials were found in it. It was built probably at the same date as its neighbour.

IRON AGE

*Bigbury, Belgic fortified settlement (TR/ 117575) 2 miles w of Canterbury, 1 mile NE of Chartham Hatch. Finds in Maidstone and Canterbury Museums.

Excavation has shown that these late earthworks were built on a site occupied from the early Iron Age but of unknown extent. The main earthwork follows roughly the 200-ft. contour and encloses about 25 acres of land. To the NW there is an irregularly shaped annexe which takes in a further 8 acres. There are original entrances on the E and W. The E one, utilised by the Pilgrims Way, is defended by 2 ditches and an outer bank, the breaks through these being deliberately staggered to make entry difficult.

The main defences consist of an inner bank 8–10 ft. high, with a ditch outside it about 16 ft. wide and originally some 6 ft. deep. There is also a counterscarp bank about 8 ft. broad and 3–4 ft. high. The earthwork forming the annex on the N side is similar in design; it is broken by 2 entrance-gaps which may be original. It probably served as a cattle pound.

Many domestic and other objects of Belgic culture have been found within the earthworks from time to time, suggesting permanent occupation here by a considerable farming community. Of these things, perhaps the most interesting is an almost complete iron slave chain with barrel padlock, a reminder of the traffic in slaves between Britain and the continent shortly before the Roman Conquest.

High Rocks, hill-fort. See **Tunbridge Wells.**

*Oldbury, hill-fort (TQ/582562) ¾ mile sw of Ightham (A25, A227) on N side of A25. Finds in Maidstone Museum.

Oldbury Hill is everywhere protected by steeply sloping sides and is an ideal site for a hill-fort. Its ramparts are visible on all sides except for a break at the NE due to 19th-century levelling, and along part of the E side where precipitous slopes may never have been additionally protected by more than a stockade. The visitor will find an earthwork comprising a bank and ditch with counterscarp bank, and in places an outer ditch. It encloses 123 acres. There are in-turned entrances in the s and NE sides. Excavation has revealed 2 periods of construction.

In period 1, c. 100 BC, Oldbury had a bank and ditch, the former not revetted, the latter V-shaped and about 5 ft. deep. Entrances, not now visible in their original form, were either simple or overlapping.

In period 2, stretches of outer bank and ditch were added in places, the former faced with heavy rubble. The period 1 ditch was recut and given a broad, flat profile. The rampart behind it was heightened. The elaborate in-turned entrances were constructed. The profile of the new ditches identifies the builders with those building similar forts in N France c. mid 1st century BC. Oldbury 2 may therefore represent a Belgic consolidation of their position in Kent at this time.

*Squerryes Park, hill-fort (TQ/442522) 1 mile s of Westerham (A25, A233), ¼ mile E of road via Kent Hatch to Crockham Hill. Finds in British Museum.

A promontory has been converted into a hill-fort of c. 18 acres by provision of a bank, ditch and counterscarp bank along the s side, facing open ground, and by enclosing the E and W sides within a ditch and counterscarp bank, together with artificial steepening and heightening of the crest along these 2 sides. There is an original entrance at the sw, where the outer bank is massive, forming an ex-tended entrance passage. Here the ditch was originally 9 ft. deep and 28 ft. wide: tumbled stonework found in excavation suggests there may have been a revetment to both banks. Not dated but possibly late Iron Age and never permanently occupied.

*Tunbridge Wells, High Rocks, hill-fort (TQ/561382) 1½ miles sw of Tunbridge Wells. Finds in Tunbridge Wells Museum.

This camp has an area of about 20 acres. It is protected by the precipitous High Rocks on the NW and by double ramparts elsewhere: at the E entrance the banks and ditches are trebled. Excavation has revealed 2 periods of construction. High Rocks 1 had a single bank and rock-cut ditch, the former not faced. This is the outermost earthwork which is now visible. Date, c. 100 BC.

In period 2 the inner earthworks were added, the banks being consolidated or faced with stone rubble and the ditches shallow and flat-floored (as at Oldbury 2, above). The E entrance was elaborated at this stage. Date, mid 1st century BC.

Lancashire

BRONZE AGE

*Bleasdale, palisade barrow (SD/577460) 5½ miles E of Garstang (A6, B6272, B6430), ¼ mile NE of Bleasdale Church. Grave goods in Preston Museum.

This site (fig. 38) comprised a small mound of turf 36 ft. across and nearly 3 ft. high, surrounded by a ring of 11 oak posts (marked by concrete pillars) with a ditch around this, lined with birch poles. There is an entrance through the latter at the E, with 2 parallel rows of 3 posts leading to the outer circle. At the centre there was a grave, 4 ft. long, 1½ ft. deep. It contained 2 collared urns, both filled with cremated human bones and charcoal; there was also an incense cup in one.

Around this grave there was an outer circle with a diam. of 150 ft., with large posts marking an entrance at the SE. The palisade forming this ring comprised closely spaced small posts set between larger ones 14–16 ft. apart. This part of the site cannot now be seen: the inner mound was not at its centre but almost touched it at the E. There were no other features within the outer circle. Date, c. 1,900–1,720, C14 determination.

IRON AGE

*Castercliff, hill-fort (SD/885384) 1¼ miles ssw of Colne (A56, A6068, B6250), ¾ mile ESE of Bott Lane Station (Nelson).

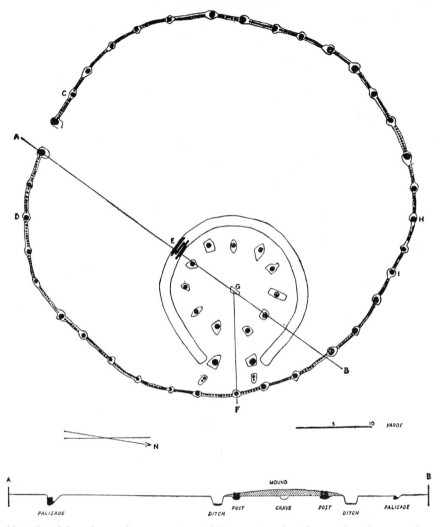

38   *Bleasdale: plan and cross-section of Bronze Age burial mound and surrounding palisade*

This denuded hill-fort is oval and encloses almost 2 acres. The defences comprise triple circuits of bank and ditch, with scarps representing outworks to the NE. The innermost bank is the slightest and may represent an earlier, univallate fort. It is complete, but shows only as a scarp or a very low bank. The middle bank and ditch are the stoutest, rising 3–5 ft. above the interior and falling 9 ft. to the present ditch floor. There are many gaps in it. The outer bank is the counterscarp to the central rampart and is discontinuous, but is well-preserved along the S and E sides. Outworks, which show as scarps, with short isolated lengths of bank, can be seen around the E and NE sides, about 70 ft. beyond the main defences.

The interrupted middle earthwork suggests that this, the second phase of the hill-fort, was never finished. Not dated. **Planes Wood,** hill-fort. See **Portfield.**

*Portfield, promontory fort (SD/745355), 6 miles NW of Burnley, ¾ mile SE of Whalley (A59, A671). Finds in Manchester University Museum.

The steep-sided promontory along the SE and SW has made defence here unnecessary, although a single rampart follows the edge of the c. 3½ acres of the site, with 2 additional lengths of rampart around the SE. The main defences face N, where the ramparts are triple. Excavation has revealed that the earliest rampart, at least along the N, had a clay base 13 ft. wide, with a kerb of stones set on edge along the front: it had no ditch. Later, this defence was absorbed into the triple ramparts visible today. The main rampart was at least 20 ft. wide and originally c. 8 ft. high. It was of clay, revetted back and front with stones. Outside its counterscarp bank, along the N, are traces of a third bank. Undated.

*Warton Crag, hill-fort (SD/492728), 1½ miles NNW of Carnforth (A6, B6254), ½ mile NW of Warton.

Covered densely with undergrowth and trees, this is nevertheless perhaps the most impressive prehistoric earthwork in the county. It is best visited in winter months. Its SE and SW sides protected by precipitous slopes, 3 wide-spaced ramparts cover approach from the N, defining a very roughly D-shaped space of c. 15 acres. The inner bank, which has no ditch, encloses c. 7 acres. Near its E end it crosses an 8 ft. cliff formed by a geological fault: it is not clear whether any of the breaks in this bank is an original entrance but the gap c. 50 ft. SE of the 8 ft. cliff is likely to be so, the cliff helping in its defence. Little can be seen of the middle rampart, c. 150 ft. beyond the inner one. Its NW end may have curved back and joined the inner rampart at some point. The outer rampart, over 200 ft. beyond the middle bank, is almost hidden by undergrowth. Its NW end, which incorporates a limestone outcrop, shows as a distinct bank where it lies outside the plantation. Not dated.

Leicestershire

IRON AGE

*Breedon-on-the-Hill, hill-fort (SK/406234) 5¼ miles NE of Ashby-de-la-Zouch (A50, A453, B5006, B5326), N of A453. Finds in Leicester Museum.

A quarry has cut away the SE quarter of this hill-fort. Originally it would have been roughly pear-shaped. The hill-fort, which has an internal area of about 18 acres, is protected by a single bank and ditch around the W half and by a bank, ditch and counterscarp bank along the E. This side runs 400 ft. E of the churchyard. There is an in-turned entrance near the centre of the W side (facing the W end of the church), and there was a possible entrance opposite, in the E side: the former is now damaged and the latter destroyed. The whole fort is being gradually quarried away.

Excavation has shown that there may have been Iron Age occupation on the hill before the hill-fort was built. The rampart of the earliest fort may have been timber-laced and was certainly revetted along the front and back with timbers. Rubble from its broad, shallow, flat-bottomed ditch formed a solid core. Later, the ditch was cleaned out and the material used to heighten the rampart. The front was now faced with turf while more turves were heaped at the rear and a breastwork of drystone added. The bank may have been about 10 ft. high.

Much pottery, animal bones and other domestic rubbish from inside the fort attest permanent occupation here, c. 3rd century BC–1st century AD.

39   *Burrough Hill: Iron Age hill-fort. In-turned entrance top left*

Burrough Hill, hill-fort (SK/761119) 4½ miles s of Melton Mowbray (A606, A607, B676), 1¾ miles SE of Gt Dalby (B6047).

This hill-fort is polygonal and encloses about 12 acres. Its defences comprise a massive rampart and ditch with traces of a counterscarp bank. They follow the edge of a steep-sided spur. There is a deep in-turned entrance at the SE corner, the in-turns being about 49 yds. long. This is approached by a hollow way up the hill-side from the SW which might be prehistoric. Some authorities suggest that the in-turned part of this entrance may be a later Iron Age addition to a simple entrance. The gap in the earthworks at the SW is probably fairly modern, although it is also approached by a deep hollow way

(fig. 39).

Trial excavation has shown that there were stone guard-chambers at the inner end of the entrance in-turns and that the rampart was faced with drystone walling. The interior contains storage pits but so far no huts have been identified.

This camp might have been the tribal capital of the Coritani (fig. 14), the non-Belgic, late Iron Age tribe of this area. The many gaps in its ramparts could then be attributed to the Roman Conquest and to the slighting of earthworks which so often followed their capture. Date of construction, c. 2nd century BC.

The Bulwarks, hill-fort. See **Breedon-on-the-Hill.**

Lincolnshire

*NEOLITHIC

Although there is a large concentration of long barrows on the chalk of the Lincolnshire Wolds, only one, Skendleby, has been scientifically excavated. The type of wooden structures and burials which it contained (below) may be assumed to exist beneath most of the others in this area.

Ash Hill, long barrow (TF/209962) 10 miles NW of Louth (A16, A157), 1½ miles

N of Binbrook (B1203), W edge of Swinhope Park.

This is the best preserved of the Lincolnshire long barrows although at present sadly neglected. It is wedge-shaped in plan, 128 ft. long and 53 ft. wide at the E end. Here it is 7 ft. high. As is the case with all these long barrows its side-ditches are not visible though doubtless they exist. It is orientated NE/SW. It has not been excavated, but must belong to the period c. 3,500–2,500 BC.

Hoe Hill, its contemporary, lies ¾ mile to the SE.

Ash Holt, long barrow (TA/190012) 3¾ miles SW of Laceby (A18, A46), in spinny 1 mile E of Cuxwold.

Though unusually small, this is an undoubted long barrow. It is wedge-shaped and orientated S/N. It is 78 ft. long and 38 ft. wide at the S end, where the mound has been damaged by robbers. Its max. ht. is 4½ ft. Side-ditches are not now visible. Date c. 3,500–2,500 BC.

Beacon Plantation, long barrow (TF/373777) 6½ miles SE of Louth (A16, A157) on N side of A16.

The largest of these barrows, this one measures 257 ft. by 64 ft. Lying SW/NE, it is 7 ft. high at the former end; like the others in this area, the mound is wedge-shaped and the side-ditches invisible. It has been damaged in several places, particularly at the S end, due, perhaps, to its adaptation as a beacon. Originally its mound would have been regular and continuous. Date, c. 3,500–2,500 BC.

Deadman's Graves, long barrows (TF/444720) 3¼ miles NE of Partney (A16, A158), ½ mile NW of Claxby.

There are 2 long barrows here, the map reference being to the W mound. This site, placed nearly E/W, is 160 ft. long, 54 ft. wide and 6 ft. high at its larger E end. It has no visible side-ditches and has been damaged near the middle.

The second mound, 400 yds. SE, is 173 ft. long, 60 ft. wide and 6 ft. high at its E end. It is orientated E/W and has been extensively damaged and distorted. Its side-ditches cannot be seen. Both mounds must be dated c. 3,500–2,500 BC.

*Giants Hill, long barrows (TF/429712) 2 miles NE of Partney (A16, A158), ¾ mile NW of Skendleby, W of A1028. Finds in British Museum.

Though now under the plough, this long barrow is still conspicuous. It has a height of 5 ft. at each end, lessening slightly in the middle. It is 210 ft. long, orientated SE/NW, and is rectangular in plan. Side-ditches continue round both ends.

Excavation has shown that before the mound was erected a rectangular wooden structure, 189 × 37 ft., had been built as an enclosure for corpses. The E end of this was concave and was clearly intended to be a monumental facade. The remains of hurdling and other structures were found within the enclosure. A platform of chalk blocks had been built 70 ft. behind this facade and the skeletons and disarticulated remains of at least 8 persons were placed on it, haphazardly. The barrow was then built to cover the burials and the enclosure. This is likely to have been 12 ft. high. The side-ditches which provided material for the mound were dug irregularly to a depth of 8–12 ft. and a width of 15–25 ft. Pottery and other finds suggest that this long barrow was built c. 2,000 BC.

There is a second long barrow 250 yds. to the S. It is almost ploughed flat but still shows as a slight ledge.

Hoe Hill, long barrow (TF/215953) ¾ mile SE of Ash Hill (above, p. 163), W of Hoehill Farm and B1203.

This barrow is well preserved. Lying nearly E/W and wedge-shaped, it is 180 ft. long, 60 ft. wide at the E end and here 11 ft. high. It is protected by a small wood. It has slight damage near the centre, and side-ditches cannot now be seen.

Early in this century there was another long barrow on the same axis, 70 yds. to the W. This has disappeared. Date, c. 3,500–2,500 BC.

Spellow Hills, long barrow (TF/402723) 2½ miles NNW of Partney (A16, A158), W of A16.

This barrow is orientated SE/NW. It is wedge-shaped, 182 ft. in length, 40 ft. in width and 7 ft. in ht. at its S end. It has been badly damaged and has the misleading appearance of 3 conjoined round barrows. Many human bones are reputed to have been found beneath this long barrow in the past. Date, c. 3,500–2,500 BC.

Tathwell, long barrow (TF/294822) 3¾ miles SW of Louth (A16, A157), 1¾ miles w of Tathwell, ¼ mile NW of junction of A153 and road to Tathwell. Not marked on 1-in. O.S.

A single large tree marks the position of this barrow. The mound, wedge-shaped, lies SE/NW. It is 105 ft. long, 52 ft. broad at the SE end and here 5½ ft. high. It has been badly damaged by rabbits. Date, c. 3,500–2,500 BC.

BRONZE AGE

Bully Hills, barrow cemetery (TF/330827) 2¾ miles s of Louth (A16, A157), ¾ mile SE of Tathwell, E of road to Hangham.

This cemetery consists of 7 bowl-barrows. They are arranged in a line, 6 close together and the seventh a little apart. Their hts. range from 4–10 ft. and their diams. from 50–80 ft. The second and third from the NE stand on a rectangular platform and are themselves more rectangular than circular. They are spaced along a local skyline and are extremely impressive. Nothing is known of the contents of these barrows. Date, c. 1,700–1,400 BC.

Butterbump, barrow cemetery (TF/493724) 2¾ miles w of Hogthorpe (A52), 1½ miles E of Willoughby, ½ mile SE of Bonthorpe.

There are 7 barrows in this cemetery.

They are arranged in 2 widely spaced lines nearly E/W. Now under the plough and denuded, their diams. are about 30–80 ft. and their hts. 2–4 ft. Their contents has not been recorded but at least 1 is currently under excavation. Date, c. 1,700–1,400 BC.

Haugham, round barrows (TF/338817) 3½ miles s of Louth (A16, A153, A157), on N side of Haugham village.

These 2 prominent bowl-barrows are 65 ft. and 30 ft. in diam. and 8 ft. and 3 ft. high respectively. Nothing is known of their contents. Date, c. 1,700–1,400 BC.

IRON AGE

Honington, hill-fort (SK/954424) 4¾ miles NE of Grantham, ¾ mile SE of Honington (A153, A607); NW of Barkston Heath Farm.

This site must owe its position to the Witham R. which in Iron Age times it would have commanded. It is an irregular 4-sided earthwork enclosing about 1 acre. Its defences, unusually elaborate for so small a camp, consist of 2 banks and ditches and an outer bank. The gap through the middle of the E side may be the original entrance. Not dated.

Norfolk

NEOLITHIC

*Arminghall, sacred site (TG/240060) 1½ miles s of Norwich, 1¼ miles NW of Arminghall. Finds in Norwich Museum.

There is nothing to be seen of this site on the ground except a slight depression but a brief description is necessary, because it is marked on the O.S. maps. It consisted of a central circular setting of 8 upright oak logs, 40–50 ft. in diam. surrounded by an inner ditch 90 ft. across,

20 ft. wide and 7–8 ft. deep, and a slighter outer ditch. There was a bank between them, made of gravel obtained from their excavation; the inner ditch and probably also the outer ditch were broken by 1 entrance facing SW. It is not known whether the wooden uprights were free-standing or supported lintels or even a roof. Occupation material from the floor of the inner ditch places Arminghall c. 2,520–2,220 BC (C14). Aerial photographs have shown that a cemetery of round

barrows accumulated around this sacred site. One of these has recently been excavated and has yielded beakers and other contemporary grave goods.

ft. deep, with a series of galleries radiating from their bases, and shafts which are shallower and were not undercut in this way (concentrated N of the custodian's

40　　*Grimes Graves: Neolithic flint mine galleries*

*Grimes Graves, flint mines (TL/817898) 5¼ miles NW of Thetford (A11, A134, B1107), ¾ mile S of A134/B1108 crossroads. Department of the Environment guardianship. Some finds at ticket office, others at British Museum, Ipswich Museum, Norwich Museum and Thetford Museum.

More than 360 mine shafts and shallower workings have been recorded (many visible as hollows) in this area of 34 acres; 2 have been cleared and made accessible to the public (fig. 40) (1 closed recently because unsafe: a third pit shortly to be opened). They are among the more remarkable prehistoric structures to be seen in England. Grimes Graves was probably the most important of the groups of flint mines which have been found widespread in the chalk country of England. Here, the mine shafts were of 2 types, those up to 30

hut). As elsewhere the red deer antler pick was the chief mining tool, the flint nodules being shovelled into baskets and lifted to the surface. Flint and stone axes were also used for cutting the chalk.

On the surface the miners roughed out their wares – mainly axe-heads – which were then exported, to be polished and finished by those who bought them.

One of the shafts on view (but closed recently) contained the most compelling religious deposit found in prehistoric England. This shaft had failed to find good flint. As if to ensure more success for further shafts, the miners built an altar of flints in it, heaped antlers around the altar and set before it a carving of a pregnant woman, together with a phallus and balls, all of chalk. A chalk lamp was placed at the base of the altar.

This mining community seems to have

flourished within the period 2,500–1,400 BC (C14).

The British Museum is engaged (1972 onwards) in an extended programme of survey and excavation at this site. It is likely that Grimes Graves will prove to be even more extensive than it is at present.

Flint knapping is still continued 3 miles to the SW, at Brandon.

*West Rudham, long barrow (TF/810254) 7½ miles SW of Fakenham (A148, A1065, B1355), 1½ miles SE of Harpley (A148), N of road to Weasenham St Peter. Finds in Norwich Museum.

This mound is about 210 ft. long and 70 ft. wide. It is orientated nearly N/S and is roughly oval in plan. Its max. ht. is nearly 7 ft. Excavation has revealed that the mound is surrounded by the ditches of 2 rectangular enclosures. The S one, which is the smaller and narrower, adds 45 ft. to the length of the whole barrow. At the junction of these structures, both covered by the mound, a platform was found on which a corpse may have been cremated. The mound itself was mainly of turf. Date, c. 2,500 BC.

BRONZE AGE

Bircham Common, barrow cemetery (TF/ 775316, NW end) 3½ miles SSE of Docking (A1067, B1153, B1155), ¾ mile SSE of Great Bircham (B1153, B1155).

These barrows are in a rough line and wide-spaced, running NW/SE. The mound at the NW end (map ref.) is a bell-barrow, its structure 90 ft. in diam. and 5–6 ft. high. It has a bank outside the ditch.

Across the road, SE, there is a line of 3 mounds, 2 bowls and a bell. The bowls are 6–7 ft. high and over 100 ft. in diam. The bell-barrow SE of these is about 150 ft. across and 7–8 ft. high. At its centre cremated human bones were found, protected by an inverted collared urn. With them was a bronze awl and several beads or buttons covered in gold sheet decorated with incised lines. Finds now lost. Date c. 1,700–1,400 BC.

Hill Field, barrow. See **Little Cressingham.**
*Little Cressingham, barrows (TL/867992) ¾ mile S of Little Cressingham, on W side of Hard Clump, S of road from Clermont

to Hopton House. Other barrows to W, in Seven Acre Plantation. Grave goods in Norwich Museum.

Though levelled by the plough, the bowl-barrow at TL/867992 is important because of the unusually rich grave goods deposited with the male burial beneath it. The skeleton had been buried W of the barrow centre, its knees drawn up. It had been deposited dressed, with an elaborate amber necklace and a rectangular gold plate (fig. 41) sewn to clothing on the chest. There were other gold ornaments together with a knife and a dagger of bronze. These grave goods are as rich as anything from Wessex: date, c. 1,700–1,400 BC. Other bowl-barrows, probably contemporary and part of one cemetery, are N of Seven Acre Plantation. That at TL/861986 is enormous, being over 200 ft. in diam. and about 15 ft. high. Another to the NE is under the plough; it is about 120 ft. across and 3–4 ft. high.

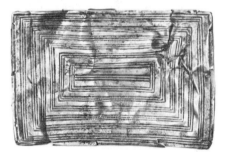

41   *Little Cressingham barrow : gold plate (3½ × 2¼ ins.), c. 1,700 BC*

Seven Acre Plantation, barrows, see **Little Cressingham.**
Seven Hills, barrow cemetery (TL/904814 centre) 2¼ miles SE of Thetford (A11, A134, A1066), SE of Great Snarehill Belt.

There were at least 11 mounds in this cemetery, in a line E/W. Only 6 barrows survive, in 2 groups of 3. The W group has 2 bowls, with a bell at the E. The latter is about 7 ft. high; the others are 3–4 ft. high and all are over 100 ft. across. The E group has recently been cleared of trees. It comprises 3 bowls, of which the central one is at least 7 ft. high. Recent damage has exposed the interior of the mound, showing that it has a core of sand, covered with chalk derived from the surrounding ditch. This is probably the structure of all these mounds. Nothing is known of their contents. Date, c. 1,700–1,400 BC.

Weasenham Plantation, barrow cemetery (TF/853198, centre) 7 miles NNE of Swaffham (A47, A1065, B1077), 1 mile S of Weasenham All Saints (A1065).

This group is scattered, but may be considered a cemetery in the Wessex manner. It contains examples of bell-, bowl-, disc- and saucer-barrows. At the NW end of the group, NW of the A1065, there is a saucer and a bell ('tumuli' on 1-in. O.S.), covered with vegetation but both about 150 ft. across. To the SE, between these and the A road (at TF/849201) there is a saucer-barrow about 140 ft. across and a bowl-barrow 3 ft. high and about 50 ft. in diam. South-east of the plantation there is a fine bell, 7 ft. high and 140 ft. in diam. It has a bank 11 ft. wide outside its ditch. Just to the S there are 2 bowl-barrows, they are now under the plough. At the E end of the plantation there is a group of 3 bowl-barrows, 60–90 ft. in diam. and 3–4 ft. high. At TF/868202 there was a disc-barrow, now destroyed. Date of cemetery, c. 1,700–1,400 BC.

IRON AGE

Holkham, lowland fort (TF/875447) 3 miles ESE of Wells-Next-the-Sea (A149, B1105), ½ mile N of A149/B1155 junction.

This camp is built on an island in a tidal salt marsh. It encloses about 5½ acres and is roughly oval. Steep natural scarps and water protect the W side. On the NE there is a single bank and ditch; on the S and SE there are 2 banks with a ditch between them. An original entrance faces S. Not dated.

This site probably protected a coastal trading station.

***Warham,** lowland fort (TF/945409) 7¼ miles N of Fakenham (A148, A1067, B1355), 2½ miles N of Little Walsingham, E of B1105. Finds in Norwich Museum.

This camp is nearly circular, its earthworks enclosing 3½ acres. These comprise 2 banks and ditches, reduced to 1 bank beside the river. While the NNW entrance may be original, the other gaps in the earthworks are modern: access may also have been obtained via the river. Excavation has shown that the inner ditch is roughly flat-bottomed and that both banks are now 8–9 ft. high. Date, 1st century BC–early 1st century AD, with Romano-British occupation.

Northamptonshire

NEOLITHIC

Thornhaugh, sacred site (TF/066008) 4½ miles SE of Stamford (A1, A43, A606, A6121), N of Manor Farm.

This site closely resembles the circles N and S of Ripon (p. 247) and is probably the same type of monument. It has a diam. of 275 ft. and consists of a broad low bank set between 2 concentric ditches. There appears to be a second bank inside the inner ditch. There are entrance causeways across the inner ditch at the NNW and SSE.

These are narrow and carefully squared off. They do not appear to have been left across the outer ditch. Its low-lying position is a classic one for a henge monument. There is the possibility, however, that this site may be a 17th or 18th century AD water garden. Date, if prehistoric, c. 2,500–1,700 BC.

IRON AGE

Borough Hill, hill-fort (SP/588626) 1 mile

E of Daventry (A45, A425, B4036, B4038). Finds in Northampton Museum.

The earthwork crowning this hill and enclosing 16 acres must be of 2 periods. At the N end there is a hill-fort with an immensely strong bank, ditch and counterscarp bank which encloses 4½ acres and also contains the E end of the golf course. Where it crosses the hill, its s side is protected by 2 banks and ditches. The original entrance appears to be at the SE: here one bank and ditch runs behind the other to form an overlapping approach to the area within. Later a very much slighter earthwork comprising a bank, ditch and counterscarp bank was built to enclose the whole hill. This is best preserved on the W, close to the golf course. It appears as a slight ledge on the E side. Not dated.

*Hunsbury, hill-fort (SP/737584) 2 miles SW of Northampton, ½ mile W of A43. Finds in Northampton Museum.

This site is important because of the variety of bronzes and other objects found when the area within it was worked for iron in the last century. The defences consist of an imposing bank, ditch and counterscarp bank, which enclose about 4 acres. The rampart was faced with drystone walling, reinforced with timber uprights; the ditch was c. 22 ft. deep. An original entrance faces SE.

The iron working has lowered the entire interior by nearly 8 ft., making the main rampart appear higher than it really is. During this process an enormous number of storage pits, many stone-lined and 6 ft. deep, were recorded. Also, at this time the presence of an outer ditch was established, almost doubling the area of the fort. This is not now visible. The richest finds, iron and bronze work and decorated pottery, show that the fort was flourishing in the 1st century BC. Other pottery, however, suggests a beginning in the 4th–3rd century BC.

*Rainsborough Camp, hill-fort (SP/526348) 5¾ miles SE of Banbury (A41, A361, A422, A423, B4035), 1¼ miles NE of Aynho (A41, B4031), W of Camp Farm on road to Charlton. Finds in Ashmolean Museum, Oxford.

This oval hill-fort has 2 banks and ditches, the outer not now visible except as weed growth along the W, enclosing 5½ acres. The original entrance, slightly inturned, is at the W. Excavation, 1961–5, has revealed a pre-hill-fort phase no later than the 6th century BC. In the 5th century BC the defences were built, comprising an inner bank of stepped construction, both sides drystone-faced and with a timber breastwork. The inner ditch was 8–14 ft. deep in bedrock. The outer bank was a dump of turf and rubble, its ditch 6–14 ft. deep. The entrance had a wood-lined passage, 60 ft. long leading to a pair of C-shaped guard chambers and sentry-box recesses and having double gates with a bridge over. Early in the 4th century BC the fort seems to have been burnt and perhaps abandoned. Late in the 2nd century BC the ramparts were rebuilt as dumps and the ditches were redug to great widths (32–34 ft. and 20–26 ft.), with depths of 5–10 ft. The entrance was also redesigned to provide a double-arched gate, without in-turns. The site was again abandoned, but re-occupied in Romano-British times and landscaped in the 18th century AD, to which belongs the drystone walling visible around the inner rampart.

Northumberland

NEOLITHIC

*Bellshiel Law, long cairn (NT/813014) 2¼ miles NW of Rochester (A68), on S side of Bellshiel Law, with round plantation at E end.

This mound is 367 ft. in length and is orientated E/W; it is 60 ft. wide at the E, narrowing to 29 ft. at the W. Its greatest ht. is about 4 ft. A large stone can be seen 70 ft. from the E end and on the N side of the barrow. It may belong to a burial chamber. Excavation showed that the barrow has a carefully built kerb, retaining a mound of boulders and smaller stones. At the E end, the N and S corners of the mound project slightly, suggesting the horns found commonly at the E end of long barrows in Scotland. Just within the mound at this end, a central grave was found which may have contained the main burial. No other burials or structures have been found. Date, c. 3,500–2,500 BC.

Coupland, sacred site (NT/940330) 4½ miles NW of Wooler (A697, A6111, B6348), ½ mile SE of Milfield (A697), on W side of A road.

Though damaged by the plough, this sacred site is still visible. Slightly oval in plan, its diam. is about 330 ft. Its ditch lies within its bank and both are broken by entrances 40–50 ft. wide at the N and S. Like most henge monuments this circle is on low ground close to water. Date, c. 2,500–1,700 BC.

Devil's Lapful, long cairn and Bronze Age cairn (NY/642928) 1 mile ESE of Kielder, Cheviot Hills. Cairn at NY/638922 (called 'Long Cairn' on 1-in. O.S.).

This long cairn has a mound of stones and boulders, those at the centre being larger than the stones along its sides. It is orientated NNE/SSW, and is highest at its S end, where it is about 40 ft. wide. In length it is at least 200 ft., with an average ht. of 5 ft. A series of sheepfolds along the W side obscures the outline of the mound and also makes it difficult to decide whether there are true horns or projec-

tions at the N end defining an entrance to a tomb. The 3 pointed cairns on it are modern like the sheepfolds. Date, c. 3,500–2,500 BC.

There is a cairn ½ mile SW called the Deadman. It is of large natural boulders, 60 ft. in diam. and nearly 5 ft. high. It has been opened at the centre but there are no burial records. Date, c. 1,700–1,400 BC.

Kielder Long Cairn, Bronze Age cairn. See **Devil's Lapful.**

Kirkhaugh, round barrow. See Bronze Age.

Rayheugh Moor, round barrow. See Bronze Age.

BRONZE AGE

*Blawearie, barrow circle (NU/082223) 6¾ miles SE of Wooler (A697, A6111) 2¼ miles NW of Eglingham (B6346). Grave goods in British Museum.

The stone circle here, 36 ft. in diam., is the retaining wall of a mound which covered 4 burial pits. The mound has been removed probably to provide material for nearby walls. The burial pits were dug into the ground, lined with slabs and each covered with a capstone. One contained a food vessel, another a necklace of over 100 jet beads. No burials survived, the bones having decayed. Two cists still show at the SW. One retains its coverstone. Date, c. 1,700–1,400 BC.

Deadman, cairn. See Neolithic, **Devil's Lapful.**

Doddington Moor, ring-marked stones. See Late Prehistoric, **Dod Law Camps.**

Dod Law, ring-marked stones. See Late Prehistoric, **Dod Law Camps.**

Duddo, stone circle (NT/931437) 7 miles SW of Berwick, ¾ mile NNW of Duddo (B6354).

Like so many prehistoric sacred sites in England, this circle is set in low ground, close to the Tweed R. It stands on an isolated knoll. It has a diam. of about 28 ft. and consists of 5 rather large stones. It is likely that the original number of stones would have been greater. The hts. of the survivors are 5–7½ ft. All are naturally shaped blocks of the local sandstone. Date, c. 2,200–1,400 BC.

Five Barrows, cairn cemetery (NT/953020) 6½ miles w of Rothbury (B6341, B6342, B6344), ½ mile s of Holystone. Grave goods in British Museum.

There are 9 cairns here with traces of 5 others. They have diams. of 12–60 ft. and hts. 1–4 ft. Some have been opened and yielded cremations, inhumations, collared urns, food vessels, bone pins and flint tools. Date, c. 1,700–1,400 BC.

Goatstones, stone circle (NY/829748) 9½ miles NW of Hexham (A69, A6079), 2¾ miles NW of Simonburn (B6320); SW of Ravensheugh Crags.

This small circle has 4 stones, equally spaced and facing the centre. One stone at the E has a flat top on which there is a group of 13 cup-markings. The centre of the ground within the circle is slightly raised, suggesting that a burial may lie there. Date, c. 2,200–1,400 BC.

Hepburn Moor, cairns (NU/083231) 6½ miles SE of Wooler (A697, A6111), 1½ miles NE of Old Berwick. Grave goods in British Museum. See also **Blawearie.**

This group contains at least 27 cairns. Their diams. are 9–18 ft. and hts. 1–2 ft. There are no surrounding ditches. One cairn contains 2 burial cists. In the larger a contracted burial has been found with a beaker. The coverstone of this cist still survives. Date, c. 1,700–1,400 BC.

Hethpool, stone circle (NT/892278) 6½ miles w of Wooler (A697, A6111), ½ mile sw of Hethpool, on w side of College Burn.

This irregular, almost U-shaped setting of 8 upright stones has a max. internal width of 200 ft. The stones range in ht. from 5½–6½ ft. All are fairly cylindrical in shape except the most N stone, which is squat and, alone of these stones, remains almost upright.

There are 3 other stones to be seen NE of the circle, which may originally have belonged to it. The s of these is ring-marked. Date, c. 2,200–1,400 BC.

*Kirkhaugh, barrow (NY/704494) 2 miles NNW of Alston (A686, B6277, B6292, B6293); SE of Kirkhaugh School House. Grave goods in University Museum,

Newcastle.

This mound is 22 ft. in diam. and about 3 ft. high. It has been built upon a natural knoll which makes the barrow look larger than it is. Excavation showed that the mound has an earthy core with a rubble capping. Decayed traces of an unburnt body were found at the centre and among the offerings in the mound near the burial there was a basket-shaped gold ear-ring of a type found with beakers in Britain. Date, c. 2,000–1,700 BC.

Lordenshaw, ring-marked stones. See Late Prehistoric.

Ravensheugh Crags, stone circle. See **Goatstones.**

*Rayheugh Moor, barrows (NU/118268) 4½ miles s of Belford (A1, B6349), 1¼ miles wsw of Rayheugh (w of A1). Grave goods in British Museum.

These 3 mounds were opened in 1862. That at the NW is about 60 ft. in diam. and originally 10 ft. high. A stone-built burial cist was found at the centre. It contained a skeleton placed on its left side, with a beaker behind its shoulders. The barrow mound was composed of stones, with traces of a carefully made kerb.

The central barrow in this group, about the same size, was also found to cover an inhumation, but without any grave offerings.

A stone-built burial cist was found at the centre of the SE mound. The bones in it had decayed completely. Date of all these mounds, 1,700–1,400 BC.

Roughtinglinn, ring-marked stone and late prehistoric promontory fort (NT/984367) 5½ miles NNW of Wooler (A697, A6111), 2 miles E of Ford (B6353); near camp.

Of the series of cup- and ring-marked stones in the county, this is the most spectacular. One surface of a rock measuring 60 × 40 ft. is covered with several dozen markings; some are simple cup-shaped impressions, others are enclosed within concentric circles, sometimes with single or pairs of lines leading from them. Date, c. 2,200–1,400 BC.

There is a late prehistoric promontory fort at NT/983367, N of minor road, Milfield (A697) to Lowick (B6353). It encloses a sub-rectangular area of about 1¾ acres. There are 3 main banks at the E, with part of a fourth at the SE and traces of a fifth, innermost, along this side. Outside the fourth bank there is a ditch, to which the outermost bank at the SE is a counterscarp.

There is an entrance at the NE, beyond which there are only 2 main ramparts. On the S side of this entrance, the fourth rampart is in-turned to define a passageway.

The streams on the W and S which form this promontory would have been a convenient water supply.

Swinburn Castle, standing stone (NY/935753) 7 miles N of Hexham (A69, A6079), 1¼ miles NW of A69/A6079 crossing.

This fine stone is in the grounds of Swinburn Castle, to the S of it. The stone is 12 ft. high and is deeply grooved down the sides. There are some cup-markings on its faces. Date, c. 2,200–1,400 BC.

Threestone Burn, stone circle (NT/972205) 5 miles SSW of Wooler (A697, A6111), tracks from South Middleton or Ilderton, W of A697.

There are 13 stones in this circle, though only 5 remain standing. The circle is not perfectly round, its diam. being 96–118 ft. The tallest stones are over 5 ft. long. Date, c. 2,200–1,400 BC.

Weetwood Moor, ring-marked stones, cairn (NU/023281, cairn) 2 miles E of Wooler (A697, A6111, B6348), 2 miles W of Chatton (B6348), 200 yds. NNW of gate from plantation on to moor.

The cairn is about 22 ft. across and 2 ft. high. Nothing is known of its contents.

The main sculptured rock (about 425 ft. O.D., NU/022282) has 6 carvings and many natural hollows. The carvings comprise cups each surrounded by 2–6 rings, the latter often cut by a duct leading to the cup. Their diams. are about 7–25 ins.

Centred at NU/023282 there is a rock face 60 ft. long, lying NW/SE, covered with cups and rings. Some of the former are without surrounding rings.

At NU/010280 there is a rock facing S with 13 well-cut cup-and-ring marks. Date of all sites, c. 2,200–1,400 BC.

LATE PREHISTORIC

Northumberland possesses no sites which can yet be referred to a specifically iron-using culture of the prehistoric period because only a little archaeological excavation has been carried out. It contains, however, a very great number of settlements and numerous hill-forts, many of which (including all the hill-forts) must belong to the last 6–8 centuries of the pre-Roman period. It is noticeable that the huts and paddocks of several settlements can be seen to overlie hill-forts and it is clear that this style of native settlement continued into the Christian era. No precise dating has therefore been attempted.

Alnham Castle Hill, hill-fort (NT/980109) 7½ miles NW of Rothbury (B6341, B6342, B6344) ¾ mile W of Alnham Church.

Triple banks and broad, intervening ditches, the innermost bank robbed out, enclose less than 1 acre. Oval in plan, the hill-fort has an entrance at the E, where traces of a slight bank between the middle and outer ramparts indicate a work of 2 periods. The NE defences are overlaid by huts, paddocks and rectangular boundary walls of a later settlement.

Castlehill, Alnham, hill-fort. See **Alnham Castle Hill.**

Castle Knowe Camp, hill-fort. See **Clinch Castle.**

Clinch Castle, hill-fort (NU/032147) 8¾ miles SSE of Wooler (A697, A6111) 2¼ miles WSW of Powburn (A697).

This fort follows the contours and is roughly oval in plan, enclosing ¾ acre. Its defences are triple except along the SE where they become double. The entrance faces NE, where the central and outer defences curve in. In the interior there are traces of hut platforms.

Coldbury Hill, settlement (NT/970273) 1½ miles SW of Wooler (A697, A6111, B6348) on SE side of Hill.

This site comprises an oval enclosure at the NE, max. width about 75 ft., containing at least 2 huts, and a slighter stock enclosure at the SW, of similar size but with a smaller-scale earthwork. The NE enclosure has been cut back into the hillside; its bank of earth and stones is 3 ft. high in places and 16 ft. wide. Both have entrances facing E or SE.

Dod Law Camps, settlements and Bronze Age ring-marked stones (NU/004317—W Camp) 2¼ miles NNE of Wooler (A697,

A6111), ¾ mile SE of Doddington (A6111).

The W site encloses about ½ acre. It comprises a main enclosure, D-shaped, its straight side at the SW, with a slight annexe at the NW. The first has 2 banks of earth and stones, 15–20 ft wide and 1–9 ft high. The outer of these is in most places the stouter. The annexe has only 1 rampart, 10–15 ft. wide and 1–2 ft. high. The main enclosure has entrances at the SE and NW. The annexe has a possible entrance at the W. There are 6–10 huts in the former, 12–18 ft. across. The rectangular buildings at the E may be modern. There are no certain huts in the annexe but outside it, at the NE, there is a circular hut with traces of 2 sub-rectangular structures E of this.

This site (fig. 42), a farmstead with stock enclosure, is probably contemporary with that to the E.

The E site on Dod Law (NU/006317) encloses 1½ acres. It is sub-rectangular and is fortified with a bank and ditch, with traces of an inner bank at the N. The main bank is 9–15 ft. wide and 1–4 ft. high. Original entrances may be those at the NE and SW. The latter is out-turned and funnel-shaped, and is restricted by a short length of bank running down its central axis. There being no traces of huts within, this enclosure was probably for stock.

Many cup and ring-marked stones can be found in the area, for instance at NU/ 011312, NU/004318, NU/005317. All comprise cups, many with varying numbers of surrounding rings. Date of carvings, c. 2,200–1,400 BC.

Fentonhill Camp, hill-fort (NT/979354) 4½ miles NNW of Wooler (A697, A6111, B6348), ¾ mile NW of Fenton.

Oval earthworks enclose about 1 acre. There are 3 banks and 2 ditches, with a main entrance at the W. This is staggered. The innermost bank is 18–25 ft. wide but all have been lowered by ploughing.

Fordwood, cliff-fort (NT/972365) 5¼ miles NNW of Wooler (A697, A6111, B6348), 1¾ miles SE of Ford (B6353).

A steep hill-slope protects the S side of an oval area of 2 acres, defended elsewhere by 1 main bank and traces at the NE, of 2 inner banks and at the SW of an outer bank. At the latter there is a ditch between the banks. In places the main bank is 4 ft. high and 18 ft. wide. No entrance can now be identified.

Gleadscleugh, promontory fort (NT/ 951291) 2¾ miles W of Wooler (A697, A6111, B6348), ¾ mile SW of Akeld (A697, B6351).

Set on a spur of Akeld Hill, the neck of land is cut off by 3 banks, the middle one 9 ft. high in places. The entrance is at the NE end of these earthworks, where the outermost curves in to meet the central bank. It is possible that the defences in-

42 *Dod Law : Late Prehistoric hill-fort*

corporate more than 1 period. Within are several hut platforms and paddocks, scattered over an area of ½ acre.

Great Hetha Camp, hill-fort (NT/885274) 6¾ miles w of Wooler (A697, A6111, B6348), 1 mile sw of Hethpool.

This site is protected by steep slopes on all sides except the sw. It has 2 roughly oval ramparts of earth and stone enclosing about 1¼ acres.

Both ramparts include traces of facing stones along the outer sides: the presence of intervening ditches has not been established. At the E, where the hill-slope is less arduous, the outer bank extends well beyond the inner bank. Here there is an entrance through both banks, slightly staggered in plan, with the ends of the inner bank increased in width. There are traces of hut platforms within and there is also a later 2-celled stone structure between the banks at the entrance.

*Greaves Ash, settlement (NT/966164) 7½ miles ssw of Wooler (A697, A6111), 6 miles w of Powburn (A6111), NE of Linhope, below Greenshaw Hill.

This complex of sites, extending over 20 acres, incorporates structures of 3 different periods. Earliest, perhaps the only site which is pre-Roman, is the hill-fort at the w end. It comprises 2 ramparts, roughly circular but making contact at the SE, the inner one having an entrance facing E, the outer having entrances at the E, N and NW. The two ramparts are joined by several cross-walls and they enclose c. 2 acres.

This for is overlaid by a nucleated settlement of at least 22 huts, many enclosed by walls incorporating paddocks, which have accumulated over a lengthy period. About 100 ft. to the E is another group of huts partly enclosed within 2 paddocks. A further 300 ft. NE is a large accumulation of huts in paddocks including yards.

These huts are all circular, 20 ft. in average diam., with entrances mainly facing SE. Excavation has shown that their floors were paved and the doorways were fitted with stone stops for doors opening inwards. Along the s edge of this complex, field walls can be seen associated with rectangular hut foundations. This group is probably post-Roman.

Harehaugh Hill Camp, hill-fort (NY/970998) 5¾ miles sw of Rothbury (B6341, B6342, B6344), ¼ mile sw of Harehaugh (B6341).

An area of c. 3 acres is enclosed by oval earthworks. Steep hillsides protect the N and S. At the E there are 2 banks and 2 ditches; at the w there are 3 banks with ditches between them. Along the s there are 2 banks and a ditch. An entrance at the sw is approached by a hollow way. There is another entrance at the NW and a third at the NE. The interior is divided by a steep scarp facing E. This is the E side of a univallate first fort, whose entrance was probably that at the NW.

Harehope Hill, cliff-fort (NT/956285) 2¼ miles w of Wooler (A697, A6111, B6348), ¾ mile s of Akeld (A697, B6351).

This is a triangular fort, its E side protected by a steep cliff-face. About 1 acre is enclosed. There is 1 rampart along the crest of the cliff at the E, 3 banks along the N and E and 2 along the s. The innermost bank is 4 ft. high in places. There is an oblique entrance at the w and another at the SE (leading to a valley and water supply). There are transverse banks sealing off the rampart-ends at the former. At the NE a gap at the end of the innermost bank gives access to the wide space between it and the middle rampart. Three huts can be found near the centre, and traces of rectangular structures which, with the slight annexe outside at the NW, may be modern.

Hetha Burn, scooped enclosures (NT/881275, 878276) 7 miles w of Wooler (A697, A6111, B6348), 1¼ miles sw of Hethpool.

There are 2 separate settlements, each formed by scooping into the hillside a series of platforms for huts and other structures. Ruined earth and stone walls are associated with the platforms. Both settlements are roughly rectangular. The lower site contains a series of interconnecting, variously shaped scooped yards, with traces of at least one hut, and an entrance at the NW. The upper site, also rectangular, has 3 main terraces, all bearing traces of huts. There is an entrance at the NW. Scooped enclosures are likely to be late prehistoric, perhaps extending into the Roman period.

Humbleton Hill, hill-fort (NT/966283) 1½ miles w of Wooler (A697, A6111, B6348). On crest of hill.

This stone fort encloses nearly 9 acres. Its nucleus, segment-shaped and occupying the high ground, has an unusually massive wall with entrance facing E. This leads into a slightly smaller annexe, with entrances at N, E and SE, whose S side extends in a wide circuit on lower ground to provide a large, weakly defended area, perhaps a stock enclosure, whose wall rejoins the annexe E of its N entrance. This enclosure has entrances at the E and SW. Hut circles can be seen within these defences.

The Kettles, Wooler; promontory fort, see **Wooler.**

Linhope, settlement, see **Greaves Ash.**

Lordenshaw, hill-fort, Bronze Age ring-marked stones, cairns (NZ/055993) 1½ miles S of Rothbury (B6341, B6342, B6344).

This fort is roughly oval in plan and encloses a habitation area of under 1 acre. The defences comprise a main inner bank, 4–6 ft. high, with 2 other banks and ditches and an outermost counterscarp bank. There are entrances at the E and W, each a narrow, walled passageway across the defences. About 200 ft. to the SW a slight bank and ditch run NW/SE across the spur of the Simonside Hills. Within the camp a series of circular hut circles can be found, some of them built into the inner rampart along the SW, others, perhaps Romano-British, overlying part of the SE defences.

Nearly 900 ft. SW of the centre of the fort, 100 ft NE of the outermost fortification, there are 2 groups of cup-marked stones of presumed Bronze Age date. The larger and more intricate group is on a big rock W of the Deer Park wall; the other is 154 yds. NW of the last. The marks on the rock at NZ/051992 appear to include a phallus. Another large series of cup marks can be seen on rocks to the E of the fort.

There are 6 cairns centred on NZ/056993, on the NE slope of this hill. One of these is 21 ft. in diam. and 1 ft. high. At its centre is a cist 3½ × 2 ft. and 2¼ ft. deep. Its coverstone is beside it. To the SW there is a cairn with traces of a re-

taining circle of stones around it. Close by, another cairn shows the same feature.

Maiden Castle, Wooler; promontory fort. See **Wooler.**

Newton Hill Camp, hill-fort. See **West Hill Camp.**

Old Bewick, hill-fort and Bronze Age ring-marked stones (NU/075216) 6½ miles SE of Wooler (A697, A6111), ¾ mile NE of New Bewick (B6346). Ring-marked stone in Alnwick Castle Museum.

This earthwork lies on the S side of a spur. Precipitous hill-slopes to the S are a sufficient protection there: massive ramparts face the flat ground to the N. In shape the fort comprises 2 pairs of banks and ditches arranged spectacle-fashion at the edge of the spur. These earthworks are enclosed by a continuous and smaller semicircular bank and ditch 200 ft. to the N. A slight bank runs along the S edge of the whole fort, overlooking the hillside.

The W inner enclosure has simple entrances at the NW and NE. The other has an entrance at the SE.

Excavation has revealed that the ramparts have a clay core, faced and covered with rubble derived from the ditches. Hut circles can be seen in the W enclosure and traces of later quarrying for millstones in the E enclosure. This unusual promontory fort is presumed late prehistoric.

Just SE of the fort, 5 or 6 isolated rocks bear cup-and-ring markings. That at NU/078216 is a large rock covered with many such symbols. Another marked rock from within the fort is in Alnwick Castle Museum. Date, c. 2,200–1,400 BC.

Ringses Camp, enclosure (NU/013328) 3 miles NE of Wooler (A697, A6111), 1 mile ENE of Doddington (A6111).

About ¾ acre is enclosed by multiple ramparts. Oval in plan but irregular, there are 3 main ramparts, with traces of a ditch and counterscarp bank at the S. The slight innermost bank may be a later addition. Some of the ramparts are widely spaced, providing areas for stock-pounding. At the S these are divided by transverse banks. The main entrance is at the SE, a passage defined by transverse banks. That at the S may also be an entrance. There are 4 huts at the centre of the site.

There are parts of 2 earthworks N of the main site, weak outworks which are difficult to interpret.

Roughtinglinn, promontory fort. See Bronze Age.

Torleehouse, settlement (NT/913287) 5 miles w of Wooler (A697, A6111, B6348), 1 mile s of Kirknewton (B6351). On NW slope.

There are 2 roughly oval enclosures here, arranged NW/SE and touching. The NW has a max. width of about 90 ft. The surrounding banks, of earth and rubble, are 9–10 ft. wide and nearly 2 ft. high. Each has an entrance facing NE, defined by upright stones. There are no traces of huts within these earthworks.

Tosson Burgh, promontory fort (NU/ 023005) 2¼ miles sw of Rothbury (B6341, B6342, B6344), ½ mile w of Great Tosson.

This oval fort encloses 1 acre. It commands the Coquet R. and is protected by steep hill-slopes on the N and sw. The defences round the N half are formed mainly by scarping the natural hillsides. Along the s and E there is a stout bank and ditch, the former in places 9 ft high. The main entrance is in the s side, where the gaps through bank and ditch are staggered. The latter is approached by a hollow way.

West Hill Camp, hill-fort (NT/909295) 5¼ miles w of Wooler (A697, A6111, B6348), ½ mile ssw of Kirknewton (B6351).

This site comprises an oval, inner walled enclosure of c. ¾ acre, with an entrance facing E. It is surrounded by an outer wall, roughly sub-rectangular, with an entrance near the centre of the E side. At least 8 huts can be found in the inner enclosure, some linked by paddock walls; they have diams. c. 12–25 ft.

Overlying the outer enclosure at the NW is a more rectangular enclosure with an entrance through its E side and containing 4 circular huts. The earthwork immediately to the NE is post-Roman. This site had a long life, probably including the Roman period.

Wooler, promontory fort (NT/984273)

¾ mile sw of Wooler (A697, A6111, B6348). s of Wand Ho.

This fort encloses 4½ acres. It is divided by triple ramparts which cross the promontory E/W. The NW half of the fort has a single bank of stones along the sw but at the N there is an outer broad rampart and a slighter scarped bank between that and the inner rampart. Here there is a simple, central entrance. On the s side of this half, an in-turned entrance leads through triple ramparts to the SE half of the fort. There are 2 banks and a central ditch here, with an entrance facing SE. There are dividing walls inside this half of the fort but no huts have yet been located.

Yeavering Bell, hill-fort (NT/928294) 4 miles wNw of Wooler (A697, A6111), 1 mile SE of Kirknewton (B6351).

This substantial hill-fort encloses 2 heights with an intervening saddle, is c. 13 acres and is defended by a stout stone wall. Entrance gaps occur near the centres of the N and s sides, with a third entrance facing NE. The main entrance, widest and with traces of a holloway inside, is at the s. There is an annexe wall at the E and w ends, the latter with its own entrance. Excavation has shown that the surrounding wall of the fort had an original width of 10–12 ft. and it would have been at least 8 ft. high. There are traces of a palisade trench around the E height, c. 160 ft. in diam. which appears to be earlier than the huts it impinges upon; it also encloses a Bronze Age cairn.

Inside, the foundations of at least 130 circular huts, 18–30 ft. across, can be located, grouped around each height. It is likely that more exist in the saddle between, covered now with hill wash. At least 4 different types of hut foundations can be noted, all of them set on level platforms made by scooping into the hill-slope and heightening the front edge: some scoops contain a circular groove cut into the subsoil to support the frame of a timber hut.

Nottinghamshire

BRONZE AGE

Robin Hood's Pot, barrow. See Iron Age, Oxton Camp.

IRON AGE

Oxton Camp, hill-fort and Bronze Age barrow (SK/635532) 1¼ miles NNE of Oxton (A.6097, B6386), on Robin Hood Hill.

This hill-fort is roughly triangular and encloses 1½ acres. It is defended by a bank, ditch and counterscarp bank along the W and by 3 banks and ditches on the E. There is a central entrance through the NW side and apparently another, approached by a sunken road from the stream, at the SE. Not dated.

Outside the NW entrance there is a barrow over 90 ft. across and about 20 ft. high. Roman coins in a pot and a Saxon burial have been found here, but the mound is either a barrow of c. 1,700–1,400 BC or else perhaps a natural hillock.

Oxfordshire

NEOLITHIC

Hoar Stone, chambered long barrow (SP/378236) 4½ miles SE of Chipping Norton (A44, A361, B4026) in Enstone Plantation, close to junction of Enstone–Ditchley/B4022 roads.

This structure is the remains of a stone burial chamber set originally at the end of a long mound. This mound has now disappeared. The chamber consists of a U-shaped setting of 3 uprights with an opening to the E. In front of these are 3 fallen stones which must originally have formed part of the chamber; one may have been a capstone. The date of this tomb would be c. 3,500–2,500 BC.

Hoar Stone, chambered long barrow (SP/458241) ¾ mile SE of Steeple Barton, ¾ mile SW of A423/B4030 junction.

This barrow still possesses a mound at least 50 ft in length. A pile of broken stones of reddish sandstone at the E end is all that remains of a burial chamber recorded in 1843. Like the other Oxfordshire long barrows, this site was probably built c. 3,500–2,500 BC.

King's Men, stone circle (SP/296308) close to Whispering Knights burial chamber and King Stone standing stone, on Warwickshire/Oxfordshire border, ½ mile N of Little Rollright.

This circle consists of 53–54 stones (folk tradition asserts that they cannot be counted), with a diam. of 105 ft. Though not yet dated by scientific excavation, the circle may be contemporary with some of the other sites N and E of it, c. 2,200–1,400 BC.

King Stone, standing stone (SP/295309). An integral part of the Rollright Stones complex, some have regarded this stone as part of a long barrow which they claim lies to the N of it. This hill is probably natural. The stone, 8 ft. high and 5 ft. wide, must be one of those single uprights so often found associated with stone circles and other religious sites.

Lambourn, chambered long barrow. See Berkshire.

Lyneham, long barrow (SP/297211) NW side of A361, 1¾ miles NE of Shipton railway station.

This barrow is about 170 ft. long and orientated NE/SW. At the N end there is set a single upright stone with a ht. of 6 ft. above the surface of the barrow. South of this, excavation has revealed the presence of at least 2 chambers but with no clear evidence of a passage linking them. Probably they are lateral chambers, each entered through the side of the mound. Burials are said to have been found in them.

The single upright stone may be the remains of a blind entrance. Date c. 3,500–2,500 BC.

Rollright Stones, see **King's Men, King Stone, Whispering Knights.**

Slate-pit Copse, chambered long barrow (SP/329165) in Wychwood Forest, 1 mile NE of Leafield Church, E of road joining Leafield to B4437.

The mound of this barrow is about 100 ft. long and 45 ft. broad, lying E/W. It stands about 6 ft. high. At the E end there is a ruined burial chamber of which only 3 stones survive. Three human skulls are supposed to have been found in it. Date, c. 3,500–2,500 BC.

*Wayland's Smithy, earthen (earlier) and chambered long barrow (SU/281854), 1 mile NE of Ashbury (B4000, B4507). Finds in Reading Museum.

The later and visible mound of this 2-period long barrow measures c. 180 ft. × 48 ft., is 4 ft. high and orientated SE/NW. The trapezoid mound retains much of its kerb of sarsens and the straight facade of originally 6 massive stones is broken at the centre by an entrance to an ante-chamber and 3 burial chambers laid out in a cruciform plan. Excavation in 1919–20 revealed side-ditches (not enclosing either end) set c. 25 ft. beyond the kerb of the mound whose core was earthy, with a chalk covering. A sarsen retaining wall, never visible, was found behind and following the kerb to strengthen the

mound. About 8 skeletons, including a child, were found in the disturbed chambers.

Excavation in 1962–3 revealed the existence of an earthen long barrow beneath the centre of the chambered mound, measuring 54 ft. × 27 ft., the original height about 6 ft. It had open-ended side-ditches. Near its SE end was a sarsen pavement 16 × 5 ft., flanked by boulders and including wooden uprights at the NE and SW, 4 ft. in diam., with two pairs of smaller side posts sloping inwards, all evidently forming a ridge-tent-like mortuary house which had collapsed. On the pavement within, remains of 14 skeletons were found, mostly lying in a confused mass. The mound of this earlier long barrow comprised a basal layer of sarsen boulders, c. 1 ft. in diam., covered by chalk rubble. Probably the 2 largest posts of the mortuary house projected through this mound to form free-standing features, doubtless carved and decorated.

This is the only recorded example of a chambered long barrow superimposed upon an unchambered long barrow: date (C14) of earlier mound, c. 2,850 BC, later c. 2,500 BC.

Whispering Knights, chambered long barrow (SP/299308) 2½ miles N of Chipping Norton (A44, A361), ½ mile NE of Little Rollright.

This group of stones, 4 set vertically to define a chamber about 6 ft. square, and the fifth, a capstone, resting at an angle, must be the remains of a portal dolmen originally set at the end of a long barrow. No traces of such a mound now exist; probable date c. 3,500–2,500 BC.

BRONZE AGE

Although only two barrows are listed here, it should not be thought that in the Bronze Age this area was without a population. On the contrary, the Upper Thames with its sheets of well-drained gravels supported a very large and prosperous society closely linked by land and river routes with Wessex and East Anglia, not to mention the Thames Estuary – a point of departure for NW Europe. Extensive agriculture and gravel-working has, however, removed virtually all traces on the ground of the many hundreds of round barrows, often large, elaborate and richly furnished with grave goods, which bore witness to these people. Every effort should be made to visit the Ashmolean Museum, Oxford, where there is an incomparable collection of air photographs revealing these barrows, and where the finest objects found in them are displayed.

Aston Upthorpe, disc-barrow (SU/542838) 3½ miles NW of Streatley (A329, A417, B4526), 1¼ miles SE of Blewbury (A417, B4016): in copse s of Sheepcot Farm.

The unusually large mound of this barrow classifies it as intermediate between bell and disc. Its total diam. is 174 ft. The mound is 3 ft. high and 54 ft. across. The berm is 30 ft. wide. Nothing is known of burials beneath the mound. Date, c. 1,700–1,400 BC.

Churn Farm, barrow cemetery (SU/515837) 1½ miles sw of Blewbury (A417, B4016), NE of Churn Farm.

There are 4 mounds here, arranged in a line E/W. They have diams. of 75–100 ft. and are 4–6 ft. high. The 2 central mounds touch and are joined to the w bowl by a slight col. The mound at the E may be the one in which a cremation was found in 1848. Date, c. 1,700–1,400 BC.

IRON AGE

*Alfred's Castle, hill-fort (SU/277823) and 'Celtic' fields, 2 miles SE of Ashbury (B4000, B4507) on NE edge of Ashdown Park.

This small camp is polygonal and encloses some 2½ acres. Its defences consist of a main bank and ditch, with traces of an outer rampart at the SE. There is an original entrance at the NW and perhaps at the SE. This site has not been excavated but there are surface indications that the main bank was faced with sarsen boulders. A recent aerial photograph has disclosed a very much larger enclosure at the NE perhaps added to the camp late in its history. Occupation here is likely to go back to the 4th century BC at least.

NE of Ashdown Park, particularly in the area of Knighton Bushes, there are abundant traces of 'Celtic' fields. It is possible that those tilling the fields may have occupied Alfred's Castle.

*Castle Hill, hill-fort (SU/569925), 1¼ miles ssw of Dorchester (Oxon) (A423); between A423 and A4130. Finds in Ashmolean Museum, Oxford.

The defensive earthwork of this camp was built to take advantage of the steep, isolated hill which it surrounds. A counterscarp bank has been heaped up from a single deep ditch within. There is a probable entrance at the w. The area so defined is about 10 acres. Undated.

*Chasleton Burrow Camp, plateau-fort (SP/259283) 4¼ miles NW of Moreton-in-the-Marsh (A44, A429), ¾ mile SE of Chasleton. Finds in Ashmolean Museum, Oxford.

In plan this camp is roughly circular, the area enclosed being 3½ acres. Its defences are unusual in that there is no surrounding ditch, only a single bank. The latter was faced with large stone blocks and may have a rubble core. Originally it was about 20 ft. wide at its base. There are simple entrances through the E and NW sides. Plentiful evidence for occupation has been found: the pottery here is of unusually early date, c. 8th century BC.

*Cherbury Camp, lowland fort (SU/374963) 2½ miles wsw of Kingston Bagpuize (A415, A420), ¾ mile s of A420. Finds in Ashmolean Museum, Oxford.

This site is located relatively close to the Thames. It is set on the edge of the naturally well-drained Corallian Beds and is surrounded, and so protected, by marshy clays. A narrow bridge of Coral Rag leads N from the camp to the dry North Berkshire Corallian ridge, via Race Farm. This constitutes the only dry route to the camp.

Cherbury Camp is oval in plan, an area of 9 acres being fortified. The defences consist of 3 banks and ditches, well-preserved on N, s and w. The construction of the bank depends on the local geology. Excavation of the innermost bank on the s side showed that it was made of sandy material, with a fine drystone revetment on the outside. Elsewhere the bank was made of tightly packed oolitic rubble, also faced with drystone walling.

The original entrance is half-way along

the E side. Gate-posts flanked this gap in the ramparts and a well-laid metalled roadway led through to the settlement within.

This camp was probably built in the 5th–4th centuries BC and was abandoned c. 1st century BC.

Dyke Hills, promontory fort (SU/574937) ½ mile sw of Dorchester (A415, A423), in angle of the Thames.

Though on low ground, this site may be described as a promontory fort because it cuts across a piece of land (114 acres) defined on S, W and E by the Thames and Thame. A rectangular area is protected at the NE by 2 enormous banks (the outer the larger) with a medial ditch and traces of an outer ditch. The other sides to the S are defended by the rivers. The gaps in the ramparts are all modern. The original entrance may have been at the E end, where the defences appear to curve S close to the junction of Thames and Thame. Air photographs have revealed many pits and ditches in the area so defined. Although the location of this site and the existence of 2 large ramparts separated by a ditch are unusual, the fort is presumed to be of Iron Age date.

*Grim's Ditch, enclosure (Kiddington sector, SP/402215; Callow Hill sector, SP/412194; Blenheim Park sector, SP/427183; Model Farm, Ditchley sector, SP/383209; Out Wood – Berrings Wood sector, SP/413208; refs. to centre of each sector). All sectors lie within sw angle of Charlbury–Kiddington/Kiddington–Woodstock (A34) roads. Finds in Ashmolean Museum, Oxford.

Grim's Ditch consists of a series of sectors each comprising a bank and ditch, built in the first half of the 1st century AD by a Belgic tribe on the move w from the Essex region. These sectors defended patches of open ground in country otherwise protected by woods and small valleys; some 22 square miles were thus enclosed and fortified by a group of people perhaps uneasy in newly conquered territory. In the Callow Hill sector 2 additional lines of earthworks can be seen, both crossing B4437, where the ground was particularly exposed. A mid 1st century AD Romano-British farm shows as a slight platform N of

this B road and w of these ditches. Both butt-ends of the ditch in Out Wood and Berrings Wood can be seen, as can the E butt-end of the ditch in the Model Farm sector, ¼ mile w of Ditchley House. In the sector in Blenheim Park – approached through Ditchley Gate (on the B4437) – a gap in the earthwork was utilised by the Romans when Akeman Street was being laid out.

When built, each sector of Grim's Ditch consisted of a bank about 20 ft. broad and 6 ft. high, with a V-shaped ditch in front of it usually 20 ft. across and 6 ft. deep.

Letcombe Castle. See **Segsbury Camp.**

*Lyneham Camp, hill-fort (SP/299214) 3¾ miles ssw of Chipping Norton (A44, A361, B4026, B4450), 2 miles w of Chadlington. On w side of A361. Finds in Ashmolean Museum, Oxford.

This camp is roughly oval, its S side now destroyed by A361 and a quarry. Its defences consist of a bank and ditch enclosing nearly 4½ acres. Except in the plantation, the ditch is now filled in. Excavation has shown that the ditch is U-shaped, 7 ft. deep and about 18 ft. wide. The bank behind it is at least 6 ft. high: on either side it has a revetting wall of drystone masonry. The gap in the earthwork facing N has not yet been proved to be an original entrance. The site may have been a cattle kraal. Date, c. 3rd–2nd century BC.

*Madmarston Hill, hill-fort and Roman road (SP/386389) 4½ miles wsw of Banbury (A41, A361, A422, A423), ¾ mile NW of Tadmarton (B4035), approached by track to Lower Lea Farm and Farmington Farm. Finds in Ashmolean Museum, Oxford.

This camp has suffered from cultivation, but it is important because it is one of the few hill-forts in the county which has been scientifically excavated. The site is oval in plan, following the crest of the hill. Its earthworks enclose 7 acres. On the sw and SE sides there are 3 banks with 2 ditches between them. On the N and E sides there are 2 banks and 1 ditch. Here, the ramparts are best preserved, being in part tree-covered. The entrance can be made out on the S side, looking across the valley to Swalcliffe: it faces visitors approaching from this direction, coming through the field gate. The entrance gap through the outermost bank and ditch lies slightly E of that through the middle and inner earthwork. The approach to the interior was thus staggered to facilitate defence. A pit, perhaps dug as a dedication, was found close to the innermost entrance gap. It contained bones of several animals and a gigantic stewpot.

Excavation has revealed that on the SW side the inner ditch was U-shaped, 30 ft. wide and 11 ft. deep. The rampart behind it, now almost level with the surface of the interior, had originally been about 11 ft. high.

must have reached Bloxham, where a Romano-British settlement has long been known.

*Segsbury Camp, hill-fort (SU/385845) 2¼ miles SSW of Wantage (A338, A417), ¾ mile SE of Letcombe Bassett.

This fortified site is D-shaped in plan, the area within its defences being 26¼ acres. Today only 1 bank and ditch are well preserved, but there are indications of an outer rampart or counterscarp on the NW side. The original entrance faces E. The main rampart may have been revetted with sarsen.

This site was probably built in the 2nd century BC.

Sinodun Hills, hill-fort. See **Castle Hill.**

43   *Uffington Castle: Iron Age hill-fort with Late Iron Age White Horse*

A water spring exists, and would always have existed in the NE part of the hill-fort. Many pits have been located inside the hill-fort. Built for grain-storage and utilised for rubbish when foul, they indicate permanent occupation here c. late 1st century BC–early 1st century AD. A hoard of currency bars, an axe-head, blacksmith's poker and horse-bit, all of iron, are evidence of relative prosperity.

The Roman road follows the line of the present track on the S side of the hill, between Lower Lea and Farmington Farms. It lies immediately N of this track. Its *agger*, which is about 30 ft. wide, shows plainly, with a ditch on the S side. The whole course of this minor road has not been worked out. South-eastwards it

*Uffington Castle, hill-fort (SU/299864) 6 miles W of Wantage (A338, A417); 1¾ miles SW of Kingston Lisle, S of B4507.

This camp consists of a roughly oval area of 8 acres defended by a bank, ditch and counterscarp bank. There is a single entrance facing NW. Here the main bank appears to run outwards, along the edges of the entrance causeway, to join the counterscarp bank. Alternatively, this may be an illusion caused by a deeply hollowed way of entry (fig. 43).

Excavation about 1850 has suggested that the main rampart was faced with sarsen. It also appears from this digging that at one period the rampart was either timber-faced or may have at one stage had a timber palisade defence. A silver coin of the Dobunni has been found outside the fort. Undated.

*Uffington White Horse, chalk-cut figure (SU/302866), ¼ mile NW of Uffington Castle (above).

This may be the earliest chalk-cut hill figure in Britain and is certainly the oldest 'white horse'. It has been cut down to natural chalk in broad terraces; it is 360 ft. long and has a max. ht. of 130 ft. (fig. 43).

In Iron Age times there is much evidence of animal worship: the horse figures repeatedly on pre-Roman coins in Britain and on buckets ånd other objects of the period. A series of horses resembling the Uffington one can be seen in bronze on the sides of a wooden vat from Marlborough, in Devizes Museum; similar horses appear on a bucket from Aylesford, Kent, now in the British Museum.

It seems likely that at a late stage in the 1st century BC this horse was cut in the hillside as a tribal emblem by those living nearby. For a suggestion of an altogether later date for the horse, however, see the Bibliography.

Shropshire

BRONZE AGE

Cwm Mawr, axe factory. See **Mitchell's Fold.**

*Hemford, stone circle and barrows (SO/324999) 5½ miles N of Lydham (A488, A489), W of road off A488 (Hope Valley) to Hemford and Bromlow.

Set in low marshy ground, this circle is of interest because it has a single stone near its centre. It has a diam. of about 75 ft. and at least 37 stones can be counted. Most of these are now obscured by peat which post-dates the circle. The highest, that at the centre, is 2 ft. 6 ins. above ground. Like those at **Mitchell's Fold** (below), these stones appear to be naturally shaped blocks. Date, c. 2,200–1,400 BC. Immediately N and NW of the circle there are 2 mounds, about 12 ft. across and 1 ft. high. These may be barrows.

Hoarstone, circle. See **Hemford.**

Marshpool, circle. See **Hemford.**

*Mitchell's Fold, stone circle and axe factory (SO/305984) 5 miles NW of Lydham (A488, A489), ½ mile NW of Whitegrit.

This circle commands an extensive view, particularly towards Wales. At least 14 stones can still be seen and it has a diam. of 75 ft. Many of the stones are now stumps reduced to turf level: those that still survive have hts. of 2–6 ft. All are natural, unworked blocks. Date, c. 2,200–1,400 BC.

South of the circle rises the great Corndon Hill. A lesser hill S of this (centre SO/304951) was the source of a volcanic rock quarried and traded extensively into the Midlands and beyond in early Bronze Age times for the manufacture of axe-heads. The exact sites of the prehistoric quarries have not yet been identified, but may have been on the NE side of this hill, facing Woodgate.

*Old Field, round barrows (SO/495776) 2¼ miles NW of Ludlow (A49, A4117), between B4365 and river and E of The Butts.

The barrow called Robin Hood's Butt (SO/490779) is c. 14 ft. high and 90 ft. in diam. It covered the bones of a child of 12–14, perhaps burnt on the spot. The blade of a bronze knife accompanied the burial. A line of 4 mounds lies E of B4365, within the NE corner of the racecourse. The 3 N mounds, which covered cremations, have been flattened. That at the S was 8 ft. high in 1884 and over 100 ft. across. Near its top a collared urn was found, containing a cremation. At the base there was an oval stone-lined cist containing bones burnt at or near the spot. Another barrow, under plough but still c. 3 ft. high, is as SO/497770, with other crop-mark sites s of A49. Date, c. 1,700–1,400 BC.

The Wrekin, round barrow. See Iron Age.

IRON AGE

Burrow Camp, hill-fort (SO/382831) 3¼ miles W of Craven Arms (A49, B4368), ½ mile W of Hopesay.

This hill-fort is pear-shaped and encloses 5 acres. On the NW, where the hill is steepest, there is a bank, ditch and counterscarp bank, with an isolated bank inside, 300 ft. long. Elsewhere there are 4 banks and ditches. There appear to be 4 original entrances. That at the SW is a passageway through the 'apex' of the fort, protected on both sides by the converging ramparts. It resembles the arrangement at **Croft Ambry** (below). There is an elaborate entrance in the S side, where all the rampart ends are in-turned, the innermost turning N for nearly 100 ft. Further to the E a third gap in the defences seems to be original because the ends of the ramparts are slightly staggered as they face each other across the causeway. The fourth entrance faces NE. Here the approach to the interior is blocked by the innermost rampart which is in-turned at an oblique angle; this prevents direct access to the interior.

There are traces of additional earthworks at the centre of the camp. These cannot be explained until the site has been excavated. Not dated.

Bury Ditches, hill-fort (SO/327836) 2½ miles NE of Clun (A488, B4368), 1 mile SW of Lower Down.

This tree-covered hill-fort is roughly oval in plan, enclosing 6½ acres. Steep hillsides everywhere except at the NE add to the man-made defences. These consist of 2 banks and a ditch around the S half and 4 banks and ditches facing N and NW. At the NE, where the ground is least helpful to defence, there are 5 banks. There are 2 elaborate entrances, one facing NE, the other SW. The first has a deeply in-turned innermost rampart, the other banks and ditches having a simple break in them. Changes in alignment of the

ends of these in-turns suggest a guard-chamber. The other entrance has unusual features. The 2 ramparts on the S side are deeply in-turned: opposite them, the innermost bank stops short and the bank in front of it is out-turned. The entrance passage is slightly oblique. Not dated.

*Bury Walls, hill-fort (SJ/576275) 4 miles ESE of Wem (A5113, B5063), 1¾ miles E of Lee Brockhurst (A49). Reached via Bury Farm.

This site occupies the spur of a hill, its W and SE sides receiving added protection from steep slopes. A rectangular area of 13½ acres is thus enclosed. An unusually stout bank follows the edges of the spur, in most places still 10 ft. high. Where the fort is approached by flat ground to the NE, there are 2 banks and ditches. The original entrance is at the NE corner: it is in-turned, the passage through to the interior being cut deep into the living rock. Not dated.

Caer Caradoc, hill-fort (SO/477953) 1¾ miles NE of Church Stretton (A49, B4370).

This hill-fort is oval in plan and encloses 6 acres. Steep hill-slopes on all sides afford good natural protection, particularly on the W and SE. Around the N half of the site there are 2 banks and a ditch. There is a hollow within the inner bank, which may have been a quarry to provide extra material for this bank. There is 1 bank around the S half of the camp except at the S end, where there are 2 banks and a ditch. The original entrance was at the SE corner where a hollow way comes up the hillside and meets an in-turned entrance through the single bank. This is unusually wide and may include a guard-chamber on its S side. Undated.

Caer Caradoc, hill-fort (SO/310758) 2½ miles NE of Knighton (A488, A4113), ½ mile SW of Chapel Lawn.

This fort commands the Redlake R to the N. It is roughly oval in plan and encloses 2¼ acres. On the S side there is a bank, ditch and counterscarp bank. On the N side there are 2 banks and ditches which become triple towards the centre. There are 2 widely spaced banks and ditches at the W end, where flatter ground menaced the defenders of the camp: s of the entrance here an extra bank and ditch was added. This entrance, and that opposite it at the E end of the fort, is in-turned. The gaps in the earthworks at the former are staggered slightly so that a direct approach to the interior is avoided.

Several circular depressions indicating hut sites and perhaps grain-storage pits can be seen in the NE part of the camp. Not dated.

*Caynham, hill-fort (SO/545737) 2¼ miles SE of Ludlow (A49, A4117), ½ mile E of Poughnhill. Finds in Birmingham University and City Museum and Art Gallery.

The main defence of the hill-fort, rectangular in plan, comprises a massive inner bank, ditch and counterscarp bank along all except the N and NW sides, where a single bank sufficed. About 100 yds. within the W end a cross-bank defines an annexe here, the bank itself perhaps representing the original W end of the fort: its entrance near the S end is modern. The original main entrance is through the E end, deeply in-turned. About 75 yds. outside the W end there is a denuded cross-bank with possible in-turned entrance at its N end and there are faint traces of a second cross-bank a further 100 yds. to the W.

Excavation has shown that the earliest rampart was timber-laced, with a rock-cut ditch 10–12 ft. deep, lying inside the present line of defences. It was replaced first by a small rampart revetted roughly with stone, then by an enlargement of the latter including a better-built stone facing, followed by a further raising of ht. Air photographs and excavation have revealed storage pits all over the interior and one large building, apparently D-shaped. Date, perhaps 7th–5th century initially, with a long life.

Coxall Knoll, hill-fort. See Hereford and Worcester.

The Ditches, hill-fort (SO/563943) 5 miles SW of Much Wenlock (A458, B4371, B4376, B4378), ¾ mile SW of Easthope.

Oval in shape, this fort encloses about 5½ acres. It is fortified by 3 banks and ditches. In places the innermost bank is 15 ft high. The entrance faces NE. Here the innermost bank on the S side curves outwards, sealing off the ends of the 2 ditches S of it and providing a well-protected entrance passageway. The gap

in the earthworks at the SW has not yet been proved prehistoric. Not dated.

*Earl's Hill, hill-forts (SJ/408046) 1 mile SE of Pontesbury (A488).

The main hill-fort encloses c. 3 acres of the hill-top, a bank, ditch and intermittent counterscarp following the W side and both ends. Defences along the E side are unnecessary. The entrance is at the N where the short length of E rampart is in-turned and that on the W out-turned. A further 4 acres are enclosed by an annexe whose W bank and intermittent counterscarp follows the 900 ft. contour: E defences are not needed. There is a cross-ditch with outer bank 300 ft. N of the main hill-fort, with central entrance, and another, bank only, 400 ft. further N. with an in-turned entrance near its N end. Both outworks may be unfinished. A multivallate camp enclosing ¾ acre is 300 ft. down the slope to the N, its entrance facing up the slope. Neither is dated.

Nordy Bank, hill-fort (SO/576847) 7½ miles NE of Ludlow (A49, A4117), ¾ mile E of Clee St Margaret (N of B4364).

The camp is D-shaped and encloses 7 acres. Its defences comprise a single bank and ditch, and there are traces of an outer defence c. 100 yds. N and NW. In most places the rampart is at least 6 ft. above the level of the ground within. There are several entrance gaps. That to the SW is in-turned and must be original. Of the other gaps in the defences, that at the NE may also be prehistoric. Not dated.

Norton Camp, hill-fort (SO/447819) 1 mile SE of Craven Arms (A49, B4368).

This camp is roughly oval in plan, its NW and SW sides being straight. It encloses 13 acres. A steep hillside protects the NW along which there is a single rampart. Elsewhere there are 2 banks and ditches, becoming triple at the SW. These earthworks are all massive. There are entrance gaps facing E and SE; both may be original. The ends of the ramparts defining the former are broadened. The passageway through the earthworks at the other entrance is at an oblique angle to their line. Not dated.

*Old Oswestry, hill-fort (SJ/296310) 1 mile N of Oswestry (A483, A495, A4083). Finds in private hands (1959).

The long history of this hill-fort is reflected in its complicated defences. At first, 2 banks and ditches, roughly rectangular in plan, enclosed an area of 15 acres. There were 2 entrances, facing E and W. At both, the inner rampart was in-turned, a design which was not changed during the 3 ensuing periods of alteration.

In stage 2 the ramparts were rebuilt and a third bank added on all except the SE side (where alone the hillside made it unnecessary).

In stage 3 the E end of the fort was unaltered but the W entrance was redesigned. In the new plan, outworks were added enclosing a series of storage pits (? for water), and the entire passage through to the interior, now 300 ft. long, was flanked by a bank.

Finally, the whole hill-fort was enclosed by an extra pair of earthworks and the E entrance had its passageway protected by a flanking bank.

Excavation has shown that this hill was inhabited in c. 6th–5th century BC before the earthworks were built. These were developed from the 4th century BC to the Roman Conquest.

Pontesford Hill, hill-fort. See **Earl's Hill.**

The Roveries, hill-forts (SO/325925) 19 miles SW of Shrewsbury (A5, A49), 2¼ miles N of Bishop's Castle (A488, B4385). Finds in Shrewsbury Museum.

This oval hill-fort with outlier across the valley to the N, encloses 6 acres. It is defended by a drystone-faced rampart and no ditch. A deep in-turned entrance, with rock-cut post-holes for gate with bridge and rectangular guard-chambers, is near the centre of the N side and is open for inspection, as the pre-1939 excavators left it. A well-marked ancient track approaches it up the hillside. A second entrance, an addition to the original plan, is opposite on the SE side. Here an out-turned arm, drystone-faced, was added running down the hill to the E and a gap was cut through the original line of rampart. The length of unfilled causewayed ditch within the camp near the W end may represent the original W side, abandoned in favour of the present plan.

*Titterstone Clee Hill Camp, hill-fort

(SO/592779) 5½ miles NE of Ludlow (A49, A4117), 1¾ miles E of Bitterley.

This unusually large hill-fort (71 acres enclosed) is at 1,749 ft. O.D. and commands extensive views. It is defended by a single rampart without ditch, showing in most places as a heavy spread of stones. Polygonal in plan, it is well preserved around the E half but has suffered from quarrying at the SW, the site of a deeply in-turned entrance with guard-chambers and bridge over the gates, excavated in 1934. Here a section across the bank is exposed in the quarry face. Excavation revealed that the first rampart had been faced with timbers, including the passageway to the gates. After a period of decline the rampart was refaced with drystone walling and heightened. Date of construction unknown, but dismantled perhaps by the Romans.

*The Wrekin, hill-fort and round barrow (SJ630083) 2½ miles SW of Wellington (A5, A442, A518).

This hill-fort commands the surrounding country for great distances. In all probability it was the tribal capital of the Cornovii who in Roman times were re-settled at *Viroconium Cornoviorum* (Wroxeter) 4 miles to the W.

The fort on the Wrekin is elongated, taking in most of the hill. It consists of a central area of 7 acres with a series of outworks to the E and W which enclose a total of 10½ acres.

The central site is defended by a main rampart, the hillsides below it being artificially steepened, and remains of a slight counterscarp bank. The entrances at the E and W ends are in-turned, with traces of guard-chambers leading off the passageways. Where the ramparts cross the hill they and the counterscarp banks are more imposing: along the hillsides they appear as a series of terraces.

Beyond the main fort, the hogsback is encircled by slighter earthworks which also appear as terraces except where they lie across the hill. At the E end these fortifications consist essentially of 2 banks, the steep hillsides making further elaboration unnecessary. In places there are gaps in one or other rampart. The most E entrance has strong in-turned banks and additional banks.

The defences W of the main fort are slight because of the steep landfall. The entrance is not in-turned but there are bulbous ends to the inner bank.

Excavation has revealed that the inner fort is of 2 periods, its rampart being built as a flat-topped broad bank faced on the outside with drystone walling. This had collapsed. Later more rubble had been added to it, perhaps supporting a timber palisade breastwork. The outer defences appear to have undergone the same development.

The entrances have also been altered. At first the ramparts were not in-turned but ended with bulbous swellings and well-built drystone walling. Later the in-turns and guard-chambers were built,

the masonry now being very shoddy. The guard-chambers had wooden roofs.

Traces of permanent occupation – hut floors, post-holes, gutters and storage-pits – have been found inside the main camp. Evidence also shows that the hill-top was occupied by Iron Age people before local wars and land hunger made necessary the building of the hill-fort. This probably took place in the 5th or 4th century BC, its development perhaps being spread over several centuries.

At the SW end of the hill-fort there is a low circular mound which is probably a barrow of the Bronze Age (c. 1,700–1,400 BC). Nothing is known of its contents.

Somerset

PALAEOLITHIC

The limestone gorges of Mendip, pitted with deep, narrow caves, offered shelter to Old Stone Age hunters who were living in this area in small numbers during the period 100,000–6,000 BC. The caves to be described are the most interesting of these.

*Flint Jack's Cave, Cheddar Gorge (ST/ 463538) SW end of Gorge (B3135), on S side. Finds in Weston super Mare and British Museum.

Most of the caves in the gorge have been utilised as shelters by the small bands of hunters who existed precariously on Mendip during the last cold phases of the Ice Age. A series of flint tools has been found in this cave which indicates that people took brief shelter here c. 12,000 BC.

*Gough's Cave, Cheddar Gorge (ST/ 466538). Finds in cave-mouth museum.

As elsewhere, excavations in this cave and the laying of hard floors for tourists have obscured its original appearance. The uppermost layers, now removed, con-

tained evidence of occupation in Romano-British and Iron Age times. The lower levels down to bedrock yielded several hundred flint implements, tools and ornaments of bone and shell and associated animal bones which indicate extensive occupation here c. 12,000–8,000 BC.

Human bones have also been found, including what may have been a deliberate burial of an adult male furnished with part of a tool – or ceremonial staff – of reindeer antler called by French archaeologists a *bâton de commandement* – a length of bone with a large, carefully drilled hole at one end, the shaft usually decorated with engraved patterns. This burial can be seen at the museum on the site. A second, complete, specimen of a *bâton*, made from a human arm-bone, has also been found in this cave. Perforated shells and fox teeth were associated with the burial and the other objects.

*Hyaena Den, Wookey (ST/531480) 60 yds. s of the Great Cave of Wookey Hole, 2 miles NW of Wells (A39, A371). Finds in Wells Museum and University Museum, Oxford.

This cave consists of a large main chamber with a narrow passage leading further into the rock. It was inhabited during the last cold phases of the Ice Age both by wild animals, mainly hyaenas, and by hunters. The former had dragged into this cave huge quantities of dead animals whose gnawed bones were recovered in 1863. The hunters, who may often have fought with the animals for possession of the cave, left remains of fires, food bones and tools of bone, fllint and chert. The shapes of some of their flint tools suggest that occupation may have begun here c. 35,000 BC and lasted until c. 12,000 BC.

*Soldier's Hole, Cheddar Gorge (ST/467538) 100 ft. above road, on s side of Gorge, 200 yds. beyond Gough's Cave. Finds in Gough's Cave Museum.

This inaccessible cave was inhabited by Upper Palaeolithic people at a slightly earlier period than Gough's Cave, for 2 superbly worked flint blades found in it recall those typical of an earlier phase, the Solutrean, on the Continent; period of occupation here c. 30,000–25,000 BC.

NEOLITHIC

Battlegore, burial chamber or stone circle (ST/075416) ½ mile NNW of Williton (A39, A358), 600 yds. s of Fowl Bridge, carrying B3191 to Watchet.

There are 3 large prostrate stones of New Red Sandstone here, for which 2 stone-holes were found by excavation in 1931. It is not yet certain, however, whether they had formed part of a burial chamber or belong to a circle. Date, c. 3,500–2,500 BC.

Devil's Bed and Bolster, chambered long barrow (ST/815532) 3¾ miles sw of Trowbridge (Wilts.), 1 mile NE of Beckington (A36, A361), N of Seymour's Court Farm.

The mound of this ruined long barrow, originally at least 85 ft. in length, is orientated E/W. About 20 sarsens are scattered along most of its length, 8 or 9 perhaps still in position. They suggest that this mound covered at least 3 burial chambers, 2 of them entered from the sides of the barrow. Date, c. 3,500–2,500 BC.

Giant's Cave, chambered long barrow (ST/678513) 2¼ miles sw of Radstock (A362, A367), 1 mile NE of Holcombe. At Charmborough Farm. Finds in Taunton Museum.

This damaged barrow is NE/SW. It was explored in 1909 and the broken-up bones of several individuals were discovered, concentrated at the E end. It seems that they were in groups, sometimes between or covered by slabs of stone suggesting burial in scattered cists. Larger vertical stones at the E end may indicate the presence of a proper chamber or perhaps a blind entrance. The mound now has a length of 115 ft. Only re-excavation can determine the architectural features of this tomb. Two leaf-shaped flint arrowheads were among the finds. Date, c. 3,500–2,500 BC.

*Gorsey Bigbury, sacred site (ST/484558) 2¼ miles NE of Cheddar (A371, B3135), 1 mile W of Charterhouse, on land of Lower Farm. Finds in museum of University of Bristol Spelaeological Society.

This sacred site is not conspicuous on the ground but it is one of the few henge monuments of any size to have been excavated thoroughly. Moreover the finds made from 1931–4 were prolific and of unusual interest.

This site comprises a circular denuded bank, roughly 200 ft. in diam. and in places 5 ft. high, surrounding a rock-cut ditch dug originally in a series of 5 contiguous sections. An entrance-gap, 13 ft. wide, faces N. These features define a fairly flat plateau about 75 ft. across. Excavation revealed that the ditch had a width of 12–21 ft. and a depth of 4–8 ft.

Before the site had acquired any great sanctity, it had been abandoned for a short time and then re-used by a group of Beaker people who squatted in the SE half of its ditch, lighting fires, cooking their food and leaving behind fragments of nearly 100 beakers. Whether this rubbish was domestic or represents sacred usage of the site, is not clear. Immediately W of the entrance, at a point where the ditch had been dug deep and pit-like, parts of a human skeleton accompanied by bone needles, knife and arrowhead of flint and a sherd of pottery had been deliberately buried and covered over, perhaps a foundation deposit to dedicate the site.

Gorsey Bigbury must have been started by native Neolithic people about the time of the arrival of beakers in Somerset, c. 2,000 BC. The main Beaker occupation here may have extended into the full Bronze Age, c. 1700 BC.

*Murtry Hill, chambered long barrow (ST/763507) nearly ½ mile SE of Buckland Dinham (A362), near Nightingale Lodge, Orchardleigh Park. Finds in Taunton Museum.

The mound of this barrow is oval, set nearly E/W. It measures 150 ft. × 100 ft. and appears to be wedge-shaped. At the E end stand 2 stones of oolitic limestone; during the excavations of 1920 a few more were found scattered to the W of these. The only finds were Romano-British potsherds and coins, suggesting that the tomb had been robbed at that period. When opened in 1803-4, many human bones were found. The 2 stones (one 10 ft. high) may be the remains of a portal dolman. Date, c. 3,500-2,500 BC.

Redhill, long barrow (ST/499636) 4 miles NE of Churchill (A38, A368), ¼ mile NE of Redhill Church (A38).

The mound of this barrow, which lies E/W, is 154 ft. long and 50 ft. wide. Nowhere does it exceed 3½ ft. in ht. Several large stones are visible in the mound but the presence of burial chambers has yet to be proved. Date, 3,500-2,500 BC.

BRONZE AGE

*Ashen Hill, barrow-cemetery (ST/ 537521, w end) 4 miles N of Wells (A39, A371), 1 mile NE of Priddy; ¼ mile S of B3135. Finds in Bristol and Wells museums.

There are 8 barrows in this cemetery, arranged in a row nearly E/W. All are bowl-barrows except the fourth from the w, which may be a bell-barrow. Its ditch is no longer clear, but the mound stands on a circular platform 1 ft. above the level of the surrounding land. Mound and platform have a diam. of about 70

ft.; the mound itself is 5 ft. high. Four cremations have been found in this barrow but not by scientific excavation. All the barrows in the group have been dug into at various times: working from E to w, the following details have been recorded:

(1)   At least 3 separate cremations have been found here, including the primary burial, an urn filled with ashes and placed in a pit in the old land surface.
(2)   A central pit at the base of the barrow contained the cremated bones of an adult who had been provided with beads of amber and faience, a bronze knife in its sheath and a grape cup.
(3)   This barrow, composed almost entirely of stone rubble, covered a cist containing a cremation with (?beneath) an urn. Higher up was another cremation, in a hollow covered by a stone.
(4)   A cist at the base of this mound contained a cremation accompanied by a bronze dagger in a sheath.
(5)   This is the bell-barrow described above.
(6)   An urn, a cremation and much charcoal from the funeral pyre were found in a cist at the base of this barrow.
(7)   A cremation and the remains of a bronze knife have been found in this mound.
(8)   At the base of this bowl there was a cremation.

Period of the cemetery, c. 1,700-1,400 BC.

Beacon Batch, barrow-cemetery (ST/ 485572) 1½ miles SW of Blagdon (A368), 1½ miles NW of Charterhouse.

On the highest part of the ridge to the E of, and overlooking Black Down, there is a group of 10 barrows sufficiently close together to constitute a barrow-cemetery in the Wessex tradition. They lie in an oval, surrounding this high point, 4 to the S, 6 to the N. Of the 4 S barrows, 2 are bowls, 56 ft. in diam., 2½ ft. and 6 ft. high: the third, a bell and the most w ? the remains of a long barrow. It measures c. 90 × 50 ft., appearing today as a stony mound 1 ft high, with no visible ditch. On the N side of the hill are 5 bowl-barrows with a bell at the centre. Their diams. range from 55-68 ft., their hts. from 1-6 ft. The third from the w, a bell-barrow, appears to have a ring of stones set around the base of its mound. It stands on a platform raised 1 ft. above the surrounding ground. The mound stands about 3 ft. above its platform and is 30 ft. across, the platform being twice as wide. The ditch is now only visible on the NW. This cemetery must have accumulated c. 1,700–1,400 BC.

Brightworthy and Green Barrow, round barrows (SS/818351, SS/818346) on Exmoor, 3 miles SW of Exford (B3223), 1¾ miles SW of Withypool, N of minor road to Withypool Cross.

The 3 Brightworthy Barrows on Withypool Common are set in a line E/W, the easternmost being on the highest point hereabouts. The central mound is 7 ft. high and 36 ft. in diam. It is a bell-barrow, a 10 ft. berm separating mound from ditch. The W site may be a disc-barrow, though it has no central mound. Like many barrows in this area they are deliberately set on high ground.

Just over ¼ mile to the S is Green Barrow, a bowl 40–50 ft. in diam. and 3–4 ft. high. The contents of these barrows has not been recorded but they are likely to have been built in the period 1,700–1,400 BC.

Green Barrow (Exmoor), see above.

Hunter's Lodge, bell/disc-barrow (ST/558501) 2¾ miles NNE of Wells (A39, A371), ½ mile E of Hunter's Lodge Inn, N of road.

This is an example of a barrow intermediate in shape between bell and disc. It has been extensively damaged by leadmine shafts dug through it, but nevertheless its shape is clear. It has a max. diam. of about 154 ft. There is a well-defined ditch with bank on the outside. Within, a mound stands at the centre, 60 ft. in diam. and about 1 ft. high, separated from the ditch by a broad berm. Contemporary with the concentration of round barrows in the Priddy area, this example must have been built c. 1,700–1,400 BC.

Nordrach-on-Mendip, barrow-cemetery (ST/528547 centre) N and S of B3134, 2½ miles SW of West Harptree (A368, B3114).

Though divided by the modern road, it is permissible to regard all these barrows as part of 1 cemetery. Those N of the road comprise 4 bowls, their diams. being

about 63–80 ft. and their hts. from 4–5½ ft. South of the road there is a row of 5 barrows, 4 of them bowls and one perhaps a bell. The latter, second from the E, shows as a very irregular mound set askew within a ditch that is discontinuous and slightly oval in plan. The mound is about 7 ft. high while the ditch has a max. diam. of 150 ft. The rocky subsoil may here have proved so intractable that the ditch was never completed. The bowls in this row are 80–96 ft. across and 5½–8 ft. high: one, however, is very much smaller, being only 27 ft. in diam. and 1½ ft. in ht.

Nothing is known of the contents of these barrows; they must have been built in the period 1,700–1,400 BC.

*Pool Farm, burial cist (ST/537541) 2¼ miles SW of West Harptree (A368, B3114), ¾ mile NW of Castle of Comfort Inn (B3134), in field W of Pool Farm. Engraved stone in Bristol City Museum.

In 1930 a round barrow 100 ft. across and 4 ft. high was excavated and the mound subsequently removed. At its centre a well-made rectangular burial cist of dolomitic conglomerate was found. This measures 5½ × 4½ ft., with a ht. of 2½ ft., and had a capstone covering almost the whole of it. Three sides are built from 3 large stones, the SE end being closed by 3 smaller stones. The floor was carefully paved. On it, near the SE end, lay a small heap of cremated human bones, perhaps originally contained in a bag. The most remarkable discovery (not noticed until 1956) was a series of engravings on the inner face of the SW side-stone, representing 6 human feet, a series of circular depressions, or cup-marks and other symbols. Similar foot carvings have been found in Northumberland, Lancashire, in Denmark, Norway and Brittany.

The barrow mound covering the cist was entirely of scraped-up soil, there being no surrounding ditch.

This barrow with its cist must have been built c. 1,600–1,350 BC.

*Priddy Circles, sacred sites (ST/540527) 4½ miles N of Wells (A39, A371), 2¾ miles SW of West Harptree (A368, B3114): N of B3135, NW of Miner's Arms Hotel.

There are 4 circles each with a diam. of about 600 ft.; they are in a line N/S and extend for ¾ mile. The 3 S circles are separated by gaps of 270 ft.: the N circle is separated from the others by 500 yds.

The circles have the unusual feature of a bank within the ditch, an arrangement seen elsewhere only at Stonehenge (Wilts., below). The 2 s circles have a single entrance facing N: the third circle has a gap facing s, while that in the N circle is probably to be located in its sw side which has now been levelled. The other gaps visible in the circles are modern. Excavation has revealed that the ditch of the s circle is U-shaped, originally 3–4 ft. deep and now 12 ft. wide. The material from it forms the bank and was piled up between 2 rings of stout posts and then roughly faced with locally collected drystone walling. These wooden posts may originally have been about 10 ft. high, considerably higher than the bank itself. The s circle had been first marked out by a slight trench lying immediately within its ditch.

Priddy Circles should be considered in relation to the groups of barrows that surround them. Date, c. 2,500–1,700 BC.

Priddy Nine Barrows, barrow cemetery (ST/538518) 3¾ miles N of Wells (A39, A371), 1 mile NE of Priddy; south of B3135 and of Ashen Hill barrow cemetery (above).

There are in fact only 7 barrows in this cemetery, all bowls and set out in a line curving s from N to E. The southernmost is at 1000 ft., the highest point hereabouts. The 2 northernmost barrows are separated slightly from the rest. They should all be considered and examined in conjunction with the Ashen Hill group, immediately to the N.

The Priddy Nine Barrows are all large, with hts. approaching 10 ft. and diams. up to c. 80 ft. Most of them have been dug into in the last century; excavation records are confused, but it seems that all covered burials by cremation. This cemetery must have accumulated c. 1,700–1,400 BC.

Rowberrow, bowl-barrow (ST/448583) 2¾ miles NE of Axbridge (A371), ½ mile NNE of Shipham, s of Rowberrow rectory. Finds in private hands.

This bowl-barrow has a diam. of 65 ft. and a ht. of 7 ft. Excavated at its centre in 1813, there was found a square stone-built cist, 4 × 4 ft., with walls 3 ft. high and roofed with flat slabs, apparently standing on the original land surface – a round barrow containing a stone burial chamber. A human appears to have been cremated on the spot: with it in the chamber several ? amber beads were found, together with a dagger (? of bronze), a clay ball and perhaps an incense cup. An unburnt burial was found near the chamber.

This barrow must belong to the later Stonehenge period, c. 1,700–1,400 BC.

Setta Barrow. See Devon.

Small Down Camp, barrow-cemetery. See Iron Age.

Stock Hill, barrow-cemetery (ST/556510) 3¼ miles N of Wells (A39, A371), ¾ mile NE of Hunter's Lodge Inn, s of B3135.

This cemetery consists of about 5 large bowl-barrows. One of them is 10 ft. high. There is a possible disc-barrow to the s. Nothing is known of their contents. They must be broadly contemporary with those around them, all belonging to the later Stonehenge period, c. 1,700–1,400 BC.

*Tynings Farm, barrow cemetery (ST/469563) midway between Cheddar (A371) and Burrington (A368), on s side of Tynings Farm. Finds in Bristol City Museum and museum of the University of Bristol Spelaeological Society.

There are 5 bowl-barrows in this cemetery. Most have been examined by the University of Bristol Spelaeological Society. Unimpressive from the outside, excavation has revealed interesting internal structures and rich grave goods.

In size, these barrows have diams. of 21–74 ft. and hts. of 2½–5 ft.; four are E of the farm, the other to the w. Of the 4, 3 are arranged in a line N/s, with the fourth to the E.

The easternmost barrow has a core of earth with a capping of stones. A cremation, accompanied by a stone pendant was found in a central burial pit. Nearby, a collared urn had been deposited, containing the ashes of a woman and a child with beads of shale and faience (from Near East) and a copper awl.

Of the next 3 barrows, the N one had a core of earth enlarged later in the Bronze Age with a capping of stones. The primary burials were cremations in pits, one of them including 3 incense cups. Urns holding cremations, covered and surrounded by slabs of Old Red Sandstone, were associated with the enlargement of the mound.

The middle barrow in this line was made of stones with a retaining kerb of larger stones. Traces of burials by cremation were found at the centre, in an area surrounded by a well-built wall with an entrance through it.

The s barrow had a complicated structure. It had been begun as a circular enclosure consisting of a bank and ditch, with an entrance at the sw, 45 ft. in diam. A series of pits had been dug within and fires lit. Two or 3 cremations had been deposited in pits and a mound then built over the whole enclosure, concealing its ditch. At a later period a new ditch was dug around the mound, with an entrance facing E. Later still the mound was enlarged, the second ditch being filled in and a stone kerb replacing it. An urn containing a cremation was associated with this last phase.

The w barrow had a mound made of stones, edged with a kerb and surrounded by a rock-cut ditch with a causeway across it. At the centre, a carefully built cist was found containing a cremation. This cist was itself surrounded by boulders with a gap facing the break in the barrow ditch.

This cemetery would have been in use c. 1,700–1,400 BC.

Westbury Beacon, bell-barrow (ST/502508) nearly 1½ miles N of Westbury (A371), ¾ mile W of Priddy long barrow (above).

This barrow is of interest because it is located on Carboniferous Limestone so hard that its builders were foiled in their attempts to dig a complete and regular ditch around the barrow mound. The mound itself is about 80 ft. in diam. and 9 ft. high: it is surrounded by a berm 14 ft. broad and then by a ditch. The latter, however, bends in at the sw, avoiding an outcrop of particularly hard stone, and ceases altogether for several yards at the NE. Nowhere is it regular in plan. There are traces of a bank outside the ditch. There is a wide depression at the centre of the mound and a report of its robbing early in the 19th century suggests

that a stone cist was found, containing 12–20 bronze implements. Date, c. 1,700–1,400 BC.

West Cranmore, barrow cemetery (ST/658427) 2½ miles E of Shepton Mallet, s of A361 between Doulting and w Cranmore, on N side of railway line. Finds in museum of the Society of Antiquaries of London.

This cemetery consists of 3 barrows, 2 bells and a bowl, set out in a line E/W, the bowl being at the E end.

From w to E, the first bell-barrow has a max. diam. of nearly 160 ft. The mound is 90 ft. across and over 5 ft. high. It has a broad berm separating it from a surrounding ditch: a bank lies outside this. Both bank and ditch are damaged on the w side. A depression at the centre of the mound represents its examination by the Rev. J. Skinner about 1827. He found evidence of burial by cremation but reported no grave goods.

To the E is a second bell-barrow, the finest in Somerset. It has a diam. of 156 ft., the ditch with its bank outside being well-defined. Separated from these by a wide berm is the barrow mound, 72 ft. across and 6 ft. high.

At least 4 people have explored this and the other mounds in this group. Cremations have been recorded from the central bell, together with a grooved dagger and a knife of bronze. No details are known of burials in the bowl-barrow. This cemetery must have accumulated c. 1,700–1,400 BC.

*Wick Barrow, round barrow (ST/209455) 1¾ miles N of Stogursey, less than ½ mile from coast. Finds and model in Taunton Museum.

This barrow appears from the outside as a simple bowl, with no visible ditch, about 85 ft. in diam. and some 6 ft. in ht. Excavations in 1907 revealed that the outer mound covered a smaller internal one, 28 ft. across, revetted on the outside by a well-built circular drystone wall about 4 ft. high. The centre of the barrow had been dug out in Romano-British times and the earliest burial removed. Three contracted secondary burials were found high in the mound, each accompanied by a beaker; in addition 2 had been provided with flint implements, one a

superbly flaked knife. Date, c. 2,000 BC.
*Withypool Hill, stone circle (SS/836343) 2¾ miles sw of Exford (B3223), 1 mile sw of Withypool.

This circle has a diam. of about 119 ft. Only 37 of its stones survive. None of them exceeds 2 ft. in ht.; all could have been quarried locally. Date c. 1,700–1,400 BC.

IRON AGE

Bat's Castle, hill-fort (SS/988421) 1 mile s of Dunster Castle, off A396.

This small camp is roughly circular, the inner bank having a max. diam. of 150 yds. It has 2 banks with a ditch between them. Both banks stand in places to a ht. of 7–8 ft. There are well-defended entrances facing E and W. The inner bank is in-turned at the W while at the E entrance the outer bank is extended outwards to form a wall on either side of an entrance passage 25 yds. long – an unusual arrangement. Not dated.

Blacker's Hill, promontory fort (ST/637499) N of B road joining Gurney Slade (A37) to Stratton-on-the-Fosse (A367).

This good example of a promontory fort consists of 2 banks and ditches which cut across level ground to fortify 15 acres: the defences on the s and W sides are provided by the spur which falls 200 ft. to a valley with a stream flowing E to the Frome. Although the earthworks have been ploughed out in places, a good section can be seen at the SE where there appears to be a simple entrance. Here the inner bank stands 6–8 ft. high and the outer one 10–12 ft. On the N side the top of the outer bank is still 40 ft. above the floor of its ditch. Not dated.

*Brean Down, promontory fort (ST/300590) sw of Weston-super-Mare, reached by B road from Burnham-on-Sea.

Brean Down is an isolated, elongated, limestone promontory protected on all but the SE side by steep slopes and the sea. At the E end, an area 1,400 ft. in length has been cut off by a single bank with ditch facing W. This earthwork bends abruptly N, its s part continuing a natural defence formed by a steep slope

N of Brean Down Farm. This may be considered a small untypical promontory fort. Not dated.

Brent Knoll, hill-fort (ST/341510) 2½ miles NE of Burnham-on-Sea (B3139, B3140), ¾ mile sw of E Brent (A370).

The earthworks of this fort are roughly triangular in shape and enclose about 4 acres. On the W and S sides the hill has been artificially scarped to add to the difficulties of those attacking the camp. There appears to be an original entrance through the E side, with additional outworks and scarping to protect it. The centre of the camp has been damaged by quarrying. Not dated.

Brewer's Castle, see **Mounsey Castle.**

Bury Castle, hill-fort (SS/917472) 2 miles NE of Porlock (A39, B3225), ¼ mile NW of Selworthy.

The mass of Bossington Hill and Selworthy Beacon has a number of spurs on its s side. One of these overlooks Selworthy. It was fortified in Iron Age times by 3 separate earthworks. The easternmost, with a bank 15 ft. high, cuts off the very tip of the spur, an area under 200 ft. wide. The E side of this defence is supplied by the natural fall of the hillside. Fifty yds. to the W. a second entrenchment cuts across level ground. It is larger than the first and originally had a counterscarp bank. About 400 ft. further W the remains of a third bank and ditch can be found, badly damaged and denuded. Not dated.

Clatworthy Castle, hill-fort (ST/046315) 3¼ miles NW of Wiveliscombe (A361), ½ mile NW of Clatworthy.

This fort is approximately triangular in shape, its single bank and ditch enclosing nearly 14 acres. It has a commanding position overlooking the valley of the Tone. The E side of the fort, covering more level ground, consists of a formidable bank and ditch with a break in it which may represent an original entrance. The other sides make use of the slope of the hill – a slight rampart with the slope outside it artificially scarped so as to present a nearly vertical face to attackers. The defences are broken at the SE. Not dated.

Cow Castle, hill-fort (SS/795374) on Exmoor, 1¾ miles SE of Simonsbath (B3223), reached by road from w via Blue Gate.

Roughly oval in plan, this hill-fort encloses almost 3 acres. It is dominated by higher ground on all sides but enjoys good natural protection locally and overlooks the Barle and its tributary the White Water. Defences comprise a single bank and ditch with traces of an internal quarry ditch. There are entrance gaps at the NE and sw, with an outer bank at the former. In places the main rampart rises 6–8 ft. from the ground outside. Not dated.

Dowsborough, hill-fort (ST/160391) 2 miles wsw of Nether Stowey (A39).

This hill-fort occupies the higher end of a narrow ridge. Oval in plan, it encloses about 7¼ acres. It is defended by a bank and ditch with counterscarp bank, following the contours of the ridge. In places the inner bank is still 5 ft. above the level ground within. An entrance, obscured and damaged recently, is at the E end – a simple gap through banks and ditch. Not dated.

Elworthy Barrows, unfinished hill-fort (ST/071337) 3¾ miles NNW of Wiveliscombe (A361, B3188), 1⅛ miles sw of Elworthy (B3188).

This hill-fort is of unusual interest because it was never completed. Very roughly oval in plan, it would have enclosed about 9 acres. Along the s half, there is a ditch with bank immediately inside, interrupted by 2 gaps. There are no earthworks at the NW, but a second line of defence has been started along the N side, with a further space at the NE. Along the N, only preliminary ditch-digging has been begun, the soil for the rampart being heaped well clear, as if marking out the inner line of a rampart which was to fill the space between this dump and the ditch (as along the s, where the work is more advanced). At the E an in-turned entrance is nearly complete. Not dated.

*Glastonbury (A39, A361, B3151) and **Meare** (B3151), lakeside villages (ST/ 492409; ST/446423) 1¼ miles N and ½ mile NW of their respective modern towns. Finds at Glastonbury and Taunton Museums.

There is nothing to be seen on the ground at either place. The remains of these villages set in a peat bog have been so well preserved, however, that the objects recovered from them tell us more about everyday life in the late Iron Age than do those of most other sites of this period. The museums at Glastonbury and Taunton contain collections from Glastonbury and Meare that should not be missed.

*Ham Hill, hill-fort and Roman settlement (ST/485165, centre) 4¾ miles w of Yeovil, immediately s of Stoke-sub-Hamdon (between A303 and A3088). Finds in Taunton Museum, British Museum (currency bar).

This impressive site is famed for the quantity of ornaments, tools and weapons of the Iron Age and Roman periods found within the earthworks. It is unfortunate that the history of the fort has not yet been worked out by excavation. The earthworks enclose the whole hill, including an irregular extension to the NW (where the ramparts and ditches are best preserved). The total area thus fortified is about 210 acres, making the site one of the largest in Britain. The fortifications consist, for the most part, of 2 banks with ditches outside them: at the sw and extreme NW these are triple, covering more level ground. The ditches have all been cut into hard oolitic rock famous as building stone. There are several breaks in the lines of ramparts; original entrances have not yet been identified but there appears to be an in-turned entrance where the NW spur joins the N edge of Stroud's Hill.

Occupation here lasted from the earliest Iron Age times but we cannot yet say when the earthworks were first erected. Occupation seems to have been extensive and perhaps permanent. The discovery of a late Iron Age (early 1st century AD) cremation in a pit, furnished with, among other things, a fine iron dagger in its sheath, is of special interest. Many currency bars and Durotrigian coins have also been found here. It is possible that the main part of the hill-fort is later than the ramparts on the N extension. Not dated, but probably occupied from the early 1st millenium BC.

Occupation continued in Roman times and at least 1 substantial building has been found on the hill. Some of the Iron Age defences appear to have been refurbished after the Conquest. The circular depression in the NE corner of the N extension defences, 100 ft. across and approached by a short passage from the S has been considered by some authorities to be the site of a Romano-British amphitheatre.

*Kingsdown Camp, hill-fort (ST/719517) 2¾ miles SE of Radstock (A362, A367), ½ mile N of Mells Road railway station (SW of A362). Finds in Taunton Museum.

This site is unusually small, its defences enclosing less than ½ acre. It is heart-shaped in plan, with an entrance at the NE. Features visible on the surface are a single bank and ditch. Excavation revealed that these were built soon after the Roman Conquest and the bank, which was originally a good drystone wall, in places overlies an inner ditch which appears to have a late Iron Age origin. This ditch, hardly visible today, was rock-cut, with a width of 4–8 ft. and an average depth of 3½ ft. The outer ditch was much more regularly cut: it was V-shaped (the inner one had a flat floor), with a width of 5–10 ft. and a depth of over 5 ft. Post-holes at the NE (Roman) entrance suggested a stout timber gate. The entrance through the Iron Age ditch, at the SE corner of the camp, was a simple cause-way 25 ft. wide. Finds include currency bars and a coin of the Dobunni. Date of visible earthwork, within the period AD 43–68. Date of earlier site not yet established.

Maesbury Camp, hill-fort (ST/611472) 2¼ miles NW of Shepton Mallet, immediately N of B road to Wells.

Maesbury, like Small Down Camp (below) is a good example of those hill-forts whose ramparts follow the line of the natural contours to encircle a hill. It is roughly oval in plan, the area within the inner rampart being about 6¾ acres. Its main defence is a single bank and ditch, but on the N and SE sides there are traces of an outer bank now almost ploughed out. There is an original entrance facing SE and another facing W. In places the inner bank stands 20 ft. above the silted-up ditch outside it. The ditch today has an average width of 24 ft. Not dated.

Meare, village. See **Glastonbury.**

Mounsey Castle, Brewer's Castle, hill-

forts (SS/886295, SS/884298) 2 miles NW of Dulverton (off A396).

These camps face each other across the Barle. Mounsey Castle is the larger, its earthworks enclosing an area of about 3 acres. It is triangular in plan, with de-fences consisting of a main bank and ditch, with traces of a second bank and ditch on the S and W. There is an entrance at the SW corner, where one bank turns inwards to flank it. There may also be an original entrance at the N end of the camp. The banks seem to have been built of large stones and rubble; a thick growth of trees obscures these details.

Brewer's Castle lies to the NW. It is circular in plan and less than 1 acre in extent. Situated on high ground with steep slopes on the E and S sides, the need for artificial defences was slight. A bank, with a ditch outside it in places, can be seen on the W where the ground is least steep.

Without excavation it cannot be said whether these camps are contemporary, and whether they were built by 1 tribe to cover the river, or by rival tribes. It is not unknown for hill-forts of differing size to be close neighbours.

Ruborough Camp, hill-fort (ST/228335) 5 miles N of Taunton, 1 mile NNE of Broomfield Church.

This site is triangular in plan, being defined by a great bank and ditch with a counterscarp bank. The inner bank in places stands 18 ft. above the silted-up surface of the ditch outside it. The area thus enclosed is 27 acres. There are possible entrances through the W side and at the apex on the E: neither has been proved by excavation.

About 500 ft. to the W and SW, an addi-tional earthwork provides protection across more open country. Here the bank is still 6 ft. high and has a ditch on its W side 21 ft. wide, separated from it by a wide berm. Not dated.

*Small Down Camp, hill-fort and Bronze Age barrow-cemetery (ST/666406) 3½ miles SE of Shepton Mallet (A37, A361, A371), 1¾ miles NE of Evercreech (B3081). On W side of track from Westcombe to Chesterblade. Finds in Shepton Mallet Museum.

This site has an irregular oval plan,

expanding at its E end. An area of about 5 acres is enclosed on 3 sides by a bank and ditch with counterscarp bank: on the E there are 2 banks and ditches as well as a counterscarp bank. At this end 2 breaks through these multiple ramparts have been proved by excavation to be original entrances. In places the innermost bank is nearly 10 ft. high. Excavation has revealed that the inner ditch had an original width exceeding 20 ft. and a depth of about 10 ft. Pottery found in the ditch suggests an early beginning in the Iron Age for this hill-fort.

Along the top of the hill surrounded by the Iron Age ramparts and towards the W there is a line of 11 bowl-barrows. Their diams. range from 25–60 ft. They have been rifled at various times. Those re-excavated in 1904 yielded evidence of burial after cremation. They must have accumulated here within the period 1,700–1,400 BC.

*South Cadbury hill-fort (ST/628251) 1½ miles SE of Sparkford (A303, A359), ½ mile S of A303, SW of Little Cadbury. Finds in Taunton Museum.

Situated on a free-standing hill, with a natural water supply below the summit at the NE corner, this hill-fort has a memorable command of country. It is now one of the most important hill-forts in southern England because of the extensive excavations conducted here, 1966–70. These revealed an astonishing, almost continuous sequence of occupation, beginning with the Neolithic and ending, more than 4,000 years later, with a pre-Norman township in which King Ethelred the Unready (978–1016) set up an emergency mint.

The hill-fort is roughly sub-rectangular, its longest sides at the N and S, its W side shorter than that to the E. About 18 acres are enclosed. The defences everywhere comprise 4 ramparts with intervening quarry-ditches; the outer 2 along the E have been removed by ploughing. Extra lengths of rampart can be seen along the N and at the SE. There are original entrances at the NE and SW (usable for access from South Cadbury and Sutton Montis respectively) and also at the SE. Each is dominated by an extra-high, projecting rampart above the right-hand side of someone approaching from outside, natural high ground being utilised.

Excavations revealed traces of Neo-

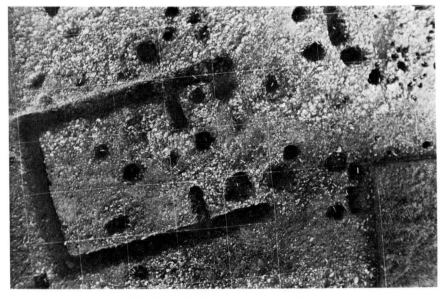

44   *South Cadbury: the apparent shrine*

lithic and Bronze Age occupation prior
to the hill-fort-building, nothing of which
can now be seen. The Neolithic, with
C14 dates c. 2,900–2,400 BC, comprised
pits and gullies with much occupation
refuse, scattered all over the hill-top.
Several pits contained human and other
remains suggestive of ritual rather than
purely domestic use.

Evidence for occupation in the 2nd
millenium BC is so far sparse. About
800 BC, however, pottery, bronzes and
half a gold bracelet show that Late
Bronze Age farmers or craftsmen were
settled on the hill. Iron Age occupation of
the hill began c. 700 BC with an undefended
settlement. No certain remains of buildings have been found but pottery, bronzes
and other finds suggest that a group of
peasants under warrior leadership mig-
rated to that area from N France at this
time. The hill-fort was begun in the 5th
century BC. At first its defences comprised
a reduced version of the innermost rampart and ditch, enclosing c. 20 acres. This
consisted of a bank of clay and rubble,
with an almost vertical facing of upright
timbers, several feet apart, holding up a
revetting wall of horizontal timbers. A
second line of vertical posts ran 5 ft.
behind the front, perhaps tied to it by
transverse horizontal beams. There was a
slight berm between the bank and quarry-
ditch outside it. Next, this rampart was
replaced by a larger earthwork, dug from
an enlarged quarry-ditch which produced
much heavy limestone. Its front was
revetted by much larger vertical posts,
between which drystone walling was built,
using lias brought from a distance. Behind
the revetment a roughly paved rampart-

walk was laid down using limestone
quarried from the ditch. Repair and minor
alterations were carried out to this rampart during the lifetime of the fort. The
outer 3 banks and ditches were added
during the final phase of the fort; the
outermost was massive, 20 ft. wide at its
base.

Only the SW gate has been excavated
and it was found to have been much
eroded and frequently rebuilt during a
life extending from the 5th century, BC to
after 1,200 AD. It provided access in a
long, slightly curved passage through the
rampart, with gates and a door-stop near
its centre, spanned by a bridge, with one
or more guard-chambers at the inner end.
A series of road surfaces had been laid
down on that belonging to the early
Roman period, evidence for a massacre
of men, women and children was found,
the bodies pulled apart by scavenging
animals. The gates were also burnt and the
defences slighted, c. 60–70 AD.

The interior of the fort is covered with
traces (not visible on the ground) of
occupation – huts, storage pits and other
structures: excavation revealed that Iron
Age inhabitants of different periods tended to live in restricted areas and not
scattered over the hill-top. Houses were
circular and rectangular and most of the
crafts necessary to an organised urban
community were practised here. One
building, evidently a shrine, was near the
centre of the fort; built after 43 AD, it was
square, with a porch. Just outside, an ox
and other animals had been buried,
together with deposits of weapons, grouped either side of a processional approach
to the shrine (fig. 44).

Staffordshire

NEOLITHIC

*Bridestones, chambered long barrow (SJ/ 906622) 3 miles E of Congleton (A34, A54, A527), N of road joining Dane in Shaw (A527) to Ryecroft Gate (A523): sw side of buildings here.

Very little can now be seen of the mound which once covered this burial chamber, but it is reputed to have been more than 300 ft. long and about 40 ft. wide. It was orientated E/W. The visible burial chamber comprises part of a parallel-sided gallery 18½ ft. in length. It is divided into 2 by a broken stone which had originally been pierced by a hole – the port-hole type of tomb entrance which is more common in the Cotswolds and in parts of France. East of this chamber there are the remains of a semicircular forecourt defined by large stones. To the W there were originally 2 side-chambers. No details of burials have been recorded.

This type of barrow belongs to a group of tombs peripheral to the Irish Sea. Date, c. 2,500 BC.

Devil's Ring and Finger, holed stone (SJ/707378) 3 miles NE of Market Drayton (A53, A529), on N edge of Oakley Park.

There are 2 stones now incorporated in the wall around the park, both 6 ft. tall. One is a square-sectioned upright, the other is D-shaped and has a large hole through it. These stones do not appear to be in their original positions. It is possible that they formed part of a chambered long barrow, the holed stone acting as an entrance or as an internal division, like that which originally sub-divided the Bridestones (above). A number of large blocks of similar local sandstone can be seen scattered in the area. Date, c. 3,500– 2,500 BC.

*Long Low,** burial mounds (SK/122539, not on O.S.) 5¾ miles NW of Ashbourne (A52, A515, A517), 1¼ miles SE of Wetton and at dead-end of road leading SE from there. Finds in Sheffield Museum.

Here 2 barrows are linked by a bank, an arrangement not recorded elsewhere in England. A modern field wall has been built along the top of the bank and across the N barrow mound. This has a diam. of 75 ft. and a ht. of 8 ft. It has been extensively robbed, its mound consisting of limestone slabs suitable for walling. Likewise, the bank joining it to a smaller mound at the sw has also been robbed. It now has a ht. of 3–5 ft. and a regular width of about 50 ft. Its edges are very straight. The sw barrow, on the N side of the field wall, is about 65 ft. in diam. and 4 ft. high. It has also been robbed, both at the centre and elsewhere.

A stone burial pit at the centre of the larger mound was found to contain the bones of 13 people, together with 3 leaf-shaped arrowheads. Traces of a cremation occurred in the other mound.

Long Low shows well on the skyline from NE and sw. Date, c. 2,500–1,700 BC.

IRON AGE

Berry Ring, hill-fort (SJ/887212) 2½ miles sw of Stafford, beside road N of A518 at Billington.

A single bank and ditch fortify an oval area of 7 acres. There appears to be a second bank and ditch around the N side of the camp. obscured by trees. The main bank is best preserved along the E side. There is a small gap in the defences facing E and a very wide break facing s. The latter has clearly been widened in recent times and may have been the original entrance. Not dated.

Berth Hill, hill-fort (SJ/788391) 7¾ miles NE of Market Drayton (A53, A529), ¾ mile N of Maer, N of A51.

Protected by trees, this fort is irregular in plan and encloses 9 acres. Its defences consist of a bank, ditch and counterscarp bank. These are particularly clear around the N side of the site. There is a fine in-turned entrance facing w, approached by a hollow way up the hillside from the NW. There is another, simple, entrance facing NE, also with a track up the hillside to it. Since this fort crowns a steep-sided hill, its main rampart is nowhere more than 4 ft. above the level of the interior; outside it falls abruptly, presenting a long steep slope within a ditch which now appears as a flat terrace. At the NNE, facing open ground, there are traces of a second ditch and bank. Here, by a modern gap in the ramparts, a spring rises inside the camp. Not dated.

Bury Bank, hill-fort (SJ/883359) 1¾ miles NW of Stone (A34, A51, A520), in angle formed by join of A51 and A34.

This fort must have been sited to command the Trent. It is roughly oval and encloses 3½ acres. The defences consist of a bank, ditch and counterscarp bank, the latter set well forward of the ditch. These do not show very distinctly because the soft subsoil has caused the banks and ditch to collapse; these features are clearest along the s and sw. There is a well-defined, in-turned entrance facing WNW, opposite the farm on A51. Not dated.

Castle Ring, hill-fort (SK/045128) 4½ miles N of Brownhills (A5, A452, B4155), N of Cannock Wood, NW of Park Gate Inn.

One of the most striking hill-forts in England, Castle Ring stands on high ground commanding the country in every direction. Its internal area is 8½ acres. It is 5-sided, its w and N sides being protected by 2 banks and ditches with a counterscarp bank. On the s and SE sides, where flat ground made extra defences necessary, there are 5 banks and 4 ditches. The original and only entrance is through the E side at the Lodge, s of which the multiplication of the defences begins. Here the innermost bank is in-turned. There appears to be a sunken track leading down the hillside NE from this entrance. Not dated.

Kinver, promontory fort (SO/835832) 4 miles w of Stourbridge (A458, A491) at N end of Kinver Edge.

An area of 7½ acres at the N end of the Edge is cut off and defended by a bank and ditch facing sw. The NW and SE sides are protected by the natural hill-slopes. In places the bank rises 10–15 ft. above the level of the interior. No entrance is now visible: access to the site may have been obtained up the hillside from a lower spur to the NE, or at the E end of the SE side. Not dated.

Thor's Cave, inhabited cave (SK/098549) 7½ miles NW of Ashbourne Wetton, reached by road off A515 at Alsop Station and by dead-end lane sw from Wetton. Finds in Derby and Sheffield Museums.

This cave is in the hillside, high above the E bank of the River Manifold. The main entrance, facing NW, is enormous. Once inside the cave several branches appear, together with a second entrance, facing w. This is a narrow cleft: to keep the cave warm it would have had to be blocked.

A large amount of Iron Age and Roman domestic rubbish has been found here, showing that occupation continued from the 2nd century BC into the 3rd century AD. Wherever suitable caves occur, prehistoric and Romano-Britons were quite willing to occupy them. They would have been drier and warmer than a hut, being impervious to the roughest weather.

Suffolk

BRONZE AGE

Brightwell Heath, barrow cemetery (TM/ 242444) 4¾ miles E of Ipswich, 1 mile NW of Brightwell (A1093).

This cemetery is unevenly scattered along the N side of a narrow E/W plantation. Originally there were at least 8 mounds. The survivors are beside and SW of the Devil's Ring (map ref. above). This has a diam. of 120 ft. and consists of a low central mound surrounded by a ditch with an outer bank – an enlarged saucer-barrow. The bank is still 3–4 ft. high. NW there are 2 bowl-barrows, the larger 110 ft. in diam. and 7 ft. high, the other 60 ft. in diam. and 6 ft. high. To the SW there were 3 bowl-barrows, destroyed after excavation.

Further SW, at the W end of the plantation, there is a bowl-barrow 70 ft. in diam. and 6 ft. high.

Unfortunately, since this account was written in 1960, all except one of these barrows have been destroyed by ploughing. The survivor, crowned with fir trees, is beside the road across Foxhall Heath. It is still 3 ft. high.

Nothing is known of the contents of these mounds. Date, c. 1700–1400 BC.
Devil's Ring. See above.

Surrey

MESOLITHIC

*Abinger, dwelling site (TQ/112459) 1¼ miles SE of junction of A25 and B2126 at Abinger Hammer; in field W of Abinger Manor Farm, Abinger Common. Pit preserved beneath building. Private museum on site.

This site consists of a pit roughly 14 ft. long and 10 ft. wide, dug to a depth of 3 ft. in the natural Greensand. It has a V-shaped cross-section. At the W end, where the floor of the pit dips to its greatest depth, a pile of stones occurred, with much burnt material suggestive of a hearth. Along the E side of the pit a slight ledge in the Greensand may represent a bench or sleeping place. Two post-holes were found just clear of the pit edge at the W end. It is possible that these held timbers supporting a flimsy roof. Two other hearths were also found during the excavations of 1950 – scatters of charcoal and burnt soil on the ground surrounding the pit, one just to the S, the other about 6 ft. to the N.

Flint microlithic implements and flakes – 1,056 in number – were found in the sandy soil filling the pit, while 6,562 other tools and flakes occurred in the soil covering the Greensand into which the pit had been dug. These finds suggest that hunters of the Mesolithic period occupied this site for some time, perhaps using the pit as sleeping quarters in the manner of some modern African tribes. There is a spring nearby (close to the farm) and the country hereabouts must have been attractive to people who depended for their existence on ability to hunt and fish, and to collect what nature had to offer. It is likely that other pits will be found close to the one described here. This site was occupied c. 5,000 BC.

*BRONZE AGE

Crooksbury Common, triple bell-barrow (SU/893450) 3½ miles SE of Farnham (A31, A287, A325), 1¼ miles NW of Elstead (B3001); 600 yds. N of Charleshill (B3001).

This is one of the rare examples of a triple barrow. In form it may be classed as a triple bell-barrow. The 3 mounds orientated roughly N/S, are surrounded by an oval ditch with a slight bank on the outside. Overall dimensions of this earthwork are c. 84×41 yds. A modern path has obscured the W side of the bank and ditch. The mounds thus enclosed are neither symmetrically placed nor the same in ht. The N mound is the smallest, being 31 ft. in diam. and 6 ft. in ht. A well-defined berm separates its N edge from the ditch. The central mound lies within the N half of the barrow. It is about 48 ft. across and 8 ft. in ht., with a pronounced pit at its centre. The S mound, the largest, is 60 ft. in diam. and 9 ft. high. There are no records of excavation, but this barrow is likely to have been built c. 1,700–1,400 BC.

*Deerleap Wood, bell-barrow (TQ/118481) 3 miles W of Dorking (A24, A25), ½ mile N of A25, opposite road S to Leith Hill.

This fine bell-barrow has a bank outside its ditch, with an overall diam. of c. 180 ft. Originally its mound measured c. 70×60 ft., with a 30 ft. berm and a ditch c. 5 ft. deep. Excavation showed that a mound of turf had been heaped up over the central area, 25–30 ft. in diam. and 3½ ft. high. This in turn had been capped with rubble. No burial was found but probably it had been an inhumation, removed by the acidic soil. Date, c. 1,700–1,400 BC.

Frensham Common, bowl-barrows (SU/853407) 3¾ miles NW of Hindhead (A3, A287), ¾ mile SE of Frensham, E of A287.

Some of the best-preserved bowl-barrows in Surrey are to be found on high ground between Frensham Great and Little Ponds. Four are situated fairly close together. From N to S, the first is 75 ft. across and 6 ft. high; the second, which has a surrounding ditch 9 ft. wide, is also 75 ft. across, but is 8 ft. high. The third has a diam. of 42 ft. and a ht. of 4 ft. The last is 54 ft. wide and 5½ ft. high. It has a surrounding ditch 8 ft. wide. Nothing is known of the contents of these barrows but they probably accumulated here between 1,700 and 1,400 BC.

Horsell Common, bell-barrows (TQ/014598, W barrow) ¼ mile NE of crossing of Basingstoke Canal and A320 on outskirts of Woking (A247, A320, A324); second barrow lies on E side of B road crossing canal here.

Two typical Surrey bell-barrows are to be found on low ground on Horsell Common. The W bell is about 160 ft. in diam.; the mound is 99 ft. across and 5 ft. high. The berm is 21 ft. wide. Its ditch is 8 ft. across and there are traces of an outer bank.

The bell-barrow to the E also has a ditch with traces of an outer bank, with an overall diam. of 128 ft. The mound, separated from this ditch by a berm 15 ft. wide, is 4–5 ft. high and about 80 ft. across.

Both barrows have been dug into but there are no records of any discoveries. Date, c. 1,700–1,400 BC.

Reigate Heath, barrow-cemetery (TQ/238505) 1 mile W of Reigate, immediately S of A25 and NE of windmill.

There is a concentration of barrows between the road to Buckland and the first windmill to the S. Moving from N to S, the diams. of the first 4 barrows are 90, 108, 75 and 78 ft; their hts. 6, 8–9, 5 and 3½ ft. respectively. The next 3 mounds – the small central one crossed by a track – are less certainly of the Bronze Age. They have diams. of 60, 27 and 50 ft. and hts. of 2, 1 and 1½ ft.

The first 4 barrows were opened in 1809 when trees were being planted. The 'largest barrow' was found to cover a pit cut into the Folkstone Beds subsoil, containing a human cremation. Another of the barrows produced a cremation in a cinerary urn. Two other mounds were excavated without result. These mounds may be dated c. 1,700–1,400 BC.

Sunningdale, bowl-barrow (SU/952665) 200 yds. S of Sunningdale railway station (A30), W of Ridge Mount Road, in garden of Heatherside. Finds in Reading and Guildford museums.

This barrow, 5–6 ft. high and about 75

ft. in diam., is of interest because urns of a Middle Bronze Age Deverel–Rimbury cemetery had been inserted into its sw side. Trenches were cut through the mound in 1901. No primary burial was found but 25 cremations, 22 of them in barrel- or bucket-shaped urns were found a few inches below the modern turf. The cremations deposited without urns were placed in shallow holes lined with pieces of sandstone and covered with slabs of conglomerate.

If the barrow mound may have been built between 1,700 and 1,400 BC, the secondary cemetery may be dated c. 1,200 BC.

Thursley Common, bowl-barrows (SU/909409, w barrow) 1 mile NE of Thursley (off A3), ½ mile SSE of Pudmore pond.

There are 2 good bowl-barrows here, situated on heathland which can have changed little since the time they were built. The w mound has a ditch which is still visible. Its full diam. is about 80 ft. and its ht. 6 ft. The second bowl, 200 yds. to the E, is of similar exterior appearance. It is 75 ft. across and nearly 9 ft. high. Its ditch is 7–8 ft. wide.

Both barrows are likely to have been built c. 1,700–1,400 BC.

West End Common, Cobham, barrow cemetery (SU/931614) 1½ miles NW of Bisley (A322), on s side of minor road joining West End (A319, A322) and Frimley (A321, A325).

Here there are 4 bowl-barrows in a row and almost touching. Those at the E and W ends are each nearly 100 ft. in diam. and 5–6 ft. in ht., with surrounding ditches 9–10 ft. wide. Between them there are 2 smaller bowls whose ditches are not clear. Each is about 80 ft. across.

This group, which has been excavated without known result, was probably built c. 1,700–1,400 BC. The juxtaposing of mounds in this manner is a common practice on the chalk downs of Wessex.

Wisley Common, bell-barrow (TQ/078592) 1¾ miles sw of Cobham (A3, A245), 1¼ miles sw of A245/A3 junction, on w side of A3.

Damaged by a parish boundary on the E and by iron working on the NE, this bell-barrow has a diam. of 144 ft. and a ht. of 10–12 ft. The berm is 18 ft. wide. The

mound appears to be set on a platform. In fact, however, it stands on the Bronze Age land surface which, beyond the ditch of the barrow, has been eroded by natural causes and by the plough so that today the land surface is 2 ft. lower than it was when the barrow was built.

A cremation has been found high up in the mound but its primary burial has not yet been found. Date, c. 1,700–1,400 BC.

IRON AGE

*Anstiebury, hill-fort (TQ/153441) 3½ miles s of Dorking (A24, A25), 1 mile NE of Leith Hill.

This camp, one of the largest in Surrey, is roughly oval in plan, following the contours of the land. Its defences enclose an area of 11½ acres. On the NE and NW there are 3 lines of banks with 2 ditches between them; there are traces of a third ditch at the NE. The innermost bank, originally stone-faced, is the highest. On the s side the land falls away sharply: if there ever was a rampart here it is now no longer visible and would never have been strictly necessary. The entrance is at the E and appears to have been unfinished. Recent excavation has suggested that the fort was built late in the Iron Age, with much earlier occupation in the area.

*Hascombe Hill, promontory fort (TQ/005387) 4 miles SE of Godalming (A3, B2130), ¾ mile SE of Hascombe, ¼ mile E of B2130. Finds in Guildford Museum.

The s end of a sand ridge was chosen for the site of this camp. North-west, sw and SE steep slopes make elaborate fortification unnecessary; only to the NE does more level ground need to be covered. For this reason, 3 sides of the site were fortified by artificaly scarping the hillside and digging a ditch 5 ft. deep, 15 ft. below the crest of the hill. To the NE, a ditch 21 ft. wide and 9 ft. deep was dug, providing material for a rampart within, 40 ft. broad at its base and nearly 5 ft. high. Through this an entrance-gap was left. No evidence for timber facings has so far been found here. Five and three-quarters of an acre are thus enclosed.

This camp seems to have been built in 2nd–1st century BC.

*Holmbury, hill-fort (TQ/105430) 1¾ miles sw of Abinger, reached by track sw from Holmbury St Mary (B2126). Finds in Guildford Museum.

This camp is nearly square in plan. Steeply sloping ground provides additional protection along the E and s sides. The area within the earthwork is about 8 acres. On the N and w sides 2 banks and ditches can with some difficulty be made out. Excavation has shown that originally the outer ditch was about 8 ft. deep and 20 ft. wide, the inner ditch about 13 ft. deep and over 30 ft. across. The outer bank was some 35 ft. broad at its base and originally about 8 ft. high. The inner bank, destroyed on the w side, would probably have been of similar size. No post-holes for timber revetting have been found. The original entrance may have been at the NW corner. The defences along the s and E sides are no longer clear but need never have been substantial because of the slope of the hillsides here.

Occupation dated (C14) late 4th century BC has been found inside the fort.

St George's Hill, hill-fort (TQ/086617) 2 miles s of Weybridge (A317), ¾ mile NW of junction of A245 and B365. Partly covered by housing estate. Surface finds in Guildford Museum.

This camp is roughly rectangular in plan, its long axis being NW/SE. The total area is 13–14 acres. Except at the NW, where the rampart is double, with a counterscarp bank, and where an original entrance was located, this camp is defended by a single bank and ditch. On the NE a later earthwork of slighter proportions has been added to the main camp, perhaps as a cattle pen.

Although not yet dated by scientific excavations, pottery recovered during building operations suggests an initial date of occupation in the 3rd century BC and extensive use (and doubtless rebuilding and enlarging) during the last 50 years before the Romans.

Sussex, East

NEOLITHIC

Clyffe Hill, long barrow (TQ/432110) 1 mile NE of Lewes (A27, A265, A275), nearly ½ mile s of A265.

This barrow, orientated E/W, is about 120 ft. long, 60 ft. wide and 6 ft. high. It has side-ditches and was probably erected c. 3,500–2,500 BC.

*Combe Hill, causewayed camp (TQ/574022) 3¼ miles NW of Eastbourne, between B2105 and A22. Finds in Lewes Museum.

The camp or cattle enclosure on Combe Hill consists of a pair of banks and ditches, interrupted in the Neolithic manner, the inner ring appearing the stouter. In plan the 2 ditches are oval, their N sides being replaced by the edge of the hill which is sufficiently steep to make

defence unnecessary. The outer earthwork measures 550 × 320 ft.

Excavation has shown that the inner ditch was U-shaped, about 12 ft. wide and 3 ft. deep. The pottery associated with the camp was not made by migrant farmers from N France, as is usually the case in camps of this type, but by local Neolithic people. Date, c. 2,500 BC.

Firle Beacon, long barrow (TQ/486058) 5 miles SE of Lewes (A27, A265, A275), 1¼ miles SE of West Firle, off A27.

This mound is over 100 ft. long and some 70 ft. wide. It stands 8½ ft. high, and has side ditches which enclose the mound except for a causeway at the SE corner. It is orientated E/W, and has a fine command of the country. Its appearance at the E end suggests that there may have been an internal wooden structure here which has collapsed. Date, c. 3,500–2,500 BC.

Hunter's Burgh, long barrow (TQ/550036) ½ mile SE of Wilmington (A27), E of the Long Man chalk figure.

Hunter's Burgh is 220 ft. long, 75 ft. wide and 6 ft. high; it lies S/N. Although its higher end is at the S, its side-ditches appear to run around this end while remaining open at the other; it must have been built c. 3,500–2,500 BC.

Litlington, long barrow (TQ/535006) 3½ miles NE of Seaford (A259, B2108), 1 mile SE of Litlington.

One of the smallest long barrows in Sussex, this example is 60 ft. in length, a little over 30 ft. in breadth and 4 ft. high. It lies SW/NE. Side-ditches, if they ever existed, are not visible today. Date, c. 3,500–2,500 BC.

Long Burgh, long barrow (TQ/510034) 3 miles N of Seaford (A259, B2108), 1 mile W of Alfriston (B2108).

This long barrow measures 150 × 60 ft.; orientated NE/SW, its N end is 8 ft. high. It has side-ditches and like the other Sussex long barrows is likely to have been built c. 3,500–2,500 BC.

Money Burgh, long barrow (TQ/425037) 2 miles NW of Newhaven (A259, A275), just W of A275.

This mound is 120 ft. long and 60 ft. broad; lying E/W, its E end is 6 ft. high. Side-ditches are not clear but probably exist. A skeleton, perhaps a later interment, is said to have been found in the mound. Date, 3,500–2,500 BC.

*Whitehawk, causewayed camp (TQ/330048) on Brighton Race Course. Finds in Brighton and Lewes Museums.

The 4 concentric ditches of this enclosure measure 900 × 700 ft., the outermost enclosing about 11½ acres, the innermost less than 2 acres. This is the only Neolithic enclosure with 4 encircling earthworks. The 2 outer ditches are the deepest, varying from 5 to 7 ft.; the inner ones have been dug into the chalk to a depth of 3 to 4 ft.

As on other sites of this type, the main occupation debris – broken pots, flint and bone tools, food bones and other rubbish – was found in and around the central earthwork. Among this rubbish parts of several human skulls occurred together with animal bones and potsherds in a hearth, evidence that these peasants coupled scant regard for the dead, and perhaps cannibalism, with the utmost respect for the corpses of those they buried beneath the long barrows.

Whitehawk was probably built c. 3,500 BC.

Windover Hill, flint mines and long barrow (TQ/542034) 4½ miles NE of Seaford (A259, B2108), ¾ mile SE of Wilmington (off A27).

Two small clusters of depressions and mounds can be seen just S of the crest of Windover Hill, one to the W, the other to the E of the chalk-cut figure. Both groups are cut across by a Romano-British or earlier trackway (there are also modern chalk quarries nearby). These mines have never been excavated.

The long barrow on Windover Hill, just S of the crest and of the W cluster of flint mines, is nearly 180 ft. long and about 50 ft. wide. It has side-ditches turning in at the ends, and stands nearly 7 ft. high. It lies NE/SW, and was probably built c. 3,500–2,500 BC, being broadly contemporary with the flint mines.

BRONZE AGE

Combe Hill, bowl-barrow (TQ/576023) on a NE spur of Combe Hill, overlooking Willingdon and A22. Finds in Lewes Museum.

This inconspicuous bowl-barrow (diam. 45 ft., ht. 4 ft.) W of the Neolithic causewayed enclosure (p. 202) was dug into in 1908 and just below the surface a hoard of 3 flanged bronze axes was found with the cutting-end of a fourth. The complete axes had been broken in half and the deposit must represent some form of ritual, perhaps associated with a burial in the barrow. These axes are of the type made in Ireland and exported to Britain and the Continent c. 1,700–1,400 BC.

Firle Beacon, round barrows (TQ/470060–TQ/508038) chalk scarp extending from Firle Plantation to Alfriston (B2108), parallel to and S of A27.

Apart from the Neolithic long barrow described above, this chalk ridge, which runs for 3½ miles E/W, has more than 50 bowl-barrows strung out along it, all broadly of the period 1,700–1,400 BC. None merits individual description but all illustrate the tendency among our Bronze Age tribes to erect their burial mounds with an eye for the country. A bronze pin (now lost) from one of these barrows was manufactured in N Germany and represents a trade piece, like the relatively numerous pins of N European origin found in Wessex.

Five Lords Burgh, round barrow (TQ/ 486036) 2¾ miles N of Seaford (A259, B2108), 2 miles W of Alfriston (B2108), 1 mile S of the Firle Beacon ridge.

The large hollow at the centre of this bowl-barrow indicates that it has been opened at some period; results of this work are not known. The mound, which used to be at the meeting-place of 5 parishes, is about 40 ft. in diam. and is 3 ft. high. Like those along the Firle ridge, it was probably built c. 1,700– 1,400 BC.

Hove, round barrow now destroyed, its site occupied by No. 13, Palmeira Avenue. Grave goods in Brighton Museum.

Although this barrow no longer exists, its grave goods are so rich and important that they must be mentioned here and inspected in Brighton Museum. The barrow mound was 12 ft. high in 1821 and nearly 200 ft. across. On the old land surface beneath the mound, and at its centre, an oak coffin 6 to 7 ft. long was found. In it there was a burial – whether cremation or inhumation is not recorded – supplied for the after life with a drinking cup carved from a block of amber, a stone battle-axe with shaft-hole, a bronze dagger buried in its leather-lined wooden scabbard and a whetstone for sharpening it, perforated for hanging at the belt. Apart from the amber cup, the shape of which recalls certain pottery vessels from central Europe, these rich objects are of Wessex type; such sets of essentially

45   *Itford Hill: reconstruction of Bronze Age village, c. 1000 BC*

masculine equipment are often found with burials around Stonehenge and belong to the period 1,700–1,400 BC.

*Itford Hill, Middle Bronze Age settlement (TQ/447053) 2½ miles N of Newhaven (A259, A275), 1 mile E of B2109. Finds in Lewes Museum.

Few settlements of this period have been so thoroughly excavated as this one. It comprises (fig. 45) a group of 11 huts, each within an enclosure (or platform, cut back into the hillside) and spread over an area 440 × 180 ft. Three hundred ft. SE of the main group are 2 more huts. A hollow way approaches the settlement from the W. Here we have a village of simple peasant farmers, living among the pastures they grazed, dating from c. 1,000 BC.

When excavated, these huts ranged in diam. from 15 to 22 ft. and consisted of a ring of post-holes (fig. 46), some with a central post and entrance porch; the simpler huts were probably used as workshops and for storage. One hut, larger than the rest, must have belonged to the chief of this little community. Originally a post fence seems to have surrounded the whole settlement. The 'Celtic' fields S of the settlement are probably Roman.

Lewes, platform-barrow (TQ/402110) 1 mile NW of Lewes, on W side of A275; about 350 yds. N of Floods Barn.

This fine example is nearly 90 ft. in diam., its flat top being 3 ft. high. It also has a bank *outside* its ditch.

Close to the platform barrow are 2 small bowl-barrows, each about 40 ft. across and 3 ft. high. These barrows were probably built in the period 1,700–1,400 BC.

Oxsettle Bottom, round barrows (TQ/444104–TQ/446093) ¾ mile NW of Glynde (off A27); NW of Mt Caburn (p. 206), Finds in British Museum.

There are several round barrows in the isolated, almost circular area of high ground between Lewes and Glynde. They tend to concentrate N of Mount Caburn and NW of Glynde, above Oxsettle Bottom. In one was found an inhumation accompanied by 2 collared urns, one of which contained an unusually varied series of trinkets – beads of shale, amber, faience and bronze. While the urn and the beads of shale, amber and bronze are of British workmanship, of the period

46   Itford Hill: Bronze Age hut, c. 1,000 BC

1,700–1,400 BC, the faience beads, 2 segmented and 1 a quoit-shaped pendant (a style far commoner in the N of England) may be of E Mediterranean manufacture and represent the far-flung trade contacts established by tribes living in southern Britain (Wessex particularly) at the time of Stonehenge. Material for the beads of shale and amber would have come from Kimmeridge (Dorset), and either the east coast or from Jutland.

*Plumpton Plain, Late Bronze Age settlements (TQ/358122) 4 miles NW of Lewes, 2 miles N of Falmer (A27, B2123); ¾ mile SW of Plumpton (B2116). Sites lie astride the 500 and 600 ft. contours, at base of spur projecting S from main ridge. Finds in British Museum and Brighton Museum.

One of the most important Late Bronze Age sites in Britain, these 2 settlements are hard to find in the scrub of the downs without expert guidance.

Site A, the higher of the two, consists of 4 banked enclosures set close and linked by winding roadways. All except the most W enclosure have been excavated and each shown to contain remains of a circular wooden hut, with a pound outside it. The enclosures themselves, varying in shape from rectangular to oval, are composed of chalk and soil scraped up from their interiors. Each hut was about 20 ft. in diam. and would probably have had a conical thatched roof and vertical walls. There were no hearths inside the huts but cooking holes were found outside.

Site B, ¼ mile SE of Site A, stands on a slight spur running out into Moustone Bottom. A slight bank and ditch cuts off this spur and marks the N limit of the settlement. Three huts, similar to those described above, have been found here. They do not appear to have been surrounded by enclosure-banks and no traces of them show on the surface.

Site B was probably in use after Site A had been abandoned. Deverel–Rimbury pottery from the former suggests a date c. 1,000 BC.

Seaford Head, round barrow. See Iron Age.

Windover Hill, round barrows (TQ/542033) 1 mile SW of Wilmington (A27), above the Long Man chalk figure. Finds in the British Museum.

There are several round barrows and a platform-barrow on the ridge S and E of the Long Man, too scattered to constitute a cemetery in the Wessex fashion. The very large bowl-barrow immediately S of the chalk figure (and of a small chalk quarry) is 135 ft. in diam. It appears to have contained a cremation in an urn, placed in a pit under a heap of flints. The platform-barrow, standing on the col between Windover Hill and Wilmington Hill, is 45 ft. in diam., a small but perfect example of this type of round barrow. All the circular burial mounds in this area must belong to the period 1,700–1,400 BC.

IRON AGE

*Caburn, hill-fort (TQ/444089) 2 miles SE of Lewes, ½ mile N of A27. Finds in Lewes Museum and Salisbury Museum (Wilts.).

This hill received its first Iron Age settlers about 600 BC, a group of people of the European Halstatt culture moving on to the Sussex downs either from Wessex or direct from the Continent. They lived here, without any fortification around their huts, for about 200 years.

The earliest ramparts were built on this hill about 400 BC. They consisted of the smaller bank and V-shaped ditch outside it, with an entrance at the NE and enclosing about 3½ acres of land. This earthwork, perhaps timber-laced, best seen along the N side of the camp, rises only a foot or two above the plateau within it. Originally it would have stood about 5 ft. high, having a ditch outside it the same in depth. There would have been a simple wooden gate. It is likely that this defence was built by the Halstatt settlers against newcomers of La Tène culture from W Sussex, who began expanding into the Weald at this time.

In spite of its hastily built earthwork, the Caburn must have been captured about 100 BC. Its new owners either lived here permanently or else used it as a temporary refuge in time of scare: about 140 grain-storage pits have been found inside the defences and are still visible as hollows. Shortly before the Roman Conquest, the massive outer rampart and ditch were built – against the Belgae or Romans. The new bank, which still stands 20 ft. above the bottom of the ditch outside it, is 10 ft. wide at its base and must have stood to a height of 10 ft.; both faces were lined with timbers, while tie-beams through the mound stabilised the structure. In all probability there was a timber breastwork with a flat space for defenders behind it. The ditch outside this was a massive flat-bottomed affair, 30 ft. wide and 7–8 ft. deep – a type of ditch found widely in N France. The gateway itself was remodelled but the roadway through it seems never to have been metalled. The inner bank was heightened and its ditch re-dug.

*Charleston Brow, settlements and fields (TQ/484055) 1,600 ft ssw of Firle Beacon, 4 miles N of Seaford (A259, B2108), 1½ miles SE of West Firle (off A27). Finds in Lewes Museum.

Two settlements with fields, connected by a track, lie on the E and SE side of the spur which separates Beacon Bottom from Tilton Bottom. The connecting track, which starts 1,600 ft. s of Firle Beacon, extends sw for 1,600 ft. before fading out. One settlement lies immediately w of its N end, the other 850 ft. to the s and 50 ft. E of the track. The s settlement is near the centre of a small rectangular field just over ½ acre in area and presumably contemporary. A rectangular hut roughly 20 × 15 ft. was found here with storage pits. The N site consists of several storage pits and at least 1 hut.

Both groups of dwellings belong to the period 50 BC–AD 43, the N site apparently remaining in use after the Roman Conquest. Those who lived here must have tilled the fields round about, the boundaries of which are marked by lynchets, in places still quite massive.

*Hollingbury, hill-fort (TQ/322078) 2½ miles N of Brighton Pier, ¾ mile NW of Moulscoombe (A27). Finds in Brighton Museum.

This camp is nearly square, with original entrances through its E and W sides. Its rampart was built with a base 20 ft. wide and stood to a height of about 6 ft. It was faced with a wall of timbers – horizontal logs lashed to vertical posts set 7 ft. apart – which would also have provided a parapet. There was a similar vertical facing along the rear, about 8 ft. behind the front, providing a box-like main rampart of timbers and earth having an original ht. of c. 10–12 ft. Some of these timbers have been marked by metal posts. There was considerable internal timbering to insure stability. The bank was separated from its ditch by a berm 10 ft. wide. This ditch was about 7 ft. deep, with a flat floor and almost vertical sides. At the w gate, not yet excavated, the main bank is turned in so as to provide a funnel-like entrance passage. The E gate was simpler, 2 massive posts being set either side of a 20 ft. break in the bank, on which a gate could be hung. These also are marked by metal posts.

This fort, which encloses about 9 acres and was used only in time of war, may have been built c. 550 BC and was abandoned a century or so later. It is known to have superseded a defensive enclosure of unknown date and enclosing almost as much land. The E side of this earthwork can just be seen, set about 35 yds. behind the E side of the later work and running under it on its other 3 sides. It had a ditch originally 6 ft. wide and little more than 3 ft. deep, providing material for a simple chalk rubble bank.

*Seaford Head, cliff fort and Bronze Age barrow (TV/495978) 1 mile SE of Seaford (A259, B2108), on headland overlooking golf links.

Triangular in plan, this cliff fort encloses 11¼ acres. The defences consist of a bank (6 ft. high) on the E and NW sides, the cliff providing adequate protection along the s. At the w end of the NE side there are traces of a ditch outside the bank. Excavation showed the latter to be V-shaped, 7 ft. deep. There are 2 entrance gaps in the E side and 1 in the NW but they have not yet been established by excavation. Not yet closely dated.

s of the NW entrance there is a barrow 40 ft. in diam. and about 3 ft. high. Excavated in 1876, it was shown to consist of earth and stones. No burials were found but there were 2 small pits containing votive offerings – 2 flint axes, scrapers and saw blades, hammer stones. Date, c. 1,700–1,400 BC.

Sussex, West

*NEOLITHIC

*Barkhale, causewayed camp (SU/976126) 8¼ miles NE of Chichester, 1¼ miles SW of Bignor, on Bignor Hill.

This is an oval enclosure of 6–7 acres, its interrupted bank and ditch almost destroyed by the plough except at the N and NE. Around this arc of its earthwork at least 15 ditch segments have been recorded, not all matched by corresponding breaks in the bank. Small-scale excavation c. 1960 yielded Neolithic pottery of c. 2,500 BC, confirming that this is an example of a causewayed camp, though apparently of later date than usual for the class.

Bevis's Thumb, long barrow (SU/789155) on Telegraph Hill, 7 miles SW of Midhurst (A272, A286), 1 mile NE of Compton, close to Fernbeds Farm.

This fine barrow is 210 ft. long and about 60 ft. wide. It is orientated E/W, rising some 6 ft. at the E end. Its side-ditches are visible. Date, c. 3,500–2,500 BC.

*Blackpatch, flint mines (TQ/094089) on S spur of Blackpatch Hill, 1¼ miles W of Findon (A24, A280), ¼ mile NE of Myrtle-grove House. Finds in Worthing Museum.

There is not much to be seen here on the surface, but in Neolithic times about 100 shafts were dug into the chalk and a seam of flint, 10–11 ft. below the surface, dug out. A number of burials by cremation and inhumation have been found in the filling of worked-out mine shafts. Some small mounds erected over other burials have been found to overlie contemporary mine shafts. Nearby, traces of the miners' village have been recorded.

While these mines were probably begun c. 3,200 BC, evidence from excavation makes it clear that they continued in use into the Bronze Age (c. 1,700 BC onwards).

*Church Hill, flint mines (TQ/112083) on top of hill, ¾ mile W of Findon (A24,

A280), ¼ mile E of A280. Finds in Worthing Museum.

This is a small group of mines, with flaking-sites interspersed among the mine shafts. One typical mine consisted of a shaft 16 ft. deep and 17 ft. wide, cutting through 2 seams of flint before it reached and exploited 2 more. The chalk hereabouts being soft, elaborate galleries radiating from the foot of the shaft were not attempted. Near the top of this mine a cremation was found in a late type of beaker, accompanied by 2 flint axes of the pattern made here by the flint miners. As at Blackpatch (above), these mines were evidently flourishing into the Bronze Age, trading their products for several generations. A radio-carbon determination suggests a beginning c. 3,300 BC.

*Cissbury, flint mines (TQ/137079) at W end of the Iron Age hill-fort (below) and outside its S entrance, 1 mile E of Findon (A24, A280). Finds in British, Lewes and Worthing Museums.

A cluster of pits and mounds estimated at more than 200 in number lies within the W part of the later Iron Age earthwork, while a line of about 39 shafts can be seen outside the S entrance of the hill fort. The natural chalk being firm, some of the shafts go down over 40 ft., cutting through 6 or 7 seams of flint and exploiting these with galleries radiating horizontally from the main shafts. Two mine shafts have so far yielded burials (one perhaps an accidental fall). Pottery found during excavation suggests that these mines belong to the early part of the Neolithic (c. 2,900–2,500 BC) and did not extend into the Bronze Age.

Harrow Hill, flint mines (TQ/081100) 2¾ miles NW of Findon (A24, A280), 1 mile NW of Blackpatch flint mines (above). Finds in Worthing Museum.

This large group of mines lies immediately NE of a small rectangular enclosure of later date (Iron Age, p. 211) which, indeed, overlies some of the shafts. Here there are over 100 mines, one of which was proved by excavation to be 22 ft. deep and 20 ft. in diam.; 6 galleries radiated from its base into solid chalk. Some open-cast mining had taken place in its shaft at a depth of 5 ft. Pottery and other finds confirm that this group of mines is broadly contemporary with those at Cissbury and did not last into the Bronze Age. It must have been trading its products c. 3,000 BC.

Stoughton Down, long barrows (SU/823121) 5 miles NW of Chichester, 1¼ miles E of B2146. Close to Bow Hill flint mines (below).

The NW of these 2 indistinct mounds appears to measure 120 × 78 ft. Set SE/NW, its E end rises 7 ft. It has side-ditches which probably do not curve around either end.

The other barrow, about 200 yds. SE, is 80 ft. long and 45 ft. wide. It lies N/S, rising 5 ft. at the N end. Its side-ditches are certainly absent around the ends. Date of both mounds, c. 3,500–2,500 BC.

*BRONZE AGE

Bow Hill, barrow cemetery (Devil's Humps SU/820111) and twin bell-barrow (SU/807107); 5 miles NW of Chichester, cemetery ¼ mile SW of highest point of hill, twin bell-barrow 1 mile SW of cemetery, ½ mile SE of Stoughton.

The cemetery consists of 2 bowl-barrows at the NE, and 2 bell-barrows at the SW; they are in a line and between each pair of mounds there is a small depression with a bank around it, resembling the pond-barrows of Wessex but on a much smaller scale. They appear to be contemporary with the bell- and bowl-barrows here. The W bell-barrow is 120 ft. across and its mound is 12 ft. high. The bell next to it is 150 ft. in diam. and the same ht. The first bowl-barrow is about 90 ft. in diam., the second nearly 70 ft.; both are 10 ft. high. All these barrows have been dug into, and a cremation with a whetstone has been recorded from the most E bowl. They were probably built in the Early Bronze Age, c. 1,700–1,400 BC.

The twin bell-barrow SW of this cemetery, the only barrow of this type in

Sussex, has mounds each 60 ft. in diam. and 6 ft. high, set within an oval ditch and separated from this by a berm 12 ft. wide. This double barrow is likely to have been erected within the same period as the cemetery.

Devil's Humps, barrow cemetery. See **Bow Hill.**

Devil's Jumps, barrow cemetery (SU/824173) 4½ miles SW of Midhurst (A272, A285), ¾ mile S of Treyford.

This is perhaps the finest cemetery in Sussex. It comprises 5 very large bell-barrows set in a line and the remains of a sixth, probably also a bell. The diams. of these barrows range from 85 to 114 ft. and their hts. from 6 to 16 ft. Cremations have been recorded from 2 of the mounds. This cemetery must be contemporary with those around Stonehenge, all c. 1,700–1,400 BC.

Didling Hill, barrow (SU/828177) 4 miles SW of Midhurst (A272, A286), ¾ mile SW of Didling: at trig. point 771.

This barrow, on the hill E of the Devil's Jumps barrow cemetery (above), is interesting because its mound, 18 ft. in diam. and 2 ft. high, is set within a square ditch. There is an entrance in the middle of the E side. This site is undated; although it is described in this section it is possible that it was built to cover an Iron Age burial.

Graffham Downs, round barrows (SU/915163) central area of ridge joining Cocking (A286) to Duncton Down (A285).

There are several bowl-barrows on this stretch of downland, situated so as to command the country, as on Firle ridge. No details survive of burials or grave goods found in any of these mounds. Two bowl-barrows close together (map ref. above) are noteworthy. Each is about 60 ft. in diam., one 5 ft. high and the other 3 ft., with surrounding ditches. Date, c. 1,700–1,400 BC.

Heyshott Downs, round barrows (SU/895165) on ridge, 1¼ miles SE of Cocking (A286).

There are 9–10 bowl-barrows on this down, almost close enough together to constitute a barrow cemetery in the Wessex style. Most vary from 30 to 60 ft. in diam. and from 1 to 5 ft. in ht.; one, with a clear ditch around it, is nearly 100 ft. across and is 7 ft. high. No records survive of their contents though all appear to have been opened. Date, c. 1,700–1,400 BC.

Park Brow, settlement. See Iron Age.

Treyford Hill, barrow within square ditch. See **Didling Hill.**

Waltham Down, barrow cemetery (SU/ 929144) midway between Chichester and Petworth (A272, A283, A285), 1 mile NW of Up Waltham (A285).

This cemetery consists of a row of 4 bowl-barrows extending NW; there is a bell-barrow at the E end. The bowls range in diam. from 40 to 80 ft. and in ht. from 2 to 6 ft. The bell is 10 ft. high and has a distinct ditch around it. Nothing is known about the contents of these barrows but they may be assumed to have been built between 1,700 and 1,400 BC.

IRON AGE

Chanctonbury Ring, hill-fort (TQ/139121) 2½ miles NW of Steyning (A283), 1¼ miles SE of Washington (A24, A283). Finds in Lewes Museum.

This small fortified enclosure, not yet dated by excavation, probably belongs to the period 400–300 BC. It encloses 3½ acres and comprises a bank with traces of an outer ditch at the SW. Here there is a simple entrance. There is a bank and ditch facing W, 1,100 ft. W of the hill-fort. Presumably this is a contemporary outwork.

Two late Roman buildings, one a square temple, the other a pear-shaped building of unknown use, and other associated structures have been found at the centre of the hill-fort.

***Chichester Dykes,** earthworks 2 miles N of Chichester.

These banks and ditches are the remains of more than 10 miles of defensive earthworks which cut across the landward side of the late Iron Age tribal centre of the Atrebates, a territory of c. 60 sq. miles between Chichester and Selsey Bill, whose S, E and W boundaries were formed by the sea and by rivers. The tribal capital itself has probably been destroyed by the sea.

Built at different periods, the earliest earthwork is probably that from SU/921084–SU/865085: SU/859081–SU/826083, well preserved along much of this line. SE of Lavant House the ditch was shown to be V-shaped, 9 ft. deep and c. 13 ft. wide. About 1 mile to the S there are remains of a second line, built later; it follows a course along SU/841067–SU/818066. At Chichester Barracks it turns south, parallel to a N/S extension of the earliest earthwork, both parallel to the Lavant. Subsequently, short stretches of E/W dyke were added further S. General date, 1st century BC/AD.

Cissbury, hill-fort (TQ/139081) 1 mile E of Findon (A24, A280), 3¼ miles N of Worthing. Finds in Worthing and Brighton Museums.

This earthwork encloses c. 60 acres of ground. Roughly egg-shaped, its defences consist of a main inner bank with ditch outside it, and an outer bank, or counterscarp. There are original entrances facing E and S. A large group of Neolithic flint mines (p. 208) was enclosed at the W end by the Iron Age people who erected their fortress about 350 BC.

In its first form, the rampart comprised a chalk rubble bank 30 ft. broad at its base, standing to a ht. of 15 ft. and faced with vertical timbers which would also have provided a parapet. This bank was held rigid by internal tie-beams. It was separated from its ditch by a berm some 10 ft. wide. The ditch was dug more than 10 ft. into native chalk; it had a flat floor and was about 25 ft. wide at ground surface. The little counterscarp bank may have been put up at this time.

Three hundred years later this great temporary refuge was in decay and probably no longer used. In the Roman period its interior came under plough; the banks of 'Celtic' fields can be seen within and around the hill-fort. Soil-creep from these later fields has filled the angle between the level ground and the inner slope of the main rampart along its S side.

At the end of the Roman occupation of Britain the hill-fort was hastily refortified, perhaps against marauding Saxons. A turf capping was added to the now slumped Iron Age earthwork and at the entrances the counterscarp bank was removed so that the main ditch could be widened. The small enclosures inside the ramparts may date from this time, while a number of very late Romano-British rubbish pits have been found dug into (i.e. later than) some of the field banks.

Devil's Ditch, Chichester. See **Chichester Dykes.**

Didling Hill, barrow within square ditch. See Bronze Age.

*Goosehill Camp, hill-slope fort (SU/ 830127) 5¼ miles NW of Chichester, 2 miles W of West Dean (A286), ¼ mile W of Brick Kiln Farm (B2141). Finds in Lewes Museum.

A fairly recent boundary bank runs across this fort, NE/SW, with close woodland E of this. Goosehill is oval in plan, its 2 concentric earthworks enclosing altogether 4½ acres. It lies on a hill-slope, its E side tilted towards the valley. The inner ring comprises a bank, ditch and counterscarp bank, with a simple entrance at the SE. The inner bank is everywhere higher than its counterscarp bank. The outer earthwork is separated from the inner one by a space of 60–100 ft. Badly damaged around the SE quarter, it is everywhere a slighter work, its counterscarp bank in places being as large as its inner bank and replacing it altogether at the NE. There is an original entrance gap at the W, approached by a track which enters at an oblique angle. A second gap at the N with a track running through it, appears to have been inserted shortly after the fort was built. At the SW the outer earthwork cuts across an earlier bank and ditch of slight proportions: this runs in an arc from N to SE for about 240 ft. Several slight circular terraces in the SW quarter of the inner enclosure mark the sites of huts or shelters.

Excavation has shown that both ditches are roughly V-shaped, 4–5 ft. deep and about the same in width. The banks are of chalk dug from the ditches and were devoid of timber reinforcements or palisades. Pottery suggests that this site, a typical example of those enclosures apparently intended for the herding and pounding of cattle, was in use late in the 3rd century BC.

*Harrow Hill, hill-fort (TQ/081100) 2¾ miles NW of Findon (A24, A280); finds in Worthing Museum.

This small earthwork resembles that on Thundersbarrow Hill (p. 212), likewise belonging to the period 600–500 BC. It is roughly rectangular, 65 × 57 yards, and comprises a single bank and ditch; there are entrances through the W side and at the NE corner. The ramparts in places overlie or cut through the shafts of Neolithic flint mines already described (p. 208). The Iron Age ditch seems originally to have been V-shaped and about 5 ft. deep. It provided material for a bank 12 ft. broad at its base and standing to a ht. of some 5 ft. This was faced and stabilised by timbers. The W gate was revealed by excavation as a square setting of four stout posts, 10 ft. apart, connected to the timber rampart-facing. Such a structure would have provided for a large gate swinging across from one side, with some form of bridge over the rop.

This enclosure was probably used for collecting livestock belonging to the several open settlements hereabouts.

*Park Brow, settlement with 'Celtic' fields (TQ/153088) 2 miles E of Findon (A24, A280), 1 mile NE of Cissbury (above). Finds in British Museum.

The area of Park Brow has been farmed by early man from the Late Bronze Age to Roman times and evidence for this activity can still be seen. Because of excavations in the 1920s, the Iron Age site here is one of the more important in Britain.

The Late Bronze Age settlement consisted of a group of 8 or more round huts, wig-wam-shaped, with wattle-and-daub walls, situated at the SW corner of the spur (TQ/153086). These huts now show as slight terraced patches of broken ground. Storage pits and domestic rubbish were revealed when excavations were carried out in 1924. Some of the 'Celtic' fields which can still be seen round about must have been started by those who lived here about 1,000 BC; they cannot be distinguished from those which were added in Iron Age and Roman times.

The first Iron Age settlement at Park Brow (TQ/153088) lies about 800 ft. NNE of the Late Bronze Age site and some 200 ft. E of the droveway which runs down the spur from N to S, curving round E just below this settlement. Here, the remains of 2 wooden huts and many storage pits were found, together with a silver finger-ring of the continental early La Tène culture (c. 325–250 BC) and many domestic objects of more local origin. This farmstead, its owners working in the fields around it, probably flourished c. 400–250 BC.

By the first century BC the early Iron Age settlement had been abandoned and a new community was living 400 yds. down the hill. Of this second Iron Age site nothing now shows; it was represented by rubbish pits containing characteristic decorated pottery, discovered when the Romano-British huts on top were being excavated in 1924.

When Britain fell under Roman rule, life at Park Brow continued unchanged. A group of rectangular huts of wattle-and-daub, with roof tiles, painted wall plaster and window glass was built over the site of the second Iron Age farm, probably by the descendants of these people. The fields and the sunken track-ways (which were fenced on each side from Iron Age times) appear today in their final Romanised form. Towards the close of the 3rd century AD the settlement was destroyed by fire: occupation by farmers, which had lasted for 1,000 years, ceased.

*Thundersbarrow Hill, hill-fort and settlement (TQ/229084) 2¼ miles N of Shoreham Beach, 1 mile NW of Mile Oak. Finds in Lewes Museum.

The prehistoric and Romano-British sites on this hill have suffered much from medieval and later ploughing but are none the less important. The main camp, where single bank and ditch protect an area 3 acres in extent, contains remains of an earlier, rectangular enclosure of about 1½ acres. The smaller enclosure was probably used for penning livestock, c. 8th century BC; c. 5th century BC it was replaced by a true hill-fort. The larger camp has entrances N and S, the ends of the rampart at each apparently in-turned to define and protect these passage-ways. The inner enclosure is of feeble construction; it has entrances on its E and W sides. The ramparts of both sites consist of bank and outer ditch; no evidence for timber facings or tie-beams has been found by excavation.

The group of 'Celtic' fields which surrounds the camps (and in places has ploughed away the ramparts) must belong to a Romano-British settlement lying immediately to the E of the larger camp. These fields are laid out in relationship to the magnificent example of a roadway with bank on either side, 80 ft. wide, which runs away SE. Today, this later settlement shows as a series of depressions in the ground, 15–30 ft. in diam. One corn-drying furnace was found 50 yds. NE of the main entrance of the camp; there was another dug into the ditch of the camp midway along its E side. A well was found close to the second furnace. Fragments of wattle-and-daub suggest that the houses of this farmstead were of the flimsy Romano-British native type. Farming here continued until the end of the Roman period.

Medieval strip fields NE and E of the camp have done much to flatten the earthworks of the earlier peiods.

Treyford Hill, barrow within square ditch. See Bronze Age, **Didling Hill.**

*Trundle, hill-fort and Neolithic causewayed camp (SU/877111) 4 miles N of Chichester, 1½ miles SE of West Dean (A286). Finds in Lewes Museum.

One of the most elaborate causewayed camps in Britain, the Neolithic site lies within the Iron Age earthwork, with part of its outermost ditch running under and outside the later bank and ditch. Roughly circular, the causewayed camp is nearly 1,000 ft. in diam. Its innermost ditch, 400 ft. in diam., is surrounded by a second ditch which, in plan, forms a spiral, creating 2 ditches on the NW. There is an unusually large number of gaps through this ditch. The outermost ditch, of which only the N sector has been recorded, would have enclosed about 18 acres of downland. None of these earthworks is clear on the ground.

Excavations have revealed that while the inner ditch is seldom deeper than 5 ft., the outermost was at least 9 ft. in depth. Evidence of occupation came mainly from the area enclosed by the inner earthwork, where pottery and other obobjects indicated a date near 3,500 BC for the construction of this camp. The body of a young woman had been buried in the outer ditch under a pile of chalk blocks, after it had begun to silt up.

Among the objects found at the Trundle, a carved bone phallus is of special interest, recalling those of chalk from Wessex (Avebury and Dorchester Museums) and reminding us of the fertility cult which played a major part in the religious activities of these simple peasant farmers.

The Iron Age hill-fort is an octagonal structure consisting of a stout bank with outer ditch and a smaller counterscarp bank. There are 2 entrances facing each other, NE and SW. At both, bank and counterscarp are turned in to provide funnel-like passage-ways. Twelve and a half acres of downland are thus enclosed, the ramparts themselves occupying a

further 6 acres. This fortification took place in the 3rd century.

So far, excavation has been restricted to an examination of the Neolithic earthworks and of the E gate of the hill-fort. This gate was redesigned twice. At first it consisted of gate-posts for 2 doors swinging in on to a central latch-post; these were placed half-way along the entrance-passage. In stage 2 this passage was narrowed by timber revetting, the original gates were made smaller to fit it and a second pair of gates was added at the inner end of the passage. The final stage, begun after 50 BC but probably never finished, saw a return to a wider, dual-carriageway and the designing of 1 huge pair of gates at the inner end of the entrance gap – gates probably never set up.

Tyne and Wear

NEOLITHIC

*Copt Hill, round barrow (NZ/353492) ¾ mile SE of Houghton-le-Spring (A182, A690, B1404). s of B road and SE of New Town. Grave goods in British Museum.

This barrow is about 60 ft. in diam. and 8 ft. high. It has a few trees on top of it. There is no trace of a surrounding ditch. The mound is composed of limestone and sandstone chips. Excavation in 1877 showed that near the centre of the barrow an unknown number of corpses have been collected, their flesh already decayed and bones separated after storage elsewhere. Wood and limestone blocks had been heaped over them and the whole pile (measuring 34 × 6 ft.) burnt thoroughly. The barrow mound was then erected over this structure, c. 2,500–2,000 BC.

In the Bronze Age 8 burials were added to the mound. Four were after cremation, 1 deposited in a collared urn; the others were inhumations, 1 of a child in a stone-lined hollow, another furnished with a

food vessel. Date of later burials, c. 1,700–1,400 BC.

BRONZE AGE

*Hasting Hill, round barrow (NZ/353544) 3¼ miles SW of Sunderland, 1 mile NW of East Herrington (A690, B1286). On E side of road to Offerton. Finds in Sunderland Museum.

This barrow is about 40 ft. across and 3 ft. in ht. It had no surrounding ditch. Excavation showed that the mound is of earth and stones. Ten burials were found in it, 3 in well-built stone slab cists (reconstructed in Sunderland Museum). These were inhumations. There was a fourth inhumation in an unlined grave N of the centre. The crouched inhumation in a cist W of the centre, buried with a beaker, bone pin and flint tools, was the primary burial. There were also 6 human cremations, 4 in small stone-lined cists, 2 in collared urns. A food vessel and other pottery, with flint tools and animal bones, were scattered at random in the material of the mound. Date, c. 1,700–1,400 BC.

*Warwickshire

NEOLITHIC

King Stone, standing stone. See Oxfordshire.

IRON AGE

Beausale, hill-fort (SP/246702) 4 miles NW of Warwick, 1½ miles SE of Wroxhall (A41), ½ mile SE of Beausale.

This is an oval camp, enclosing 5½ acres. It overlooks a stream to the E and commands the country locally. Its interior is under the plough and its defences are denuded. They consist of a bank, ditch and traces of a counterscarp, well preserved on the S side. The entrance cannot now be identified. Not dated.

*Burrow Hill Camp, hill-fort (SP/304850) 2 miles SE of Fillongley (A423, B4102), on SE side of Corley (A423).

This camp is nearly square in plan and encloses 7 acres. Its defences consist of a bank over 6 ft. high in places, and ditch, with traces of a counterscarp bank on the N side. There is a simple entrance near the centre of the W side, now damaged by the plough. Excavation has shown that the rampart is of earth and rubble, faced on the outside with a well-built masonry wall. Of particular interest was the discovery that small logs of oak had been laid criss-cross in the wall while it was under construction, to hold it together (timber-lacing). Not dated.

*Corley, hill-fort. See above.

Meon Hill, hill-fort (SP/177454) 4 miles NE of Chipping Campden, 1½ miles NE of Mickleton (A46).

These earthworks crown the top of an isolated hill which rises to 600 ft. The remains of 2 banks and ditches and a counterscarp bank follow the contours to enclose about 24 acres. On the WNW, where the hill falls steeply, there is a single bank. Around the N side the innermost bank and ditch are ploughed out: here, a drystone wall which is visible around the outer side of the middle bank may be original. The ramparts are best at the SW. Original entrances cannot now be identified. A hoard of 394 currency bars was found near the centre in 1824. Not dated.

Nadbury Camp, hill-fort (SP/390482) 3¾ miles SE of Kineton (B4086, B4451), crossed by B4086, 1½ miles W of Warmington (A41).

One of the largest hill-forts in the county, both sides of this roughly oval site are protected by steep hill-slopes. It encloses about 17 acres. Now badly denuded, the defences consist of a bank, ditch and counterscarp bank. The original entrance faced W, being approached by a hollow way now obscured by the modern road. This lies in the ditch along the N side of the camp, the main rampart rising high above it. Air photographs have revealed the presence of a large annexe at the SE, now ploughed flat. Not dated.

Oldbury Camp, hill-fort (SP/314947) 3½ miles NW of Nuneaton, 1 mile NW of Hartshill (between A47 and A4131).

This site has a rectangular plan and encloses some 7 acres. Traces of a once massive bank and ditch can be seen on all sides except the SE. The bank is still 6 ft. high in places. Without excavation it is impossible to say which gap in the earthworks is an original entrance. Not dated.

*Wappenbury, lowland fort (SP/377693), 4¼ miles NE of Leamington Spa (A425, A452), 1¾ miles SW of Princethorpe (A423, B4453). Finds in Coventry Museum).

This defensive site occupies an unusual lowland position. Roughly rectangular in plan, it lies immediately N of the Leam and is overlooked by slightly higher ground on 3 sides. Two fords across the river opposite the SE and SW corners of the fort may account for its position. The defences comprise a bank and ditch, well preserved at the NW and along the E: here there is a possible entrance. Excavation has shown that the rampart may originally have been c. 9 ft. high and the roughly V-shaped ditch about 13 ft. deep. Finds suggest that the earthworks were built c. 1st century BC–early 1st century AD. Domestic debris covered by the rampart belonged to an earlier Iron Age occupation of the site, perhaps c. 4th–3rd century BC.

West Midlands

IRON AGE

*Berry Mound, hill-fort (SP/095778) on s edge of Birmingham, 1¾ miles w of Shirley, ½ mile NW of Major's Green.

This hill-fort is oval in plan and encloses about 11 acres. It has a bank and ditch, well preserved by trees around the s side and everywhere visible as a scarped boundary to the field it encloses. The breaks in the s side are probably modern: an original entrance may have existed in the E side, facing the gravel pit. This appears to have been in-turned, but is now ploughed out. Not dated.

Birmingham, Berry Mound, hill-fort. See above.

Wychbury Hill Camp, hill-fort, see under Hereford and Worcester.

*Wiltshire

NEOLITHIC

Adam's Grave, long barrow (SU/113634) on Walker's Hill, 3¾ miles NE of Pewsey (A345, B3087), 1 mile NNE of Alton Barnes.

This mound is 200 ft. in length and 20 ft. high. It lies SE/NW. A burial chamber of sarsens, traces of which can still be seen at the E end, was opened in 1860 and found to contain 3–4 skeletons and a leaf-shaped flint arrowhead. The barrow seems to have had a kerb of sarsens, with the spaces between filled with dry-stone walling as at West Kennet. The ditch around the mound can still be seen on the ground. Date, c. 3,500–2,500 BC. The site has been damaged by quarrying.

Avebury, sacred sites and avenue etc. (SU/103700) 6 miles w of Marlborough (A4, A345, A346), on A361. Finds in the museum at Avebury.

Avebury, one of the largest ceremonial monuments in Europe, encloses 28½ acres (fig. 47). It consists of a circular bank of chalk, 1,400 ft. in diam., 20 ft. high, 75 ft. broad at its base, with an inner facing of chalk blocks quarried from a ditch within 30 ft. deep, 40 ft. wide at ground level and with a flat floor 15 ft. across (fig. 48). The ditch today is half filled with silt and the bank, originally gleaming white, is now grass-grown. There are 4 original entrances, N, S, E and W; the E entrance has not yet been proved by excavation.

Around the edge of the plateau so defined stands a circle of about 98 blocks of

47 *Avebury henge monument: Kennet Avenue follows road leading towards top left of illustration; Silbury Hill off top right*

48 *Avebury henge monument: ditch showing original profile and size*

sarsen, a silicified sandstone obtained locally. Inside this are 2 smaller stone circles, the N. 320 ft. in diam. with 27 stones, the S 340 ft. across with 29 stones. At the centre of the S stood a large stone (marked by a large concrete pillar), with smaller boulders around it forming 3 sides of a square. The N circle contains a U-shaped setting of 3 large stones (one now destroyed) – the Cove. Three stones of a supposed N circle have been found but recent excavation failed to reveal traces of further stones and this circle is now discounted. The Ring stone, a single sarsen, stood formerly within the ditch and main stone circle at the S entrance; on the E side of the entrance causeway here, the socket for a large timber post has been found.

The sinuous **Kennet Avenue** 50 ft. wide consisting of pairs of sarsens 80 ft. apart, broad stones facing narrow, links Avebury with the 2-period temple of wood and stone, the Sanctuary, on Overton Hill (below), 1 mile to the E. Burials, 2 accompanied by beakers and 1 with a bowl of the same period, were found beside 4 of the Avenue stones and must be contemporary.

The bank, ditch and stone settings of the Avebury monument are probably broadly contemporary, c. 2,000 BC. The Avenue, a monument of the Beaker people, would have been completed during the next 300 years. These people may also have played at least a part in the construction of the Avebury circles.

The Long Stones – Adam and Eve – standing stones (SU/089693) ¾ mile SW of Avebury village, ¼ mile NE of the Beckhampton cross-roads (A4, A361); objects in Devizes Museum.

These are 2 sarsen stones of natural shape, Adam the larger, the other called Eve; it has recently been established that they belonged to an avenue leading from the Avebury monument W to the Kennet. When Adam fell in 1911, the crouched skeleton of a middle-aged male with a beaker was discovered; it had been buried by the side of the upright stone.

The Sanctuary, wood and stone circles (SU/118679)S of A4, on Overton Hill, 5 miles W of Marlborough. Finds in Devizes Museum.

This was a wooden building erected for ritual purposes in late Neolithic times. It was replaced by a double stone circle by the Beaker Folk and at that stage joined to Avebury by the Kennet Avenue. Remains of the wooden building consisted of 6 concentric rings of post-holes (marked by concrete pillars) with 1 central post. The diam. of the largest ring was 65 ft. This structure may have been rebuilt several times. Of the 2 circles of sarsen stones (rectangular concrete blocks) which apparently replaced it, the outer one was 130 ft. across, the inner 45 ft. Against the inner face of 1 stone of the latter the excavators found a grave containing the crouched skeleton of a youth, a beaker of Rhineland or Low Countries design near its knees. This may represent a dedication, as at Woodhenge; similar burials beside some of the Kennet Avenue stones and beside Adam (above) have already been noted. The group of prominent round barrows N of the Sanctuary is probably a little later (p. 228).

Bowl's Barrow, long barrow (ST/942468) 2¾ miles NNE of Heytesbury (A36, A344, B3095), 3½ miles NW of Chitterne (A344). Finds in Salisbury Museum.

The mound of this long barrow is 150 ft. in length and 10 ft. high. It lies E/W. The site is important because a block of bluestone (of which Stonehenge phases 2–3 is made) from Pembrokeshire was found with skeletons at its E end. These burials were primary; there were about 14, their disarticulated bones placed in disorder on a layer of flints. Sarsen stones and oxen skulls were lying on top of the deposite. Date, c. 3,500–2,500 BC.

Bratton, long barrow. See Iron Age, **Bratton Castle.**

Devil's Den, long barrow (SU/152696) just E of Fyfield. (A4), 2,300 ft. N of A4.

The visitor will find a setting of 4 sarsen uprights with a capstone. These are set at the E end of a mound about 230 ft. long and 120 ft. broad, now virtually removed by ploughing. Restored last century, these stones are probably the remains of a simple chamber set at the end of a long barrow. Eighteenth-century drawings suggest that there may also have been a curved stone facade. Date, c. 3,500–2,500 BC.

*Durrington Walls, sacred site (SU/

150437) immediately N of Woodhenge, lying astride A345. Finds in Salisbury Museum.

The denuded bank and ditch of this, the largest henge monument in Britain, recently damaged by road-straightening, enclose a dry valley. With a max. diam. of 1,600 ft., it has entrances at the NW and SE, the latter close to the Avon. Recent excavations and survey have revealed that in detail the earthworks include slight changes of alignment and that the bank is separated from its ditch by a berm up to 150 ft. wide in places. The ditch reached a depth of 20 ft., with a width of nearly 40 ft. Just within the SE entrance, a setting of 6 concentric rings of post-holes of varying sizes was found which represents the remains of a complex timber building having a max. diam. of 65 ft. This structure had 2 main periods, the second of which, like Woodhenge (p. 222), may have included a centre open to the sky. Of the first building, the close-spaced post-holes of a timber facade were found on the SE; to the NE of this building there was an oval hollow, over 40 ft. long, with arcs of stake-holes around its ends, which had been a massive rubbish dump, whether for ritual purposes or simply domestic was not established. A second timber building or circle was excavated about 475 ft. to the N (geophysical survey indicated that this henge must contain several buildings). Also of 2 phases, the first may have been an open circle about 90 ft. in diam.; the second was probably a building, nearly 50 ft. across. Each structure was approached from the S by an avenue of timbers. The mass of pottery from the excavation was mainly grooved ware and C14 determinations suggest a date c. 1,700 BC for construction of this henge.

East Kennet, long barrow (SU/116669) 1 mile SW of West Kennet (A4).

Being covered with trees this mound has never been excavated scientifically. It is slightly larger than West Kennet and stands 20 ft. at its E end. Here sarsens may be seen showing through the soil, indicating the presence of burial chambers. This mound would be broadly contemporary with West Kennet, c. 3,500–2,000 BC.

Giant's Cave, long barrow. See **Luckington.**

Giant's Grave, long barrow (SU/189583) 2 miles SE of Pewsey (A345, B3087), 1¼ miles S of Milton Lilbourne (S of B3087).

This barrow is 315 ft. in length and 7 ft. high, with side-ditches which do not go around the ends of the mound. It is orientated NE/SW. A pile of disarticulated bones was found at the E end, representing 3–4 adults. The skull of one had been cleft before burial; with another a flint leaf-shaped arrowhead was found. This barrow must have been built c. 3,500–2,500 BC.

*Knap Hill, causewayed camp and Iron Age enclosure (SU/121636) 3½ miles NW of Pewsey (A345, B3087), 1½ miles NE of Alton Barnes. Objects in Devizes Museum.

The flattened top of Knap Hill, about 4 acres in extent, was enclosed in Neolithic times by a curved length of bank and ditch along the W side, interrupted by 5 causeways. The E side of the hill has precipitous slopes and it is not clear whether the earthwork originally encircled the hilltop. Excavation in 1908–9 and 1961 has shown that the ditch is irregular but roughly flat-floored, nearly 9 ft. deep in places and originally about the same in width. Windmill Hill pottery is associated with the construction of this causewayed camp, dated by radio-carbon to c. 2,700 BC.

At the N end of the camp a roughly triangular earthwork encloses about 1 acre, which contains additional subdivisions. This is Romano-British but has also yielded pagan Saxon finds.

In 1908–9, this was the first site to reveal a typical Neolithic causewayed ditch; and here too the early character of Windmill Hill pottery was suspected for the first time.

Lake, long barrow. See Bronze Age.

*Lanhill, long barrow (ST/877747) 3 miles W of Chippenham on S side of A420. Objects in Devizes Museum.

This chambered long barrow, orientated E/W, was originally about 185 ft. long and 75 ft. wide: there are 2 small burial chambers, one on the N side, the other (the only one visible) on the S side and there may have been 2 more within the mound. There seems to have been a blind entrance at the E end. The mound and chambers have been built from the local limestone. The E and W ends of this barrow were recently destroyed. Twenty burials have been found in the chambers; evidence from the bones in the N chamber suggests that this was used by one family. Architecturally, Lanhill belongs to the Cotswold tombs. Date, c. 3,500 BC.

Luckington, long barrow (ST/820830) 1 mile SE of Luckington, at SE corner of Badminton Park.

This site is about 130 ft. long and its width some 80 ft.; it is orientated SE/NW and is 8½ ft. high. There were at least 4 side-chambers, arranged in pairs on the N and S sides; 11 interments have been found in these. There is a forecourt and blind entrance at the E end; the W end is now damaged. Perhaps late of its type, this Cotswold tomb is c. 3,000 BC.

Lugbury, long barrow (ST/831786) 1 mile NW of Castle Combe, about ½ mile S of B4039.

The mound of this long barrow is 190 ft. long and about 90 ft. wide. It lies E/W. There is a blind entrance at the E end. Along the S side, towards this end 4 burial chambers have been found; these were apparently isolated within the mound, having no approach passages. They contained 26 skeletons. This barrow is unlikely to have been built before 3,000 BC.

Manton, long barrow (SU/152714) 2¾ miles NW of Marlborough (A4, A345, A346), 2,700 feet NW of Manton House. Objects in Devizes Museum.

Ruined in the 17th century and now almost destroyed, this barrow was built as a mound about 60 ft. long and 40 ft. broad, with a single burial chamber at the E end, opening directly on to a forecourt; a kerb of sarsens edged the mound. Excavation has revealed a large ritual pit in the forecourt, containing the skeleton of an ox. Neolithic pottery found on the site sets this tomb in the period 3,500–2,500 BC. Its single chamber suggests that it is late in the chamber-tomb series.

***Marden,** sacred site and round barrows (SU/091584) 4¾ miles WSW of Pewsey (A345, B3087), NE side of the Avon, astride road to Woodborough. Objects in

Devizes Museum.

Set in the Vale of Pewsey beside the Avon, a bank with internal ditch encloses a roughly oval area of 35 acres. The S boundary of this huge henge monument must always have been the river; its E side is a gently convex earthwork with a near-central entrance, bending W, sharply at the N end (cut by the modern road), to form a more curved NW side with a second entrance. Excavation has shown that the ditch was originally about 40 ft. wide and some 6 ft. deep. Immediately within the N entrance were 21 post-holes of a circular wooden building c. 32 ft. in diam., with 3 central posts supporting the top of the roof. Its location, and the presence of pit and midden outside the hut to the S recall directly the layout of the S building and midden at Durrington Walls (p. 217). Much grooved ware at Marden confirmed the close relationship of the two henges and it has yielded a radio-carbon determination of c. 1,900 BC.

Hatfield Barrow, a mound now destroyed, was situated between Hatfield Farm and the road, NE of the circle's centre. It was claimed to be 20–50 ft. high and over 200 ft. in diam.

A low mound, c. 200 ft. in diam., can be seen SW of this farm. Resembling Woodhenge before that site was uncovered, it may cover a similar timber building.

Milston Down, long barrow (SU/217463) 2 miles SW of South Tidworth (A338), on N side of military road to Bulford Camp.

It is unusual to find 2 long barrows so close together. Both lie E/W. The larger, 170 ft. in length and 7 ft. high has a flat space separating its surrounding ditch from the mound within.

The smaller barrow lies a few yards to the N. It is only 90 ft. long and 4 ft. high. Both barrows must have been erected between 3,500–2,500 BC.

Normanton, long barrows. See Bronze Age.

Norton Bavant, long barrow (ST/926459) on Norton Down, 2 miles N of Heytesbury (A36, A344, B3095). Objects in the British Museum.

This site is 180 ft. long, 9 ft. high and orientated E/W. The quarry-ditches do not continue around the ends of the mound but appear to project beyond it in both directions. Excavation in 1866 at the E end revealed a group of bones representing 18 people, 8 male, 5 female, 5 children. These were packed into a space 8 ft. × 5 ft. on the old land surface, all flesh and sinew having already decayed. Here was good evidence for the Neolithic custom of storing corpses for considerable periods before burial. With the bones from this long barrow a Neolithic pot of the earliest form had been deposited (fig. 2), together with a flint hammerstone. Date, c. 3,500 BC.

Pertwood Down, long barrow (ST/872374) 4¾ miles S of Warminster (A36, A350, A362), 1 mile E of Monkton Deverill (B3095).

This barrow is about 260 ft. long and 6 ft. high, placed SE/NW. Its shape is unusual in that a berm separates the inner edge of its quarry-ditch from the base of its mound. It can be dated c. 3,500–2,500 BC.

Stonehenge, sacred site. See Bronze Age.

*Stonehenge Cursus, processional avenue (SU/124430, where S ditch is cut by track from Stonehenge car-park to Larkhill), ½ mile N of Stonehenge, running E and W of map ref.; finds in Salisbury Museum.

This cursus has a parallel pair of banks and ditches, the latter on the outside, set 400 ft. apart. The ditches, which were originally some 6 ft. wide and 2–6 ft. deep, form rounded ends, thus enclosing a rectangular piece of ground 1¾ miles long; there are several gaps through this earthwork. The W end is set just W of Fargo Plantation; the E end stops short of a long barrow lying at right-angles to the cursus and today ploughed almost flat. This cursus spans a valley. It runs towards Woodhenge and may be considered as a ritual site associated with the latter. Date, c. 2,000 BC.

A smaller cursis, the **Lesser Cursus** (SU/103435), has been located immediately W of Fargo Plantation, parallel to the Stonehenge Cursus and on a line ¼ mile N of it. This is now almost obliterated by the plough. It has never been excavated.

Tidcombe, long barrow (SU/292576) 7¼ miles NW of Andover (A303, A343,

A3057), about ½ mile S of Tidcombe.

This barrow is nearly 200 ft. long and 10 ft. high, and is orientated N/S. A burial chamber built of sarsen stones formerly existed at the S end and remains of it are still visible; it comprises 3 uprights with 2 roofing slabs and contained 1 skeleton. The ditch around this long barrow is now no longer visible. Date, c. 3,500–2,500 BC.

Tilshead Old Ditch, long barrow (SU/023468) over ½ mile W of Tilshead White Barrow, S of Tilshead Lodge.

Old Ditch (so named from the later boundary ditch that carefully skirts its S side) is one of the largest long barrows in this country, being 380 ft. long. It lies NE/SW, with a quarry ditch around it. At the E end (11 ft. high) 2 bodies have been found, buried under a pile of flints; one was partly burnt, the other unburnt and with evidence that the skull had been cleft at or before death. Three more skeletons have been found at the W end, lying on a pavement of flints covered with much burnt ash. Beside one of these a ritual pit had been dug in the chalk. Date, c. 3,500–2,500 BC.

Tilshead White Barrow, long barrow (SU/033468) S of Tilshead, nearly ½ mile along track leading SW from A360.

This barrow, visible from the main road, is orientated E/W. It is about 250 ft. long and is widest at its E end, where it stands over 7 ft. high. A ditch runs around it. White Barrow must have been built about 3,500 BC. Nothing is known about the burials under it.

*West Kennet, long barrow (SU/104677) 1,000 yds. SW of the centre of West Kennet (A4). Track S from A4, W of village. Objects in Devizes Museum.

One of the largest long barrows in Britain, this consists of a wedge-shaped mound of chalk 330 ft. long and 8 ft. high at its E end, dug from a massive quarry-ditch (originally 10 ft. deep and 20 ft. wide) running around the mound but not across the E end, and separated from it by a berm about 30 ft. wide. Excavation has revealed that the core of this mound was built of large sarsen boulders, each a load for 1 man. A kerb of sarsens ran around the edge of the mound. At the E end a gallery gives access to 5 burial chambers, leading in from a concave forecourt defined by large stone uprights; this is closed by 1 enormous blocking stone and several smaller ones which hide the concavity of the original facade. This straight facade which confronts the visitor was set up when the last Neolithic funerals had taken place. Behind the blocking stones will be found a parallel-sided gallery, 2 pairs of side-chambers leading off it, with a fifth chamber at its end. Walls and capstones are of sarsen from the Marlborough Downs. The drystone walling found filling gaps between many of the uprights is of oolitic limestone from the region of Calne, 12 miles to the w. On several uprights of the chambers (noticeably on the N face of the stone separating the sw chamber from the gallery) areas of polishing can be found. Here stone axes were sharpened by those building the tomb – great quantities of timber being used during this work. About 30 adults and children were buried here

early in the Neolithic period (fig. 49). Pots deposited with some of the dead are identical with many found at Windmill Hill (p. 222). The tomb must date from c. 3,500–2,500 BC. Subsequent deposits of pottery, ornaments and food in the gallery and chambers suggest that native Neolithic people, including Beaker Folk, came here at intervals to perform rituals (figs. 1, 4–5). The architecture of West Kennet belongs exactly to that of the Cotswold chambered tombs and can be derived from long barrows at the mouth of the Loire.

Whitesheet Hill, causewayed camp and Bronze Age round barrow (ST/802352) $2\frac{1}{2}$ miles s of Maiden Bradley (B3092), $1\frac{3}{4}$ miles NNW of Mere (A303). Objects in Devizes Museum.

This camp consists of a single bank and ditch, the latter with at least 21 causeways across it, oval in shape and enclosing 4 acres. Excavation has revealed that the ditch was dug originally with an

49   *West Kennet: Neolithic chambered long barrow. Primary inhumations, south-west chamber*

average width of 10 ft., its depth ranging from 1 to 4 ft. Pottery from the ditch-bottom shows that this site was built about 3,500 BC. A bowl-barrow overlies the causewayed camp ditch at the s. This is about 8 ft. high and nearly 60 ft. in diam. It has been opened more than once but no primary burial has been recorded. Date, c. 1,700–1,400 BC.

*Windmill Hill, causewayed camp and Bronze Age barrow cemetery (SU/087714) 2½ miles N of Avebury Trusloe (off A361). Finds in Avebury Museum and Devizes Museum (barrows).

Windmill Hill is crowned by 3 irregularly planned, roughly concentric ditches which altogether enclose about 20 acres of downland. These earthworks are all pierced by a series of gaps in the Neolithic manner of ditch-digging. The outer ditch is the deepest, averaging 8 ft. The inner one and the N half of the others were excavated by the late Alexander Keiller between the 2 world wars. Finds in the ditches, mostly domestic but some ritualistic, suggest that the camp had been used for regular gatherings of people and livestock – a sort of fairground – involving the dumping of refuse in the ditch. A dwarf had been buried in the outer ditch soon after it was dug. Windmill Hill was built c. 2,900 BC and continued in use for several centuries.

Excavation (1957–8) has revealed that this hill was cultivated by Neolithic farmers before they erected these earthworks: post-holes belonging perhaps to a house were also found beneath the outer bank of the camp on the E side.

A Bronze Age barrow cemetery of c. 1,700–1,400 BC extends E from the causewayed camp. The mounds lie in an irregular line beginning on top of the hill (at SU/086713), between the inner and central ramparts of the Neolithic site. The barrow here, Picket Barrow, is a bell-barrow, 8 ft. high and with a mound 80 ft. in diam. The ditch around it was cleared out during the excavation of the camp and found to contain much domestic debris from the latter. Nothing is known of any burials beneath this barrow. Next to the E come 2 bowl-barrows, both 6 ft. high and about 60 ft. in diam. The second was found to cover a burial accompanied by a grape cup and

battle-axe made of stone quarried at Cwm Mawr, Montgomeryshire (p. 182). Further E, below the crest of the hill, there are 2 fine saucer-barrows (SU/089714). The first is 83 ft. across, the second 86 ft. The mound, ditch and outer bank of both are very clear. Nothing is known of burials beneath them.

Winterbourne Stoke Cross-Roads, long barrow. See Bronze Age.

Woodhenge, sacred site (SU/150434) 1 mile N of Amesbury, on the A345. Finds in Devizes Museum.

Woodhenge is one of the few Neolithic wooden buildings so far found in Britain. It may safely be regarded as a temple, incorporating the henge monument idea in its surrounding ditch with outer bank and entrance. Within this earthwork, which has a max. diam. of 220 ft., a setting of 6 concentric circles of post-holes (today marked by concrete pillars indicating their original diams.) has been found: 4 other post-holes occurred at the entrance through the earthwork. Within the inner post-ring there was a grave (now marked by a pile of flints set in concrete) which contained the skeleton of a child about 3 years of age, whose skull had been cleft.

Assuming that the posts represent the roof-supports for a large building, it seems likely that the ring with the largest posts held the roof ridge, while the smaller posts supported the roof as it sloped outwards and inwards, perhaps to an open centre.

Pottery found at the bottom of the ditch and sealed beneath the earthwork bank includes grooved ware and several fragments of the earlier Neolithic pottery (belonging to those who built the causewayed camps and long barrows). Higher in the ditch and all over the interior, beaker sherds were found together with grooved ware. The builders were thus worshipping here from c. 2,000 BC.

Among the ritual objects found were 2 axe-heads carved out of chalk.

Immediately s of Woodhenge 4 contemporary burial circles have been excavated. In one occurred the crouched skeleton of a male provided with a fine necked beaker and a battle-axe of pink granite from the Teignmouth area of

Devon. **Durrington Walls** (p. 217) should be considered a part of this group.

*BRONZE AGE

Aldbourne Four Barrows, barrow cemetery. See **Sugar Hill.**

Amesbury Down, triple bell-barrow (SU/ 148394) E of the Avon, 1½ miles S of Amesbury (A303, A345).

This is an example of the rare type of barrow which has 3 mounds enclosed by an oval ditch. The mounds are 2–3 ft. high and the major axes measure 189 × 140 ft. The surrounding ditch has an outer bank. The contents of these mounds are not know. Date, c. 1,700–1,400 BC.

Cow Down, barrow cemetery (SU/ 229515) 1½ miles N of North Tidworth (A338, A3026), ½ mile SW of A342/ A338 cross-roads. Grave goods in Devizes Museum.

There are at least 14 bowl-barrows and a disc-barrow in this cemetery (fig. 10). The bowls lie in a ragged line NE/SW, crossing the N end of the wood, with the disc-barrow and 4 bowls forming an even more ragged line to the N.

From W to E the main line of barrows possesses the following features.

(1) Large mound overlapped by a smaller, probably covering cremations.

(2) No burials yet found.

(3) Main burial not found. Probably enlarged c. 1,200 BC to contain an urn-field of Deverel–Rimbury culture. These first 3 are W of the wood.

(4) The main burial was a crouched inhumation, the hands and 1 arm missing. About 1,200 BC, 13 cremations, 3 of them in urns, were added by Deverel–Rimbury people. This mound is 7 ft. high and about 80 ft. in diam.

(5) At the base of the mound a cremation had been placed in a wooden coffin and furnished with an antler mace-head. About 1,200 BC a cemetery of 8 cremations, 2 in urns, was added by Deverel–Rimbury people on the S and SE sides.

(6) The main burial was of a child of 3–4 years, furnished with a food offering in a collared urn and with a food vessel. On the S side there were 18 cremations and

at least 45 urns of Deveral–Rimbury culture. This barrow is 12 ft. high and about 100 ft. in diam.

(7) A cremation was the earliest burial here. Higher in the mound were parts of an inhumation on a wooden plank; above this there was a second cremation with beads of amber and shale. This mound is 6 ft. high and about 60 ft. in diam. Nos. 4–7 are at the N end of the wood.

(8) No burials have been found here. The mound is 6 ft. high and about 60 ft. in diam.

(9) This mound covered a cremation.

The disc-barrow is 158 ft. in diam. and its central mound 1 ft. high. Nothing is known of its contents. Of the other bowls N of the wood, that farthest S covered a child's skeleton, furnished with a cup with handle, of central European derivation. Date of cemetery, c. 1,700–1,400 BC.

Cursus Group, barrow cemetery (W end SU/115428) ¼ mile N of Stonehenge. Grave goods in Devizes Museum.

This group, part of the Stonehenge complex, is laid out in a straight line E/W and consists, from W to E, of a bowl-barrow, 3 bell-barrows, a double-bell and another bell-barrow. More scattered barrows extend W into Fargo Plantation. In the main group the bowl, which has an outer bank (and diam. 136 ft., ht. 3 ft.) contained a cremation and beads of amber, faience and stone. Moving E, the first bell (diam. 124 ft., ht. 10 ft.) covered a simple cremation. The next one (diam. 137 ft., ht. 6 ft.) contained a cremation with a bronze knife. The third bell, still 11 ft. high and 194 ft. in diam., yielded a cremation. In the double-bell the W mound covered a pit containing a cremation with 6 bone beads. The burnt bones of a girl, placed in an urn, were found under the E mound; with them were many beads of faience, amber and shale, one with sheet gold on it. There was also a bronze knife and an awl. The long axes of these mounds are 158 × 120 ft. The mounds are 6–7 ft. high. There are no records of the contents of the last bell in this group (185 ft. in diam., 10 ft. high). Date, Stonehenge period, c. 1,700–1,400 BC.

Enford, bowl-barrow (SU/129516) 2¼ miles SSW of Upavon (A342, A345),

$\frac{3}{4}$ mile w of Enford (A345).

This bowl-barrow is nearly 150 ft. in diam. (excluding its now silted-up ditch) and 17 ft. high. It is one of the largest round barrows in Britain. It has been dug at the centre but nothing is known of its contents. Date, c. 1,700–1,400 BC.

Everleigh Barrows, barrow cemetery (SU/184561) 1 mile NNW of Lower Everleigh (A342), on the track to Down Farm. Grave goods in Devizes Museum.

There are 2 fine bells (diams. 147 ft., 162 ft., hts. 11 ft., 10 ft. respectively), a disc (diam. 185 ft.) and a bowl (diam. 60 ft., ht. 1 ft.) in this little cemetery. The larger bell-barrow covered a simple cremation, the smaller a cremation with a bronze knife. Nothing has yet been found in the others. Date, c. 1,700–1,400 BC.

Gopher Wood, barrow cemetery (SU/139639) $2\frac{3}{4}$ miles NW of Pewsey (A345, B3087), $\frac{1}{2}$ mile NW of Huish.

This cemetery consists of 5 small bowl-barrows extending raggedly N from a disc-barrow and commanding a fine view to the s. The disc is about 87 ft. across, with a central mound 3 ft. high. It contained a burial in an urn, with an incense cup, bone pin and bronze awl. There were 2 other cremations, both enclosed by flints. Among the bowl-barrows there are 2 groups, one of 3 mounds, the other of 2, which are contiguous. All the mounds are 30–50 ft. in diam. and 2–3 ft. high. Cremations have been recorded from some. Date, c. 1,700–1,400 BC.

Grafton, disc-barrows and 'Celtic' fields (SU/271563) 2 miles E of Collingbourne Kingston (A338), approached by a track passing Hill Barn.

These 2 disc-barrows, excavated without record, are noteworthy because they overlap. They have diams. of 152 ft. and mounds 2–3 ft. high. Overlying part of both is one lynchet of a 'Celtic' field system. These fields have been laid out so as to avoid the disc-barrows – a deliberate regard for the earlier burial places so frequently found in prehistoric England.

A third disc-barrow will be found a short distance up the hill. It is 144 ft. across and its mound 2 ft. high. All 3 are c. 1,700–1,400 BC.

Grim's Ditch, enclosure ditch. See Hampshire, p. 136.

Lake, barrow cemetery and Neolithic long barrow (SU/109402) $1\frac{1}{2}$ miles sw of Stonehenge, E of green path leading past the Normanton cemetery (p. 225) to Druids Lodge, on A360. Grave goods in Devizes Museum and the British Museum.

This group (fig. 10) is part of the Stonehenge complex and has no noticeable plan. It contains 15 bowls (hts. 1–10 ft.; 20–100 ft. diams.), 4 bells (diams. 120–150 ft., hts. 10–11 ft.), 2 discs (diams. about 180 ft.) and a long barrow. One of the N bowl-barrows, called Prophet Barrow, covered a wooden coffin let into a pit in the chalk, containing a cremation, a slate pendant and a bronze dagger. A child aged 3 or 4, with a beaker, lay beneath 1 of the bells.

Most of the barrows in this cemetery covered cremations; grave goods included beads of shale, amber, faience and bone, bronze daggers, knives and awls, bone pins and an incense cup (fig. 9, top right). These burials must have been made c. 1,700–1,400 BC. The long barrow lies SE/NW. It is 140 ft. long, 75 ft. wide and 8 ft. high at the SE. It has not been excavated. Date, c. 3,500–2,500 BC.

Lake Down, barrow cemetery (SU/117393) nearly $\frac{1}{2}$ mile s of the Wilsford cemetery (p. 235). E of Westfield Farm.

There are at least 16 barrows in this cemetery (fig. 10), of which 5 are pond-barrows (diams. 59–81 ft.) – an exceptional concentration of a rare form. There is also a disc-barrow (diam. 181 ft.), and 10 bowls. Excavation records are scanty. The disc contained a cremation in a miniature urn and a cremation also occurred in 1 of the pond barrows. Similar burials, 1 with ashes contained in a collared urn, have been found in 2 of the bowls. Part of the Stonehenge complex: date of cemetery, c. 1,700–1,400 BC.

Maizey Down, Middle Bronze Age enclosure. See **Marlborough Downs.**

Manton, round barrow (SU/168689) 1 mile w of Marlborough, 100 yds. N of the Marlborough Youth Hostel (on A4). Grave goods in Devizes Museum.

Though inconspicuous, this bowl-barrow, the mound of which was surrounded by 2 ditches and is some 60 ft. in diam., covered the crouched skeleton of an old woman buried with one of the richest groups of grave goods in Wessex. She had been interred in a dress or shroud, for traces of cloth were noticed in the clay beneath the bones. Personal possessions included a bronze knife with pommel of amber, a necklace of 150 shale beads graded in size, a large shale barrel-shaped bead with gold bands around it, another bead of gold and bronze shaped like a halberd and a third consisting of a disc of amber with gold sheet around the edge. A bead resembling the latter has been found in Crete. Besides other beads and a clay stud, 3 bronze awls, 2 incense cups (one a grape cup, fig. 9, bottom right both) and a collared urn with a food offering had been placed with the body. This important person must have been buried c. 1,700–1,400 BC.

Marlborough Downs, Enclosures and fields: Ogbourne Down (3 enslosures, SU/172744; SU/175744; SU/177744), ½ mile E of Four Mile Clump and nearly ¼ mile s of Smeath's Plantation. Finds in Devizes Museum.

These lie in a valley. They can probably be associated with the 'Celtic' fields round about. The w enclosure is about 200 ft. by 350 ft., its long axis NE/SW. The ditch defining it was originally v-shaped, 10 ft. wide at the top and some 4 ft. deep. There is an entrance at the sw, 30 ft. wide; a post-hole was found at its s end, perhaps for a gate. A 200 ft. gap on the E side could originally have been blocked by brushwood. This site can be interpreted as a cattle enclosure.

The central enclosure is about 185 ft. by 145 ft., with an entrance through the w side.

The E enclosure consists of 2 curved lengths of ditch with wide gaps on the N and s, enclosing an area 165 ft. by 140 ft.

Ogbourne Maizey (SU/158747), 1¾ miles NW of Rockley, ½ mile w of Four Mile Clump. Finds in Devizes Museum.

This enclosure is 220 ft. × 200 ft., with an opening about 15 ft. wide to the E. It consists of a bank and ditch which have been built on top of slightly earlier 'Celtic' fields. This may be either a cattle pen or else the defences of a settlement.

Preshute Down (SU/142743), 2¼ miles SE of A361, just N of the road from Broad Hinton to Marlborough. Finds in De-vizes Museum.

This enclosure lies at the foot of a steep northerly slope. It measures 150 ft. × 135 ft., its long axis N/S. There is a 90 ft. gap through the ditch at the sw. This V-shaped ditch resembles that at Ogbourne Down (West). Within, a pit and a post-hole have so far been found; much late Bronze Age pottery is scattered over the area and the chalk surface was said by its excavator to be much trampled, perhaps by cattle stalled inside. The 'Celtic' fields surrounding this enclosure are a little later in date.

All these earthworks and fields were the work of indigenous farmers of the Middle Bronze Age, c. 1,400–1,000 BC. They developed the first settled farming here and their huts and fields are the earliest we can see in Wessex.

New King Barrows, barrow cemetery. See **Old** and **New King Barrows.**

50   *Normanton: grape cup, c. 1,700–1,400 BC*

*Normanton, barrow cemetery, Neolithic long barrow and mortuary enclosure (SU/115413) ½ mile s of Stonehenge, approached by a grass track off A303. Grave goods in Devizes Museum.

This group (figs. 9, 10, 50–52), perhaps the finest in Britain, begins in the square plantation w of the green road from Stone-henge. Here are 2 bowl-barrows (1–2) with a disc-barrow (3) between them. North of this plantation is a bell-barrow (4) 11 ft. high and 174 ft. in diam., which covered a burial with beaker and bronze daggers placed inside what appeared to have been a wooden hut. Moving E, a disc-barrow lies on either side of the track; the first (5) contained a cremation accompanied by beads of Near East faience, amber from our own east coast and shale from Dorset. Both have total diams. of about 200 ft. Next we find the celebrated Bush Barrow (7), a bowl 11 ft. high, covering the inhumed corpse of what must have been one of the most powerful of Wessex chiefs. The body had been buried clothed: on the chest was sewn a lozenge-shaped plate of sheet gold (fig. 52); a belt was furnished with a gold-plated hook-and-eye. The warrior's weapons consisted of 3 daggers, 1 having a handle inlaid with hundreds of tiny gold pins. All were in sheaths of wood, leather-lined. There was also a bronze axe wrapped in cloth and the remains of a shield. As a symbol of authority a mace had been put in the grave. It consisted of a wooden shaft decorated with bone rings and fitted with a head made from a fossil pebble of Devon origin.

The next 3 barrows lie in a line N/S.

The northernmost (8) is a bell 10 ft. high and 135 ft. in diam. which covered a cremation with rich grave goods. Among these were an incense cup (fig. 9, top centre), a gold-plated shale button, gold-edged amber beads and a model halberd of amber and gold. South-west of this is a saucer-barrow (9) and just SE of that a bowl (10), 8 ft. high, the inhumation burial beneath which was accompanied by a grape cup (fig. 50), beads of gold, amber, shale and fossils and an urn with a food offering. Moving E we pass 3 insignificant bowl-barrows (11–13), Neolithic long barrow and a disc-barrow (14) (diam. 220 ft.) which covered a cremation. The long barrow is 65 ft. in length, 3 ft. high and orientated NE/SW. It has not been excavated.

Another small bowl (15) separates us from a fine twin bell-barrow (16) – 2 mounds within one ditch, with overall measurements of 125 ft. N/S and 188 ft. E/W; their hts. are 8–9 ft. These have yielded a cremation, beads of shale and amber and a bone belt-hook.

The group ends with a bell-barrow (17) touching the last and a group of 4 bowl-

51   *Normanton: Bronze Age barrow cemetery*

barrows (18–21), 3 disc-barrows (22–24) and a saucer (25). No details of burials or grave goods survive for these.

This great cemetery, the burial area for a rich Wessex tribe, must have accumulated c. 1,700–1,400 BC. It is undoubtedly sited in relation to Stonehenge, like all the barrow-cemeteries hereabouts.

There is a long barrow 300 yds. SW of Bush Barrow, at SU/114411. It lies E/W, is 126 ft. long and 6 ft. high. Its side-ditches are still visible. Four skeletons were found close together near the E end, on the old land surface below the barrow.

*Immediately S of the mound aerial photographs have revealed a rectangular enclosure defined by a ditch, smaller than the long barrow. This is a mortuary enclosure, a place where corpses were accumulated until the long barrow was built to cover them. It can just be seen in a low sun.

this group set in wood on N side of A303, 1½ miles W of Amesbury (A303, A345).

The Old and New King Barrows, 2 groups of 7, are laid out in straight lines. The S group, the New King Barrows, consists, moving N, of 5 bowl (100–120 ft. in diam. and 9–12 ft. high) and 2 bells (about 140 ft. in diam. and 8–9 ft. high) aligned N/S and stopping short of the Stonehenge Avenue (p. 232). The Old King Barrows begin N of the Stonehenge Avenue and extend NE. These are all bowls (40–80 ft. in diam. and 4–6 ft. high). We have no record of what lies beneath these barrows which, by 1,400 BC, must have formed an impressive line of chalk-covered mounds forming part of the Stonehenge complex.

Overton Hill, barrow cemetery (SU/119682) astride A4 E of The Sanctuary (p. 217), and 4¼ miles W of Marlborough. Grave goods in Devizes Museum.

52 *Bush Barrow,*
Normanton: gold plate
(7¼ × 6¼ ins.),
c. 1,700 BC

Ogbourne Down, Middle Bronze Age enclosure. See **Marlborough Downs.**
Ogbourne Maizey, Middle Bronze Age enclosure. See **Marlborough Downs.**
Old and **New King Barrows,** barrow cemetery (S end SU/135421) S end of

Records of the contents of these mounds (fig. 10) are scanty. The bowl immediately S of A4, 12 ft. high and about 60 ft. in diam., contained an inhumation crouched in a wooden coffin and furnished with a bronze knife and an axe-head and pin of German design. The first mound N of A4 is a bell which covered burnt bones and an incense cup. Its berm can now only be seen on the w. It is 11 ft. high. Next come 2 bell-barrows with a bowl-barrow between them and just overlapping their ditches. Each contained a cremation: there was a bone pin with that under the central mound, and a bronze knife and bone belt-hook under the N bell. Both bells are 10 ft. high and about 130 ft. in diam. The bowl is $3\frac{1}{2}$ ft. high. The last barrow in this cemetery, a bowl, covered a cremation.

The Overton Hill group, with the scores of isolated barrows on Avebury Downs to the N (and next entry), must be referred to the period 1,700–1,400 BC, the Stonehenge phase of our Bronze Age. **Overton Hill,** bell-barrow (SU/118692) 1 mile SE of Avebury (A361), $\frac{3}{4}$ mile N of The Sanctuary (p. 217).

Of several bell-, bowl- and disc-barrows scattered on Overton Hill and Avebury Downs, this bell is an exceptionally fine example of one of these specialised Wessex forms. It is 12 ft. high and 168 ft. in diam. The berm between mound and ditch is 27 ft. wide. Nothing is known of burials beneath it. Date, c. 1,700–1,400 BC.

Preshute Down, Middle Bronze Age enclosure. See **Marlborough Downs.**

Silbury Hill (SU/100685), on A4, $5\frac{1}{2}$ miles w of Marlborough; finds in Devizes Museum.

This mound is about 130 ft. high, its base covers c. $5\frac{1}{4}$ acres and its flat top is 100 ft. across. It has been built on a spur, its lowest 25 ft. being undisturbed chalk: the heaped-up mound comprises about 9 million cu. ft. It is surrounded by a ditch, about 100 ft. wide beside the A4 and here interrupted by 2 causeways. Around the NW–SE, the ditch widens to c. 150 ft. and there is a huge extension to the w.

Excavation has shown that Silbury was evolved in 3 stages. First was built a mound of turf and soil of normal barrow form, 120 ft. in diam. and 16 ft. high, apparently retained by a ring of wooden posts. Next, this mound was covered by chalk dug from a surrounding ditch with a minimum diam. of c. 350 ft. This stage was abandoned before completion and its ditch refilled, to be replaced by the mound in its present form, its quarry ditch at least 20 ft. deep. The mound was built as a stepped cone, all except the top step smoothed out by chalk derived from the w quarry. No burials or objects have yet been found; a C14 sample indicates construction from c. $2,145 \pm 95$ BC.

*Snail Down, barrow cemetery (SU/218522). Between Everleigh and Tidworth, approached by several tracks leading s from A342. Grave goods in Devizes Museum. (N.B. Though on W.D. property, it is usually possible to visit this cemetery when there is no military training in the area.)

A semi-circle of mounds over $\frac{1}{4}$ mile

53 *Silbury Hill: presumed burial mound of the Bronze Age*

54   *Snail Down, showing chalk crust over turf mound of Bronze Age bell-barrow (4) and broad berm (with figures) separating mound from ditch. C14 date, 1,540 ± 90 BC*

long, Snail Down (fig. 10) includes all Bronze Age types. Archaeological excavation following damage by tanks during World War II has now obliterated 10 barrows, but 1 of these, a disc-barrow, excavated completely in 1953, is preserved (1976) in the state in which its Bronze Age builders had it immediately before the central tumps were erected.

There used to be 29 barrows in this cemetery, with more examples, isolated, to the sw. Beginning at the w end we find a saucer-barrow (1), overlapped by a modern track and excavated in 1953. It contained a central grave with a cremation, bronze awl and 2 incense cups (fig. 9 top left). Beside it was a second pit, with the burnt bones of a youth whose skull had been trephined. Moving NE we come first to a bowl-barrow (2) which, like 2 others in this group, contained an

empty grave. Beyond it is another bowl (3) (with a cremation in a wooden box), followed by a bell-barrow (4) destroyed by excavation in 1955 (figs. 54, 55). It had covered a pit which held an urn filled with human ashes; there was clear evidence that an adult male had been cremated at this spot before the barrow had been built (C14 determination, 1,540 ± 70 BC). Secondary burials in the mound included 4 urns (fig. 6) and beads of shale, amber and faience. This mound had been 8 ft. high and about 120 ft. in diam. A track running E/W crosses the s lip of the barrow-ditch and is faintly discernible in the turf. It is probably Romano-British, linking several farms with the main Roman road from Old Sarum to *Cunetio* (Mildenhall).

Between this bell and the next, an enormous one, lies a group of 9 small

55   *Snail Down: Bronze Age bell-barrow (4). Details of mound, showing turves; nineteenth-century excavation pit at centre of barrow (right)*

bowls (5–13), some touching. They lack surrounding ditches, being composed of scraped-up topsoil. Excavation in 1957, which has almost destroyed them, showed that some at least contained burials after cremation. Also, it was found that these mounds had been built over the remains of an earlier occupation site. The post- and stake-holes of flimsy tents or huts were found in large numbers, together with potsherds of beakers and grooved ware, and implements of flint and stone.

The barrow at the w end of this little group (5), totally excavated in 1957, contained a cremation in a large collared urn. Evidence for burial ritual suggested that a corpse had been laid out on a platform for a considerable period before the bones were removed, burnt and then brought back to the site of the barrow. The collared urn was ritually smashed after being placed in the burial pit; then the bones were put in the pit and the barrow mound heaped over them. Later a small collared urn was brought to the barrow, in pieces, and buried in a pit at the w edge of the mound.

The bell-barrow (14) beyond these mounds is the largest in the cemetery, being 160 ft. in diam. and 11 ft. high. No burials have yet been found in it. Next comes a disc-barrow (15), almost touching the bell on its NE side. A cremation has been found at its centre. There are 2 bowl-barrows to the NE (16–17), both covering cremation burials.

Now the main line of barrows swings SE, beginning with a bowl called Hunter Barrow (18), 80 ft. in diam. and 9 ft. high. Here a cremation was found, covered with a pile of antlers and furnished with 4 flint arrow-heads. Above it was the skeleton of a dog. Almost touching this barrow on the SE is another bowl (19), from which no burial has been recorded. Beyond that there is a bell-barrow (20) covering an *empty* grave. It is 120 ft. in diam. and 11 ft. high.

There is a disc-barrow (21) in the angle formed by the 3 last; originally with 2 mounds within its ditch, it was excavated in 1953 and left open. Its central cremation pit was robbed before the 19th century. Beneath the other mound an enormous pit has been found, which must

have been intended for rituals. Immediately to the s is a low bowl (22) made of scraped-up soil, 90 ft. in diam. and 2 ft. high. A fine urn filled with human ashes has been found in it.

Going back to the main line of mounds we find 2 excavated in 1955; the first (23) is a bowl made from top-soil; beside it is one of those flat barrows (24), more familiar in the Upper Thames, consisting of a ditch with outer bank and no mound within. The first was found to cover a ring of stout posts 50 ft. in diam. enclosing a space containing a cremation pit. The other barrow, 100 ft. across, contained 3 ritual pits but no burials.

56　*Snail Down: typical Bronze Age contracted inhumation, bell-barrow (26)*

To the s there is a double bell-barrow (25), its N mound 4 ft. high, its s mound 9½ ft. high. A cremation was found in the former, while beneath the latter a wooden coffin was found to contain a cremation with a bronze dagger and pin with ring attachments, of central German origin. Excavation in 1957 showed that a ring of short stout posts surrounds each mound, acting as retaining circles to preserve their shape. The N/S diam. of this double barrow is 192 ft. There is another bell (26) to the s, 10 ft. high and 175 ft. in diam. On the N side of its berm there is a small mound which is probably a secondary feature. Neither mound has yet yielded a primary burial, but in 1957 the crouched skeleton of a youth was found (fig. 56), added as a secondary burial to the small mound. Beads of amber and perforated sea-shell were

57   Snail Down: Bronze Age pond-barrow (28). Pegs mark post-holes of enclosure containing ritual pits

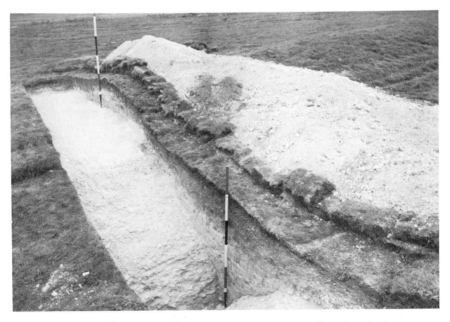

58   Snail Down: Middle or Late Bronze Age ranch boundary ditch

found round its neck. About 450 ft. to the w there is another bell-barrow (27), 10 ft. high and about 120 ft. in diam. No burial has yet been found in this mound.

A pond-barrow (28), found and excavated in 1957 (fig. 57), lay about 150 ft. w of the last bell-barrow. It was 40 ft. across and about 1 ft. deep. Three pits were uncovered near its centre; they were surrounded by the holes of a ragged fence. Each pit contained a few fragments of burnt human bone. This cemetery belongs to the period 1,700–1,400 BC.

Immediately N of the Snail Down cemetery there is a substantial ditch with its bank on the s side (fig. 58). It runs E/W, bearing s at Weather Hill Firs, and E again after ¼ mile, to run s of the barrow cemetery to disappear about SU/224518. This was shown by excavation to be V-shaped, 11 ft. wide at surface level and 5 ft. deep. It is an example of those boundary ditches dug by the indigenous Middle Bronze Age farmers who, by c. 1,250 BC, had begun to practise settled agriculture and stock farming on a large scale. Through respect for the dead, the ditch system on Snail Down was dug to protect the cemetery from the system of 'Celtic' fields which surround it. Thus the ditch deliberately bends N to avoid the most NW bowl-barrow in the cemetery (at SU/217523).

*Stonehenge, sacred site and avenue (SU/ 123422) 2 miles w of Amesbury (A303, A345) between A303 and A344. Finds in Salisbury Museum.

Stonehenge (fig. 59) must be understood as the vital part of the complex of religious sites which surround it. Geographically, it lies at the centre of a slight depression, dominated by King Barrow Ridge to the E, Normanton Down to the s, Winterbourne Stoke Down to the w, and to the N by Larkhill. These features all support barrow cemeteries, tribal burial grounds erected within sight of the greatest Bronze Age temple in Europe. This archaeological setting, which should be appreciated before Stonehenge itself is visited, can best be viewed from King Barrow Ridge, crossed by A303 from Amesbury.

When building began at Stonehenge, c. 2,200 BC, the existing centre for religious ceremonies in the area was at Woodhenge

and Durrington Walls (pp. 217, 222), just out of sight to the NE. The Stonehenge Cursus and the Lesser Cursus (p. 220) must also have existed, probably in connection with the latter. Neolithic long barrows and a causewayed camp near Robin Hood Ball, would have already become distinctly ancestral when the work at Stonehenge was started.

Stonehenge phase 1 comprises a circular earthwork about 380 ft. in diam., with an entrance facing NE and outside it a single standing stone of sarsen, The Heel Stone (on the s edge of A344). This stone is the only naturally shaped sarsen on the site. Immediately inside the earthwork there is a ring of 56 pits, the Aubrey Holes, marked today by concrete patches, They are 2–6 ft. in diam. and 2–4 ft. in depth. These appear to have been filled soon after they were dug and many incorporated human cremations. Their purpose must have been part ritual, part burial and the whole of phase 1 a cremation cemetery of a design matched elsewhere in Britain, but nowhere so large. It is also unusual to find the main bank *inside* the ditch of a Neolithic cemetery or henge monument; at Stonehenge there is a slight outer bank in addition.

Stonehenge phase 2 saw the erection of a double circle of bluestones from Pembrokeshire at the centre of the earthwork, the digging of the Avenue up to the entrance from the Avon at Amesbury and the widening of the entrance to fit it. This may have taken place c. 1,600 BC.

About 80 naturally-shaped blocks of bluestone (various varieties of volcanic ash and lava) were set up in 2 concentric rings (diam. 72 ft., 86 ft.) with additional pairs of stones inside at the NE to define an entrance. This faced the gap in the phase 1 earthwork and down the avenue of phase 2. The NW side of this structure was never finished and nothing can now be seen of it, except those unshaped bluestones which were incorporated in the next and final phase.

The avenue runs downhill to the NE, then bears E between the 2 hills of King Barrow Ridge (and between the Old and New King Barrows, p. 227) and reached the Avon 1 mile w of Amesbury. It comprises 2 parallel banks and ditches,

59 *Stonehenge: looking north. Aubrey Holes in arc foreground. Period of construction,*
c. 2,200–1,200 BC

the latter on the outside, with a total width of 80 ft. This feature shows clearly between Stonehenge and the road, and as a crop-mark for several hundred feet further NE.

A slight ditch surrounds the Heelstone. It is believed that this was dug by the avenue builders to preserve the sanctity of the stone while the bluestones were being dragged past on their final journey from the river to Stonehenge.

In Stonehenge phase 3, first, the bluestone double circle of phase 2 was demolished and the ground levelled. Then about 80 sarsen blocks, many weighing 20–30 tons, were dragged across from the Marlborough Downs near Avebury, 24 miles to the N. They were set up as we see them today, an outer circle about 100 ft. in diam. with a continuous ring of lintels on top, and a U-shaped setting within, with 5 pairs of uprights each with a lintel (the 'trilithons'). Two sarsens were set up at the entrance to the earthwork (one is now lost, the other fallen and called the Slaughter Stone). Finally, 4 small sarsens were erected at intervals close to the inner edge of the bank of phase 1. One of these stood up through a barrow-like mound

of earth (the 'South Barrow'; stone now lost); its opposite, also now lost, was set within a circular bank and ditch (the 'North Barrow'). The other pair of stones survives and was unsupported by such earthworks. It is thought that, since lines joining these pairs meet at the centre of the circle of sarsens, they may commemorate the elaborate laying out which must have been necessary before the sarsen circle and horsehose setting were erected.

The bluestones of phase 2 had now to be incorporated in this final structure. Recent excavation suggests that at first about 22 of the longest stones were dressed to rectangular shape and set up inside the sarsen horseshoe. The plan of this arrangement is not known but it included at least 2 pairs of uprights with lintels and 2 others joined longitudinally by a tongue-and-groove (the grooved stone is N of the tallest trilithon upright and one of the lintels can be seen, fallen, N of the NE trilithon). Meanwhile a ragged double circle of holes had been dug outside the sarsen circle (the Z and Y holes, not now visible) to receive the remaining 60 bluestones of phase 2. A change of plan then saw the abandoning of these before stones had been set in them, the dismantling of the dressed bluestone feature and the arrival at a layout which can be seen today – a circle of standing bluestones between the sarsen circle and horseshoe, and a horseshoe of uprights inside the trilithons. Finally, at the centre of the bluestone horseshoe the Altar Stone was erected – a large block of Pembrokeshire sandstone now fallen.

Features to note:

(1) The lintels of the sarsen ring are fitted end to end by tongue-and-groove joints and attached to the uprights by tenon-and-mortice.

(2) These lintels are all dressed on a curve. Their upper surfaces are all flush.

(3) The trilithons are graded in height, the tallest at the centre of the horseshoe.

(4) The upper surface of the lintels of the trilithons, also cut on a curve have a larger area to counteract the foreshortening by perspective which would otherwise appear.

(5) The lintels of the trilithons are attached to their uprights by tenon-and-mortice (notice huge tenon on top of central trilithon, mortice holes on under side of its fallen lintel).

(6) All sarsens have been hammered to a rectangular shape and their surfaces, especially inner surfaces, smoothed.

The Carvings. The outlines of some scores of axe-heads, a dagger and other symbols have been recorded. These can be pointed out on application to an attendant. The carving of these symbols of wealth and authority was clearly a ritual act and has been noticed on stone tombs and religious sites elsewhere in Britain. Though it used to be said that the outline of the dagger resembled Mycenaean weapons, it now seems more likely that the dagger portrays a native weapon, just as the temple itself was probably locally inspired. C14 determinations for phase 3: $1,720 \pm 150$ BC, $1,240 \pm 105$ BC.

Sugar Hill, barrow cemetery (SU/249773) $1\frac{1}{2}$ miles NW of Aldbourne (A419), $\frac{1}{4}$ mile E of A419. Grave goods in British Museum.

This cemetery is in a line, NW/SE. At the N there are 3 bell-barrows, all touching.

At the s end there is a bowl-barrow, separated by a few yards from the others. From N to S the diams. of the bells are 124–131 ft., and their hts. 8–10 ft. The first contained a cremation at the base with an incense cup, amber beads and a bone pin. The middle bell covered a skeleton in a grave 7 ft. long, furnished with a bronze dagger and flint arrowhead. The s bell covered a cremation with a decorated bone pin copying a style current in central Germany. The bowl-barrow is about 60 ft. in diam. and 6 ft. high. An adult had been burnt here before burial.

A short distance sw (at SU/247771) there is a famous bowl-barrow nearly 100 ft. in diam. and 6 ft. high. It covered a cremation placed on a wooden plank and furnished with the finest specimens of a type of incense cup – the Aldbourne cup – which took its name from this barrow. There was also a bronze knife and awls, beads of faience, amber, shale and fossils, and other pendants and a button of shale. N of the main burial there was a second cremation, also with an Aldbourne cup and flint arrowheads. Date of all barrows, c. 1,700–1,400 BC (fig. 7).

Thorny Down, Middle Bronze Age habitation site (SU/203338) $4\frac{1}{4}$ miles NE of Salisbury, 250 yds. N of A30, opposite turning s of Winterslow. Finds in Salisbury Museum.

This site stands in an area of open downland sheltered to the N by Thorny Down Wood. Among a group of low banks and hollows excavation has revealed a rectangular enclosure, bounded on the N, s and w by a bank and outer ditch, enclosing nearly $\frac{1}{2}$ acre of ground on which stood 9 circular huts. Among these huts some storage pits, cooking holes and many other post-holes were found. Pottery, a spearhead and bracelet of bronze and other objects show that this settlement was built by indigenous farmers settled on the land from c. 1,250 BC.

This enclosure is probably associated with the complex of linear earthworks extending N to **Snail Down** (p. 232) and to **Quarley Hill** (Hants., p. 142).

Upton Great Barrow, bell-barrow (ST/ 955423) $1\frac{1}{2}$ miles NE of Upton Lovell (s of A36), $\frac{1}{2}$ mile s of A344 to Chitterne. Grave goods in Devizes Museum.

This bell-barrow (diam. 175 ft., ht. 10 ft.), which used to have a bank outside its ditch, is one of 2 survivors of a scattered group famous for a quantity of gold and amber ornaments from one (fig. 60), and of bone pendants from another. With a cremation under the Great Barrow was found a particularly fine necklace of shale, amber and faience beads. These mounds range in date from c. 1,700–1,400 BC.

as wide a range as those from the Lake cemetery (p. 224), the richest things concentrated in the disc-barrows; they must have been deposited here c. 1,700–1,400 BC.

Winterbourne Stoke Cross Roads, barrow cemetery and Neolithic long barrow (SU/101417). In the NE angle formed by the junction of A303 and A360, 1½ miles W of Stonehenge. Grave goods in Devizes

60   *Upton Lovell golden barrow: gold plate (6 × 3 ins.), c. 1,700 BC*

West Everleigh Down, barrow cemetery. See **Everleigh Barrows.**

Wilsford, barrow cemetery (SU/118398) nearly ¾ mile SE of the Lake cemetery. Grave goods in Devizes Museum.

A cemetery (fig. 10) noted for some rich grave finds and poor present-day preservation, Wilsford includes 5 disc-barrows (diams. 150–200 ft.), a pond-barrow (diam. 94 ft.) and a saucer-barrow (diam. 118 ft., ht. 1 ft.), 9 bowls (diams., 30–100 ft., hts. 6 ins–7 ft.) and a bell (diam. 150 ft., ht. 11 ft.).

The bell-barrow covered the bones of a particularly tall man, accompanied by a stone battle-axe, a bronze axe, a bone musical instrument and a knife-handle, and a stone for smoothing the shafts of arrows. With these was a unique pronged object made of twisted bar-bronze, with 3 links of a chain hanging from it. One disc-barrow has 3 mounds inside it (today almost ploughed away). The objects from the other barrows in this group have

Museum.

This cemetery (fig. 10), which includes all barrow-types, is set out in 2 parallel lines, orientated NE/SW. The Neolithic long barrow described below is at the SW end of the group and seems to have influenced the siting of the later mounds. Moving NE from it, one comes to a bowl-barrow (1) and then to a bell-barrow with a pond-barrow (2–3) 66 ft. in diam. overlying the S edge of its ditch – presumably a deliberate imposition. The modern pond immediately S of the latter should not be mistaken for a pond-barrow. Beneath this bell-barrow, which is 12 ft. high and 178 ft. in diam., a cremation has been found, placed there in a wooden box and accompanied by a large bronze dagger, a smaller knife, bone tweezers and other objects. To the NW is another fine bell (4), 10 ft. high and 164 ft. in diam. which covered an inhumation and grave goods consisting of an urn and 2 bronze daggers of Breton form. Away from these bells stretches a line of 6 bowl-barrows (5–10); beneath the second (ht. 5 ft., diam. 80 ft.) lay an inhumation, with grave goods including a grape cup and beaver teeth. A beaker was found in the fourth.

In the parallel line of barrows to the W, the southernmost (11) is a bowl, and then a disc with a central tump, 170 ft. across and containing a cremation. Touching it NE is another disc-barrow (12) with 3 tumps which have yielded cremations, amber beads and 2 incense cups (fig. 9, bottom left). The disc is 175 ft. in diam. In the next (13), a bowl 6 ft. high, a cremation in an urn was a later addition to the mound, whose earliest burial was an inhumation. A stone mace-head of late Neolithic type was found in the material of this barrow. The row of barrows is completed by a pond-barrow (14) 96 ft. across, and then by another bowl (15).

About 100 yds. NW there is a second group of round barrows to be included in this cemetery. They are on the E side of A360, around SU/100418. There are 5 bowl-barrows (16–20), that at the W partly covered by the modern road, and 2 saucer-barrows (21–22) N of these. One of the latter is almost destroyed by the plough, but the other is a perfect example, about 100 ft. in diam., its mound 2 ft. high and its outer bank well preserved. Both saucers covered cremations. The bowl-barrows have diams. of 25–60 ft. and hts. of 2–6 ft. They covered cremations, one with an incense cup. This cemetery belongs to the period 1,700–1,400 BC.

The earliest barrow in Cross Roads Cemetery is a long barrow (at SU/100415), lying NE/SW, about 240 ft. long and broader at its NE end where it is 10 ft. high. The quarry-ditch skirting it does not continue around this end. Here we have a rare example of a long barrow which apparently covered only 1 primary burial – the flexed skeleton of a male on the old land surface at the broader end.

Winterslow, bell-barrows (SU/229353) 600 yds. N of the Pheasant Inn, on A30, 6 miles NE of Salisbury. Grave goods in Ashmolean Museum, Oxford.

This bell-barrow (ht. 4 ft., diam. 108 ft.) lies E of 2 of the largest mounds (both bells) in Britain (diams. 178 ft., 206 ft., hts. 18 ft., 12 ft. respectively). The burial at its base was an inhumation furnished with a fine bell-beaker, a slate wrist-guard, flint arrowheads and a copper knife of W European origin. Near the top of the mound a secondary cremation was found, wrapped in cloth and placed in an urn of Cornish design. With this was another urn of Wessex type. In the first were beads of amber, a bronze awl and a bronze razor; fragments of hair found with these have been identified as human eyebrows – perhaps belonging to the mourners.

If the primary burial may be dated c. 2,000 BC, the urns higher up may have been deposited c. 1,250–1,000 BC. It is possible that there may have been another secondary cremation in this barrow, situated between the burials already described and intermediate in date. Nothing is known of the burials beneath the other bell-barrows here.

IRON AGE

*****Barbury Castle,** hill-fort (SU/149763) 2½ miles S of Wroughton (A361), reached by track – the Ridgeway – crossing Broadhinton–Marlborough road. Finds in Devizes Museum.

An oval hill-fort commanding much country, Barbury consists of 2 ramparts and ditches with entrances E and W. The E entrance has additional outworks. Aerial photographs have revealed the existence of huts and storage pits within the 11½ acres so enclosed. Casual finds from inside include fittings for chariots. Eastward, along the slope below the chalk scarp, the 'Celtic' fields tilled perhaps by those who lived here may be seen (see also p. 237, **Burderop Down**). Not dated.

Battlesbury Camp, hill-fort (ST/898456) 1½ miles E of Warminster (A36, A350, A362), 1¼ miles along the road to Imber. Finds in Devizes Museum.

Battlesbury is irregular in shape, its defences following the contours of the hill. Its triple ramparts, double on the SE, enclose 23½ acres. There are entrances with outworks NE and NW. Pits found within the fortifications contained late

Iron Age pottery, the hub of a chariot wheel, an iron carpenter's saw and a latch-lifter for a hut door. These indicate permanent occupation. That its inhabitants came to a violent end is indicated by the discovery of many graves containing men, women and children outside the NW entrance. It is not yet known whether the Roman legions put the villagers to the sword or whether this was the result of inter-tribal warfare before the Roman Conquest. Not dated.

Bratton Castle, hill-fort and Neolithic long barrow (ST/901516) 2 miles E of Westbury (A350, B4098), 1 mile SW of Bratton (B3098).

Bratton Castle is roughly rectangular in plan and has a commanding view in all directions. It has 2 banks and ditches except on the E where there is only 1. They enclose 23 acres. There are entrances NE and S utilised by the modern road; both have outworks. The date of construction of this hill-fort is unknown. The famous white horse, re-cut in 1778, lies outside on the W side.

Near the centre of the hill-fort there is a barrow 230 ft. in length, orientated E/W and 12 ft. high at the E. Its side-ditches are now silted up and hollows in the mound indicate 19th-century excavations. Only 2 adults appear to have been buried beneath this great mound. They lay on a platform at the E end and had been partly burnt. Date, c. 3,500–2,500.

Burderop Down, field system (SU/164762 centre) 5 miles NW of Marlborough (A4, A345, A346), 2¾ miles SE of Wroughton (A361, B4005).

This is one of the finest groups of 'Cel-

61   *Burderop Down: 'Celtic' field system overlaid by medieval enclosure. Barbury Castle, Iron Age hill-fort, top right*

tic' fields in England (fig. 61). It extends along the hillside E of Barbury Castle (p. 236) for over 1 mile, covering an area of about 140 acres. These fields have not been dated by excavation but are likely to have been started in the Iron Age. Romano-British pottery on the surface suggests continuation into Roman times. At SU/160765 an enclosure, probably medieval, overlies the fields. It is likely that those tilling the fields may have lived in Barbury Castle.

Casterley Camp, enclosure (SU/115535) 1½ miles SW of Upavon (A342, A345), reached by track off A345. Finds in Devizes Museum.

This is an irregular 4-sided enclosure of 68 acres, defended by a bank and ditch with original entrances at the N, S and W. The latter is approached by a hollow way which leads to 'Celtic' fields. At the NE the defences bulge outwards to enclose the head of a dry valley and cover otherwise hidden ground. Excavation has shown that at the centre there are sub-rectangular and pear-shaped enclosures, with evidence that they may have contained temples and are earlier than the surrounding earthworks. The latter also are unfinished. The bank of the earthwork is at least 5 ft. high around the SE and the ditch was shown to be V-shaped, 4–5 ft. deep. Post-holes for a simple gate were found at the S entrance. Date, early 1st century AD.

Castle Ditches, hill-fort (ST/963283) ¾ mile N of Swallowcliffe (A30), approached by track off road to Tisbury.

Double banks and ditches, triple on the SE, where the ground is flatter, enclose 24 acres. This hill-fort is roughly triangular in plan. There are original entrances E and possibly W. This fort is not dated.

Figsbury Ring, hill-fort (SU/188338) 3½ miles NE of Salisbury, ¼ mile N of A30. Objects in Devizes Museum.

The outer bank and ditch enclose a nearly circular area of 15 acres. Some way within there is a second ditch, dug to provide more chalk for the main bank. Excavations have shown that the outer bank was heightened twice. There are entrances E and W, with outworks damaged by ploughing. No traces of permanent settlement have been found here but

the construction of this unusual fort can safely be placed in the 5th or 4th centuries BC.

Fyfield Down, 'Celtic' fields (SU/142710) S of the path linking Avebury and Marlborough over the downs; 2¼ miles E of Avebury.

This group is undated but likely to be Iron Age with Romano-British and medieval additions. Some of the field banks have been augmented by sarsen boulders cleared from the fields by the original farmers. A sunken trackway along the S edge of the system must have joined it to a settlement not yet located.

Grim's Ditch, boundary ditches. See Hampshire, p. 136.

Knap Hill, enclosure. See Neolithic.

Liddington Castle, hill-fort (SU/209797) 5 miles SE of Swindon, ¼ mile S of the Ridgway which joins A345 and A419. Finds in Ashmolean Museum, Oxford.

The roughly oval hill-fort of 7¾ acres has a bank, ditch and counterscarp bank, with traces of sarsens as a bank-facing. There is a SE entrance; on the opposite side of the fort there is a dip in the bank and slight rise in the ditch which suggest a former NW entrance slightly in-turned, blocked in antiquity. Date, 5th–4th century BC.

Martinsell Hill, hill-fort (SU/177639) 1¼ miles NE of Oare (A345).

A well-sited but weakly defended rectangular camp of about 33 acres is set in the SE corner of Martinsell Hill. Without excavation its original entrances cannot be identified but one may be at the NE It has not yet been dated by excavation.

In Withy Copse, outside the N rampart, a large Belgic rubbish pit was excavated in 1907. Finds in Devizes Museum.

Membury. See Berkshire.

Ogbury Camp, enclosure (SU/143383) 2 miles SW of Amesbury, ¼ mile NE of Durnford.

This is a weak, many-sided enclosure of about 62 acres. Today its bank stands 8 ft. above the centre of its ditch which is now completely silted up. The gap on the E side may be original. The area enclosed has been divided up into a series of fields, but these may not be contemporary. Not dated.

Oldbury Camp, hill-fort (SU/049693) 3¼ miles SE of Calne (A4, B3102), 1 mile SE of Cherhill (A4). Finds in Devizes Museum.

This triangular hill-fort of 25 acres is defended by 2 banks and ditches, with an in-turned entrance on the E. It is not known whether the SE entrance is original. The area enclosed is divided across by a small bank and ditch running N/S; this is probably not contemporary. Pottery of the 2nd–3rd centuries BC has been found in rubbish pits inside. The white horse is not more than 200 years old.

Olivers Camp, hill-fort (SU/001646) 2 miles NNW of Devizes (A342, A360, A361), W of path from Roundway to Heddington. Finds in Devizes Museum.

This almost rectangular earthwork consists of a bank and ditch enclosing about 3 acres and commanding much country. There is an entrance-gap through the NE side which excavation showed to have had a wooden gateway. On this side the V-shaped ditch had been dug to a depth of 14 ft. Datable pottery found under the bank suggests that this camp was built about 450 BC and may never have been permanently occupied.

Pewsey Spectacles, habitation site (SU/177574) 1¾ miles SE of Pewsey (A345, B3087), ¾ mile NW of Down Farm, on S side of Pewsey–Everleigh minor road.

The Spectacles comprise 2 roughly oval banks and external ditches, 450 ft. apart and joined by a ditch. Both are slight and have been damaged by the plough. The E circle of the Spectacles is roughly 400 ft. in diam. and has been ploughed flat except near the road, where its NE arc still shows. The other circle lies to the W and has axes of 300 and 400 ft. It has an entrance facing W. Depressions can be seen within both circles. Excavations 160 years ago yielded much pottery and other domestic rubbish. It is likely that both earthworks (each enclosing about 3 acres) surrounded farm buildings like those excavated at Little Woodbury, near Salisbury (models, etc. in Salisbury Museum). This specialised form of settlement enclosure, well represented in the S of England, appears to have been evolved in the 1st century BC.

Scratchbury Camp, hill-fort (ST/912443) 1¼ miles NW of Heytesbury (A36, A344), reached by track off A36. Finds in Devizes

Museum.

This superbly placed hill-fort, looking across at Battlesbury Camp, encloses 37 acres within a bank and ditch with a counterscarp bank. Its irregular 4-sided shape follows the contours of a steep hill. There are 2 entrances on the E side and possibly a third on the NW. Remains of a central inner earthwork of much smaller size can be seen. This resembles the earlier enclosure at Yarnbury and has recently been dated c. 350 BC. A bank and ditch can also be seen running across the hill in a NE/SW direction. This may belong to an early phase of the hill-fort. A Romano-British or later ditch, running E/W and turning S sharply at the SW corner of the hill-fort, overlies the Iron Age earthworks and encloses the S side. The main ramparts have not yet been dated by excavation.

Whitesheet, hill-fort (ST/804346) 1½ miles NW of Mere (A303, B3095), reached by track off B3092.

Precipitous ground on the S and W is defended by a single rampart but towards the N this triangular fort of 15 acres is protected by 3 lines of ramparts. There are several entrance-gaps through these, none yet established by excavation. Not dated.

*Winkelbury Camp, promontory fort (ST/952218) ¼ mile SE of Berwick St John (S of A30). Finds in Salisbury Museum.

This camp shows 3 phases of design, none completed. The earliest is the bank and ditch across the spur at the S, with staggered near-central entrance. Next came the bank and ditch designed to enclose the whole of the spur to the N, an area of 12½ acres. Finally, a small, almost circular hill-fort was begun at the N end of the spur, with entrance at the SE and another, perhaps of phase 2, at the N. Date, as known at present c. 5th–4th century BC: the fort is (1976) under large-scale excavation by the Department of the Environment.

Yarnbury Castle, hill-fort and 'Celtic' fields (SU/035404) 2½ miles W of Winterbourne Stoke (A303). Finds in Devizes Museum.

Perhaps the most rewarding site in Wiltshire, the massive outer earthworks (2 banks and ditches with a slighter third bank and ditch) having a very elaborate in-turned entrance on the E, enclose an almost circular area of 28½ acres. Inside this there are traces of an earlier fort of about 9 acres comprising a single bank and V-shaped ditch with a known entrance on its w side. Excavation has revealed remains of a wooden gate here and shown that the ditch was 8–9 ft. deep. The inner fort was built in the 7th–5th century BC. The outer fortifications must belong to the 2nd century BC with occupation running through the Belgic phase to the arrival of the Romans.

A small enclosure added outside to the main ramparts on the w is probably a late Romano-British stock enclosure.

Remains of the pens of an 18th-century AD sheep fair can be seen overlying the SE part of the first Iron Age fort, and the inner face of the inner rampart of the later hill-fort has been dug into along the SE to provide more pens (fig. 62).

In the morning or evening a system of 'Celtic' fields can be seen on either side of the shallow valley extending NE from the main entrance to Yarnbury Castle.

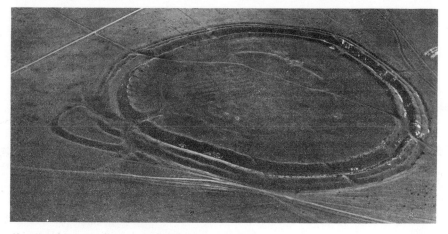

62   *Yarnbury Castle: Iron Age hill-fort. Earlier hill-fort at centre, partly overlaid by grid of eighteenth-century sheep pens. Romano-British kite-shaped enclosure added to later hill-fort, top right*

Yorkshire, North

MESOLITHIC

*Star Carr, dwelling site (TA/027810) 4¾ miles s of Scarborough, 1 mile NNE of A64/A1039 junction. Finds at Scarborough Museum, Museum of Archaeology and Ethnology, Cambridge and British Museum (Natural History).

This site is not now visible but since its position is recorded on the 1 in. O.S. map it must be briefly described. It comprised a rough platform of birch brushwood situated close to the edge of a prehistoric lake. Two birch tree trunks extended towards the water and may have been a jetty for fishermen's canoes. The area of settlement was about 200 sq. yds. In it was found a dense concentration of flint, bone, wooden and other implements and ornaments, the richest collection of Middle Stone Age material so far found in Britain. These had been left by a community of hunters and fishermen who camped at this spot for several years, c. 7,500 BC.

*Victoria Cave, inhabited cave (SD/838650) 1¾ miles NE of Settle (A65, B6479). Finds in Tot Lord's Pig Yard Museum, Settle, British Museum.

During the last phases of the Ice Age this cave, which comprises 3 chambers, had been a den for hyaenas: with their bones were found those of hippopotamus, elephant and woolly rhinoceros. Higher up, bear, fox and red deer were represented. Above these deposits the remains of Palaeolithic and Mesolithic hunters have been found – animal bones, flints and a typical double-edged barbed harpoon of fossilised red-deer antler: date, c. 10,000–8,000 BC.

NEOLITHIC

*Ayton East Field, long barrow (TA/000864) 2¾ miles sw of Scarborough, ¾ mile NE of East Ayton (A170, B1262). Grave goods in British Museum.

This barrow is about 85 ft. long and orientated N/S. It is higher and wider at the N. No side-ditches now show. A deposit of human bones was found beneath a pile of stones on which a great fire seems to have been burnt in the manner of several Yorkshire long barrows. With some of the bones a series of typical Neolithic flint tools had been deposited – leaf-shaped arrowheads, 3 axe-heads and an adze-head, flint knives with polished edges, boar's tusks and an antler handle. This is one of the very rare grave deposits in an unchambered long barrow. Date, c. 3,500–2,500 BC.

Cana, sacred site. See Bronze Age.

Castle Dykes, sacred site (SD/982873) 3½ miles SE of Bainbridge (A684), 1½ miles sw of Aysgarth (A684), s of track to Haw Head.

This site is slightly oval, its max. diam. being 195 ft. It has a bank with a ditch inside and 1 original entrance facing E. Two other gaps in its bank are probably modern. Date, c., 2,500–1,700 BC.

*Duggleby Howe, round barrow (SE/881669) 2¼ miles ESE of North Grimston (B1248, B1253), SE of Duggleby, on N side of B1253. Grave goods in Transport Museum, Hull.

This is perhaps the most spectacular Neolithic round barrow in Britain. It is about 120 ft. in diam. and still 20 ft. high. Originally it would have been over 30 ft. high. Excavation has shown that this barrow consists of an inner chalky mound, sealing a deep grave pit and covered in turn by a layer of clay with an outer capping of chalk. In the upper part of this mound there were 22 cremations, 1 buried with a bone pin. In the lower part of the mound and in the pit beneath there were 10 inhumations of adults and children. Grave goods placed with those included long bone pins, a flint knife with ground edges, other flint tools, a macehead of antler, a flint axe-head and an early Neolithic bowl.

Other cremations found in this barrow make a total of 53; it is likely that the original total might have been about 100. All appear to have been deposited at one time. Date, c. 2,500–2,000 BC.

Hanging Grimston, long barrow. See Bronze Age.

*Hedon Howe, round barrow (SE/784665) 3¼ miles S of Malton (A64, A169, B1248, B1257), ¾ mile SW of Langton. Grave goods in Transport Museum, Hull.

In 1893 this mound was 8 ft. high and 50 ft. in diam. It is one of the few Neolithic round barrows in Britain. There were 5 stone slab-lined burial cists beneath the barrow, each 4–9 ft. long. The unburnt remains of 1–3 adults were found in each cist, including a cremation in the central cist. The pottery in the cists and in the mound included a round-based Neolithic bowl, a beaker and a food vessel. Joints of meat and flint tools also occurred in the mound. Date, c. 2,500–1,700 BC.

*Helperthorpe, long barrow (SE/963679) 3 miles WNW of Langtoft (B1249), ½ mile NE of Belle Vue Farm.

Little now remains of this long barrow. It lies E/W, 96 ft. long, 48 ft. wide at the E and 42 ft. across at the W. There are side-ditches. Five burials were found here in 1868, 2 being connected by a trench and 1 being a cremation. Much wood ash was found on the old land surface sealed by the mound. Date, c. 3,500–2,500 BC.

Howe Hill, Duggleby, round barrow. See **Duggleby Howe.**

Howe Hill, Scambridge, long barrow. See **Scambridge.**

Jubilee Cave, inhabited cave (SD/838656) 1¾ miles NE of Settle (A65, B6479), 1,500 ft. N of Victoria Cave (see Mesolithic).

This is a small cave with 2 entrances. Apart from Iron Age and Romano-British pottery, some Neolithic Peterborough ware has been recorded which suggests habitation, c. 1,800 BC.

*Kepwick, long barrow SE/492904) 6¼ miles NE of Thirsk (A19, A61, A168, A170), 1¼ miles ESE of Kepwick, on Little Moor.

This barrow is 100 ft. long, 30 ft. wide at the E and 25 ft. wide at the W. It is uniformly about 4 ft. high. The incomplete and disarticulated skeletons of 5 adults and youths were found 15–25 ft. from the E end, at the base of the barrow. Date, c. 3,500–2,500 BC.

Nunwick, sacred site. See Bronze Age, **Thornborough Circles.**

*Scambridge, long barrow (SE/892861) 5 miles NE of Pickering (A169, A170), 2¼ miles NNW of Ebberston (A170), ¼ mile NW of High Scambridge Farm.

This long barrow is orientated E/W. It is 165 ft. long, 9 ft. high at the E end and tapering from 54 ft. at the E to 46 ft. at the W, where it is 7 ft. high. The burials were at the E end, on a bed of yellow clay. The disordered bones of 14 people were found, spread over 40 ft. down the centre of the mound. They had been burnt in a crematorium trench 40 ft. from the E end covered by limestone boulders and rubble. Clearly the bones had lost all flesh and sinew long before burial: the skulls of several seem to have been battered, perhaps before death. Date, c. 3,500–2,500 BC.

Thornborough, sacred sites and cursus. See Bronze Age.

*Willerby Wold, long barrow, Bronze Age round barrow (TA/029761) 2¼ miles S of Staxton (A64, A1039, B1249) 1¼ miles E of Willerby Wold House (B1249). Grave goods in British Museum.

Excavation has shown that the original dimensions of this trapezoidal long barrow, lying NE/SW, were 122 ft. in length and 35 ft. in width at the E. It had side-ditches and its max. ht. today is 3 ft. The mound covers a mortuary enclosure defined by a narrow, continuous ditch, the E end being concave and marked by timber uprights set in a trench. This had been burnt down early in the burial sequence. Here at least 3 bodies had been stored prior to burial. A crematorium had been built at the E end of this enclosure after the burning of the latter. The long-barrow mound was built over the enclosure and finally the crematorium had been fired. Date, c. 3,000 BC (C14).

BRONZE AGE

*Acklam Wold, round barrows (SE/796620 centre), 5¾ miles S of Norton (A64, A169, B1248, B1257), 1 mile E of, and overlooking Acklam and Leavening. Grave goods in Transport Museum, Hull.

There were originally at least 17

barrows between Leavening Brow and Stone Sleight. All are now denuded by the plough. Burials by cremation and inhumation have been recorded from these mounds: a skeleton beneath the barrow at SE/802620 had been buried with 2 pairs of fine jet buttons at its feet – perhaps originally fastened to leggings. At SE/795622, the w of 3 mounds covered at least 6 inhumations, with 1 of which a flat bronze dagger blade 5 ins. long had been deposited. A superb flint knife 7¼ ins. long was found placed in the hand of a skeleton beneath the mound at SE/794624. These barrows were accumulating c. 1,700–1,400 BC.

Allan Tops, settlement, cairns (NZ/828028 centre) 6¼ miles sw of Whitby (A169, A171, A174), 1 mile NW of Goathland, ½ mile NE of Beck Hole.

At the centre of this overgrown complex there is a series of embanked enclosures together with long banks running N/S at the E end of the area. Scattered among these earthworks there are over 70 small stone cairns. Some of the enclosures are probably fields, stones forming their banks having been cleared from the areas to be cultivated. Larger stones can be found in some banks which appear to have been built in and these may have been associated with dwellings. The cairns are not necessarily contemporary nor have they been proved to cover burials. Date of complex, c. 1,700–500 BC.

Blakey Topping, stone circle (SE/873934) 7¼ miles NE of Pickering (A169, A170), 2¾ miles NE of Lockton. There are the remains of a circle 50 ft. in diam. on the sw side of Blakey Topping. Three stones survive, each about 6 ft. high. Some of the holes in which others stood can still be seen. Date, c. 2,200–1,400 BC.

Boltby Scar, round barrow. See Iron Age.

Bridestones, barrow circle (NZ/576978) on Bilsdale East Moor, 5½ miles SE of Broughton (B1257), ½ mile NE of Oak House.

This circle of stones, about 40 ft. in diam., is probably the remains of a retaining wall to a barrow or some other form of burial. There are over 40 small stones, originally touching each other around the circumference of the circle. There are traces of an outer earth bank.

Date, c. 2,000–1,400 BC.

Cana, sacred site. See **Thornborough Circles.**

Cass Hill, settlement, cairns. See **Allan Tops.**

Castleton Rigg, settlement (NZ/682041) 8½ miles SE of Guisborough (A171, A173), 2½ miles ssw of Castleton.

This long narrow spur is cut across at map ref. above and at NZ/684048 by 2 earthworks. The more southerly, High Stone Dyke, has a series of large stones along the crest of its bank which would originally have formed a close-set wall. The banks themselves were stone-faced. Traces of huts, fields and barrows occur on the spur thus protected: all are believed to be contemporary and c. 1,000–500 BC.

Crown End, settlement and cairns (NZ/668075) 6½ miles SE of Guisborough, 1½ miles sw of Castleton; on Westerdale Moor.

An accumulation of small (and some larger) burial mounds are here associated with compact walled settlements but may not necessarily be contemporary. The small mounds are 6–12 ft. in diam. and recall those on **Danby Rigg** (below). The settlement itself is in 2 parts, a large triangular walled enclosure containing many circular huts and paddocks (at map ref. above), and a circular embanked site sw of this, with large stones incorporated and entrances facing NE and sw. It is 129 ft. in diam. and its purpose obscure. There are 3 larger barrows 400 ft. to the sw. An earthwork cuts across this spur between the Esk and Baysdale Beck at NZ/658070. Originally it had comprised a bank, ditch and counterscarp bank, both banks having a line of close-set stones along their crests. Since settlement and cairns disappear to the w, the whole group of sites may be broadly contemporary, c. 1,250–1,000 BC.

Danby Rigg, cairns, circle, fields and earthworks (NZ/710065, centre of cairns), 8½ miles SE of Guisborough (A171, A173), 1½ miles s of Danby.

This steep-sided spur contains over 800 minute circular mounds, the purpose of which has not yet been established. Presumably they are associated with

Bronze Age burial rites but burials have not been found beneath them. At NZ/708065 there is a broad standing stone over 5 ft. high which is the only survivor of a circle set inside an earth bank, recorded in the last century as having a diam. of 42 ft. At the centre of this circle

fields with which the earthworks on Danby Rigg above may be associated; these all belong to the later Bronze Age or even the Iron Age.

Date of mounds and circles, c. 1,700–1,400 BC. Earthworks and fields contemporary or c. 500 BC–1st century AD.

63   *Devil's Arrows, Boroughbridge: Bronze Age standing stones*

a cremation was found beneath 2 collared urns. Other single standing stones can be found among the cairns. Nearly 500 yds. s of this circle there are 2 barrow mounds of more normal size, one with a stone retaining wall around it. Danby Rigg is cut across by 2 groups of earthworks which protect the burial ground. The first of these has its centre about NZ/708061. It is a stone rubble structure without a ditch. There are 3 banks and 2 ditches 700 yds. further s, the **Double Dyke.** Between these 2 earthworks there is a second circle of earth and stones which may have contained a central burial; it is 70 ft. in diam. It is noticeable that the inner earthwork encloses the majority of the cairns; it has not yet been proved, however, that the earthworks and cemetery are contemporary. At NZ/718064 there is a group of large rectangular field banks, probably 'Celtic'

Devil's Arrows (W.R.), standing stones (SE/391666) sw of Boroughbridge (A1, A1167).

These 3 naturally shaped stones are almost in a line N/S, 200 and 370 ft. apart (fig. 63). They have hts. of 18 ft. (at N) and 22½ ft. They are made of millstone grit quarried at Knaresborough, 6½ miles to the sw. The grooves at their tops are the result of uneven weathering. They should perhaps be considered as part of the line of sacred sites extending 11 miles to the N, along the course of the Ure – the Thornborough, Nunwick, Hutton Moor and Cana circles (pp. 247–249). Date, c. 2,200–1,400 BC.

Flat Howe (N.R.), round barrow (NZ/855046) on Sleights Moor, 4½ miles sw of Whitby (A169, A171, A174), between **High Bridestones** and A169.

There is no record of the contents of Flat Howe but it is important because its mound is contained by a ring of stones still clearly visible. Date, c. 1,700–1,400 BC.

*Folkton (E.R.), round barrow (TA/ 059777) 4¼ miles sw of Filey (A1039), 1½ miles SSE of Flixton (A1039); NW of Long Plantation. Grave goods in British Museum.

Never a large mound, this barrow covered 3 carved drum-shaped chalk objects, among the most remarkable things from Bronze Age England (fig. 64). The mound covered 2 circular ditches. Between these a grave was found containing the bones of a child, the chalk 'drums' and a bone pin. Within the inner ditch the skeletons of 4 adults and a child were found near the level of the old land surface. At the centre of the barrow a mound of flints covered the bones of a male and female with a bell-beaker. These skeletons appear to have been reburied in antiquity after their skulls had been removed. Date of burials, c. 1,700–1,400 BC.

The chalk 'drums' are carved with geometric patterns and each is 4–5 ins. in diam. They appear to be solid copies of the incense cups of this period.

64　*Folkton: carved chalk ritual object (diam. 4 ins.), c. 1,700 BC*

*Hanging Grimston, round barrows and Neolithic long barrow (about SE/810608) 7 miles s of Malton. Grave goods in Transport Museum, Hull.

This group of barrows lies on either side of the Roman road between SE/805614 and SE/819601. There is a long barrow at SE/808608. Now denuded by the plough,

it is about 80 × 50 ft., orientated E/W and 2–3 ft. high. It must originally have been nearly 10 ft. high. It has flanking ditches 27 ft. wide and 6 ft. deep. Excavation exposed a ritual pit outside the E end of mound, while the latter appears to have been faced by an incurving line of timbers. The remains of more than 20 pigs were found scattered in the mound, together with other animal bones and 4 early Neolithic bowls, but no human burials. Date, c. 3,500–2,500 BC.

All the round barrows in this group are now almost levelled. They have yielded cremations and inhumations, beakers, collared urns, a food vessel, a stone battle-axe, flint tools and a jet button. The central mound of 3 contiguous barrows (SE/ 806613) covered an internal stone ring 21½ ft. in diam., enclosing 11 skeletons, one cremated. There was a beaker with 1 of these. The remains of a funeral pyre were found beneath one of the 4 most southerly mounds. Date of round barrows, c. 1,700–1,400 BC.

Hawthorn Hill, settlement, cairns. See **Allan Tops.**

High Bridestones, stone circles (NZ/ 850046) 5 miles sw of Whitby (A169, A171, A174), 1½ miles ESE of Grosmont, s of road from latter to A169.

There are the remains of 2 circles, both originally 30–40 ft. in diam. Each circle has only 3 of its stones standing, with a few survivors fallen. The tallest stone is 7 ft. high. There are single standing stones outside these circles, 1 to the s, 3 to the N. Date, c. 2,200–1,400 BC.

Hutton Moor, sacred site. See **Thornborough Circles.**

John Cross Rigg, cairns and earthworks (NZ905025) 5¼ miles s of Whitby (A169, A171, A174), 1¼ miles sw of A171/B1416 junction, on Fylingdales Moor.

There are more than 1,200 very small mounds in this burial ground, an accumulation characteristic of the Cleveland Hills. They are assumed to be connected with burial. The cemetery is cut across at NZ/ 905023 by an earthwork comprising 4 banks and 3 ditches. Originally there was a wall of close-set stone uprights along the crest of each bank. The s rampart also had facings of large stones. The cairns are c. 1,700–1,400 BC. The earthworks have not yet been dated, but may be Iron Age.

*Loose Howe, round barrow (NZ/703008) on Danby High Moor, $4\frac{3}{4}$ miles s of Danby, E of road over Rosedale Moor to Rosedale Abbey; $3\frac{1}{4}$ miles NW of latter. Grave goods in British Museum.

This barrow is 60 ft. in diam. and 7 ft. high. It does not appear to have a surrounding ditch. Excavation has shown that the mound has an earthy core covered by stones, which had a circular stone retaining wall. The main burial lay NW of the centre. It consisted of a corpse buried fully dressed (including leather shoes and linen materials), laid extended in a wooden coffin, upon a layer of reeds, rushes and straw, with a grass or straw pillow. Branches of hazel with hazel husks suggested burial in the autumn. A flat bronze dagger was with the corpse. The oak coffin it lay in had a wooden lid which, like the coffin itself, seems to have been built as a canoe; alongside them in the grave-pit there was a third; all are about 9 ft. long. Two ft. E of the centre of the barrow there had been a secondary burial after cremation, the bones contained in a collared urn and furnished with a stone battle-axe, a heavy bronze dagger and a bronze T-shaped pin of central German origin. Date of barrow, c. 1,700 BC; later burial, c. 1,400 BC.

Maiden Castle, earthwork and barrows (SE/023981) 11 miles w of Richmond, $1\frac{1}{4}$ miles sw of Reeth (B6270), s of Ivy House.

This site cannot be matched closely in England, except perhaps by the bank and ditch of phase 1 at Stonehenge. It is roughly circular, with a diam. of about 300 ft. and consists of an earth bank with a ditch outside; an entrance faces E. The latter is approached by an avenue of stones 120 yds. long.

The large barrow approached by the avenue is probably contemporary, though nothing is known of its contents. Date of sites, c. 1,700–1,400 BC.

Nunwick, sacred site. See **Thornborough Circles.**

*Sharpe Howes, barrow cemetery (TA/049777) $4\frac{1}{2}$ miles sw of Filey (A1039), $1\frac{1}{4}$ miles s of Flixton (A1039), sw of Folkton Wold Farm. Grave goods in

65   *Sharpe Howes: food vessel, diam. 7 ins.*

British Museum.

Of the 6 barrows in this cemetery, 1 at the E has been destroyed. Of the others, that at the s has a diam. of 80 ft. and a ht. of 8 ft. The others extend N in a ragged line. From s to N, the mounds contained the following burials:

(1) The core of this large mound was of chalk blocks on a chalk 'platform', revetted with chalk slabs. Over it there was earth, followed by an outer jacket of chalk rubble. At the centre of the mound a large chalk-cut cist contained a crouched female skeleton with a food vessel (fig. 65).

(2) A mound NE now destroyed. A food vessel was found with the skeleton of an old man.

(3) A small mound NW of (1). An inhumation of an adult male lay in a cist, furnished with a flint knife. Similar tools and a food vessel were found in 3 other graves, in 1 of which there was also a cremation.

(4) NE of the last, this barrow had a lower mound of earth, with an additional heap of chalk surrounded by a chalk 'wall' with an entrance s. Together with a male skeleton and a food vessel, there was an empty grave here.

(5) Nothing is known of the contents of the next mound, NW of the last.

(6) The northernmost mound covered a scattered cremation and another in a cist. The latter included a food vessel, flint knife and bone pin. A second pit contained an inhumation. Date of cemetery, c.

1,700–1,400 BC.
Shooting House Rigg, cairns and earthworks. See **John Cross Rigg.**
*Snowdon Carr, carvings, settlement (about SE/177512) 4 miles NNW of Otley (A659, A660, A6039, B6451).

A small series of carvings can be found on open moorland at Snowdon Carr (fig. 66), all within 1½ mile radius of the map ref. above. There are hollows, a few with circles around them, and many lines. An outlying carved stone can be found at SE/182496, midway along and just N of the northernmost wall of Greystone Plantation.

The settlement, which may be later than the carvings, lies at SE/179514. On the spur overlooking Low Snowdon there is a D-shaped enclosure 70 × 80 ft. This has a bank and slight trench inside it sufficient to support a stockade. A series of circular huts lies NW of the enclosure, the westernmost of them being isolated, 30 ft. in diam. At least 30 small cairns have been located near the huts. No burials have yet been found beneath these. Traces of paddock and field boundaries

can also be found NW of the main enclosure. Date, c. 2,200–1,400 BC.
Standing Stones Rigg, circle (SE/983969) 6 miles NW of Scarborough, 2¼ miles NW of Cloughton (A171). Finds in Scarborough Museum.

This circle has a diam. of about 32 ft. and contained at least 24 stones, 1½–2 ft. high. Central features including, perhaps, a burial have been recorded. Four stones from this feature bearing cup-and-ring marks are now in Scarborough Museum. Date, c. 2,200–1,400 BC.
Thompson's Rigg, cairns (SE/882922) 7 miles NE of Pickering (A169, A170), 2¾ miles NE of Lockton (off A169); N of Staindale Forest.

This is a cemetery of small mounds of the type peculiar to the Cleveland Hills. It contains more than 100 mounds concentrated on a spur overlooking Crosscliffe Beck. Date, c. 1,700–1,400 BC.
*Thornborough, Hutton Moor and **Cana,** sacred sites, cursus and barrows (SE/285795; SE/353735; SE/361718) 5½ miles N of Ripon, 1 mile NE of West Tanfield (A6108) for the Thornborough Circles:

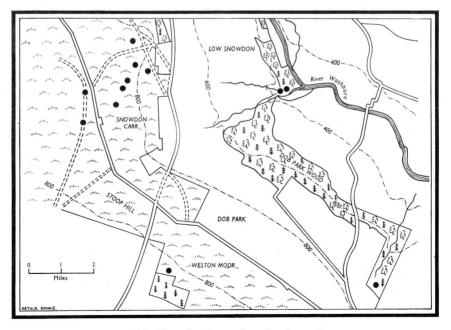

66 Snowdon Carr: plan of rock carvings

3¼ miles E of Ripon, N and S of minor road through Sharrow, joining A61 to A168, for other sites.

Early in Bronze Age times the land about Ripon, between the Ure and the Swale, became a religious centre. Six enormous sacred sites were built in an area 7 miles long; among them at least 28 round barrows were accumulated.

The most impressive henge monu-ments are the 3 Thornborough Circles (fig. 67). Of these, the central one is the most accessible, the N one the best pre-served (because it is protected from the plough by trees). Each circle, like those E of Ripon, has a max. diam. of about 800 ft. They are all nearly circular, with en-trances NW and SE. Each has a massive bank, originally about 10 ft. high, with a ditch inside and outside it, about 65 ft.

67   *Thornborough Circles: henge monuments in line (North Circle under trees, bottom left)*

wide and 8–10 ft. deep. The outer ditch of each circle is now filled up by ploughing. Broad spaces about 40 ft. wide separate the banks from their ditches – an architectural refinement found nowhere else in England on such a scale. These circles have been built in a straight line orientated NW/SE: they are ¼ mile apart.

Excavation in 1952 suggested that when first built each bank had been coated with a deposit of gypsum crystals in an attempt to whiten it. This may have been inspired by the blazing white of similar circles built in the chalk country of Wessex or the Wolds. The gypsum occurs in large deposits a few miles down the Ure.

A ceremonial avenue, or cursus, has recently been discovered from the air. It lies beneath the central circle and is at least a mile in length. It is straight, running NE/SW and ending in the gravel pit SW of this circle, close to the railway line. It is not visible on the ground, excavation in 1952 showing that it had become silted up and grass-grown when the circles were built. But sometimes it can be seen as a dark green pair of lines when covered by cereal crops. Its ditches are about 100 ft. apart. A cross-section through the N ditch can be seen (1959) in the N corner of the quarry, close to the track to Camp House and the N circle.

These avenues are of late Neolithic date in Britain; the presence of one beneath – therefore earlier than – the Thornborough Circle suggests that the latter is of early Bronze Age date, c. 1,700–1,400 BC. This date is borne out by the concentration of round barrows in the vicinity of the circles (below).

The circles on Hutton Moor and at Cana are less impressive because they have been reduced by ploughing. They should be seen nevertheless, since they are part of a concentration of sacred sites unmatched in the N of England. Recently aerial photographs have revealed the remains of a third circle here, at Nunwick, still visible on the ground about SE/323747. This appears to be a smaller circle with no outer ditch, aligned on the 3 Thornborough Circles. Its diam. is 300 ft. These sites must be contemporary with the Thornborough Circles. They are identical in design but their entrances are orientated N/S.

Many barrows can be found close to the circles – the resting places of those chiefs whose people worshipped there. Most are now sadly reduced by ploughing and their surrounding ditches cannot be seen. The Centre Hill barrow (SE/287791), between the central and southern Thornborough Circles, is 90 ft. in diam. and 3 ft. high. A skeleton was found at its centre, buried in a wooden coffin and furnished with a food vessel and flint knife. There are 3 barrows close together (SE/286801) E of the northern Thornborough Circle, S of B6267. One is 80 ft. in diam. and 3½ ft. high, the others are 60 ft. across and 1 ft. high. They covered cremation burials. There are 3 badly damaged mounds NW of Hutton Grange (on A61), about SE/347755. These covered cremations, associated with incense cups and larger pots.

There is a fine barrow, tree-covered, N of Copt Hewick Hall (SE/348724).

All these mounds belong to the period 1,700–1,400 BC.

Westerdale Moor, settlement and cairns. See **Crown End.**

*Western Howes, round barrows (NZ/682023) on Danby High Moor, 4¼ miles SSW of Danby, E of road from Castleton to Hutton-le-Hole. Grave goods in British Museum.

There are 3 mounds here. The largest, 32 ft. in diam., had a central core of stones about 14 ft. in diam., among which 2 collared urns were found about 1863. One contained a cremation, incense cup, bone pins and other tools and a stone battle-axe. The smallest mound in the group covered a cremation. No burial has been located in the third mound which is 28 ft. in diam. and 3–4 ft. high. Date of group, c. 1,700–1,400 BC.

*Wharram Percy, barrow cemetery (SE/837636) 2½ miles S of North Grimstone (B1248, B1253), ½ mile W of Wharram Percy House. Grave goods in Transport Museum, Hull.

Nine barrows are within ½ mile of each other, 6 of them in a line which might be considered as a linear cemetery in the Wessex manner. From E (SE/842636) to w (SE/836635) these mounds covered the following:

(1) Simple cremation.
(2) Simple cremation.
(3) Cremation and inhumation in grave with food vessel, flint and bone tools.
(4) Cremation burial, with collared urn added later.
(5) A central grave, marked by an upright stake, contained the skeleton of a 14-year-old boy, with 2 jet ear-plugs.
(6) Collared urn with cremated bones in pit at centre: second collared urn near top of mound at centre, also containing burnt bones.

These barrows were built c. 1,700–1,400 BC.
Willerby Wold, round barrow. See Neolithic.
*Willerby Wold House, round barrow (TA/015763) 2 miles ssw of Thaxton (A64, A1039, B1249), ¼ mile SE of Willerby Wold House (B1249). Grave goods in British Museum.

Originally 45 ft. in diam. and over 2 ft. high, this mound covered a central burial of 2 skeletons in a pit; a later pit had been dug through this, containing an inhumation with a beaker. This area, where a great fire had been lit before the first burial took place, was surrounded by a shallow ditch. Near the edge of the mound, but apparently of the same date as the first burial, there were 4 decorated bronze axes of Irish origin, lying on the Bronze Age land surface. Date, c. 1,700–1,400 BC.
Yockenthwaite, stone circle (SD/899794) 6¼ miles NW of Kettlewell (B6160); 700 yds. NW of Yockenthwaite, on N bank of river Wharfe.

This circle has a diam. of 25 ft. and is almost a true circle. It comprises 20 stones, most set edge to edge and with a gap facing SE (perhaps modern). At the NW, 4 more stones lie immediately outside the circle and on an arc concentric to it. A slight mound at the centre suggests the presence of a burial.

All the stones could have been found in the bed of the Wharfe; the circle, like so many sacred sites, is situated as near as possible to the river. Date, c. 2,200–1,400 BC.

IRON AGE

Boltby Scar, promontory fort, Bronze Age round barrows (SE/506857) 7 miles w of Helmsley (A170, B1257), 1¾ miles NW of Cold Kirby. Finds in Yorkshire Museum, York.

A semicircular area of 2½ acres has been cut off by a bank and ditch on the E side. A steep hillside protects the w. An original entrance has not yet been identified. There are 3 barrows within the earthwork. One covered a primary burial in a collared urn, c. 1,700–1,400 BC. The camp may have been built c. 500–100 BC.
Casten Dyke, promontory fort. See **Roulston Scar.**
Castle Steads, hill-fort (NZ/112075) 6¾ miles SE of Barnard Castle (A67, B6277, B6278), ¾ mile w of Gayles.

This hill-fort occupies a local spur and has an area of nearly 4 acres. Its defences comprise a stone-built rampart, ditch and a counterscarp bank, now badly preserved. An original entrance has not yet been identified. Not dated.
Castleton Rigg, promontory fort. See Bronze Age.
Danby Rigg, fort. See Bronze Age.
Double Dykes, Danby Rigg, promonotry fort and 'Celtic' fields. See Bronze Age.
Roulston Scar, promontory fort (SE/ 514816) 5½ miles E of Thirsk (A19, A61, A168, A170), ¾ mile s of Sutton Bank (A170).

The largest and strongest of NE Yorks. promontory forts, Roulston Scar (erroneously called Casten Dyke on the 1-in. O.S. as if part of that altogether later earthwork) encloses about 53 acres. In places its rampart, which cuts off the spur to the sw, still stands 11 ft. high. There is a ditch on the NE side. Air photographs show that the E end of the rampart continues SE, along the side of the valley in that quarter. This appears, on the ground, as a terrace. Not dated.
Selside, settlements (SD/775780, SD/ 777772) 9 miles NNW of Settle (A65, B6479), 1¼ miles (s settlement) SE of Ribbleshead Station. w of B6479.

These sites have the finest 'Celtic' field system in Yorks. – the s settlement is the better preserved. There is a series of circular huts (diam. 20 ft.) each in a small walled enclosure. The remains of at least 1 pond (in a triangular yard) can be seen. Field walls extend over 200 acres, crossing B6479 and railway but not reaching the river. Some fields measure 300 × 200 ft. but most are smaller. Tracks can be traced through them to the settlements. There are many springs of water in the area. Stone robbing for modern walls accounts for the many gaps in the ancient field boundaries. Not dated.

*Stanwick, fortified area (NZ/180115 centre) 3¼ miles sw of Piercebridge (A.67, B6275), between Forcett (B6274), Carkin Fields, Park House and Carlton Park. Finds in British Museum, Yorkshire Museum, York.

This earthwork (fig. 68) encloses about 750 acres, a prehistoric feat of engineering unrivalled in Britain. Excavation in 1951–2 revealed that it had been developed in 3 phases.

Phase 1. The enclosure at the centre of the whole work, The Tofts, s of Stanwick Church and Mary Wild Beck, was built first. It can be described as a hill-fort and encloses 17 acres. It is well preserved only on the w side in a plantation. It was found to have a V-shaped ditch about 18 ft. wide and a simple bank behind it. There is a counterscarp bank on the N side, facing the stream, and a stone-flanked entrance (obscured by the end-wall of the plantation) near the NW corner. This fort was built early in the 1st century AD. Circular huts indicated permanent occupation. In Phase 2 the N side of this hill-fort was levelled when The Tofts was incorporated in an altogether larger work.

Phase 2. About AD 50–60 an enclosure of 130 acres was added N of The Tofts. Except where the new earthwork joins on to the N side of The Tofts, the former lies N of Mary Wild Beck. This brook acts as the only protection to the enclosure of Phase 2 between The Tofts and the w side of Henah Hill. The main entrance to this work is s of its w corner. The defences comprise a flat-bottomed ditch 16 ft. deep and originally about 40 ft. wide, and an earth and rubble rampart faced with a drystone wall (fig. 70).

Phase 3. Nearly 600 acres were added c. AD 72 when an area s of Mary Wild Beck was enclosed by a bank and ditch with an entrance near the middle of the s side. This ditch was V-shaped, 33 ft. wide and 15 ft. deep. The earth and rubble bank behind it was faced with a drystone wall. The s entrance is defined by a slight in-turn of the bank on the w and a deep in-turn on the E. Excavation revealed that before this entrance had been finished it was abandoned – due no doubt to some sudden alarm – and the ditch was made continuous. Amost the whole circuit of the defences is visible from The Tofts, making possible a central command of this vast area. This explains why Henah Hill was deliberately left outside the defences which it would otherwise have obscured.

It is generally supposed that these earthworks mark the rallying-point of the Brigantes, the great Iron Age tribe of the N, whose king, Venutius, had become a confirmed opponent of Rome (fig. 14). His queen, Cartimandua, was pro-Roman and the loyalties of the tribe were shared between them. After AD 51 Venutius set himself at the head of a resistance movement while his queen received the support of the Roman legionaries during the struggles that were fought between the supporters of husband and wife. During this period it seems likely that Venutius and his supporters were developing the Stanwick defences, while Cartimandua may have set up her house in the hill-fort of Almondbury, near Huddersfield (p. 257).

In AD 69 Emperor Vespasian established his hold upon Britain. The Brigantes rose in open revolt at this time and Cartimandua sought safety outside her kingdom. An energetic governor, Petillius Cerialis, campaigned against the followers of Venutius between AD 71 and 74 and completed the conquest of this area at an exact date still unknown.

Of the finds from Stanwick, the most important is an Iron Age sword in a scabbard of ash with mounts of bronze (fig. 69), and a wooden bowl of oak.

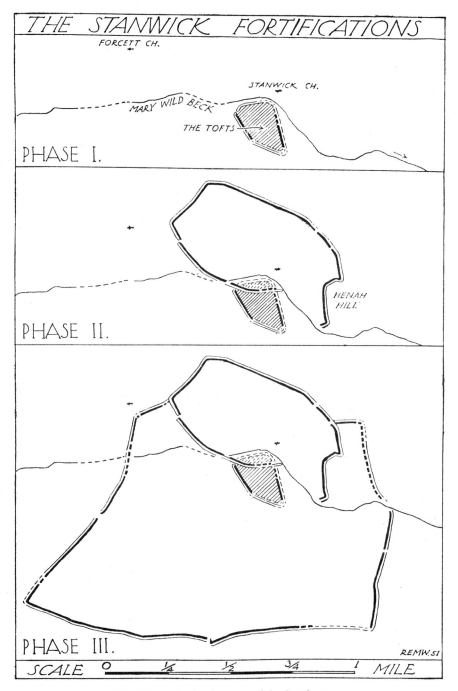

THE STANWICK FORTIFICATIONS

FORCETT CH.

STANWICK CH.

MARY WILD BECK

THE TOFTS

PHASE I.

HENAH HILL

PHASE II.

PHASE III.

REMW.51

SCALE 0   1/4   1/2   3/4   1   MILE

68   *Stanwick: development of the fortifications*

69 Stanwick: iron sword (length 34 ins.)
in wooden scabbard with bronze mounts,
1st century AD

70   *Stanwick: ditch and bank, excavated, restored and maintained by the Department of the Environment*

Yorkshire, South

IRON AGE

Caesar's Camp, Scholes Wood; hill-slope fort. See **Scholes Wood.**

*Carlwark, settlement (SK/260815) 5 miles sw of Sheffield, 1¾ miles E of Hathersage; (A622, A625); on Hathersage Moor.

This is a nearly rectangular enclosure of 2 acres protected on all but the w by natural slopes. It is fortified on the w and s, and perhaps originally all round, by a turf and soil rampart faced on the outside with a masonry wall still 9½ ft. high on the w. Though leaning inwards now, this facing wall would have been built verti-

cal. There is a fine in-turned entrance at the sw corner. It is 6 yds. long and 5 ft. wide at its inner end. There is a simple entrance in the E side. Date, perhaps 1st century BC, but many authorities regard it as post-Roman (Dark Age) in date.

Roman Ridge, defensive earthworks, Sheffield centre to Mexborough (A6023, A6092).

Though not yet dated by excavation, these earthworks are likely to be pre-Roman, perhaps part of a defensive system dug by the Brigantes against enemies (Romans or other natives) advancing from the SE. They follow fairly low ground, never far from the river Don. They start about SK/358880, run as a single earthwork NE through Grimesthorpe, E of Wincobank hill-fort (right) to Hill Top (SK/397927). Here they fork, the W branch running ½ mile E of Scholes Wood hill-slope fort (below) to Wentworth Park where it is well preserved, showing 2 banks and a medial ditch. It bends E at SK/420985, can be found in the S part of Wath Wood and E of A633; it is visible across Bow Broom and ends W of Mexborough hospital. The E branch crosses Greasborough and runs through the E end of Wentworth Park where it is visible until Upper Haugh. It bends here towards Piccadilly where it disappears at SK/448981.

Scholes Wood, hill-slope fort (SK/395953) 5½ miles NE of Sheffield, 2½ miles NW of Rotherham, ½ mile ESE of Scholes, N of A629.

This is an oval site of about 1 acre. It is protected by a bank and ditch and has an original entrance at the NE. The main bank rises 3 ft. above the interior. The site is overlooked by higher ground NE, W and S. Date, c. 1st century BC–1st century AD: but some believe that the site is not prehistoric.

*Wincobank (W.R.), hill-fort (SK/378910) 2½ miles NE of centre of Sheffield. Finds in Sheffield Museum.

This is an oval fort with an internal area of 2¼ acres. A bank, ditch and counterscarp bank are continuous around it except on the N side where ditch and counterscarp have been destroyed. The banks now nowhere exceed 3 ft. in ht. There is an entrance on the NE side, where one end of the main bank is thickened and the other end runs out across it for 30 ft., forming a type of out-turned entrance.

Excavation in 1899 showed that the ditch had an original depth of 5–6 ft. The main bank has a rubble core with stone facings. It had contained much timberwork holding it together; at some period this had been burnt, accidentally or otherwise, until much of the rampart had been fused into a solid mass by heat. Not dated.

Yorkshire, West

NEOLITHIC

*Bradley Moor, long cairn and Bronze Age round barrow (SE/009476) 5 miles NW of Keighley (A629, A650, B6143), 1 mile N of Kildwick (A629). Highest point of Black Hill.

This long barrow is about 230 ft. in length. It is orientated SE/NW. Its E end is expanded in plan and is noticeably higher than the W half of the mound, rising from 4 ft. to 8 ft. Excavation has revealed a burial cist 6¼ ft. long and 3 ft. wide, 60 ft. from the E end and entirely covered by the mound. It had a heavy capstone. On its floor a smaller slab was found to cover a depression filled with unburnt human bones broken to fragments. They represented an adult. Also in the cist were burnt human bones. A few feet S of the cist a series of large upright stones was found, 3 of which appeared to be a blind entrance to the cist while 2 others were set up on edge as plain uprights. A third upright was found near the central axis of the mound, 100 ft. W of the E end. These stones may have had a phallic meaning.

Long cairns like this are closely related to earthen long barrows: date c. 3,500–2,500 BC.

A round barrow can be seen 114 ft. to the S. It has been robbed, its contents not recorded. It is 89–99 ft. in diam. and 6 ft. high.

BRONZE AGE

Addingham High Moor, carved stone. See **Ilkley Moor.**

Bradup, stone circle (SE/090440) $2\frac{1}{2}$ miles NE of Keighley, at Bradup Bridge, on w side of road across moor from Keighley to Ilkley.

This circle lies s and w of Bradup Bridge, in Brass Castle pasture. It has a diam. of about 30 ft. Twelve stones remain, less than half its original complement. They are irregularly arranged and are of the local millstone grit. Date, c. 2,200–1,400 BC.

Bull Stone, standing stone (SE/206435) $1\frac{1}{4}$ miles NE of Guiseley (A65, A6038), 1 mile w of East Carlton: $\frac{1}{3}$ mile s of Royalty Inn, The Chevin.

Bull Stone stands 6 ft. above ground. It is made of millstone grit probably derived from an outcrop $\frac{1}{2}$ mile N, on The Chevin. The stone is unshaped, with a cross-section changing from rectangular at the base to almost circular near the upper end, where it is naturally weathered. Date, c. 2,200–1,400 BC.

Grubstones Circle. See **Ilkley Moor.**

Horncliffe Circle. See **Ilkley Moor.**

*__Ilkley Moor,__ carvings, circles and cairns; s of Ilkley and A65. Casts in Leeds Museum.

This area contains an unusual number of rock carvings and circles. Barrows, however, are rare. The carvings on the millstone grit are in 2 groups, Addingham High Moor and Green Crag Slack. These are at or above 1,050 ft., following the edge of the steep slopes around this moorland area (about SE/086472 and SE/132463, and Pancake Stone, SE/133462). The carvings consist of circular hollows, many with concentric rings around them and some joined up by meandering lines: circles and hollows are under 12 ins. in diam. The most elaborately carved stone, the Panorama Stone, is in the public gardens opposite St Margaret's Church, Ilkley (SE/115472). It includes hollows, some encircled, and ladder patterns. At Upwood House, Morton, there is a stone from Rumbalds Moor with a hollow and concentric rings, with 2 parallel lines attached to the latter.

More remarkable, but perhaps of Iron Age date, is the Swastika Stone (SE/094470). This shows the double outline of a swastika, with a cross-shaped arrangement of hollows incorporated in it. There is a hollow within an open circle close to it. The first motif is common on Celtic art of the last 3 centuries BC, which may be the date of this carving.

There are 5 circles in this area, of which 3 need description. All are dated c., 2,200–1,400 BC:

Twelve Apostles Circle (SE/126451). Twelve stones, most now fallen, have been set in a bank of earth and small stones 52 ft. in diam. The stones are irregularly placed and originally there would have been many more.

Grubstones Circle (SE/136447). This site is 33 ft. in diam. and is almost perfectly circular. Its stones, of which at least 20 survive, are set edge to edge in a slight bank. The circle has been damaged by a shooting butt at the s side.

Horncliffe Circle (SE/134435) is oval in plan, its long axis being N/S. It has a max. diam. of 43 ft. The stones are set very close together and at least 46 can still be seen. Remains of a smaller circle around the centre suggest the presence of a burial. It has been disturbed, but no discoveries have been recorded.

There are also cairns and circles SE of the Grubstones. From NW to SE these are as follows:

(1) **Skirtful of Stones,** a cairn 85 ft. in diam. and 5–6 ft. high. Nothing is known of the burial beneath it.

(2) An earth circle, 93 ft. diam. $2\frac{1}{2}$ ft. high, with entrances E and W, 300 ft. SE of the last.

(3) An earth circle like the last but 80 ft. across, 1,500 ft. SE of Skirtful.

(4) A small cairn with no burial records.

These remains represent a cemetery and sacred sites all broadly contemporary with the carvings, c. 2,200–1,400 BC.

Rumbolds Moor, carved stones, circles. See **Ilkley Moor.**

Skirtful of Stones, cairn. See **Ilkley Moor.**

Swastika Stone, carved stone. See **Ilkley Moor.**

Twelve Apostles Circle. See **Ilkley Moor.**

IRON AGE

Addingham High Moor, carved stone. See Bronze Age, **Ilkley Moor.**

***Almondbury,** hill-fort (SE/153141) 1¾ miles SE of centre of Huddersfield: 1 mile NE of Honley railway station. Finds in Tolson Memorial Museum, Huddersfield.

This hill-fort is oval in plan, its earthworks tending to follow the contours and enclosing about 16 acres. Excavation has revealed that its present and final shape was reached in successive stages, ending with its adaptation as a medieval castle. Essentially, the site shows 2 groups of earthworks, an inner oval with the highest part of the hill at its sw end, 900 ft. long and 8 acres in extent, and an outer, less distinct pair of banks and ditches lower down the hillsides.

In phase 1 the sw end of the summit plateau was fortified by a single bank and V-shaped ditch; there was a slightly in-turned entrance facing NE, at the centre of the rampart which cuts across the plateau (a building now stands at the N end of this cross dyke). The rampart was of earth, faced front and back by a stone retaining wall. In phase 2 the rest of this plateau was enclosed by a bank, ditch and counterscarp bank to fortify 8 acres. An entrance at the NE end was built,

approached by the hollow way up the hillside from the N. The rampart was built like that of phase 1. Some minor banks and ditches were added lower down the hillside E of the new entrance, including a rectangular 'annexe' of unknown purpose. These stages were probably begun c. 8th century BC.

In stage 3 the hill-fort remained the same size but the inner rampart (of phase 2) was reconstructed to include timber-lacing.

Finally, the area of the hill-fort was doubled by the addition of a pair of banks and ditches surrounding the hill further down; a deep in-turned entrance through the latter was built at the w end. This probably occurred at the end of the 1st century BC.

Castle Hill, Almondsbury. See **Almondsbury.**

South Kirby Camp, hill-fort (SE/435105) 1¾ miles SSE of Hemsworth (A628, B6273), on w edge of South Kirby (B6422).

On fairly low ground between 2 streams, this fort encloses 4½ acres. It is roughly oval in plan and is defended by a bank and ditch, the former 8–10 ft. high where it is well preserved at the sw and NE. The original entrance may be the break near the centre of the N side. Not dated.

Swastika Stone, carved stone. See Bronze Age, **Ilkley Moor.**

BIBLIOGRAPHY

All sites for which there is additional information in a published excavation report or reliable field survey are listed here by counties alphabetically, and are indicated by an asterisk in the Gazetteer. The following abbreviations have been employed:

A.	*Antiquity*
A.C.	*Archaeologia Cantiana*
Ant.J.	*Antiquaries Journal*
Arch.	*Archaeologia*
Arch.J.	*Archaeological Journal*
Arch.Ael.	*Archaeologia Aeliana*
A.W.	R.C. Hoare, *Ancient Wiltshire*, 2 vols., 1812–19
B.A.	*Bedfordshire Archaeological Journal*
B.A.J.	*Berkshire Archaeological Journal*
B.B.	W. Greenwell, *British Barrows*, 1877
C.	E.C. Curwen, *Archaeology of Sussex*, 1954
C.A.	*Cornish Archaeology*
C. and E.	I.Ll. Foster and L. Alcock, Eds., *Culture and Environment*, 1963
C. and K.	O.G.S. Crawford and A. Keiller, *Wessex from the Air*, 1928
D.A.J.	*Journal of the Derbyshire Archaeological and Natural History Society*
E.M.	F. Elgee, *Early Man in North-east Yorkshire*, 1930
I.A.H.F.	D. Hill and M. Jesson, *The Iron Age and its Hill-forts*, 1971
J.B.A.A.	*Journal of the British Archaeological Association*
L. and B.	F. Lynch and C. Burgess, *Prehistoric Man in Wales and the West*, 1972
L.B.C.	O.G.S. Crawford, *Long Barrows of the Cotswolds*, 1925
M.	J.R. Mortimer, *Forty Years' Researches in Bri-*

	tish and Saxon Burial Mounds of East Yorkshire, 1905
N.A.	*Norfolk Archaeologist*
O.	*Oxoniensia*
P.C.A.S.	*Proceedings of the Cambridge Antiquarian Society*
P.D.A.E.S.	*Proceedings of the Devon Archaeological Exploration Society*
P.D.A.S.	*Proceedings of the Dorset Natural History and Archaeological Society* (previously *Antiquarian Field Club*)
P.H.F.C.	*Proceedings of the Hampshire Field Club*
P.I.W.N.H.S.	*Proceedings of the Isle of Wight Natural History Society*
P.P.S.	*Proceedings of the Prehistoric Society*
P-R	Pitt-Rivers, *Excavations in Cranborne Chase*, 4 vols., 1887–98
P.S.A.L.	*Proceedings of the Society of Antiquaries of London*
P.Som.A.S.	*Proceedings of the Somerset Archaeological Society*
P.U.B.S.S.	*Proceedings of the University of Bristol Spelaeological Society*
P.W.C.F.C.	*Proceedings of the West Cornwall Field Club*
R.C.H.M.	*Royal Commission on Historical Monuments*, reports
Rel.	*The Reliquary and Illustrated Archaeologist*

R. of B.   Records of Buckingham-
shire

R.R.   Research Reports of the
Society of Antiquaries

S.   I.M. Stead, *The La Tène
Cultures of Eastern
Yorkshire,* 1965

S.A.C.   Surrey Archaeological
Collections

S.A.T.   Shropshire Archaeological
Transactions

Sx.A.C.   Sussex Archaeological
Collections

T.B. and G.   Transactions of the Bristol
and Gloucestershire Ar-
chaeological Society

T.B.A.S.   Transactions of the Birmingham Archaeological
Society

T.C.W.A.S.   Transactions of the Cumberland and Westmorland
Antiquarian Society

T.D.A.   Transactions of the Devon-
shire Association

Ten Years   T. Bateman, *Ten Years'
Diggings in Celtic and
Saxon Grave Hills,* 1861

Thom   A. Thom, *Megalithic Sites
in Britain,* 1972

T.L.C.A.S.   Transactions of the Lancashire and Cheshire Anti-
quarian Society

U.P.B.   D.A.E. Garrod, *The Upper Palaeolithic Age in
Britain,* 1926

V.C.H.   Victoria County History

Vestiges   T. Bateman, *Vestiges of
the Antiquities of Derby-
shire,* 1848

W.A.M.   Wiltshire Archaeological
and Natural History
Magazine

Y.A.J.   Yorkshire Archaeological
Journal

AVON

Bury Hill, *P.U.B.S.S.* 1, No. 3, 1926, 8ff.

King's Weston, *P.U.B.S.S.* 8, No. 1, 1956–7, 30ff.

Lansdown, *P.S.A.L.* 20, 1903–5, 6ff., 252–4.

Maes Knoll Camp, *P.U.B.S.S.* 10, No. 1, 1963, 9ff.; *Arch. J.* 115, 1958, 1ff.

Stanton Drew, Ministry of Works Guide, 1956.

Stokeleigh Camp, *P.U.B.S.S.* 14, No. 1, 1975, 29ff.

Worlebury, C.W. Dymond, *Worlebury, An Ancient Stronghold in the County of Somerset,* 1902.

BEDFORDSHIRE

For Neolithic and Bronze Age sites, see *B.A.* 2, 1964, 16ff., and below.

Five Knolls, *Arch. J.* 68, 1931, 193ff.

Maiden Bower, *B.A.* 2, 1964, 23.

Waulud's Bank, ibid., 1ff.

BERKSHIRE

For long and round barrows, see L.V. Grinsell, *B.A.J.* 39–43, 1935–9.

Hill-forts, see *B.A.J.* 60, 1962, 30ff.

Lambourn Long Barrow, *B.A.J.* 62, 1965–6, 1ff.

Lambourn Seven Barrows, *B.A.J.* 40, 1936, 59ff; ibid. 55, 1956–7, 15ff.

BUCKINGHAMSHIRE

Beacon Hill, *R. of B.* 18, 1968, 187ff.

Cholesbury, *J.B.A.A.* 39, 1934, 187ff.

Cop, *R. of B.* 13, 1934–40, 313ff.

Whiteleaf, *P.P.S.* 20, 1954, 212ff.

CAMBRIDGESHIRE

Wandlebury, *P.C.A.S.* 50, 1956, 1ff.

CHESHIRE

Castle Ditch, *Arch. J.* 111, 1954, 89ff.

Kelsborrow and other hill-forts, *T.L.C.A.S.* 72, 1962, 9ff.

Maiden Castle, *Arch. J.* 111, 1954, 87ff.

Sponds Hill, *T.L.C.A.S.* 30, 1912, 184ff.

CLEVELAND

Eston Nab, *Y.A.J.* 42, 1967–9, interim reports.

CORNWALL

Bodrifty, *Arch. J.* 113, 1956, 1ff.

Carn Brea, *C.A.* 9–11, 1970–2, interim reports.

Carn Creis, *Arch.* 49, 1885, 185ff.

Carn Euny, H. Hencken, *Archaeology of Cornwall and Scilly Isles,* 1932, 139ff.

Carn Gluze, *Arch.* 49, 1885, 189ff.

Castle an Dinas, *C.A.* 2, 1963, 51ff.

Castilly, *P.W.C.F.C.* 1, 2, 1953–4, 35ff.

Castle Dore, *J.R.I.C.* 1, Appendix 1951.

Castlewitch, *Ant.J.* 32, 1952, 67ff.
Chapel Carn Brea, *Arch.* 49, 1885, 195ff.
Chun Castle, *Arch.* 76, 1926, 205ff.
Chysauster, *Arch.* 83, 1933, 237ff.
Fernacre Circle, *Arch.* 61, 1906, 33ff.
Gurnard's Head, *Arch. J.* 97, 1940, 96ff.
Hurlers, *P.P.S.* 4, 1938, 319.
Leaze Circle, *Arch.* 61, 1906, 29ff.
Maen Castle, *P.W.C.F.C.* 1, 3, 1953–5, 98ff.
Pelynt, *J.R.I.C.* 1845, p. 33: W.C. Borlase, *Naenia Cornubiae,* 1872, p. 188; *P.P.S.* 17, 1951, p. 95; 18, 1952, 237; *W.A.M.* 65, 1970, 93ff.
Rillaton, *Arch.J.* 24, 1867, 189; L.V. Grinsell, *Ancient Burial Mounds of England,* 1953, 125–6.
Stannon Circle, *Arch.* 61, 1906, 36ff.
Stripple Stones, *Arch.* 61, 1906, 1ff.
Tregeare Rounds, *J.R.I.C.* 16, 1904, 73ff.; *Arch.J.* 109, 1952, 1ff.
Tresvennack, W.C. Borlase, *Naenia Cornubiae,* 1872, 102ff.
Trevelgue Head, *P.P.S.* 5, 1939, 254.
Trewey Foage, *Arch.J.* 98, 1942, 3; *P.W.C.F.C.* 1, 2, 1953–4, 45–6.
Trippet Stones, *Arch.* 61, 1906, 25ff.

CUMBRIA

See *R.C.H.M. Westmorland* for sites formerly in that county, and below.
Birkrigg Common, *T.L.C.A.S.* 12, 1912, 262ff.
The Carles, Thom, 145ff.
Carrock Fell, *T.C.W.A.S.* 38, 1938, 32ff.
Castlehead, *T.L.C.A.S.* 72, 1962, 32ff.
Castle How, *T.C.W.A.S.* 24, 1924, 78ff.
Eskdale Moor, *T.C.W.A.S.* 5, 1881, 55ff; Thom, 63–5, fig. 6.5.
Grey Croft, *T.C.W.A.S.* 57, 1958, 1ff.
King Arthur's Round Table and Mayburgh, *T.C.W.A.S.* 37, 1937, 227ff.; 38, 1938, 1ff; 40, 1940, 169ff.
Lacra, *T.C.W.A.S.* 48, 1948, 1ff.
Lanthwaite Green, *T.C.W.A.S.* 24, 1924, 117ff.
Mecklin Park, *T.C.W.A.S.* 37, 1937, 104ff.
Mount Hulie, *T.C.W.A.S.* 40, 1940, 162ff.
Swinside, *T.C.W.A.S.* 2, 1902, 53ff.
Threlkeld Knott, *T.C.W.A.S.* 43, 1943, 20ff.

DERBYSHIRE

For all chambered tombs see *D.A.J.* 78, 1958, 25ff, and below.

Arbor Low, *Arch.* 58, 1903, 461ff.; *Vestiges,* 64–5.
Ball Cross, *D.A.J.* 74, 1954, 85ff.
Beeley Moor, *D.A.J.* 89, 1969, 1ff.
Bull Ring, *P.P.S.* 16, 1950, 81ff.
Castle Naze, *D.A.J.* 74, 1954, 9; ibid, 77, 1957, 49ff.
Creswell Crags, *U.P.B.,* 122ff.
Doll Tor (Stanton Moor), *D.A.J.* 13, 1939, 116ff.
End Low, *Vestiges,* pp. 36, 45.
Fin Cop, *D.A.J.* 74, 1954, 5–6.
Five Wells, *Rel.* 1901, 229ff.
Gib Hill, *Vestiges,* 31–2; *D.A.J.* 88, 1968, 100ff.
Green Low, *D.A.J.* 85, 1965, 1ff.
Harthill Moor, *D.A.J.* 13, 1939, 126ff.
Hob Hurst's House, *Ten Years,* 87–9.
Lean Low, *Vestiges,* 35–6, 102.
Mam Tor, *D.A.J.* 74, 1954, 3–4; ibid. 87, 1967, 158ff.; D.W. Harding (ed.), *Hillforts, a Survey of Research in Britain and Ireland,* publication forthcoming.
Markland Grips, *D.A.J.* 74, 1954, 4–5; ibid. 89, 1969, 59ff.
Minninglow, *Vestiges,* 39–40; *Ten Years,* 54–5, 82.
Ringham Low, *A.* 26, 1952, 41ff.
Stanton Moor, *D.A.J.* 4, 1930, 1ff; ibid. 10, 1936, 21ff.; ibid. 13, 1939, 105ff; 74, 1954, 128ff.
Swarkeston Lowes, *D.A.J.* 75, 1955, 123ff.; ibid. 76, 1956, 10ff.; ibid. 80, 1960, 1ff.

DEVONSHIRE

For barrows, see *P.D.A.E.S.* 28, 1970, 95ff., and below.
Archerton Newtake, *V.C.H.* 1, 1906, 361.
Blackbury Castle, *P.D.A.E.S.* 5 (2–3), 1954–5, 43ff.
Broad Down, *P.D.A.E.S.* 4 (1), 1948, 1ff.
Chapman Barrows, *T.D.A.* 27, 1905, 92ff.
Clovelly Dykes, *Arch.J.* 109, 1952, 12ff.
Cranbrook Castle, *P.D.A.E.S.* 30, 1972, 216ff.
Dartmoor, see p. 86.
East Hill, *P.D.A.E.S.* 3 (2), 1938, 86ff.
Hameldown, *Ant.J.* 17, 1937, 313–14.
Hembury, *P.D.A.E.S.* 1 (1) 1929, 40–63, 90–120, 162–90; 2 (3), 1935, 135ff.; *Arch.J.* 114, 1957, 144ff.
Kent's Cavern, *U.P.B.,* 25ff.; *P.D.A.E.S.* 5 (2–3), 1954–5, 68ff.
Kestor, *T.D.A.* 86, 1954, 21ff.

Milber Down, *P.D.A.E.S.* 4 (2–3), 1949–50, 27ff.
North Molton, *P.D.A.E.S.* 4 (1), 1948, 13; *Ant.J.* 31, 1951, 25ff.

DORSETSHIRE
For all sites, see *R.C.H.M.*, w, central and SE; for all barrows, see L.V. Grinsell, *Dorset Barrows,* 1959, and below.
Afflington Barrow, *P.D.A.S.* 77, 1955, 149–50
Badbury Rings, C. and K., 58ff.; *Ant.J.* 45, 1965, 41ff.
Badbury Barrow, *Ant.J.* 19, 1939, 291ff.
Bindon, *Ant.J.* 33, 1953, 1ff.
Buzbury, C. and K. 64ff.
Chalbury, *Ant. J.* 23, 1943, 98ff.
Clandon, *P.D.A.S.* 58, 1936, 18ff.
Dorset Cursus, *A.* 29, 1955, 4ff.; *Arch.J.* 130, 1973, 44ff.
Eggardun, *A.* 13, 1939, 152.
Grey Mare and Her Colts, *P.D.A.S.,* 67, 1946, 30ff.
Hambledon Hill, C. and K., 44ff.
Hampton Down, *P.D.A.S.* 88, 1966, 122.
Hengitsbury Head, *R.R.* 3, 1915.
Hod Hill, C. and K., 36ff.; J.W. Brailsford, *Hod Hill,* Vol. 1, 1962; I.A. Richmond, *Hod Hill,* Vol. 2, 1968.
Kingston Russell, *A.* 13, 1939, 142.
Knowlton Circles, ibid. 152ff.
Litton Cheney, ibid. 143ff.
Maiden Castle, *R.R.* 12, 1943.
Maumbury Ring, *A.* 13, 1939, 155ff.
Mount Pleasant, *A.* 13, 1939, 158.
Nine Stones, ibid. 146ff.
Pilsdon Pen, *P.D.A.S.* 92, 1971, 126.
Poor Lot, *P.D.A.S.* 76, 1954, 89.
Poundbury, *Ant. J.* 20, 1940, 429ff.
Rempstone, *A.* 13, 1939, 148.
Ridgeway, *P.D.A.S.* 58, 1936, 20ff.; *P.P.S.* 23, 1957, 124ff.
Spettisbury Rings, *Arch.J.* 96, 1939, 114ff.; 97, 1940, 112ff.
Thickthorn, *P.P.S.* 2, 1936, 77ff.
Wor Barrow, P-R IV, 58ff.

DURHAM
Batter Law, *Arch. Ael.* 11, 1914, 158ff.
Murton Moor, ibid., 167.

ESSEX
See *R.C.H.M.*
Colchester, *R.R.* 14, 1947.
Lexden Tumulus, *Arch.* 76, 1927, 241ff.

GLOUCESTERSHIRE
For all long barrows see *L.B.C.,* for round barrows see *T.B. and G.* 79, 1960, 1ff., and below.
Avening, *P.P.S.* 6, 1940, 133ff.
Bagendon, Mrs E.M. Clifford, *Bagendon: A Belgic Oppidum,* 1960.
Belas Knap, *T.B. and G.* 51, 1929, 261; 52, 1930, 123ff., 295ff.
Crickley Hill, P. Dixon, *Crickley Hill, Interim Reports,* 1969ff.
Leckhampton, *T.B. and G.* 47, 1925, 81; ibid. 90, 1971, 5ff.
Lydney, *R.R.* 9, 1932.
Minchinhampton, *T.B. and G.* 59, 1937, 287ff.
Notgrove, *Arch.* 86, 1937, 119ff.
Nympsfield, *P.P.S.* 4, 1938, 188ff.
Oxenton Hill, *T.B. and G.* 55, 1933, 383ff.
Rodmarton, *P.P.S.* 6, 1940, 133ff.
Salmonsbury, *A.* 5, 1931, 489ff.
Snowshill, *Arch.* 52, 1890, 70–2.
Soldier's Grave, *P.P.S.* 4, 1938, 214ff.

GREATER LONDON
Caesar's Camp, *Arch.J.* 102, 1945, 15ff.
Keston, *A.C.* 84, 1969, 185ff.

HAMPSHIRE
For all barrows see *P.H.F.C.* 14, 1938–40, and below.
Buckland Rings, *P.H.F.C.* 13, 1936, 124ff.
Bury Hill, *P.H.F.C.* 14, 1938–40, 291ff.
Butser Hill, *A.* 4, 1930, 187ff.
Danebury, *Ant.J.* 51, 1971, 240ff.
Grim's Ditch, *A.* 18, 1944, 65ff.
Ladle Hill, *A.* 1931, 474ff.
Martin Down, P-R, IV, 190.
Quarley Hill, *P.H.F.C.* 14, 1939, 136ff.
St Catherine's Hill, C.F.C. Hawkes, J.N.L. Myres, and C.G. Stevens, *St Catherine's Hill,* 1930.
Stockbridge Down, *Ant.J.* 20, 1940, 39ff.

HEREFORD and WORCESTER
See *R.C.H.M. Herefordshire* for sites formerly in that county, and below.
Aconbury, *Arch.J.* 110, 1953, 25–6.
Bredon Hill, *Arch.J.* 95, 1938, 1ff.
Credenhill, ibid., 127, 1970, 82ff.
Croft Ambrey, S.C. Stanford, *Croft Ambrey,* 1974.
Dinedor, *Arch.J.* 110, 1953, 23ff.
King Arthur's Cave, *P.U.B.S.S.* 2, No. 3, 1925, 221; 3, No. 2, 1927, 59.
Sutton Walls, *Arch.J.* ibid., 1ff.

HERTFORDSHIRE
St Albans, *R.R.* 11, 1936.
Therfield Heath, *P.P.S.* 1, 1935, 101ff.

HUMBERSIDE
Callis Wold, M. 153ff.
Dane's Graves, *Arch.* 60, 1906, 251ff.; M., 359; S.
Kilham, B.B. 553ff.; **A.** 45, 1971, 50ff.
Towthorpe, M., 1ff.
Willy Howe, *Arch.* 52, 1890, 22ff.

ISLE OF WIGHT
See *P.I.W.N.H.S.* 3, 1941, 179ff. for all barrows, and below.
Chillerton Down Camp, *P.I.W.N.H.S.* 4, 1947, 51ff.
Long Stone, *A.* 31, 1957, 147ff.

KENT
Bigbury, *Arch.J.* 59, 1902, 211ff.; *A.C.* 48, 1936, 151ff.
Chestnuts, *A.C.* 76, 1961, 1ff.
Coldrum, R.F. Jessup, *South-East England*, 1970, 108.
Julliberrie's Grave, *Ant.J.* 19, 1939, 260ff.
Oldbury Hill, *Arch.* 90, 1944, 127ff.
Oldbury Rock Shelters, Institute of Archaeology *Bulletin*, 8, 1970, 151.
Ringwold, A.C. 9, 1874, 16ff.
Squerryes Park *A.C.* 86, 1971, 29ff.
Tunbridge Wells, *Sx.A.C.* 106, 1968, 158ff.

LANCASHIRE
For all hill-forts, see *T.L.C.A.S.* 72, 1962, 9ff., and below.
Bleasdale, *Ant.J.* 18, 1938, 156ff.
Portfield, *T.L.C.A.S.* 67, 1957, 115ff.

LEICESTERSHIRE
Breedon-on-the-Hill, *Transactions of the Leicestershire Archaeological Society* 26, 1950, 17ff.; *Ant.J.* 44, 1964, 122ff.

LINCOLNSHIRE
See *Arch.J.* 89, 1933, 174ff. for long barrows, and below.
Giant's Hills, *Arch.* 85, 1936, 37ff.

NORFOLK
Arminghall, *P.P.S.* 2, 1936, 1ff.
Grimes Graves, *Ant.J.* 1, 1921, 81ff; *P.P.S.E.A.* 3, 1922, 434ff., 548ff.; 4, 1924, 113ff., 182ff., 194ff.; 5, 1927, 91ff.; 7, 1934, 382ff.; *A.* 7, 1933, 166ff.; *P.P.S.* 39, 1973, 182ff.

Little Cressingham, *N.A.* 3, 1852, 1–2; *P.P.S.* 4, 1938, 92–3.
Warham, *Ant.J.* 13, 1933, 399ff.
West Rudham, *Transactions of the Norfolk Archaeological Society* 26, 1940, 315ff.

NORTHAMPTONSHIRE
Hunsbury, *Arch.J.* 93, 1936, 57ff.
Rainsborough, *P.P.S.* 33, 1967, 207ff.

NORTHUMBERLAND
For all hill-forts and settlements, see *Arch. Ael.* 43, 1965, 21ff.; G. Jobey, *A Field Guide to Prehistoric Northumberland,* Part 2, 1974, and below.
Bellshiel Law, *Arch. Ael.* 13, 1936, 293ff.
Blawearie, *B.B.,* 418ff.
Greaves Ashes, *Arch. Ael.* 42, 1964, 41ff.
Kirkhaugh, *Arch. Ael.* 13, 1936, 207ff.
Rayheugh, *B.B.,* 413ff.

OXFORDSHIRE
For ring-ditches, see *Oxon.* 28, 1963, 1ff.; for Iron Age sites from the former Oxfordshire, see *O.* 31, 1966, 28ff., and below.
Alfred's Castle, *B.A.J.* 60, 1962, 51.
Castle Hill, ibid., 46.
Chastleton Burrow Camp, *Ant. J.* 11, 1931, 382ff.
Cherbury Camp, *Oxon.* 5, 1940, 13ff.
Grim's Ditch, *A.* 4, 1930, 303ff.; *O.* 2, 1937, 74ff.; ibid. 22, 1957, 11ff.
Lyneham, *O.* 22, 1957, 1ff.
Madmarston, *O.* 25, 1960, 3ff.
Uffington White Horse, L.V. Grinsell, *White Horse Hill and Surrounding Country,* 1939; *Trans. Newbury District Field Club* 11, No. 3, 1965, 3ff.
Wayland's Smithy, *Ant.J.* 1, 1921, 183ff.: *A.* 39, 1965, 126ff.

SHROPSHIRE
Bury Walls, *S.A.T.* 46, 1931, 85ff.
Caynham, *S.A.T.* 57, 1962–3, 91ff.
Earl's Hill, *Arch.J.* 119, 1964, 66ff.; L. and B., 345ff.
Hemford, *C. and E.,* 127.
Mitchell's Fold, *P.P.S.* 17, 1951, 159ff.; *C. and E.,* 125ff.
Old Field, *S.A.T.* 8, 1884–5, 445ff.
Old Oswestry, *Arch. J.* 105, 1948, 41ff.
Titterstone Clee, *Archaeologia Cambrensis,* 89, 1934, 83ff.
The Wrekin, *Arch.J.* 99, 1942, 99ff.

SOMERSET

For all barrows, see *P.Som.A.S.* 113, 1969, 1ff. and ibid. 115, 1971, 43ff., and below.

Ashen Hill, *P.Som.A.S.* 85, 1940, 159.

Brean Down, *P.U.B.S.S.* 8, No. 2, 1958, 109.

Flint Jack's Cave, *P.U.B.S.S.* 7, No. 1, 1954, 23ff.

Glastonbury and Meare, A. Bulleid and H. St G. Gray, *Glastonbury Lake Village,* 2 vols., 1911–17; *Meare Lake Village,* 2 vols., 1948, 1953; *P.Som.A.S.* 112, 1968, 21ff.

Gorsey Bigbury, *P.U.B.S.S.* 5, No. 1, 1938, 3ff.; 6, No. 2, 1951, 186ff.

Gough's Cave, *P.U.B.S.S.* 7, No. 1, 1954, 23ff.

Ham Hill, *P.Som.A.S.* 58, 1913, 45ff.; 70, 1925, 104ff.; 71, 1926, 57ff.; *Ant.J.* 2, 1922, 381–2; 3, 1923, 149–50; 4, 1924, 51–3; *Arch.J.* 107, 1950, 90–1.

Hyaena Den, *P.U.B.S.S.* 7, No. 1, 1954, 23ff.

Kingsdown Camp, *Arch.* 80, 1930, 59ff.

Murtry Hill, *P.Som.A.S.* 67, 1922, 38ff.

Pool Farm, *P.Som.A.S.* 76, 1930, 85ff.; *P.P.S.* 23, 1957, 231ff.

Priddy Circles, *P.U.B.S.S.* 8, No. 1, 1957, 7ff.

Small Down Camp, *P.Som.A.S.* 50, 1905, 32ff.

Soldiers Hole, *P.U.B.S.S.* 7, No. 1, 1954, 23ff.

South Cadbury, L. Alcock, *By South Cadbury is that Camelot . . .,* 1972.

Tynings Farm, *P.U.B.S.S.* 2, No. 2, 1924, 136ff.; 4, No. 2, 1933, 67ff.; 6, No. 2, 1951, 111ff.

Wick Barrow, *P.Som.A.S.* 54, 1908, 1ff.

Withypool Hill, *P.Som.A.S.* 52, 1906, 42ff.

STAFFORDSHIRE

Bridestones, *T.L.C.A.S.* 53, 1939, 14ff.

Long Low, C.W. Phillips, *O.S. Map of the Trent Basin,* 1933, 9–10.

SURREY

See *S.A.C.* 40, 1932, 56ff. for all barrows, and below.

Abinger, *Surrey Archaeological Society, Research Report No. 3,* 1951.

Anstiebury, *S.A.C.* 12, 1895, 157ff.

Deerleap Wood, *S.A.C.* 60, 1963, 1ff.

Hascombe Hill, *S.A.C.* 40, 1932, 78ff.

Holmbury, *S.A.C.* 38, 1929–30, 156ff.

SUSSEX

See *Sx.A.C.* 75, 1934, 216ff.; 81, 1940, 210ff.; 82, 1942, 115ff. for all barrows, and below.

Barkhale, *C.* 89.

Blackpatch, *C.* 117ff.

Caburn, *Arch.* 46, 1881, 423ff.; *Sx.A.C.* 68, 1927, 1ff.; 79, 1938, 169ff.; 80, 1939, 193ff.

Charleston Brow, *Sx.A.C.* 74, 1933, 164ff.

Chichester Dykes, *R.R.* 26, 1971, 17ff.

Church Hill, *C.* 114ff.

Cissbury, *C.* 106ff., 238ff.; *Ant.J.,* 11, 1931, 14ff.

Combe Hill, *Sx.A.C.* 79, 1950, 105ff.

Goosehill Camp, *Sx.A.C.* 94, 1956, 70ff.

Harrow Hill, *Sx.A.C.* 78, 1937, 230ff.

Hollingbury, *Ant.J.* 12, 1932, 1ff.

Itford Hill, *P.P.S.* 23, 1957, 167ff.

Park Brow, *Ant.J.* 4, 1924, 347ff.; *Arch.* 76, 1927, 1ff.

Plumpton Plain, *P.P.S.* 1, 1935, 16ff.

Seaford Head, *Sx.A.C.* 32, 1882, 167ff.

Thundersbarrow Hill, *Ant.J.* 13, 1933, 109ff.

Trundle, *Sx.A.C.* 70, 1929, 33ff.; 72, 1931, 100ff.

Whitehawk, *Sx.A.C.* 71, 1930, 57ff.; 77, 1936, 60ff.

TYNE and WEAR

Copt Hill, *Arch. Ael.* 11, 1914, 123ff.

Hasting Hill, ibid. 135ff.

WARWICKSHIRE

For all sites, see *T.B.A.S.* 86, 1974, 16ff., and below.

Burrow Hill Camp, *T.B.A.S.* 52, 1927, 282ff.

Wappenbury, ibid. 76, 1958, 1ff.

WEST MIDLANDS

Berry Mound, ibid. 75, 1957, 93.

WILTSHIRE

For all sites, see V.C.H. 1(i) 1957 and 1(ii) 1973, for Neolithic and Bronze Age sites, see also F.K. Annable and D.D.A. Simpson, *Guide Catalogue of the Neolithic and Bronze Age Collections in Devizes Museum,* 1964; and below.

Barbury Castle, *W.A.M.* 58, 1963, 394ff.

Durrington Walls, G.J. Wainwright and I.H. Longworth, *R.R.* 29, 1971.

Knap Hill, *W.A.M.* 60, 1965, 1ff.

Lanhill, *P.P.S.* 32, 1966, 73ff.
Marden, *Ant.J.* 51, 1971, 177ff.
Normanton mortuary enclosure, *P.P.S.* 27, 1961, 160ff.
Snail Down, *W.A.M.* 56, 1955, 127ff.; ibid. 57, 1958, 5ff.
Stonehenge, R.J.C. Atkinson, *Stonehenge,* 1960.
Stonehenge Cursus, *W.A.M.* 58, 1963, 370ff.
West Kennet, S. Piggott, *The West Kennet Long Barrow,* 1962.
Windmill Hill, I.F. Smith, *Windmill Hill and Avebury,* 1965.
Winkelbury, *I.A.H.F.* 32ff.

YORKSHIRE, NORTH
Acklam Wold, M., 83ff.
Ayton East Field, *E.M.,* 40–1.
Duggleby Howe, M., 23ff.
Hanging Grimston, M., 96ff.
Hedon Howe, M., 346ff.
Helperthorpe, M., 333ff.
Kepwick, *B.B.,* 509–10; *E.M.,* 47.
Loose Howe, *P.P.S.* 15, 1949, 90ff.
Scambridge *B.B.* 484ff.

Snowdon Carr, *Y.A.J.* 33, 1936–38, 291ff.
Stanwick, *R.R.* 17, 1954.
Star Carr, J.G.D. Clark, *Excavations at Star Carr,* 1971; Addison-Wesley Modular Publications 10, 1972.
Thornborough, Hutton Moor, Cana Circles, *Y.A.J.* 38, 1955, 425ff.; ibid. 40, 1959–62, 169ff.
Victoria Cave, *University of Durham Philosophical Society* 9, 1936.
Western Howes, *Gentleman's Magazine,* 15, 1863, 548ff.
Wharram Percy, M. 44ff.
Willerby Wold, *P.P.S.* 29, 1963, 173ff.
Willerby Wold House, *Arch.* 52, 1890, 2ff.

YORKSHIRE, SOUTH
Carlwark, *A.* 25, 1951, 210ff.
Wincobank, *Arch.J.* 111, 1954, 87.

YORKSHIRE, WEST
Almondbury, *Arch.J.* 105, 1948, 46–8; 111, 1954, 86–7.
Bradley Moor, *Y.A.J.* 34, 1939, 223ff.
Ilkley Moor, *Y.A.J.* 29, 1929, 356ff.

INDEX